DUKE

THE LIFE AND TIMES OF

JOHN WAYNE

DUKE
THE LIFE AND TIMES OF
JOHN WAYNE

by *DONALD SHEPHERD*
and *ROBERT SLATZER*
with *DAVE GRAYSON*

DOUBLEDAY AND COMPANY
GARDEN CITY, NEW YORK
1985

LIBRARY OF CONGRESS CATALOGING IN PUBLICATION DATA
Shepherd, Donald.
Duke, the life and times of John Wayne.

Filmography: p. 335
Includes index.
1. Wayne, John, 1907–1979.   2. Moving-picture actors and
actresses—United States—Biography.
I. Slatzer, Robert F.   II. Grayson, Dave.   III. Title.
PN2287.W454S54   1985   791.43′028′0924 [B]
ISBN 0-385-17893-X
Library of Congress Catalog Card Number 84-26004

In addition to the sources cited, the dialogue presented here has been reconstructed from memory and from the extensive journals of Dave Grayson. Duke Wayne was a man of blunt words and hauntingly rhythmic speech patterns, so the dialogue attributed to him will be substantially what he said.

—D. S., R. F. S., and D. G.

CONTENTS

vii

CONTENTS

ACKNOWLEDGMENTS

O_{NE} of the pitfalls for those who approach the writing of show-business biography with integrity and who feel that film celebrities are worthy of earnest biographical treatment is mistaking the apparent for the real, in accepting often-repeated and seemingly factual information as truthful. In no other field of endeavor is so much said and written about its notables as the entertainment business. And in no other field—not even politics—is so little of what is said and written the truth.

Information disseminated about entertainers is usually fashioned by publicity and public relations people and show-business columnists and fan-magazine writers whose job it is to promote or to entertain rather than to inform. So they fashion "facts" to an end: toward creating or reinforcing images. This is often done quickly and with less than scrupulous regard for truth. Author Norman Mailer was frustrated by such "facts" in researching *Marilyn*, his novel biography of actress Marilyn Monroe; he called such attractively shiny information-retrieval nuggets "factoids," a wonderfully appropriate and slick alloy of a noun that has the look and feel of the stuff it's named for. As Mailer discovered, factoids were the fundamental building blocks of Hollywood filmmakers and of the illustrious humanoids they manufactured once upon a time.

It is in the area of secondary research, then—an area that writers of general biography find familiar and comfortable and secure —that show-business biographers are frustrated at every turn. The difficulty of the task before them is found not in unearthing, analyzing, organizing, and interpreting reliable information, but in scaling the mountains of factoids that stand between them and

ACKNOWLEDGMENTS

their subjects and that often collapse when tested for footing. Thus, serious show-business biographers are all the more indebted to those who help them find solid footholds and vantage points from which they can get a relatively unclouded view of the stars. Therefore, in addition to our editor, Adrian Zackheim, and our literary agent, Dominick Abel, for whom we have enormous respect, we hereby acknowledge the following people, whose guidance has been of inestimable value:

The late *June Kaser*, former president of the Madison County Historical Society of Winterset, Iowa, a wonderfully charming woman who was devoted to truth and who left no factoid unturned or uncracked; *David E. Trask*, Chairman of the John Wayne Birthplace Committee of Winterset, Iowa; *Kathy and Randall Lee*, Winterset, Iowa; *Miriam B. Jenkins*, Registrar, Simpson College, Indianola, Iowa; *Dr. Milton J. Bowman*, Registrar and Professor of biology, Monmouth College, Monmouth, Illinois; *Dean Nelson*, Associate Registrar, Iowa State College, Ames, Iowa; *Philip L. Patton*, Associate Registrar, University of Northern Iowa, Cedar Falls, Iowa; *Delpha Trindle*, Secretary of the John Wayne Birthplace Committee, Winterset, Iowa; *Paul Christopher*, Archivist, University of Southern California, Los Angeles; *Carol Ann Nix*, South Bend, Indiana; *Blaine Miles*, Winterset, Iowa; *Anthony Slide*, Hollywood researcher; the *staff* of the Margaret Herrick Library of the Academy of Motion Picture Arts and Sciences, Beverly Hills, California; *Barbara Boyd*, Special Collections Librarian, Glendale Public Library, Glendale, California, a factoid cracker without peer; *Esther Guzman*, Administrative Secretary, Glendale High School, Glendale, California; *Vic Pallos*, Director of Public Information, Glendale Unified School District, Glendale, California; *Ellen Perry*, feature writer, the Glendale *News Press;* the *staff* of the American Film Institute Library, Hollywood, California; *Lillian Clary*, Santa Maria Library, Santa Maria, California; *Howard D. Saperston*, Director, Registration and Records, University of Southern California, Los Angeles; *Anthony LaScala, Steve Tragash,* and *Ralph Rivet* of Great Western Savings, Beverly Hills, California; the Lancaster Historical Society, Lancaster, California; the Palmdale Chamber of Commerce, Palmdale, California; *Milton*

ACKNOWLEDGMENTS

Stark of Leona Valley, California; the late *Sylvia Picker McGraw;* *Floyd C. "Babe" Herman; Dorothy Gulliver; Wilson S. Hong; Doral Chenoweth; Mary Ellen Hunt; JoAnn Goldberg* and *Nick Lombardo* of Barwell Productions; *Sarah Rozen* of the Bettmann Archive; *Rina Cascone,* Manhattan free-lance copy editor extraordinaire; the incomparable *Barbara Walters;* and finally, *Woodrow W. Slatzer, Barbara Kevern Shepherd,* and *Paula Grayson.*

PART ONE

1

AN EVENING WITH THE DUKE—1972

*I*T was almost four thirty in the afternoon when we turned off Alameda Avenue into the artists' parking lot of the NBC television studios in Burbank. Duke was scheduled to do Johnny Carson's *Tonight Show* there at five thirty and had called us from NBC on impulse. He had also alerted the gate guard to our arrival, so we were waved in and told to park next to Duke's green Pontiac station wagon. The Pontiac was easily recognized; it had a specially designed roof—a raised section above the front seats, which Duke had had installed to accommodate his height and the Stetson hat he often wore when driving.

We parked and walked up the ramp and through the main entrance to the studio complex. A young NBC page cleared us at the reception desk before we turned down the narrow corridor that led to the dressing rooms and to Studio One, where the *Tonight Show* is taped. Duke opened the door within seconds of our knock, his six-foot-four frame filling the doorway. He was dressed in a tuxedo, and he already had a drink in hand. "What'd you come by, *horse?*" he said, his voice booming down the corridor. "It sure as hell took you long enough!"

"Heavy afternoon traffic," we told him.

He scowled and fixed us with blue eyes for a moment, then

3

broke into a broad grin and stepped back, motioning us in and shaking hands as we entered. He had invited us for a drink to help him celebrate the *Photoplay* magazine award he would receive later that evening at the Beverly Hills Hotel; *Photoplay*'s readers had voted him the most popular male actor of 1971. In those days, it was customary for Johnny Carson to have the award winners on his talk show the evening of the presentations. Robert Mitchum's youngest son, Christopher, was receiving a *Photoplay* award, too—as the year's most promising young male actor—and he was scheduled to appear on Carson's show that evening. Duke remembered that Bob Slatzer had given Chris his first starring role in a motion picture—a low-budget film Slatzer had directed two years earlier—and it seemed to Duke that Slatzer ought to be present.

Duke closed the dressing room door behind us and strode to the makeshift bar he had set up on a credenza, where there was a nearly full bottle of Wild Turkey bourbon, some clear plastic cups, and a champagne bucket filled with melting ice. "I'll be bartender," he said, lining up the cups and pouring the bourbon. He poured what in those days we jokingly called "John Wayne Cocktails": tumblerfuls of straight liquor.

It was never an easy task to remain relatively sober in Duke's company, for he was an attentive host who believed in share and share alike with his guests. When an evening was young, he realized that not everyone could stomach the amount of alcohol he himself could put away with little effect, but as the spirits continued to flow, he'd often forget this fact and begin taking offense if one didn't keep up with him drink for drink. "Listen," he'd say, "if you're gonna drink with *me*, you're gonna *drink* with me!" We had learned to appoint a driver from our ranks whenever we went drinking with Duke Wayne.

Duke had been alone in his dressing room when we arrived, which wasn't unusual, since he didn't travel with a pack. We had expected Dave Grayson to be there, though. Grayson, Duke's personal makeup man and a friend of ours, had arrived early to apply Duke's makeup and toupee. We noticed his makeup case on the credenza, and Duke was already made up. We asked where Dave was. "Hell, I don't know," Duke said, filling the last cup with bourbon. "He's wandering around here somewhere. I'm pouring him a drink, but if the little bastard isn't back by the time we finish ours, we'll drink *his*, too."

We had to laugh. It was a typical Duke Wayne remark. At five foot ten, Grayson was neither little nor a bastard, but Duke usually referred to his friends and co-workers by such affectionate sobriquets. What was particularly funny, though, was his threat of action toward Grayson. Grayson had done his job, and there was no need for him to be at Duke's side at the moment, but he was Duke's personal makeup man and, when asked, Duke didn't know where his makeup man was. Ordinarily he wouldn't have cared, but in Hollywood circles, where one's popularity and power are often judged by the length of one's entourage and the obsequiousness of one's attendants, an absence like Grayson's could be misconstrued as inattention and, therefore, disrespect. Duke rejected the more absurd embellishments of Hollywood power, but he was very sensitive about his dignity and about how he was perceived by others, whether such perceptions were well or ill founded.

This kind of petulance was very much a part of Duke's character; it was a childlike quality that added to the vulnerability fans found so attractive in him and that those who truly knew him found incongruous, but disarming and even charming.

Duke finished pouring Dave's drink and glanced over his shoulder at Wilson Hong, a mutual friend whom we had appointed as driver for the evening. "Throw some ice in these drinks for me, Wil," he said.

Hong looked into the ice bucket; it contained mostly water now, and what little ice there was had fused into a lump. "I'll need an ice pick," he said.

"An ice pick?" Duke said, brushing past Hong and peering down into the bucket. "Well, for Christ's sake! Here I've been sweating my ass off in this dressing room, and I thought it was *me!* I guess the network can't afford decent air-conditioning."

He distributed the cups of bourbon. "To hell with the ice," he said. "It just dilutes good liquor, anyway." Then he raised his cup in a toast that we had often heard him make, in Spanish: *"Salud y tiempo, y amor, y dinero, para gastarlos."* (Here's to health, and time and love, and money to enjoy them.)

The dressing room was long and narrow and painted white. Besides the credenza and a dressing table that sat before a mirrored wall at one end, it was furnished with a couch and matching easy chair and several director's chairs. There was a television monitor opposite the easy chair; it was tuned in to the Carson taping, but the sound was off. Duke motioned for us to be seated as he settled into the easy chair with his drink. We had been seated only a moment or two when Dave Grayson joined us. Dave hadn't planned to attend the awards ceremony at the hotel that evening; he'd be going home to dinner with his family soon, so he declined the drink Duke offered him.

"Good," Duke said. "We're running out of liquor, anyway, and it's all we have to stave off the interminable heat." He got up and poured a little bourbon into each of our cups from the cup Grayson had declined. "What's that W. C. Fields line?" he said to no one in particular. He paused for a moment, thinking, then broke into a grin at the recollection. "Ah, yes," he said, doing a barely passable vocal impression of Fields. "We wandered for days with nothing but food and water."

Duke laughed and downed the remainder of Grayson's bourbon as a young woman tapped on the door and opened it slightly, peeking in. She was one of the Carson show assistants. "You'll be on in half an hour, Mr. Wayne," she said.

"You're just the lady I'm looking for," Duke said to her, pulling a roll of bills from his pocket and handing her a twenty. "Have someone get us another bottle of Wild Turkey, will you?"

The assistant seemed a little troubled by his request, as though she had visions of big John Wayne plowing onto the *Tonight Show* set roaring drunk from the booze she had gotten him. She took the money, only to return a minute or two later.

"That was a quick trip!" Duke said. There was more than a touch of sarcasm in his voice, for the woman still had his money in her hand, with no bottle in evidence.

"I can't leave the premises," she said, laying the money on the dressing table.

"I didn't ask you to," Duke said. "I asked you to find someone who *can!*"

"But you're going on in less than half an hour, Mr. Wayne."

"And that would give us almost half an hour to have a couple of drinks—*if* we had something to drink!" Duke said, glaring down at her. "Listen, I know there are liquor stores nearby. Do I have to go get it myself?"

Rattled, the assistant left the room without taking the money. Duke looked at the money, glanced at us with a "do you believe this?" look on his face, then paced the length of the dressing room, angry. "A fella could get a bill through Congress quicker than he could get a drink around here," he said.

Hong offered to go get a bottle, but Duke said he wasn't going to send his guests out into the streets. Seconds later there was another knock at the door and a different assistant asked him what he wanted.

Duke picked up the twenty from the dressing table and pulled another from his pocket, handing them both to the assistant. "Two bottles of Wild Turkey," he said. "And if you can't get them *now*, I'll go out and get them myself!"

"No problem, Mr. Wayne," she said, taking the money. "We do have some champagne, though. Would you prefer a couple bottles of that?"

"If I had wanted champagne, I'd have asked for it," Duke said.

"Oh. Okay. I'll be back as quickly as I can."

"That's the kinda talk I like to hear," Duke said.

When the woman returned, she brought two cardboard buckets of ice along with the bourbon, and Duke set about happily tending bar again. Chris Mitchum stuck his head in the doorway to say hello. Duke invited him in for a drink, but Chris politely declined, saying he had just been called from the Green Room and was on his way to the set; he'd be going on in a minute. When Chris left, Duke turned the sound up on the monitor and kept his eye on it as we continued talking.

Another production assistant stopped by and told Duke he'd be on in ten minutes. Grayson checked Duke's toupee; a couple of shiny spots had developed on his forehead from perspiration, so Duke moved to the dressing table, where Grayson touched up the spots. When Grayson finished, Duke stood and remained standing until he went on. He sipped his bourbon and gave his full attention to the television monitor when Carson introduced Chris Mitchum. Shortly thereafter, a production assistant interrupted and told Duke they were ready for him on the set. Duke downed the rest of his drink, straightened his tie, buttoned his coat, and started from the dressing room with Grayson. "Fix yourselves another drink," he said. "I won't be long."

He was very relaxed on the *Tonight Show*. He didn't visit the show often, but he always enjoyed himself when he did. He and Carson never had occasion to socialize, but their respect and liking for one another was apparent. Duke was disarming on such shows, displaying a lively intelligence and wit that one seldom associated with him and that often surprised his host. On this particular night, Duke was more serious than usual; the subject was the *Photoplay* awards, and Duke always took awards seriously. He graciously thanked the publishers of the magazine and its readers for acknowledging his contribution to the motion picture industry. On an appearance a few months later, though, he cracked Carson up when, as he was leaving, he waved at Carson and said for the benefit of Carson's millions of viewers, "Goodnight, *Merv*," as though he had mistaken Carson for another well-known talk-show host, Merv Griffin.

Duke did his four- or five-minute appearance, then returned to the dressing room, loosening his collar and saying, "Now we can get down to some serious celebrating!" He was pouring himself another drink when Carson's associate and announcer, Ed McMahon, stopped by the dressing room. McMahon and Duke were known to hoist a few together in such fashionable Sunset Boulevard watering holes as Sneaky Pete's. Duke poured McMahon a drink, and the two of them had a brief, private conversation before McMahon waved to us and went back to the taping.

We talked for a while longer as Duke relaxed with his drink; then Grayson reminded him that he had only half an hour or so before he was due at the Beverly Hills Hotel. We got only as far as the corridor before being stopped by a distinguished-looking man who asked Duke if he would make an appearance in an adjacent studio, before a live audience. It was June 6, Primary Election Day, and the network had already begun its coverage.

Duke agreed to do a quick walk-on, and the man escorted us to the studio. Outside the studio door, Grayson checked Duke's makeup and toupee for the last time; they would be fine for the rest of the evening—in natural light—but they required special attention for television's harsh, flat lighting.

"Okay, you're looking good," Grayson told him.

"You're just saying that because you wanna get home to Paula and the kids," Duke said.

"True," Grayson said. "Actually, you look like hell, but I can't work miracles."

"It's a miracle that you're even *working*," Duke shot back. "Okay, go on home. I'll get along on my natural beauty."

"That'll get you as far as the parking lot," Grayson said.

Duke grinned. "You've just *got* to get the last word in, don't you?" he said. "All right, you got me, you li'l son of a bitch! Now get the hell out of here. And give Paula my love."

"I will," Grayson said, waving to us and heading toward the parking lot.

The executive who had escorted us to the other studio stopped Duke just inside the door and asked if he could walk on camera with him. Duke eyed the man for a moment, then said, "I'm with *friends*, here, but you're welcome to join us, if you like." Plastic cup of bourbon still in hand, Duke threw his arm around Slatzer's shoulder and walked onto the set, leaving the disgruntled network executive behind.

After the brief appearance, we walked Duke out to the parking lot, where the young chauffeur who had driven him up from his Newport Beach home was waiting. We thanked Duke for the drinks and congratulated him again on winning the award. It was our intention to go back to Slatzer's office at Columbia Studios, but Duke wouldn't hear of it. "C'mon over to the hotel," he said, "and we'll have a few more belts."

DUKE

"We don't have invitations," we told him.

"You don't need 'em. You're with *me*."

By this time, we had drunk the equivalent of at least two full glasses of one-hundred-proof bourbon, and so going to a black-tie affair without invitations and dressed in sports clothes seemed like a not-too-bad idea, and we agreed to join him.

"Get your car and follow us," Duke said, getting into his station wagon.

We followed his Pontiac west on Ventura Boulevard and then north across Coldwater Canyon, which links the San Fernando Valley with Beverly Hills. When we finally turned up the Beverly Hills Hotel drive, Duke was already out of his car. Mobs of photographers and fans and autograph seekers were clustered around him. It was Duke's practice to hand out lithographed signature cards, which he always carried for such occasions, but there were just too many autograph-seekers in the crowd this time. He ran out of cards, and we had to wait for him while he signed his way through the mob.

Inside, Duke ran interference for us against the officials who spotted our casual wear and took us for party crashers, which we were. Once we were in the bar that had been set up in a room adjacent to the Maisonette Room, where the awards dinner was to be held, we were no longer bothered. Duke asked the bartender for Wild Turkey, but there was none in stock, so he asked for his favorite, Conmemorativo Tequila. There was none of that, either.

"Well, what the hell you got back there besides beer and milk, Pilgrim?" Duke asked. "Got any Tequila Sauza?"

The bartender searched his stock and came up smiling. "Yessir, Mr. Wayne," he said, opening the bottle and reaching for a shot glass to measure with. He hadn't begun pouring when Duke reached over the bar and grabbed the bottle of tequila with his big paw (Duke had enormous hands, almost twice the size of an average man's). "Thanks, anyway, Pilgrim," he said, "but you just give us some tall glasses and we'll get out of your way, here."

The bartender laughed and handed us glasses as Duke made his way through the crowd to a relatively quiet corner table. We joined him, and he emptied the entire bottle into the glasses. A woman nearby had been watching him. She approached the table and asked if she could have the bottle as a souvenir. Duke obliged by handing her the bottle, and she asked if he'd autograph the label, which he did.

In a short while, Duke's glass was empty. He got another bottle from the bartender and emptied that one into our glasses, too. And again the woman asked for the bottle. Duke asked her name this time, then wrote something on the bottle, signed it, and handed it to her. "You must have quite a bottle collection," he said.

"I do *now*, Mr. Wayne," the woman said.

By this time, the invited guests were drifting from the bar into the Maisonette Room, and Duke got to his feet. He had put away at least four cups of straight Wild Turkey and two tall glasses of tequila. We were nearly to the point of falling-down drunk—and would have been had we tried to stand up quickly—and Duke was just beginning to feel festive. He told us that they had him seated at the long table on the dais, but that he'd make arrangements to get us seats or to have another table brought in for us. Even in our inebriated state we realized that this was just too much of an imposition, so we convinced Duke that we'd prefer finishing our drinks and watching the ceremonies from the bar.

To say that our recollection of what followed is hazy would be a colossal understatement. We had an extremely vague, four- or five-tumbler remembrance of Duke receiving his award and of his saying a few words. We were later told that we left the hotel right after Duke got his award; all we remember is that we awoke late the following afternoon at home in our own beds, fully clothed, and wishing we were dead. We had never drunk so much in one evening in our lives. Meanwhile, Duke had returned to Newport Beach in the early hours of the morning, had gotten a few hours sleep, was up early for a steak-and-egg breakfast, and was making phone calls, including a personal call to Slatzer to see whether everyone had made it home all right. Apparently Duke's only side effect from the evening was that he lost his award plaque—which he later found in the station wagon.

DUKE

Slatzer didn't even remember the phone call until Duke reminded him of it later. Considering that the members of our party were in their late thirties and early forties, we hadn't weathered the evening so well. But with Duke it had been just another evening of "cocktails." He was sixty-six years old at the time. In this respect, at least, he surpassed his own legend.

PART TWO

2

WINTERSET
AND EARLHAM

Duke's true name was Marion Mitchell Morrison. That's not the name he was given, though, when he was born to Clyde Leonard and Mary Alberta Morrison, née Brown, on May 26, 1907, in Winterset, Iowa. He was Clyde and Mary's first child, and to honor both their fathers, the couple named him Marion Robert— after his paternal grandfather, Marion Mitchell Morrison, and his maternal grandfather, Robert Emmett Brown.

When Clyde and Mary's second and last child—another son— was born four years later, the newborn was named Robert Emmett, and Duke's middle name was changed from Robert to Mitchell, thus fully honoring both grandfathers. After he gained celebrity, Duke deliberately confused biographers and others by claiming *Michael* as his middle name, a claim that had no basis in fact.

Duke was of Scottish, Irish, and English descent. His great-great grandfather, Robert Morrison, was born November 29, 1782, in County Antrim, northern Ireland, the son of John and Nancy De Scrogges Morrison, both of whom were of Scottish descent. Robert had joined an alliance of Protestants and Catholics calling itself the United Irishmen. When the alliance failed in the late 1790s and traitors within the alliance began naming names and exposing their plot against the Crown, Robert Morrison was named and had to flee for his life.

Robert was just nineteen when he arrived in New York. A weaver by trade, he headed south toward the rich Southern textile mills. At first he went to South Carolina, where he joined two uncles, also weavers, who had emigrated before him. The prospect of beginning a new life, of owning land and tilling the soil, was apparently more attractive to him than weaving, however, and he moved to Kentucky, where he settled and joined the Reformed Presbyterian Church. There he met Mary Mitchell. Robert and Mary were married shortly thereafter, on November 7, 1803, and on that day they left for Cherry Fork, Ohio, a small village taking form just across the Kentucky border, where they cleared rich forest land and began to farm.

Robert is said to have helped build the Presbyterian church in Cherry Fork and to have become a Ruling Elder in the church. For a decade, the couple led an almost idyllic life. The farm prospered and their family grew in number. Then, without warning, Mary Mitchell Morrison died in the summer of 1813 at age twenty-nine, possibly of complications following the recent birth of their sixth child.

During the War of 1812, and immediately after Mary's death, Robert left his children with relatives and joined a cavalry unit as an officer. Captain Morrison saw no action against the British, but he fought in several skirmishes against the Indians, who had sided with the British. In 1817, he was appointed a brigadier general in the Ohio militia, having declined a commission in the regular army. It was also in 1817 that Robert Morrison was elected a representative of the Ohio legislature, where he served four consecutive one-year terms before he became disillusioned with politics. Robert subsequently remarried, and by his death on February 10, 1863, he had fathered fifteen children.

Duke's great-grandfather, James, was born September 21, 1811, one of Robert and Mary's six children. He became a farmer and stayed in Cherry Fork, where he met and married Martha Purdy Ewing on February 18, 1836. Among their children was Duke's grandfather, Marion Mitchell Morrison, who was born January

20, 1845, and who was named after his father's brother, Marion, and his grandmother, Mary Mitchell Morrison.

While James farmed in Cherry Fork and began raising a family, his brother Marion followed scholarly pursuits and the family's Presbyterian leanings, and eventually became a Presbyterian minister. In 1856, he moved to Monmouth, Illinois, where he helped found Monmouth College and served as that institution's first professor of mathematics and natural sciences.

In 1861, Reverend Morrison succeeded in getting James and his family to join him in Monmouth. At the time, James was forty-one and had lived all his life in Cherry Fork. However, the thriving Illinois community that Marion described in his letters made the nearly five-hundred-mile trek west irresistible to James. The city was surrounded by fertile rolling meadowland, and there was still choice farming acreage available close to town—with a railroad to ship the produce. It was a farmer's dream, an opportunity that James couldn't resist, so he moved his family to Monmouth, where he settled for life.

Reverend Morrison enjoyed the company of his relatives in Monmouth for only a year before he felt a calling elsewhere. The Civil War had begun, and on August 7, 1862, the reverend joined the 9th Illinois Regiment of the Union forces as its chaplain. Six months later, on February 3, 1863, he was killed during the defense of Fort Donelson, in Tennessee.

In 1864, Marion Mitchell Morrison, Duke's grandfather, entered the war at age nineteen as an enlisted man in the Union forces. He saw action in several battles and was wounded and left for dead at Pine Bluff, Tennessee. He lay on the battlefield for two days and nights before he regained consciousness and crawled to a river, where he was discovered and picked up by a Union boat.[1] When he was released from the hospital, he returned to Monmouth and farmed. On November 4, 1869, he married Weltha Chase Parsons. Marion and Weltha had four children: George, Guy, Clyde, and Pearle. Their third son, Clyde Leonard Morrison (Duke's father), was born on August 20, 1884.

Clyde was about three when the Morrisons moved west to Indianola, in Warren County, Iowa. Marion was a realtor there and farmed. After the turn of the century, he and Weltha moved to Des Moines, Iowa, where they were living when their grandson, Duke, was born. In 1909, two years after Duke's birth, Weltha died, and within a year or so of her death, Marion left Iowa for California.

Little is known of Clyde Leonard Morrison's early life. He was raised on a farm in Indianola, although farming wasn't his family's chief occupation, and he was a quiet, intelligent, and gentle young man, very easygoing and soft-spoken. In the fall of 1901, at age seventeen, Clyde enrolled in a mechanical engineering workshop at Iowa State University, at Ames, Iowa, a one-semester class, which he took as a non-degree-seeking student. When his parents moved from Indianola to Des Moines in 1903, Clyde moved to Waterloo, Iowa, where he was presumably working when he met Mary Alberta Brown. Molly, as she was called, was living with her parents in Des Moines and working for the telephone company when she met Clyde Morrison. The daughter of Robert Emmett and Margaret Brown, she had been born in Lincoln, Nebraska, before the Browns moved to Des Moines, where her father was a printer.

Molly Brown was a strikingly pretty girl of English and Irish extraction. She was of medium height, with auburn hair and blue eyes and a lively intelligence. She was also a gifted mimic and had an extraordinary sense of humor, which Duke and his brother, Robert, inherited. Duke always said of his mother that she reminded him in looks and actions of comedienne Billie Burke.

Unfortunately for Clyde, Molly also had a dominating nature, a fiery temper, and a sharp tongue. Duke took after his mother in this respect, too, while brother Robert was more easygoing, like his father. Clyde and Molly were married on September 29, 1905, by a justice of the peace in Knoxville, Iowa. Clyde was twenty-one at the time; Molly was twenty.

They settled in nearby Winterset in 1905. It's the county seat of Madison County, Iowa, located thirty-five miles southwest of Des Moines, with a population of less than four thousand. Still a farming community that markets corn and soybeans and raises poultry, hogs, cattle, and horses, it's a picturesque little midwestern city that was chosen as one of the locations for the 1971 movie comedy *Cold Turkey*, which is often rerun on television these days and which features a particularly good aerial view of Winterset's courthouse.

There's a limestone quarry outside town that for more than a hundred years has yielded a unique pearl-gray stone that was much prized and used for building by the Winterset and Madison County pioneers. Many of the historic homes in and around Winterset are built of it, as is the one-room Bennet Schoolhouse north of town (which is in the National Registry of Historic Places) and the Clark Tower (a monument that sits castlelike on a high bluff in Winterset City Park) and, of course, the courthouse itself, which dominates the square around which the city is built.

Seven of the original sixteen covered bridges that spanned the creeks and rivers around Winterset in Clyde and Molly's day still stand. There are only about eight hundred covered wooden bridges still standing in the United States, and Madison County's are among the best preserved. One of them, the 1871 Cutler Donahoe Bridge, now stands in Winterset City Park. The bridges have been declared national historic structures, and Winterset honors them by hosting Madison County's annual Covered Bridge Festival, which is held the second weekend in October and draws as many as thirty thousand visitors yearly.

The city's main thoroughfare, Court Avenue, has changed a bit since Clyde and Molly's day. One of the grain elevators is gone, as are the blacksmith shops and livery stables. There's a bank now where the old gray-cement St. Nick Hotel once stood. And the Arcade Hotel, where botanist George Washington Carver once stayed, was razed in the 1970s. Carver was a graduate and faculty member of Iowa State University at Ames (where Clyde attended a semester), fifty miles north of Winterset, and he is said to have taken nature walks on the grounds that are now the site of the two-story Madison County Historical Museum in Winterset.

The changes in Winterset are really minor, considering that more than three quarters of a century have passed since the Morrisons settled there. The courthouse still stands, as do most of the commercial buildings, including the one in which Clyde worked and the boardinghouse where he and Molly stayed when they arrived.

The Morrisons first stayed in the Cottage Hotel, a boardinghouse for teachers. The house still stands, but it has been moved next door, one lot south of its original site, which was a block west of Courthouse Square, at the southwest corner of Court Avenue and Second Street, a site now occupied by a gas station.

A block east of the original Cottage Hotel site and directly across from the courthouse is the building in which Clyde worked. Two Winterset oldtimers disagree as to which of two buildings housed the Marquis and Smith Store where Clyde worked as a pharmacist's clerk until he left Winterset in 1910.[2] But both buildings still stand. Robert Barcroft, who still lives in Winterset, has no recollection of Clyde Morrison, but he remembers the store where Clyde is said to have worked as being in the building at 24 Court Avenue, now occupied by a Montgomery Ward catalog store. As a child, Mr. Barcroft visited the store daily to buy a copy of the city's newspaper, the Winterset *Madisonian*, for his parents. Blaine Miles also remembers the store. Mr. Miles is older than Mr. Barcroft, and he remembers Clyde and Molly Morrison very well; he recalls the store as being at 66 Court Avenue, a building now occupied by the Village Bootery.

While Clyde is remembered as serious, shy, and retiring, Molly was quite the Winterset socialite and made many close friends among the merchants' wives. Blaine Miles, whose family was in the livestock business, remembers seeing Molly around town with her friends and always fashionably dressed. "She always wore those big picture hats of the day," he said, "and she was the prettiest woman I'd ever seen. And Clyde Morrison was a nice fellow, a handsome man. He was about five-eleven, as I recall, and stalwart—athletically built."

Clyde and Molly had been staying at the Cottage Hotel a short time when another couple moved from Winterset, and the Morrisons rented the little house—a bungalow, really—they had vacated at 214 East Court Avenue. It was in this house that Duke was born.[3] It wasn't long before the Morrisons found a larger house of four rooms at 224 South Second Street, which they rented and made their home until they moved to Earlham three years later, in 1910.[4]

In Earlham, a city smaller than Winterset and eighteen miles to the northwest, Clyde and Molly bought a drugstore—reportedly the Rexall Drug and Jewelry Store. The following year, on December 18, 1911, Duke's brother, Robert Emmett Morrison, was born. One would have thought this the best of times for the Morrison family. They had begun putting down roots in their new community; they added a new and healthy member to the family; and they had invested in a business of their own—one that by all accounts prospered for a while. However, all was not well in the Morrison household.

Molly had always been high-spirited and headstrong, but after Duke's and Robert's births and the purchase of the drugstore, she seems to have grabbed the reins not only at home, but in the business, too. Judging from their reportedly bitter battles, Clyde wasn't giving up control without a struggle. But he was losing his grip. The impression the Earlham people got was that Clyde "feared" Molly's explosive temper and her wrath and that, at least in public, he let her have the upper hand.[5] Most of their fights involved their new business and the way Molly thought Clyde was mishandling it. Clyde, in Molly's view, was too generous. He gave credit where it wasn't warranted. He was too easygoing to be a good businessman. In Molly's eyes, his failure to rise to the challenge of his business responsibilities revealed a fundamental weakness in him that she didn't admire.

Robert, of course, was too young to have been affected by the family feuding, but the impressionable young Marion absorbed it all. He suffered from insomnia; even during naptime Molly often pressed her visiting friends into service by having them try to rock Marion to sleep while she attended to Robert. Marion was also given to temper tantrums and was high-strung and uncontrollable. Worst of all, though, was his penchant for running away from home. At age five, he hopped freight trains out of town. The Earlham telephone operator, Blanche Powell Neff, often received frantic calls from Molly when Marion was missing, and she would make calls from her central switchboard to people around town and along the railroad line, alerting them of the boy's disappearance. Young Marion obviously had no trouble sleeping on flatcars of trains; he would sometimes awaken in another town.[6]

There was lots of tension in the Morrison household, and something eventually had to snap. In a short while the Morrisons abandoned their business and their way of life and were on their way to California—under the worst conditions imaginable.

3

DESERT HOMESTEAD

IT was probably in the late summer of 1914 that Clyde Morrison
went west by train to California. He had decided to farm eighty
acres of land in Lancaster, and he left Molly and the boys with
Molly's parents in Des Moines while he went out to prepare for
their move. The Lancaster property was owned by his father,
Marion Mitchell Morrison, who had homesteaded it and had built
a house on it.

Even with the advantage of having a place to come to, the move
west was a major one for Clyde; it required uprooting his family,
giving up his profession, and starting over, at age thirty, on a
barren piece of land on the rim of the Mojave Desert. It was a
desperate move, and one that Clyde would not have made had his
circumstances in Iowa seemed less hopeless.

Duke said that his family moved west for his father's health.
This statement prompted numerous writers to speculate on
Clyde's health, and the speculations were repeated by others as
fact. The truth of the several "sickness" stories isn't substanti-
ated, however. Clyde's business was failing, and his father offered
him the use of the Lancaster farm; the health Clyde was probably
seeking to restore was more financial than physical.

It was Duke's paternal grandfather and namesake who came to
the family's rescue. Grandfather Morrison had gone west after
his wife's death in Des Moines. He was living on south Westlake

DUKE

Avenue in Los Angeles and had been in California at least four years by the time Clyde arrived in Lancaster. He was sixty-eight and couldn't have been much help to his son on the farm, but he did provide him with financial aid. In November of 1914, he opened a large account in his name with the Antelope Valley Lumber Company, purchasing enough material to enlarge the house. Clyde's family and Molly's parents were already settled in at the Lancaster farm, and the building materials were no doubt used to add a bedroom or two to the place. Molly's parents, by then, had decided to stay with them.

Molly's parents, Robert and Margaret Brown, arrived in August by train, accompanying Molly and the boys. Years later, Duke recalled that his mother had great misgivings about their desert venture, or fiasco, as she might have called it. Nothing she had ever experienced or heard could have adequately prepared her for what she saw that day. The view from her passenger car must have been demoralizing: the stark, two-story wood frame Southern Pacific depot, around which nothing grew; the railroad tracks bordered by sand-pitted telephone poles stretching flat out in both directions as far as the eye could see; and the sandy soil of the desert floor, hot and flat and sparsely mottled with brown and yellow patches of scrub brush dancing in the heat waves. The crusty tableau made the woods and creeks and rolling green prairies of the Midwest seem junglelike in comparison.

Clyde drove the horse and wagon north from Palmdale along what is now known as the Sierra Highway. The village of Lancaster was eight miles away, and the Morrison property was in the third section south of the village, or about two and a half miles from it, right on the highway. Duke no doubt rode in the back of the wagon and was probably, as usual, in charge of brother Robert, who wasn't quite three at the time. Duke had just turned seven. Up front, Molly, who was known for voicing her opinions, was no doubt telling Clyde what she thought of his father's choice of land.

Duke described the Lancaster house as "more of a shanty than a house." It was a small, four-room, wood frame place, built well enough to keep the elements out, but nonetheless demoralizing to behold. Duke's description of it is presumably as it appeared in August, before any additions had been built. The place had none of the comforts of their Winterset and Earlham homes; there was no electricity, no gas, no running water, and, of course, no telephone. Molly's kitchen had a hand pump for well water and a wood-burning stove, which served to cook meals and to heat the rest of the house. Kerosene lamps were used for light. Out back there was an outhouse and a shedlike barn to protect the Morrisons' two horses and the farm equipment—what little equipment there was.

Apparently Molly was skeptical of Clyde's decision to grow corn in Lancaster, but it was a decision based partly on necessity; the alfalfa and grain crops grown by other farmers in the area required equipment for harvesting that the Morrisons could not afford to buy and maintain. Corn, on the other hand, could be harvested by hand and would have a ready market not only with local wholesalers but also with the villagers at retail.

It wasn't a bad idea, and Duke had intimated that his father was particularly zealous in pursuing it because, as Duke said, "Mother had got it into her head that Dad was a failure," and Clyde was determined to prove otherwise. Clyde tried planting several acres of beans, too, but within a day or two of their sprouting, every sprout was eaten by the desert jackrabbits, which infested Lancaster's farming area. Clyde always carried a rifle to the fields and was constantly shooting them, but he didn't realize how many there were until he planted the beans.

It was a hard life in Lancaster. Clyde worked from sunrise to sundown on the eighty acres, and Duke wasn't old enough to be any real help—though he did shuck corn at harvesttime until his hands bled. Their nearest neighbor was at least a mile away, and there was nothing resembling the social life Molly had grown accustomed to in Iowa. As time passed and it seemed that they were making no progress at all, Clyde and Molly began fighting again, though the Browns' presence must have brought a semblance of peace to the household. Grandfather Brown was sixty-five and not much help to Clyde, but Duke remembered him fondly. He took particular delight in recalling how Grandfather

DUKE

Brown liked a taste of liquor now and then and how he kept a bottle of it hidden in the fields, where he and Duke took frequent walks so that he could take a sip and do a little jig; it was a secret Duke shared with his grandfather and one that he delighted in.

Duke often spoke of his family's hard times in Lancaster, but he also said that for him, as a boy of seven and eight, it was a good character-building experience and one that wasn't without its pleasurable moments. He started school—at age seven—in Lancaster, attending Lancaster Grammar School, on Cedar Avenue, during the 1914–15 school year. A new school building had been completed that summer, and two new teachers had been added, bringing the teaching staff to four. The school was about three miles from the Morrison homestead, and Duke used to walk the six-mile round trip on occasion. More often than not his dad let him ride the older of their two horses, particularly during inclement weather or whenever he needed to pick up a few supplies in Lancaster. The horse was so skinny that one of the villagers complained to authorities, who investigated the report. The school's principal, Mrs. A. Reed Averill, defended Duke, saying that he always carried feed and that he always fed the horse properly. It was finally determined that the horse was just too old to fatten up, and the matter was dropped. But it had been an embarrassment to Duke, one that he didn't forget. His classmates nicknamed him "Skinny" after the incident.

The village of Lancaster was a small one, and everyone knew that Marion Morrison's son had come out from Iowa to farm his spread. Clyde's poor financial condition must have been obvious to them. Duke recalled that the local dairyman offered him a cat, and as an incentive for Duke to take the cat off his hands, the dairyman insisted on providing milk to feed it; he had Duke stopping by his dairy every other day for a gallon of milk. He knew, of course, that the cat couldn't drink that much milk. It was the dairyman's way of providing the Morrison boys with the milk he felt they required, without seeming to be offering charity.

Duke also recalled his parents having to buy groceries on credit, usually just staples. Even then they didn't have much; their diet consisted mostly of the vegetables they grew and could store or can. Other than jackrabbit, which was plentiful, but tough and stringy and tiresome, they seldom had meat on the table. The Lancaster area is in one of the Pacific Flyways for migrating ducks, though, and so Clyde went duck hunting, and wild duck was a treat they always looked forward to.

Eventually, though, the farming venture was a failure. Clyde's first corn crop was a meager one. He sold all the corn he grew, but there was so little of it that Duke said he just about broke even for his twelve-hour-day efforts. The next crop or two had about the same yield, and Clyde grew very discouraged with farming. He had developed a sophisticated irrigation system and water was no problem, but there was just a limit to what one man could accomplish on eighty acres of land in a twelve-hour day.

Duke remembered that Clyde wasn't very satisfied with life on a farm and probably wouldn't have been even if the farm had prospered. Molly continued to long for the comforts and social life of the city. Aside from Clyde's wish to prove himself successful in Molly's eyes, he may have felt an obligation to his father, too, in trying to make the farm a success. If so, then he was released from this obligation on December 5, 1915, for that's the day Marion Mitchell Morrison died. Within months, Clyde gave up the farm. They left Lancaster in June of 1916, when Duke got out of school for the summer.

4

MARION MITCHELL MORRISON

DUKE'S paternal grandfather, Marion Mitchell Morrison, was a mystery figure in the Morrison family ancestry because Duke deliberately excluded him from the family history. In more than a half-century of interviews with writers and biographers, Duke made indirect reference to his paternal grandfather only once, and apparently never mentioned him by name.[1] And grandfather Morrison should have been the ancestor he was most proud of.

Marion Mitchell Morrison had been the soldier of the family and had been seriously wounded in combat; he had moved the Morrisons from Illinois to Iowa; he had been a successful local politician, serving as treasurer of Warren County, Iowa; he had become a successful businessman; he had come to the family's rescue when Clyde's business failed; and he had been instrumental in the family's move to California—a momentous move with respect to Duke's life and career. Yet it was not Grandfather Morrison but rather Grandfather Brown about whom Duke spoke fondly and often, and Grandfather Brown's achievements were relatively insignificant compared with those of Marion Mitchell Morrison.

All the more curious is the fact that Duke was so intent upon disassociating himself from his paternal grandfather that he publicly disavowed his own middle name. Once he achieved a semblance of fame, Duke told everyone that his true name was Marion *Michael* Morrison.[2] But in fact he was all the while signing his true name, Marion Mitchell Morrison, on legal documents, such as marriage licenses—which he both printed and signed in his own hand.

Duke even had an arrangement with Glendale High School, from which he was graduated in 1925, not to release any information about his attendance there unless it was cleared with him personally. This arrangement was honored by the school as a courtesy to Duke, and it was honored until his death in 1979.[3] Whenever a writer—or anyone—requested information about Duke, which was very often, the school's administrative secretary, Mrs. Esther Guzman, would call Duke's secretary (for years, Mary St. John, then Pat Stacy when Mary retired) and give her the specifics of the request. Mary or Pat would relay the request to Duke—even if he was away on location—and would get back to Mrs. Guzman with Duke's decision. Occasionally Duke himself would take Mrs. Guzman's calls. He would sometimes refuse to release any information, depending upon the writer and the publication, but more often than not he would cooperate. Duke always wanted to know exactly what information was being requested, and often he would instruct Mrs. Guzman to give out only the dates of his attendance and the year he graduated. Mrs. Guzman said that Duke was "somewhat restrictive of the kind of information given out," for reasons that she neither knew nor questioned.

Duke's scholastic, athletic, and extracurricular activities and achievements at Glendale High School were extraordinary. He is said to have graduated at the top of his class, and besides his athletic accomplishments, he was, among other things, an honor student; vice-president of his junior class; president of his senior class; a member of Comites, an honor society of Latin students; a sportswriter for the student newspaper, The Glendale *Explosion;* an actor and prop man in school plays; an orator who represented the school in a statewide Shakespearean contest; and a member and often chairman of numerous social activities committees. He had been very popular at Glendale High with both students and faculty, so why—more than fifty years after he had graduated—did he still have the high school administration call him each time someone requested information about his attendance there? The only logical answer is that the school records contained something that Duke was trying to suppress even half a century after he graduated.

Now that the restraints have been lifted from Duke's records—except for his grades, which are revealed only by transcript from one learning institution to another—and we have examined them, we found only one bit of information that Duke himself didn't make public at one time or another. And that is the fact that he was known at Glendale High by his true middle name: Mitchell. It's an apparently inconsequential fact that would have had significance only to Duke himself, had he not gone to such extraordinary efforts to hide it. The only time to our knowledge that he ever uttered the name publicly was when he did so as an apparent diversionary tactic during an interview: "I graduated from high school with a 96 average." He said; "I was salutatorian. The valedictorian was a girl named Marion Mitchell—and I was Marion Morrison!"[4]

In fact, other than Duke himself, there was no one in his graduation class named Mitchell. The girl he referred to was Marion Sears Mair. Apparently Duke assigned her the name so that if anyone checked the high school yearbook, *Stylus*, and noticed that he was listed as Marion Mitchell Morrison (which he is), it would be presumed a typographical error. Duke considered the name *Mitchell* a link to a part of his past—his paternal grandfather—that he wanted to keep hidden. This seems to be his sole reason for guarding his school records. And so attention is drawn to the mysterious Marion Mitchell Morrison.

We don't know exactly when Marion Morrison left Iowa for California, but judging from the events that followed, it must have been shortly after he made out his will in Indianola, Iowa, on July 1, 1910. Marion was sixty-five at the time; his wife, Weltha, had died less than a year earlier, and he had apparently decided to get his affairs in order and to live the rest of his years in California. He may have signed the deed to his Des Moines property over to his daughter, Mrs. Pearle K. Kirk, before leaving Iowa, for he made provisions in his will to leave her his "household goods, furniture, books, pictures, and everything contained in the home," and one assumes that the home referred to was his and Weltha's Des Moines place. Marion provided for the balance of his estate to be divided equally among his four children: George H. Morrison, who had settled in Tower, North Dakota; Guy J. Morrison, who was living in San Pedro, California; Pearle, who was the only one of his children who stayed in Iowa; and, of course, Duke's father, Clyde, who at the time the will was signed had moved, or was in the process of moving, from Winterset to Earlham.

As a wounded Civil War veteran, Marion was receiving a government pension of $21 a month, on which one could live fairly well in those days. He had apparently planned to live in semiretirement in California, for he continued to speculate in real estate there. He may have stayed with his son Guy in San Pedro upon his arrival, but shortly afterward he is thought to have settled for a while in Lancaster on the eighty-acre parcel that Clyde later farmed. But by 1914, when Clyde moved his family to California, Marion was living at 503 South Westlake Avenue in Los Angeles, and he had even remarried.

It was probably in 1912 that Marion married Emma J. Wescott; Emma was sixty-three at the time, and Marion was sixty-seven. Emma had been born in Boston, Massachusetts, in April of 1849, the daughter of Edward and Katherine Wescott, both of whom had emigrated from England. Emma was fifty years old when she moved to California in 1899, and she's thought to have been a widow when she married Marion Morrison. She was apparently a woman of means. She was active in Marion's real estate ventures, purchasing a number of properties, including a boardinghouse in Long Beach, California, with him. And she loaned him money on one occasion for the purchase of a lot in what is today Hawthorne, California, a venture that, presumably, she didn't want to participate in.

Emma also took care of Marion financially when he became ill, and after he died she made no claim on his estate (he had not written her into his will) except for the loan she had made him and the bills she had incurred in his name for his care. She apparently reached an out-of-court agreement with Clyde, who was appointed executor of his father's estate, whereby she kept the properties that she and Marion jointly owned, including the income property at Long Beach and one on Hickley Street in North Hollywood, while the several properties that Marion owned alone went into the estate.

In late 1928, Emma lost, through foreclosure, two of the properties she and Marion had purchased. By this time, she may have been confined to a convalescent home in Santa Monica, California, for it was there, on December 5, 1929—exactly thirteen years to the day from Marion's death—that she died at age eighty of pneumonia, following hip surgery.

Marion and Emma's married life was short-lived and, for Emma, traumatic. Within a year or two of their marriage, Marion began exhibiting symptoms of a debilitating mental illness. In November 1914, when Marion took a train up to Lancaster and arranged for the lumber Clyde needed to improve the Lancaster property, Marion's condition had apparently not reached the critical stage. But just four months later, in the following March, he began visiting Emma's doctor, J. R. Leadsworth, in Los Angeles. He made ten office calls before he was admitted to Thornycroft Farm, a private sanitarium on East Ninth Street in Glendale, California. Presumably, he was admitted there for observation, for he was released thirteen days later.

Between April 8, when he was released from Thornycroft, and June 3, 1915, Marion became so deranged that he was taken into custody by the Los Angeles Sheriff's Department. And on June 3, 1915, by order of the Los Angeles County Superior Court, he was escorted in the custody of Sheriff John C. Cline by train to Southern California State Hospital at Patton, a state mental institution fifty miles east of Los Angeles, near San Bernardino. On the day of his arrival, he was examined by two psychiatrists, declared insane, and formally committed. Six months later, on December

5, 1915, while still confined to the mental hospital, he died of a heart attack.

Marion's mental condition was diagnosed as senile psychosis, an illness not uncommon among the elderly; even today it accounts for about ten percent of new admissions to mental hospitals. Usually senile psychosis has a slow and insidious onset; one slips into the psychotic state almost imperceptibly. In Marion's case, however, the development of the disease may have been more abrupt, perhaps complicated and accelerated by the effects of the gunshot wound to his head he had received during the Civil War. In any case, the characteristics or symptoms of senile psychosis are often of a nature that can be extremely embarrassing to a family. And mental illness was even more a stigma at the turn of the century than it is today; Marion's commitment, for example, was arranged through the offices of what in those days was officially called the State Commission in Lunacy.

It was a pitiful ending for a man who had pulled himself from the carnage of the battlefield to marry, to raise a family, to become a successful farmer, public-office holder, and businessman. He was a man worthy of a family's veneration. Certainly Clyde must have taken pride in his father's accomplishments and must have recounted to Duke his fascinating story. But in the end, the old man had become a ward of the Commission in Lunacy.

In Duke's eyes, then, was Marion Morrison a lunatic? The skeleton in the family closet? The prevailing attitude of those who guided public figures, even in the 50s and 60s, was that mental illness in the family was somehow debasing. (In the mid-1950s, Marilyn Monroe, owing to her celebrity and on the advice of her studio and publicist, claimed to be an orphan all the while her mother was confined to a nearby mental institution.) Only fear of such an attitude would account for Duke's implicit denial of his grandfather Morrison's existence and his refusal to use the name unless it was legally necessary to do so.

Duke was only eight when his grandfather Morrison died. It must have been a shock for an eight-year-old to have a "crazy person" as a namesake. Still, judging from Duke's actions in his adulthood, there must have been more trauma than simply the shock of his grandfather's condition—more family upheaval or humiliation owing to his condition, perhaps. Consider the lengths he went to. More than half a century after his grandfather's death, at a time when mental disorders were understood to be forms of illness and not family curses, Duke was still forsaking not only his grandfather's name but also his memory!

This bewildering act is not at all consistent with Duke's character. Duke was a loving family man, an intelligent man, a basically sincere and honest man. The public controversy he occasionally stirred was always the result of his speaking the truth as he saw it —and to hell with the consequences. He wasn't the kind of man to forsake his own grandfather simply because the old man had succumbed to an illness that often affects the aged. Perhaps when he was gaining a foothold in the motion picture business he might have taken such advice from those who presumed that public knowledge of his having a "crazy person" in his family background might adversely affect his career. But for him to continue denying his own name fifty-six years later and to continue monitoring his high school records sixty-four years after his grandfather's death—and to his own death—is mystifying and sad.

It's hard to imagine what else could have occurred to make Duke, in effect, excommunicate his own grandfather. But something happened. Whatever it was, it must have wounded Duke very deeply, for the wound never healed.

5

GLENDALE

DUKE was just turning nine years old when his family moved to Glendale, California, where he spent the remaining and probably to him the most important years of his childhood. Clyde found work as a drug clerk at the Glendale Pharmacy on Broadway, across from city hall, and he rented a house just around the corner from the pharmacy at 421 South Isabel Street. Duke was enrolled at Doran Elementary School, and the family settled into the relative comfort of city life once again.

Glendale was a fine city to grow up in, a city nestled against the wooded southern slopes of the Verdugo Hills, the foothills of the San Gabriel Mountains, which border it on three sides and which form part of the Los Angeles basin's northern rim. When the Morrisons moved there in 1916, Glendale had only eight thousand residents and was surrounded by vineyards and orchards and ranches. Despite its rural atmosphere, it was a fast-growing commercial city, less than ten miles from downtown Los Angeles and only five miles from Hollywood, both of which were just minutes away by Red Car, L.A.'s then-elaborate commuter trolley system.

Although Molly was thankful at having escaped the hardships of the Lancaster farm, the move to Glendale didn't appreciably improve the quality of her life with Clyde; neither did it bring harmony or stability to the Morrison household, for although they stayed in Glendale, they never really settled anywhere. In an era when people were far less mobile than they are today, the Morrisons were looked upon as nomads by their Glendale neighbors; the city's directories and newspapers published during the nine years they lived in Glendale reveal that they moved an average of more than once a year. Duke also claimed to have lived at two undocumented addresses, bringing the total number of Morrison dwellings to at least twelve in that nine-year period. The fact of anyone moving that often around a small town in those days was considered strange, but the seemingly random pattern of the Morrisons' movements was considered even stranger. Clyde told customers that his moves were made to be nearer work or his sons' schools. In fact, all his moves were made within a ten-block radius. One of them necessitated the boys having to change schools, and most of the houses he moved to were farther from his work, not closer—which, in any case, made little difference; all four of the pharmacies where Clyde worked while he lived in Glendale were within six blocks of one another.

The frequent moves seem to indicate financial mismanagement, which had always been one of Molly's chief complaints against Clyde. Duke described his father as a "nonprosperous druggist who was lucky to clear $100 a month."[1] In those days, of course, such a sum was a fairly good middle-class income for a family of four, yet the Morrisons were considered very poor, moving from one fairly run-down rental to another. From the time Duke was twelve, he had to work at part-time jobs to keep decent clothes on his back, a situation that caused many arguments between Clyde and Molly.

When Grandfather Morrison's estate was finally settled in 1918, Clyde apparently used part of his small inheritance to speculate in the booming real estate market. In early March 1920 he purchased a six-room house at 313 West Garfield Avenue, while his family continued to live in an apartment above the Glendale Pharmacy, where they moved after selling a house at 404 North Isabel in December of 1919.[2] On June 3, 1920, the Morrisons sold a house on Christopher Street. The family apparently never occupied any of the houses, for during the time that they purchased and sold them, they were living in rentals at 315 South Geneva and 443 West Colorado Street. After the sale of the last house, they moved from Colorado Street to a rental at 815 South Central Avenue, then to 129 South Kenwood, then to 245 South Orange Street, before finally settling in an apartment at 207 West Windsor Road.

Clyde didn't seem to have profited much from his real estate ventures. He bought and sold all three houses within a two-year period, and then never again bought another piece of property. If he made any money at all on his investments, it couldn't have been much. There were no signs of prosperity; he always drove old automobiles, and the houses he rented for his family were politely referred to by his Glendalian contemporaries as "fixer-uppers." During his first nine years in Glendale, Clyde was employed full-time as a drug clerk first at the Glendale Pharmacy, then at Roberts and Echols Drugs, then at Jensen's Drugstore, and finally at Brown's Drugs. After he left the drugstore business for good in 1926, he became the manager of a Los Angeles paint store, a job he held until his death in 1937.[3]

The Glendalians' general impression of Clyde was that of an ineffective man heading an impoverished family, a man who tried to provide for his family but who was easily discouraged in doing so. They also felt that Clyde drank more than was prudent and that the Morrisons may have been forced to move frequently because they weren't prompt in paying their rent. Molly, however, was the backbone and "worker" of the family; she even took in washing to help meet the family's basic financial needs. The consensus was that Clyde was personable but inept, and a failure as the family breadwinner.[4]

Clyde Morrison was also remembered by Glendalians as a dapper and charming man, but an irresponsible one. He didn't seem to be bothered much by things like bills. His gentlemanly manner, his friendliness, and his neat and well-groomed appearance were impressive. He was always fashionably dressed. He didn't have his suits tailor-made, but he always wore a new light suit each spring and a new warmer suit in the fall. He was what old-timers called a hat-tipper, too. Glendalians found this amusing, saying that if a small crowd was gathered at the ticket office of the Palace Grand Theatre when Clyde was closing the drugstore, he practically wore his arm out tipping his hat before he reached his car. He tipped his hat with special enthusiasm for the ladies, and it was thought that there was more than one woman in Clyde Morrison's life.

Molly seemed to be a "nice woman, well-liked and rather plain." She was "sickly"—at least during the time she was in Glendale—and she seemed to enjoy her illnesses, whether they were real or imagined.[5]

From the time Duke was about ten or twelve, his parents stayed together only for his and Robert's sake. Their explosively unstable relationship probably had a worse effect on their children than a separation or a divorce would have had. The icy silences and too-formal civilities of Clyde and Molly's infrequent truces were about the best conditions that Duke and Robert could expect and hope for at home. Clyde and Molly weren't at all discreet in airing their differences. Even the presence of Duke's or Robert's friends apparently did nothing to deter their flare-ups. One of Duke's earliest boyhood friends, Ralf "Pexy" Eckles —whom Duke met in grammar school and with whom he went to high school and on to the University of Southern California— admitted that Clyde and Molly's battles were generally known and that he had been around when the Morrisons argued. Like Duke, he was just a youngster then, and so he neither understood nor was interested in the substance of the bitter arguments. Duke spent a good deal of his time at the Eckles house in order to avoid the fighting at home.

Despite an often unsettling home life, Duke's childhood was active and fulfilling once a semblance of continuity was established. The boys' maternal grandparents, the Browns, had moved from the Lancaster farm to Valentia Street in Los Angeles, about five miles south of Glendale, and Duke and Robert occasionally stayed with them on weekends. In a city whose population exploded from eight thousand to seventy thousand during their first eight years there, the Morrisons gained a modest prominence as one of the "established" (though mobile) families among a veritable hoard of strangers—a prominence brought about primarily by Clyde's position at the Glendale Pharmacy, with its city-hall clientele. This modest prominence is attested to by the following newspaper item regarding Duke, then twelve years old:

THUMB CAUGHT BY BICYCLE
CHAIN

Clyde Morrison's eldest son, Marion M., got the thumb of his left hand caught between the chain and sprocket wheel of his bicycle last Saturday while tuning it up for practice on the boys' speedway at the corner of Hawthorne and Central Avenue, in hopes of entering some of the races. The flesh was badly lacerated and the joint spread somewhat, necessitating the care of a surgeon, but the boy is getting along very favorably.

By the time the article appeared, Duke was into the mainstream of the Glendale community, but the adjustment hadn't been easy. He entered Doran Elementary School in the fourth grade, a shy and very skinny nine-year-old stranger, taller even than the school's sixth-graders. He had been mocked for his skinniness and his poverty at Lancaster Elementary, which had undermined his confidence. Being among the tallest—if not the tallest—of boys at Doran Elementary made it impossible for him to slip into their ranks inconspicuously. He was very self-conscious about his height, and he remained so until he reached high school; it was a distinct handicap in grammar school, for unlike his fourth-grade peers, Duke wasn't too small to be picked on by the school's older students, particularly the bullies. His natural shyness, his wish to make friends, and his desire for a harmony among his peers that he couldn't have at home made him vulnerable.

At first, Duke's world was a hostile one, with mocking humiliations and physical conflicts in the streets and at school, while his home remained an arena of constant and bitter battles between his mother and father. His only sanctuary was with the subjects of his studies and with the interior worlds of poets and popular novelists that he discovered at an early age. He grew to be an intelligent and docile child, and so he read a lot and excelled in school, becoming a favorite among his grammar and intermediate school teachers. He was also a sensitive and likable boy, and he had no heart for fighting. His father had taught him never to start a fight or to back down from one if provoked. So he stood his ground and took a few beatings until, at age ten or eleven, it occurred to him that his height and reach and the two large hands dangling at the ends of his arms could be used to persuade would-be toughs that their time might be better and less painfully spent at pursuits other than provoking him. By this time, however, he had grown even taller, and his size was usually sufficient deterrent in itself.

It was at Doran Elementary that Duke first met Ralf Pexy Eckles and developed a friendship that lasted long after Duke and Pexy went their separate ways.[6] It wasn't until the fifth grade that they became close friends; that was before Duke got his nickname. He was known as Marion to his family and his teachers, of course, but Pexy told us that none of his friends dared call him Marion; it was a common name for girls in those days, too, and Duke found that embarrassing. So his friends called him Morrison.

When Duke was passing into the sixth grade, in 1918, Clyde moved the family to 443 West Colorado Street, which was close enough to their old neighborhood for Duke to continue the friendships he had cultivated at Doran, but which put him in the Columbus Street School district. He was attending the Columbus Street School when he got his nickname. As he often told the story, he and Robert had an Airedale named Duke. Robert was only seven at the time, and not as active and adventurous as his older brother, so the dog naturally took to Marion and followed him everywhere. When school started, the Airedale became a problem; he persisted in following Marion to school, and school authorities had animals impounded if they were found hanging about the school grounds. The problem was soon resolved by firemen at a fire station Marion passed on his way to and from school; they took a liking to the dog and so detained him each morning until his young master was out of sight. The firemen knew the dog's name, but not the name of his tall, gangling and likable master, and so they began calling the dog Little Duke and the boy Big Duke. Marion Morrison took to the name immediately. It had a noble, dignified, and masculine sound to it. Anything was better than Marion, so he encouraged his friends to call him Duke, too, and he used the nickname the rest of his life.

The following year, Duke finished grade school and was transferred to Wilson Intermediate School, where only the seventh and eighth grades were taught and where he was reunited with his Doran Elementary classmates. "I used to tell the students to choose their own seats," Mrs. Vera Brinn, the seventh and eighth grade math teacher said. "New students always take seats way back. Not Marion. He sat down in the front row of seats, close to my desk." Mrs. Brinn taught Duke algebra and geometry during his two years at Wilson. She remembered him as a very tall and thin and handsome boy. She said he was quiet, too, and clean and neat and always well dressed. He always wore a blue serge suit, white shirt, and tie. She remembered his attentiveness and intelligence; Duke never volunteered answers in class, but he always knew them when called upon.

One thing that troubled her, though, was Duke's pale complexion and physical lethargy. He didn't appear well to her. "I spoke to Marion about it, and he said he was fine. So I sent for his mother. Mrs. Morrison was a fine lady. She was embarrassed about Marion's health. She said the reason he was tired was because he worked mornings before school. I had no realization that the family was poor, for young Marion looked so well got up in class. Marion did not tell me about the job. He was a reserved young man."[7]

Molly Morrison had cause to be embarrassed about Duke's fatigue; he was working much harder than a boy his age should. It was common for boys Duke's age to do chores for pocket money. But Duke had just turned twelve and was holding two part-time jobs—both, apparently, out of necessity. Using the bicycle he had gotten when he was seven, he was out at five thirty each morning delivering the Los Angeles *Examiner*, then off to school, then on to the Glendale Pharmacy to deliver prescriptions until sundown or later. Clyde Morrison didn't provide enough money to buy school clothes for Duke and Robert. This enraged Molly, and she finally told Duke, "Looks like you will have to go out and make some money yourself, Marion, if you expect to look decent in class."[8] So Duke went to work and provided school clothes for himself and for his brother Robert, too, whom Duke always looked after with genuine affection.

While Duke was at Wilson Intermediate, he joined the Boy Scouts of America and was apparently very active in Troop 4, for he earned numerous merit badges and became a first-class scout. He was always gregarious; he enjoyed participating with others in group activities and organizations. When he outgrew the scouts, he joined the DeMolays, a boys' organization.

Aside from the sandlot baseball and football games that Duke and friends like Pexy Eckles organized, he was involved with another group of youngsters whose consuming interest was in playing imaginary games like cowboys and Indians. Unlike the games their youthful counterparts played, though, the Louise Street Gang, as they called themselves, didn't imagine themselves to be cowboys or Indians or pirates and the like; they imagined themselves to be *actors* portraying the parts of cowboys and Indians and all manner of heroes and villains. With makeshift props and a tripod topped with a wooden box for a movie camera, they staged adventures, with one of them acting as the director of the "motion picture" and someone acting as the cameraman and the rest of them actors. Often they'd "film" scenes from the feature they had all seen that day at the Palace Grand Theatre (where Duke had seen his first motion picture when he was about ten), or sometimes they'd have "script conferences" and would make up their own stories. According to Duke, their moviemaking reached its most inspired pitch after they had seen a Douglas Fairbanks, Sr., swashbuckler. There were several actors whom Duke admired in those days, but none more than Fairbanks. He dreamed of being like him. Duke particularly admired the dazzling smile Fairbanks flashed in the face of danger and the daring athletic stunts he performed with seemingly effortless grace; Duke tried to emulate him by smiling and leaping from garage roofs to trees, giving his all for the imaginary movies.

Pretending to be actors portraying heroes and villains, rather than pretending to be the heroes and villains themselves, was a convoluted twist on the games children usually play. Unlike most children, whose movie experiences were limited to images projected on a silver screen, the kids in Glendale were privy to what went on behind the camera, too. There were two movie studios in Glendale when Duke was growing up: Sierra Photoplays and the Kalem Company. Glendale's proximity to Hollywood and its lovely setting of the purple-hued Verdugo Hills and San Gabriel Mountains made it an ideal outdoor film location. Most of the major studios filmed there, and the Louise Street Gang spent a good deal of time observing them.

Duke had learned something about the making of movies even before the Louise Street Gang was formed; in his first year in Glendale, he not only observed the business but also "worked" in it. The railroad spur in Glendale was used by most of the movie companies to film railroad sequences; Duke used to hang around whenever they were filming. He got to know the grips (movie stagehands), and they'd often let him help them with something like holding a reflector to help light a scene. As payment, he'd be given a box lunch and allowed to eat with the crew.[9]

One experience that Duke often recounted was the time he was nine years old and watching actress Pearl White film segments of her adventure serial *The Perils of Pauline*. He was astonished at the way the star was treated. "That's the first time I ever heard a man swear at a woman," Duke said. "This director was filming one of Pearl White's adventures. The star was supposed to climb a telephone pole and drop off the bottom [lower foot spikes of the pole] —she really wasn't high up at all. The director said, 'Goddamn, get the hell up there and *do* it!' I was shocked!"[10]

A few years later, Duke experienced his first boyhood crush while watching another movie company at work. The object of his first attraction to the opposite sex was actress Helen Holmes, star of the movie serial *The Hazards of Helen*. What attracted him to the actress at first was a dangerous stunt she executed at the same location that Pearl White's sequences had been filmed. Miss Holmes was bound hand and foot and placed across the railroad tracks in the path of an oncoming train. Just as the train reached her, she rolled between the tracks and the train rumbled over her, just inches above her body. A shallow pit had been dug for her to roll into. It had been an awesome stunt to behold, and Duke was captivated by Helen Holmes's courage and beauty.

What fanned young Duke Morrison's ardor for Miss Holmes was the fact that she lived in Glendale. Her lavish and sprawling estate was only a mile or so from the Morrisons' rented house on Colorado Street. Duke soon learned that it was Miss Holmes's habit to go horseback riding almost every morning, and so on summer mornings he often rode his bicycle over to her estate just to get a distant and fleeting glimpse of her. He worshipped her for the better part of a summer, until his newly awakened attraction to the opposite sex was generalized to include those nearer his own age.

In the spring of 1921, Duke graduated from Wilson Intermediate. Sixty-six students and their families attended the graduation ceremonies, and a few of the students were chosen to address them; Duke was one of them. He had written an essay in his English class titled "The World War." The apparently stirring and patriotic spirit of the piece was thought appropriate for the graduation, and so he was asked to recite it. Rather than read, Duke apparently memorized it, and although he forgot a few lines during his presentation, it was generally acknowledged that his stage presence, good speaking voice, and forceful delivery more than compensated for his relatively minor mistakes.

Duke was still acutely self-conscious about his appearance when he entered Glendale Union High School in 1921. He had yet to reach his full height, but he was over six feet and weighed only 140 pounds. His weight finally worked to his advantage, though, for in those days the football league had a "light team" class, and qualification was determined not by grade level but by weight. To a fourteen-year-old freshman like Duke Morrison, football was more important even than girls, and he soon stopped worrying about being tall and skinny. He even dieted. Anything for football. One of Duke's classmates who played substitute end on the football team, Norman Nelson, said of Duke, "He weighed 140 like me when we started high school. The C.I.F. [football league] had a ruling at the start of that year that if you weighed in at the start of the season as a flyweight, you could play all season on the flyweight. We were both doing everything we could to get our weight down so we could start on the team, including drinking Pluto Water for lunch. We both got our weight down, but then the C.I.F. changed its rule and said you had to weigh in before every game."[11]

In his second year of high school, Duke began excelling in scholastic activities, too. He earned his one and only honor pin that year, a bronze pin for maintaining a B average. He was also a member of the Latin club, Comites, which was open only to honor students, and he joined the stage crew. The rudiments he learned of stagecraft and the use of props were useful to him a few years later, but on at least one occasion he took his propping less seriously than the drama teacher expected of him. "When I was a sophomore," he recalled, "I became friends with the high school drama coach and I began propping shows for him. He'd put on two-act plays during the afternoon recess and I helped out. There was a guy I didn't particularly care for in one of the shows, so I decided to play a gag on him.

"As a prop man, I was supposed to place three phones on a desk, but I didn't. So when the guy came out and gave his first speech, I rang a bell offstage. He went over to the desk, looked at it—and then at the audience. The poor son-of-a-bitch was completely lost. The audience started laughing. At that point the director came out on stage, kicked me in the pants, and rang down the curtain!"[12]

Duke's record at high school was impressive. He was popular in his junior and senior years, and he participated in more social activities on and off campus than the average student. He was vice president of his junior class and first-semester president of his senior class. He played left guard for the school's league-winning team. He represented the school in a Southern California Shakespeare contest. He was a member or officer of numerous social and scholastic clubs, a stagehand in the drama department, an actor in two plays, a sportswriter for the school newspaper, and he graduated with very close to a B average.

This is not to say that Duke was a model citizen at Glendale High; he ran afoul of the school's principal, George U. Moyse, on at least one occasion when he and Pexy Eckles were instrumental in shutting down the school for a day. Duke showed up at school one morning with two bottles of asafetida, a gum resin derived from Asiatic plants and used as an antispasmodic; the stuff is so disgustingly foul-smelling that it can induce nausea. Duke gave one of the bottles to Pexy, and together they sprinkled the resin— a bit too liberally—about the halls and classrooms. Everyone got nauseated and the school had to be closed for the day.

The boys hadn't anticipated such an extreme reaction to their prank, and it scared them. To rid himself of the evidence, Pexy broke his bottle, buried the pieces, and even burned the label. Unfortunately, Duke was a little more casual with the evidence he had at hand. He threw his bottle into a hydrangea bush at the main entrance to the school.

The school administration called upon the student body for a confession, but neither Pexy nor Duke was of a mind to confess. Eventually the bottle Duke threw away was found and traced to the pharmacy where Clyde Morrison worked. It happened that Duke had labeled the bottle himself, so when he showed up at the pharmacy on the evening that the bottle had been turned over to his father, Clyde asked him to spell *asafetida*. Duke misspelled the word exactly as he had misspelled it on the label. The mystery was solved. When Pexy heard that Duke had been caught, he confessed his part in the incident, and both boys were made to apologize before an assembly of the entire student body before they were readmitted to school. They were put on probation for a while.

A semester or two later, Duke and Pexy were caught in another scheme. Clyde Morrison had taken a job as manager for the newly opened Jensen's Drug Store, which was owned by Bob Jensen, who also owned the Palace Grand Theatre in the same building. As usual, Duke worked for his father in the evenings, delivering prescriptions, jerking sodas, and sweeping up, and he soon became acquainted with the Palace Grand theater manager, who eventually offered him free admission to the theater at any time in exchange for distributing notices announcing the change of bill. Since the bill changed two or three times a week and there were hundreds of handbills to distribute, the manager had several boys working for him, and Duke arranged for Pexy Eckles to get in on the offer, too.

Both boys loved the movies—particularly Duke, who was an inveterate moviegoer and who saw every change of bill, often sitting though several showings of each. The distribution route was long, though, the handbills heavy, and eventually the boys hit upon a scheme to lighten their work load: they began throwing the handbills away. It wasn't long before they were caught at their deceitful practice and fired. This was particularly embarrassing for Duke, who had to continue working for his father at the drugstore and so came face to face with the theater manager more often than he cared to.

There were no fraternities at Glendale High, so Duke and Pexy and about ten other boys formed their own. Their "frat house" was the second floor of Pexy's parents' two-story garage on Orange Street. Their primary activity was trying to sneak into the Palace Grand without passes and boycotting parties unless each of their fraternity brothers was invited. They also pooled their money for bootleg booze. In spite of Prohibition, the boys found a pharmacist in town (not at the pharmacy where Clyde Morrison worked) who sold alcohol laced with wild cherry syrup at two dollars a pint, and so the boys sometimes partied at their fraternity house above Pexy's garage.

As a tall and dark and handsome young man—and a varsity football player—Duke was popular with the girls at Glendale High. According to Pexy, he was a fine dancer, too. He liked to attend the Saturday afternoon "tea dances" at the famous Cocoanut Grove of the Ambassador Hotel and the La Monica Ballroom at Ocean Park. Pexy didn't care much for dancing, but his father had two cars and Pexy could always get one of them, so Duke usually talked him into going to the dances. The Cocoanut Grove was Duke's favorite spot, for it was frequented by young Hollywood starlets like Joan Crawford, with whom Duke would one day co-star.

One would have expected a young man as popular with the Glendale High girls as Duke Morrison to have a steady girlfriend, as most of the junior and senior boys did. But Duke didn't. To go steady in those days meant having to take the girl out at least once a week, and Duke couldn't afford steady dates. Then, too, he had a bad reputation for drinking and traveling with a "fast" crowd by the time he reached the junior and senior levels of high school, and Glendale parents forbade their daughters to go out with him.[13]

Duke apparently began drinking at age sixteen, during his sophomore year. He claimed that he didn't suffer a hangover after his first drunk and that one of the effects of alcohol that he particularly liked was that it helped him overcome his shyness with girls. "After that [first drunk]," he said, "I would drink almost every weekend, and I didn't like dating girls who were against my drinking." He did have one steady girlfriend, Polly Richmond, whom he met during his sophomore year. For a while, he took her to school dances and the like, and afterward they'd go to the Tam-O-Shanter on Los Feliz Boulevard, Glendale's first fast-food restaurant. But when Duke began drinking and running with what he called "probably the toughest roughest gang of guys in the Glendale High School," Polly severed their relationship.[14]

"I didn't usually hang around with them [the rough crowd]," Duke said, "except for drinking and drag racing and picking up a certain type of girl on Saturday nights. I just kept my drinking companions separated from my refined Glendale friends."[15] His refined friends were, of course, his fraternity brothers and most of the girls in Glendale Union High School.

Duke's "double life" was no secret to his teachers, either. After Duke gained fame in the thirties, someone at Glendale High thought it a good idea to have his former teachers record their remembrances of his high school years. One teacher noted her "amazement" that owing to his "fast life," Marion often fell asleep in her class, yet he maintained good grades and set high standards of achievement in school.[16]

As his senior year began, Duke naturally looked to the future, and it didn't hold much promise. He wanted to continue his education, but had it not been for the extraordinary record achieved by the Glendale High School football team during his senior year, he would not have been able to do so.

The 1924–25 Glendale Dynamiters, led by coach Normal C. Hayhurst, were a high school phenomenon. Nearly all of the starting eleven were six feet or taller, and none weighed less than 170 pounds. By physical standards of the day, they were giants, and they totally outclassed every football team in their league. No one could beat them. No one could even score upon them in regular-season play. It wasn't until one of their two postseason semifinal games that they were finally scored upon, and they went on to win that one 15 to 10. By the time they met Long Beach Poly High School in the Los Angeles Stadium in a game to determine the Southern California high school championship, they were undefeated and had scored 189 points to their opponents' 10. They lost the championship game 15 to 8, but their team had been Glendale's finest, and the respectable loss detracted little from the record the team had compiled—a record that did not go unnoticed among college football recruiters.

One of Coach Normal Hayhurst's assistants was Vic Francy, a Glendalian himself who went on to coach Glendale's Hoover High School track teams for twenty-seven years. Francy was a student coach and was still attending USC at the time he assisted Coach Hayhurst, and it was Francy who recommended Duke to the coaching staff at USC. "One thing they insisted," Francy said, "was that he [Duke] had good grades. I checked his record, and he had 19 A's."[17] So it was owing largely to Vic Francy's recommendation that Duke was offered a two-year football scholarship at the University of Southern California—a scholarship, as it turned out, that was instrumental in getting Duke into the motion picture business.

PART THREE

6

USC AND
FOX STUDIOS

In September of 1925, Duke was enrolled as a pre-law student at the University of Southern California in Los Angeles. USC was a private, very expensive, and highly exclusive institution. Its alumni were among the most prominent and influential leaders in Southern California commerce and society, and its students were, for the most part, the children of the well-to-do and wealthy, of bankers and lawyers and doctors and corporation executives. It was into their ranks that Duke Morrison stepped one September afternoon when he crossed the threshold of his new home: the Sigma Chi fraternity house, about a mile or so from the USC campus.

Duke arrived that day with a few dollars in his pocket, the clothes on his back, and an old suitcase that contained all his worldly possessions: one suit, a couple of shirts and ties, some socks and underwear, one sweater, and perhaps an extra pair of trousers. Pexy Eckles recalled Duke's entire wardrobe because there were so few items.

The disparity between Duke's social status and that of his Sigma Chi brothers didn't trouble him in the least. The diffident boy had grown into an imposingly large and supremely self-confident young man; ambition and tenacity were two of his strongest character traits. Besides, Duke wasn't moving in among strangers; he and Pexy (also a Sigma Chi pledge) had already met most of the fraternity members on a get-acquainted outing, and Duke had liked them all.

The two-year football scholarship that had brought Duke to USC covered only his tuition and university fees; nothing more. Owing to Duke's need—and to the university's need as well—the athletic department used its considerable influence to help him earn his way. With professional football still in its infancy, collegiate football was even more a national craze than it is today. As USC did not have a winning football team, they hired a football coach named Howard Jones. Jones had a fine coaching reputation, and he eventually brought winning football and national esteem to the university. The semester that Duke started at USC was Jones's first season, and even before the season began, his staff had scouted the area for prospects who could play his style of football. Duke was one of them.

Jones's recruiters had reported that young Morrison's family was in no position to assist him financially, so the athletic department arranged with an alumnus to get Duke a few hours' work at the telephone company each week to cover his personal expenses —a job with flexible hours that didn't conflict with football practice or the season's schedule of games. They also arranged for the fraternity to provide Duke with room and board in exchange for working in the fraternity house dining room and washing dishes.

Duke thoroughly enjoyed college and fraternity life. Sigma Chi had a new house under construction nearer the campus, which wasn't quite ready for occupancy that fall, and Duke was "wedged" into the old fraternity house. It was a three-story, mid-Victorian-style building with clapboard siding. It had a meeting room on the third floor, a kitchen and dining room, a parlor, and a large communal bathroom, with open-stalled showers and several toilets and washbowls; every other inch of the old place was given over to wall-to-wall metal army-surplus bunk beds, for it was home for about twenty-five fraternity men and it was very overcrowded. It also had a sleeping porch, and it was there that Duke was given an upper bunk. Owing to the overcrowded conditions, Pexy Eckles lived at home in Glendale that first semester, though his presence was required at the Sigma Chi house the first week—traditionally "hell week" in fraternity and sorority circles.

The Sigma Chis' hazing consisted mostly of assigning its pledges menial tasks, like shining the shoes of all the fraternity brothers, washing their cars, and the like. Naturally, their treatment during hell week was more harsh. Once during the week Duke and Pexy weren't allowed to sleep for twenty-four hours, and on the final night they were subjected to a hazing practice common to most fraternities: each pledge was searched to ensure that he had no money, then he was made to lie down on the floor of an automobile and driven around campus until he lost all sense of direction, then finally taken to some distant, desolate spot and dropped off, leaving him to find his way back to the fraternity house as best he could. Pexy was left on a narrow, deserted winding mountain road late at night, a site that he eventually discovered was the Santa Monica Mountains above Malibu Beach, about thirty miles from the campus.

The general hazing of pledges continued until they were initiated into the fraternity five or six months after they pledged. Once hell week was over, Duke found that the hazing wasn't too bad unless one broke the rules of the house, most of which were adopted to ensure the continuance of common decency and consideration for others. Coming in late and disturbing the sleep of others was taboo, for example, as was drinking too much or bringing alcohol into the fraternity house—this was during Prohibition, when the sale, possession, and consumption of alcohol was against the law; the fraternity was scrupulous in keeping alcohol off the premises. Later, there were a few times when Duke and Pexy broke one or another of the rules, but in those months before initiation they were particularly careful. Then, too, Duke was too tired and too busy to get into mischief that first semester, with part-time work at the phone company, waiting table and washing dishes at the fraternity house, his studies, and football practice and the games. This hardly left him time for a good night's sleep.

Duke earned a spot as first-string guard on the USC freshman team that first season, together with four other former members of the Glendale Dynamiters championship team: Bill Bradbury, Clayton Philips, Leslie Lavell, and Darrel Elliott. The team was fielded under freshman coach Clifford Herd, who, at the direction of coach Howard Jones, drilled them in the brand of football that eventually made Jones famous in college football circles: a hard-hitting and lightning-fast running attack that buried opposing teams under mountains of points before they could even attempt to adjust to USC's fast game. After the first few wins, USC fans nicknamed Cliff Herd's freshman team "the thundering herd," and it went undefeated that season, even beating its arch rival, Stanford. Duke earned his football letter, but unfortunately he played so hard that he landed himself a position on the sidelines, too—on crutches and in a cast. During one of the last games of the season he fractured an ankle. Duke hobbled around on crutches for weeks, terribly despondent because he couldn't finish the season.

During the two-week Christmas break, Duke went home to Glendale, where he and Pexy got jobs with the Glendale Post Office. The post office was inundated with work, as it always is that time of year, so the boys could put in as many overtime hours as they wanted. Duke's job with the phone company was either phasing out or had been phased out, and he was trying to earn enough money to carry him through the spring semester and until summer, when he could find a full-time job.

In the spring, the Sigma Chi brothers and their pledges moved into their new quarters just across the street from the campus. It was a beautiful new building, designed for use as a fraternity house, a two-story California Spanish place with a red-tile roof and private two-man rooms and a larger dining room, which, like the one in the old house, doubled as a study room for students and their tutors during the nondining hours. It also featured something else that those who broke the rules didn't appreciate. In the center of its enormous communal bathroom was a specially designed bathtub used for an odious practice that came to be known as tubbing, a sadistic and dangerous form of punishment that has since been outlawed by fraternities.

"We had meetings every Monday night," Pexy recalled, "at which fraternity brothers were sentenced for transgressions. If the transgression was a major one, the offender was sentenced to the tub." In the tubbing ritual, the bathtub would be filled with cold water to which ice was added. Then the victim would be bound hand and foot. A wet pillowcase would be placed over his head, and three or four members would lower him into the tub and hold him underwater for a minute or two before pulling him out and plunging him in again before he had a chance to take a deep breath. This process would be repeated a number of times, depending upon the gravity of the offense. "It was a frightening experience," Pexy said, "and one that I believe was outlawed after a pledge was drowned—not at USC, but at one of the universities in the East, I think."

Both Pexy and Duke got tubbed on a couple of occasions. "I remember one time in particular," he said, "because during the tubbing Duke got us in worse trouble than we were in to begin with. I don't recall what we had done, but we were both sentenced to the tub. Someone had suggested to Duke that if he held some ketchup in his mouth just before the tubbing, then spit some of it out while he was underwater, the guys would think it was blood and it would scare them into pulling him out. Well, he did it, and it worked. It really scared them. But when they pulled him out and frantically pulled the pillowcase off his head, the damn fool started laughing and everyone realized what he had done. They got so mad that they redoubled their efforts and very nearly drowned *both* of us that night!"

Pexy was around to be tubbed because he had moved into the new fraternity house that spring and was Duke's roommate. Since it wasn't football season, Duke had more time, and so he and Pexy had begun hanging around together again, double-dating (and getting tubbed). Sometimes they'd take dates dancing at the Biltmore Hotel ballroom or the Cocoanut Grove, but usually they couldn't afford those places, so they'd take a stack of records and a bottle or two of pharmacy gin over to some girl's house and dance there. It was about this time, too, that Duke and Pexy made

a little money as extras in motion pictures, even before Duke
began working at Fox studios.

"Movies with college themes or backgrounds, particularly collegiate football, were very popular at the time," Pexy said.
"Nearly all the studios were making them, and so were coming
over to USC and using students as extras. Duke worked as a football player in several of them, along with other members of the
team. Being of slighter build, I was usually employed as a football
fan in the crowd scenes. I remember that one of them was filmed
in the Rose Bowl; I don't recall any of their titles, though; they
weren't important films, and there were quite a few of them.

"I do recall the title of one we worked in, though, because it
wasn't a football picture. It was a big-budget film and it starred
John Gilbert. It was called *Bardelays the Magnificent* [a 1926 MGM
release]. Duke portrayed one of the spear-carrying guards who
were gathered around the gallows where Gilbert was about to be
hanged. The script called for Gilbert's character to grab a spear
from one of the guards and use it to pole-vault over the crowd,
thereby escaping. Since I was about Gilbert's size and build, they
employed me as his double, and I did the pole-vaulting stunt.
Duke and I enjoyed such work and were grateful for the pay,
which was about eight or ten dollars a day—good money back
then."

According to Pexy, Duke never expressed interest in an acting
career during his USC days. "Duke's interest was solely in finishing college. Even when he began working at Fox, he did so only
to make enough money to stay in college. I don't think the idea of
becoming an actor even occurred to him. Certainly none of us
who knew him ever expected him to become an actor."

It was during that spring semester of 1926 that Duke met and
fell in love with the young woman who would eventually become
his first wife. The occasion of his meeting her was an Easter-week
gathering of students at Balboa, a beach resort adjacent to Newport Beach, about fifty miles south of Los Angeles.

The gathering of students at Balboa during the Easter holidays
was—and still is—a tradition. Fraternity and sorority members
rented houses or apartments there and spent the week entertain-

ing themselves by crashing one another's parties and just hanging out and getting to know one another. Activities were seldom planned; indeed, the whole point in going down there was to get away from the structured life, to enjoy the spontaneity, to drift with the flow of activity. One night Duke and a few of the Sigma Chi brothers dropped in at a dance pavilion called The Green Lantern, where Duke chanced to meet a young woman who shared his enthusiasm for dancing. Her name was Carmen Saenz; she was pleasant to be with and a very good dance partner, so she and Duke spent the rest of the evening dancing.

When it came time for Carmen to leave, Duke walked her home. Unlike the other young women gathered at Balboa that week, Carmen wasn't a sorority girl. Her family had a summer house at Balboa, and she was down from Los Angeles with her parents and sisters for the holidays. She was one of four daughters of Alicia and José S. Saenz. Mr. Saenz was a business entrepreneur and consul general for Panama in the United States.

When they got to her house, Carmen invited Duke in. They found Carmen's sister Josephine and her date sitting in the parlor. The couples talked for a while, and after getting acquainted they decided to go out for hamburgers at a nearby café. Duke had taken a liking to his date's slightly younger sister, whom they called Josie, when he and Carmen had entered the house, but it wasn't until he was seated opposite her in the beachfront café that he took particular notice of her and was suddenly overwhelmed.

Josie was lovely. She had been born in Texas, but both her mother and father had been born in Spain. She was petite, with a stunning figure, clear fair skin, raven-black hair, and enormous dark, lustrous, fawnlike eyes. It was her eyes that enchanted him that evening; when he first looked into them at the café, their effect on him was hypnotic: at that moment he had taken a spoonful of sugar for his coffee, and the instant froze for him. It wasn't until Carmen, amused, called his attention to the fact that he had been sitting there motionless, a spoonful of sugar poised above his coffee cup for an inordinately long time, that the spell was broken. But even then, before he came to his full senses, he stared down with complete detachment at the spoonful of sugar and at the hand that held it, and then suddenly and inexplicably he plunged the sugar into his mouth, rather than into his coffee.

There was no question that it was love and that Duke and Josie's feelings were reciprocal. Owing to the casual informality of those Balboa "dates," there was no problem in changing partners. Duke took Josie for a walk on the pier after they ate. They sat together on the pier and stared out at the sea, the silence broken only by the ocean's sounds; words would have diminished the profundity of their feelings.

Nearly fifty years later, Duke recalled how deeply he had been affected that night in Balboa: "I was looking out at the ocean [with Josie]. I was full of feelings I never had felt before. I was so hypnotized I don't think I said more than two words that night. I remember opening the door of the car for her, and my fingers happened to graze her arm as she was standing on the running board, kind of pulling this black coat around her. A shiver went through me. I knew I must be in love. I had read about it in stories, seen love scenes in the movies, read love poems about feelings like this, so I knew this was what it had to be. It was my first time. But they don't tell you it hurts. They never tell you how much it hurts. They don't tell you it hurts from the start and I guess it never stops hurting, but it sure is a beautiful feeling to have, and it wasn't long after that we started keeping company and she was my steady girl, and it was beautiful but it hurt a lot. . . ."[1]

The complexion of Duke's social life changed completely after that week in Balboa. The Saenz family returned to their home in the fashionable Hancock Park section of Los Angeles—not far from the USC campus—and Duke began dating Josie. Pexy didn't think Duke had ever loved anyone before Josie Saenz. "He finally gave her his fraternity pin [in lieu of an engagement ring]," Pexy said, "and he never went out with anyone but her after that. We double-dated often. Josie was a fine young lady, and we had a lot of fun on those double-dates, but even so their courtship could be best described as stormy."

The storminess was caused by Josie's extreme jealousy. Though Duke gave her no cause to be jealous, Josie imagined that he was seeing other girls, or that he was at least attracted to others. He wasn't, but he couldn't convince Josie, and they were always fighting and making up and fighting again. One night when Pexy and Duke were out on a double-date, Josie ruined the evening by getting into a jealous rage and demanding to be taken home. Jealousy was part of her nature.

There were other factors that contributed to their stormy relationship, too. Josie was three years younger than Duke when they first met, which made her only sixteen or seventeen. She had yet to finish high school, and the fact that she had fallen madly in love with an "older" college man didn't set too well with her parents, particularly her father. The fact that the Saenz family were devout Catholics and Duke was a non-churchgoing Protestant caused familial friction as well. However, Josie made it clear to Dr. Saenz that she was genuinely in love with Duke, and so an uneasy arrangement was reached. Josie could continue dating Duke so long as their dates weren't too frequent and so long as they kept restraints on their relationship until Duke graduated from college and could provide for her properly.

Duke and Josie didn't know it at the time, but their "engagement" was to last seven years, for events didn't break in Duke's favor, which only served to reinforce Dr. Saenz's opinion that Duke was a young man of no means and even less potential.

It was at about the time Duke met Josie that his parents' marriage ended. Clyde and Molly had separated in March or April, and Molly filed for divorce on May 1, 1926, charging Clyde with desertion. They had agreed to part, of course; the "desertion" charge, necessary to establish grounds for divorce, was more a legal formality than a fact. Clyde took an apartment in Los Angeles and went to work as manager of a paint store there, while Molly moved to Long Beach and kept custody of Robert, who was fifteen at the time. In accordance with the law, their divorce didn't become final until February 15, 1929. A year after that, on February 24, 1930, Clyde married Florence R. Buck, née Allen, a saleswoman at Webb's Department Store in Glendale. Clyde and Florence and her daughter by a previous marriage, Nancy, lived in Glendale for two years before moving to Los Angeles. At

DUKE

Clyde's death in 1937, Florence returned to her job at the department store and settled again in Glendale, where, two years later, Duke attended Nancy's graduation from Glendale High. Eventually Molly married Sidney Preen, a Long Beach plumbing contractor, and she remained in Long Beach until her death in 1970.

Duke was very saddened by the divorce, but he had known it was inevitable. He continued seeing his parents, of course. Clyde attended the USC football games with tickets Duke gave him, and also went to a football banquet or similar university social function with Duke. Molly visited the campus on at least one occasion; Duke though, usually went out to Long Beach, either hitching a ride with one of the USC students who lived there or taking the Red Car. He didn't see either of his parents often after their separation, and naturally there were no more family get-togethers.

His parents' separation meant that Duke no longer had a home, either, so during the summer break of 1926 he remained at the fraternity house while working full-time for William Fox Studios on Western Avenue in Hollywood. The studio job had been arranged through the university's athletic department. Tom Mix, one of the most popular and successful Western film stars of the day, was under contract to Fox and was a USC football fan. He had suggested to coach Howard Jones that if any of the USC players was in need of summer work, he would arrange for the studio to hire them. So in June, Jones sent two of his needy students—Duke and another football player—to see Mix.

As Duke often told the story, he and the other student arrived at the Fox lot with a letter of introduction from the athletic department, and Tom Mix was very cordial to them. He showed the boys his elegantly furnished studio bungalow, with its living quarters, dressing room, private gym, and steam room. Mix told them that he used the gym to keep in shape and that he had decided to put the boys on payroll as his trainers; they could help him keep fit while staying in shape themselves for the coming football season. The star also told them that he was starting another picture soon and that he'd get the boys minor parts in it, for which they would be paid in addition to their weekly salaries as his trainers. They could start work, he told them, as soon as their final exams were over.

Duke was ecstatic. The promised double paycheck might cover his expenses until the following summer, if he budgeted properly. He was very grateful for Mix's interest and generosity; he had seen most of the cowboy star's films at the Palace Grand and had admired his work, but this personal gesture won Duke's admiration for the man, too.

At the appointed time, Duke reported to the Fox studio gate and was told to see the labor supervisor, who knew nothing of Duke's understanding with Tom Mix. Duke's name had been added to the laborers' roll, and the supervisor assigned him to a swing gang, a crew of men who worked all over the lot, doing whatever labor was needed.

Duke had been working on the swing gang a week or so when he happened to see Tom Mix. "I figured there had been some kind of foul-up," he said, "so when I was hauling some furniture across the lot and saw Mix's car stopped nearby, I dropped what I was doing and went over to talk to him. He was sitting in the backseat of this big limousine that had his initials in gold on the doors, and I introduced myself and reminded him of his promise to use me as one of his trainers. Well, he just regarded me with that deadpan expression of his for a moment, then he just nodded and, without a word of explanation, looked away—as though dismissing me or as though I had already left. So I did leave. And that's the last I ever saw of Mr. Tom Mix."

It was the last Duke wanted to see of the cowboy star, too. It was Duke's first experience with the "Hollywood promise"; Duke thought it was bad enough that Mix hadn't kept his word, but for him to act as though he hadn't even *given* his word was unconscionable. He was bitterly disappointed over the episode. (Like most film stars, Tom Mix kept a tight rein on his purse strings, and what probably happened is that he tried to get the boys placed on *studio* payroll as his trainers. The studio obviously wouldn't agree to such an arrangement, and rather than having to pay the boys out of his own pocket—he was reportedly making almost $20,000 a *week* in those days—he let the matter drop.)

Duke returned to his fraternity-house job that fall, and made the varsity football team. He didn't make first string, which wasn't to be expected with so many veteran varsity players returning that year, but he made second or third string and occasionally got to play.

In the spring of 1927, Duke was notified that his football scholarship would not be extended; it would end in June. "This hurt Duke very much," Pexy said, "but Duke was really not a great football player. He tried hard as hell, but he was competing with spectacular football players at USC." The news was terribly disappointing to Duke, but he undoubtedly expected it, for he knew how he was doing against his competition on the field. He didn't rail against the decision, but he did determine to finish college, scholarship or not, for it seemed at the time that only by finishing college and making a success at law practice could he marry Josie and support her in the manner she had grown accustomed to.

When the semester ended in June 1927, Duke went back to work on the Fox lot. He moved into the room above Pexy's garage at 328 North Orange Avenue that summer—the room they had used as their high school "fraternity house"—to save the $30 or $40 a month it would have cost him to stay at the Sigma Chi house. He was trying to save every penny in order to go back to USC on his own in the fall. Pexy was aware Duke was having a hard time financially. "After the football season ended [the spring of 1927]," he said, "he started going down to the local blood bank and selling his blood for expense money. I didn't know until later that Duke had been doing this even *during* the first football season. I had noticed that he was sometimes very tired and often pale, but I attributed it to his rigorous schedule at the time; he never mentioned that he was selling his blood—and so much of it! He went down to the blood bank so often that they finally refused to take any more of his blood. And when he persisted in trying, they finally *barred* him from the place entirely."

In September 1927 Duke registered for the fall term and moved back to the fraternity house. He had lost his fraternity-house job along with his scholarship—presumably the job was promised during the summer to someone else, probably another freshman football prospect. Meanwhile, Sigma Chi extended Duke credit for a month or two for his room and board, and Duke may have used his summer savings—and perhaps borrowed money—to pay his tuition. Duke explained that he finally left the university because he couldn't even make enough to pay back the money he had borrowed in order to continue his education. Presumably the money borrowed was for the term his scholarship didn't cover, for although he was always in need of expense money, there was no need for his borrowing a substantial amount before he lost his scholarship.

Duke went out for football again, but this time he couldn't even make the team, let alone prove that he was worthy of another scholarship. "He had been injured," Pexy said. "It might have been a shoulder injury, I'm not sure, but whatever it was it kept him from getting back into the kind of shape he needed to be in to make the team."

Pexy was living at home in Glendale again at the time, but he was still in the fraternity and so dropped by the fraternity house whenever he had use of the second family car. A few weeks into the semester, he dropped by the house one afternoon and happened to find Duke standing on the front porch with a cardboard box. When Pexy got up the steps, he noticed that the box contained all Duke's belongings.

"Where you going, Duke?" he asked.

"I don't know," Duke said. "I can't pay my bills, and they said I can't live here anymore."

"He was standing there with this box," Pexy said, "and he didn't even know which side of the steps to go down. I knew from attending the [Sigma Chi] meetings that they were after him to begin paying his room and board. They couldn't keep carrying him. None of us could see how Duke could possibly make it. We figured it was just a matter of time, that his leaving was inevitable. But when he finally got the word, I guess he was too proud to ask anyone for help. He didn't even call me, which he could have, and he didn't have the faintest idea where he was going or what he was going to do. It was just a coincidence that I happened by when I did; my sister usually had use of the car, and so I didn't get over to the fraternity house on a regular basis. Anyway, I said, 'Duke, you know you're welcome to stay in that spare room above the garage.' And so he went home with me."

7

MR. FORD
AND MR. WALSH

PEXY Eckles's parents had known Duke since his grammar
school days; he had spent much time around their household.
They had known him even before he was nicknamed, when he
was still known as Marion and he and Pexy shrieked through
sultry summer evenings on their bicycles, shirttails flying. They
had known him, too, as a tall, gangling adolescent, hanging moon-
eyed around their house for the better part of one summer when
he had a schoolboy crush on Pexy's pretty older sister, Marguerite—this on the rebound from his unrequited long-distance adoration of actress Helen Holmes. They had known him as he went
through intermediate school and high school, head and shoulders
taller than his friends, ambling along with that unique walk of
his, or scampering with the others up the steps to their garage
"fraternity house."[1] They had taken particular interest in Duke
because he was among their son's closest friends and because they
had felt sympathetic toward him; they had been aware of the
smalltown gossip about Clyde and Molly Morrison's bitter marriage, which had finally ended in divorce, leaving Duke without a
home.

The Eckleses liked young Duke Morrison very much. Not that
there was anything extraordinary about him; there wasn't. But

they had liked him as a young boy, with his quick smile and ingratiating manner, and they liked what he had become: a sincere, respectful, considerate, and industrious young man. Pexy had told them of the scholarship problem and of the probability that Duke would be unable to continue his education. The Eckleses, particularly Pexy's mother, Jenny, had found the news disquieting. Jenny Eckles had taken a maternal interest in Marion since first hearing of his troubled home life, and when Pexy brought Duke home with him from the university that day in late October or November 1927, the Eckleses received him warmly. They told him he was welcome for as long as he wished to stay.

Duke was grateful for their hospitality, and at dinner that evening, he suggested to Dr. Eckles that once he found work and could get an apartment of his own, he would pay Dr. Eckles rent for the time he stayed there. It was an awkward moment, for a young man has his pride, and Dr. Eckles handled it tactfully. In effect, he said that Duke was a friend of the family and a most welcome guest, and he suggested that if Duke were in his shoes, Duke would not charge an old friend rent for the use of a vacant storeroom above a garage. Duke had to agree that he wouldn't, and with that the matter was closed.

Duke was up with the sun the following morning and out to the William Fox Studios, where he was immediately given a full-time job at $35 a week. He continued living above the Eckleses' garage for several months.

None of the Eckleses saw Duke often after he began to work. As a single man without seniority at Fox, he was at first assigned work on the less desirable location shootings—away from the studio—and so there were times when he didn't return to his garage apartment for days. Meanwhile, Mrs. Eckles saw to it that his laundry was done by their housekeeper, and on those nights when Duke did return—usually very late, for twelve- and four-teen-hour days were the rule rather than the exception in those times—she would take meals up to him to ensure that he was eating properly. Duke never forgot this kindness, and after he gained stardom, he visited the Glendale home of James and Jenny Eckles on more than one occasion.

Duke and Pexy kept in touch over the years, too. Pexy became an oil company executive in San Francisco. Duke's business didn't take him to San Francisco often, but he'd call Pexy whenever he did get up there, and Pexy would join him at the St. Francis Hotel, where Duke usually stayed and where they'd have a few drinks, bring each other up to date on their activities, and reminisce. "Our worlds were poles apart," Pexy recalled "and so our paths didn't often cross, but I always looked forward to our get-togethers. Duke was a good friend."

Owing to his experience in working on the Fox lot the two previous summers, Duke was given a job as an assistant property man, or prop man, as they are called. The job entailed dressing the movie sets with whatever furniture, equipment, fixtures, and sundry articles the script called for. Being an assistant was relatively hard work, and often tedious, but a definite promotion from the unskilled swing-gang labor he had been doing while a student.

Duke had done prop work in high school and occasionally while working the swing gangs, so he had confidence in his ability and took pride in doing the work well. After a few months, he decided to make a career of propping; skilled property men were always in demand and were being paid $150 a week or more, even in the late twenties. There were other aspects of the job that Duke capitalized on and that eventually caused him to change his career goal. As an assistant prop man he had the time and the opportunity to work on-camera as an extra in mob scenes and the like, for which he received extra pay. In addition, he was usually assigned to prop particular pictures, rather than having to work odd jobs around the entire lot, as he had done on the swing gang. This enabled him to develop friendships with influential craftsmen, actors, and directors. In time the friendships he cultivated and the on-camera experience he gained, opened another career avenue that he had not considered. Despite his brief acting experience in high school, the possibility that he could become a professional actor didn't even occur to him until he had been doing prop work in the movie industry for two years.

When Duke went back to work that fall, his first assignment

was propping for a picture called *Mother Machree*. It was probably because he lacked seniority that he was assigned to the picture, because it wasn't one of the better jobs on the lot. The director was a man named John Ford, an eccentric, self-centered, ill-tempered, and often sadistic man whom some called half genius and half Irish and who would become and remain one of Duke's lifelong friends, exerting a strong, almost parental influence on him. Ford was only twelve years older than Duke, but he seemed older than his years and was such an authoritarian that even his co-workers called him Pappy and both feared and respected him.

John Ford didn't direct, he dictated. Owing to his artistic sensibilities, he brought to the screen a superb sense of composition; every frame of a John Ford film was executed with an economy and balance that directors before him hadn't even envisioned, let alone tried.

Duke soon learned that the reason Ford's films bore his unmistakable imprint was that he was enormously talented and an absolute despot. He ran a tight ship, and he let no one forget—even for a moment—who was officer in command. He planned his films as one would plan a military assault: with precision at every step and with inordinate attention to even the smallest details. And it must be said that despite his quirky methods, and perhaps owing largely to his wonderful talent and professional standing, he attracted and inspired loyalty, which he took for granted. In effect, Ford also *commanded* loyalty, for when he notified his small group of followers (which were often referred to rather sarcastically by outsiders as "the John Ford rolling stock company") that he was ready to begin a picture, he expected them to drop whatever they were doing and go to work for him, even if it meant working for less money. A refusal to answer Ford's call resulted in excommunication. One of Ford's oldest and dearest friends, actor Harry Carey, grew weary of Ford's Irishness and clannishness and turned down one of his pictures. Ford didn't employ his old friend again for fifteen years.

Ford delegated authority well and put great trust in his chosen cameramen and technicians, but he harnessed the talents of all others working for him, and his grip on them was viselike. He rewrote writers' scripts. He bent the actors to his will. And he virtually eliminated film editors from the collaborative process; less talented or less confident directors, for example, often shot the same scenes two or more ways in order to decide later which version was best. Ford usually shot them one way, leaving his film editor with little more to do than splice the film together in proper sequence. Ford is said to have "edited" the film in his head or in the camera as he was shooting it. He often did numerous takes to get exactly what he had envisioned, but he seldom shot extra footage or variations of scenes. Such a technique took inordinate talent and egomaniacal self-confidence; John Ford had an abundance of both.

Duke was not intimidated by the director at their first encounter. One rural scene in the film called for a flock of geese to be seen in the background of an outdoor set, and he was put in charge of the geese. He acquitted himself as well as any gooseherder could, for the fowl are known to be uncooperative and ill-tempered. For technical reasons, Ford reshot the scene several times. Duke had to keep rounding up the geese between takes and putting them back in their pens, from which he would again prod them when Ford called for action. The geese wandered in and out of the scene, as they were supposed to do, but each time Ford stopped the action to reshoot, many of the geese had scattered in all directions, some hiding behind or beneath objects to avoid being caught and penned again. There's no record of John Ford taking particular notice of Duke at this time, but since he and the actors had to wait until Duke had the geese corraled again before the scene could be reshot, the spectacle of the husky, six-foot-four prop man lurching after skittering geese could hardly have escaped his attention. Duke did take notice of Ford, though. He noted how everyone fawned on the director, and he later remarked about the making of *Mother Machree*, "Everyone on the set was scared shitless of Ford, except me and the geese."

Ford took sadistic pleasure in publicly humiliating people who worked for him. He would demean them by bullying and berating them before others for mistakes both real and imagined, and by playing cruel practical jokes on them. He never pulled such stunts on influential craftsmen or stars, but rather on those who needed work and were at his mercy. On every picture he had a whipping boy or two. He was especially vigorous in employing his sadistic practices on newcomers, apparently as a test to determine whether he would admit them to his "stock company."

When *Mother Machree* was completed, Ford immediately started another picture, to which Duke was also assigned. It was called *Four Sons*, and during the filming of this picture Duke came to Ford's attention and became the subject of his hazing. *Four Sons* was a World War I story of a mother who lost three of her sons in battle. There was a particularly touching scene in which the mother received a letter telling her that her third son had been killed. The scene takes place during autumn; the mother sits on a bench, tearfully reading the letter, and the script called for dead leaves to be blowing across the lawn in the background. Duke was put in charge of the leaves and the large Ritter fan that he used to blow them across the lawn. Ford did several takes of the scene, stopping to rehearse the actress and suggesting small bits of business. Each time they broke the scene, Duke had to rake up the leaves and pile them before the fan for the next take. During one break, he was raking the leaves and happened to glance up. The actress was holding the letter and wailing. The camera was rolling. And there stood Duke in the background, squarely in the middle of the scene, holding his rake and staring directly into the camera with a shocked expression.

Ford exploded. He screamed at Duke, called him names, and ranted that he had ruined the only good take of the day. Ford pointed to one of the film's extras, who had played the part of a German officer and was in full uniform, and ordered Duke to march over to him in a military manner. Ford had the extra take the Iron Cross from his uniform and pin it on Duke. Then Ford had Duke assume his football crouch, stepped behind him, and kicked him in the hind end.

Duke often recounted the story, saying that it was one of the most humiliating moments of his professional life. Ford, too, retold the story from his point of view to writer-director Peter Bogdanovich, but he didn't tell Bogdanovich of the Iron Cross or the kicking, and he suggested that the incident had been blunderingly accidental on Duke's part. In fact it was typical of Ford's humiliating practical jokes. That was John Ford's style. Duke knew, of course, that it had been a deliberate trick, and that made it all the more humiliating to him.

The making of *Four Sons* was followed by *Hangman's House,* an Irish story starring a Ford favorite, Victor McLaglen, in which Duke propped and made a screen appearance for the first time since he had been an extra while at USC. He wasn't given screen credit, but he appeared in silhouette as a condemned man in court (a shadowy flashback in a judge's memory) and as a racetrack spectator in an action scene.

All three of the Ford films Duke propped for were released in 1928. By early 1928, having lived above Pexy Eckles's garage for three or four months, Duke moved to an apartment of his own near the corner of Western and Fountain avenues, within walking distance of the Fox lot and of Josie's house in Hancock Park.

Despite Duke's educational setback, he and Josie remained devoted to one another and continued dating. They went to the movies and to the afternoon tea dances at the Cocoanut Grove, which had become a gathering place for upcoming film stars like Joan Crawford and for USC students. Duke and Josie got around by Red Car at first, except on rare occasions when they'd double-date with Pexy and one of his girlfriends. But that summer Duke bought an old Model-A Ford so that they wouldn't be dependent on public transportation.

Duke's determination to marry Josie never wavered, but there were times when he grew very discouraged. By mid-1928, he had decided to make propping a career. He tried to build up a savings account, too; he hustled for opportunities to do bit parts and stunt work for extra money, but he was (and remained) an impulsive spender, an easy touch for loans, and he saved little. This, in turn, made him all the more impatient and frustrated that after more than a year at Fox, he was still making only $35 a week. Such a salary was more than enough for a young man to support a wife in those days, but not enough, Duke knew, to support a young Hancock Park socialite like Josephine Saenz.

DUKE

In the spring of 1929, Duke was again assigned to a John Ford picture. It was *Salute*, a naval cadet story exploiting the traditional football rivalry between the Army and Navy academies. The film was shot at Annapolis and starred one of the Fox studio's leading young actors, George O'Brien. It was also Ford's first all-talking picture, and to lend it authenticity, he decided to cast real athletes in the supporting roles. He couldn't take a chance on the Annapolis cadets delivering dialogue convincingly, or even on their being available when he needed them, so he decided to take back to Annapolis a group of college football players who could both deliver lines and double for themselves on gridiron close-ups.

Ford remembered that Duke had played football for USC, so he had him assigned to the picture and promised him a bit part. One of Duke's first assignments was to use his influence with contacts in the university administrative offices to recruit members of the USC football team. The studio had apparently tried to make such an arrangement but had failed. The problem was time; in order for Ford to meet his shooting schedule, the football players had to be en route by train to Annapolis during or slightly before the university's final examination week. Duke's task was to recruit as many players as he could, from which Ford would choose the best candidates; then to arrange for the chosen ones to take their finals early. Somehow Duke talked the administration into reversing their decision and agreeing to the plan. Then Duke headed straight to the Sigma Chi house from the administration office, to ensure that his football-playing fraternity brothers were aware of the studio offer before arranging for the athletic department to post the casting call.

On the day that Ford was to look the football players over and choose the ones he wanted to take East, Duke requisitioned a studio bus and picked them up on campus. There were numerous non–Sigma Chi players in the group, and among them was a burly, barrel-chested lineman named Wardell Bond. Bond was a pre-med student at the time, and he apparently so reminded Ford of a younger Victor McLaglen that Bond was among the first players the director chose, beating out one of Duke's Sigma Chi brothers for a spot on the roster. Bond was also immediately taken into Ford's clique and was given a better part in the film than Duke. This resulted in a slight rivalry between the two men, but it was short-lived. Duke wasn't happy about the turn of events, but he was never small about such things, and eventually Ward Bond became one of his closest friends and drinking buddies.

On location at Annapolis, Duke learned that he was recorded with the paymaster as a $35-a-week prop man and that he would be paid an additional $7.50 a day only for the few days that he worked as a bit-part player. Duke protested, saying that he had been promised more money for negotiating with USC and saving the film company several hundred dollars a week by hiring the players for $50 a week, even though he had been authorized by the studio to pay up to $75. The paymaster claimed no knowledge of such an arrangement and could get no authorization for higher pay under such a claim. Finally Duke pointed out that he, too, had a part in the film—in addition to his other duties—and that the least the studio could do would be to pay him what Ward Bond and the other students were making. The studio finally agreed to this arrangement and paid him $50 a week. Duke was sorry he had been such a good negotiator for the company; he had bargained himself out of an extra $25 a week.

Salute was released in August 1929 to very good reviews. Ironically, Ward Bond got screen credit and Duke did not. Duke wasn't even mentioned by name in the reviews, and the closest he came to being acknowledged at all in his first talkie was an indirect reference in the August 21 issue of *Variety:*

No question that the producing company has turned loose a good looking and well playing group of youngsters in this effort. That goes for . . . [Frank] Albertson and Ward Bond, a lineman from USC playing his first picture role as a light heavy and not a little responsible by his "straight" for making Albertson stand out to such an extent. Bond will probably stick in pictures after this effort. He's not unlike [Victor] McLaglen. . . .

DUKE

When *Salute* was completed in the fall of 1929, Duke went back to his propping job, but the addition of sound to motion pictures was changing the complexion of the industry drastically, and his opportunities to make additional money as a bit-part player increased. His next assignment was propping for director James Tingling. The film was *Words and Music,* a collegiate musical starring Lois Moran. Duke was given a small role as a college student named Pete Donahue, and aside from his having scenes with the glamorous Lois Moran (who was later immortalized by F. Scott Fitzgerald as the model for Rosemary Hoyt in his novel *Tender Is the Night),* the film was a milestone for Duke in that he was given his first screen credit—and it was the only time he was ever billed as Duke Morrison.

In the winter of '29, Duke went back to work for John Ford in a submarine picture called *Men Without Women* (a title apparently lifted without credit from Ernest Hemingway's 1927 short story collection). The picture was shot on location at Santa Catalina Island, about thirty miles off the Southern California coast, and at San Diego, California. Duke did stunt work in the film and played an unbilled part as one of fourteen seamen trapped in a submarine disabled on the ocean floor. One of Duke's duties as a prop man on the film was to operate an air compressor on a yacht that Ford used as a camera boat. The air was channeled by hose into the ocean, where it bubbled to the surface, simulating air expelled from a sub's torpedo tubes, through which, according to the script, the trapped sailors were to escape and be picked up by a Navy vessel standing by—the studio had arranged with the Navy to hire the services of the vessel and crew. When it came time to do the scene, however, the weather turned stormy, and the sea's enormous swells were intimidating. Ford's plan had been to have the bit players jump from the camera boat and swim underwater to surface at the spot where the air hose was churning up bubbles. However, some of the players weren't strong enough swimmers to chance doing the scene under such adverse conditions.

Ford was in a bind to complete the scene that day, while he had use of the Navy vessel, so he asked Duke if he wanted to double for a few of the players, saying that he'd receive the going stunt rate for each dive he made. Duke was a strong swimmer, and he agreed to do it. He needed the money very badly because he had placed a bet on a football game with a bookmaker the previous weekend and had lost more than he could afford to pay. Always the sentimentalist, Duke had bet on USC against the odds, and his bookmaker had connections that one couldn't refuse to pay. So Duke dove in, surfaced, was picked up by the Navy vessel, then repeated the stunt several times, doing each take a little differently. The stunts were exhausting, for the sea was rough and numbingly cold, but as Duke often intimated in telling the story, it wasn't nearly as chilling an experience as facing his bookmaker with empty pockets would have been.

When the scene was wrapped up, the boat headed back to San Diego Harbor. En route, Duke joined Ford and several others in a high-stakes poker game (a tradition on all John Ford picture locations). Duke won several hundred dollars, which was more than enough to settle with his bookmaker, and he didn't fully realize how fortunate it was that he had had a few dollars in his pocket to enter the game; a few days later the studio disallowed his claim for stunt pay, a fact that still had him fuming—even in the 1960s and 70s—whenever he retold the story.

Duke didn't work with John Ford again for almost ten years after the filming of *Men Without Women*. Ford wrapped up his five-picture contract with Fox—in preparation to free-lance with other studios—and in the meantime, Duke went to work on *A Rough Romance*, directed by A. F. Erickson. It was a logging film set in the Pacific Northwest and starring George O'Brien, who had befriended Duke when they worked together on *Salute* and who had requested that Duke prop the picture. Duke did an un-billed bit part as a card player in the film. Then from *Romance* he went to work on *Cheer Up and Smile*, a comedy-drama starring Arthur Lake, who later gained fame in the Blondie films, and Dixie Lee, whom Fox Studios was grooming for stardom before she married Bing Crosby and retired from the business. Duke played a college student in the film, and it was to be his last job as a prop man and bit-part player. By the time *A Rough Romance* and

Cheer Up and Smile were released, he was working on location in a $2 million film—as its star.

In the early autumn of 1929, Duke was unloading a truckful of furniture at the Fox property warehouse when director Raoul Walsh noticed him. What arrested Walsh's attention was the fact that Duke fit the image he had of a lead character in a film he was having trouble casting. Walsh said that Duke was carrying an overstuffed chair when he first noticed him. He stopped at a distance to watch the young prop man. And as he was watching, Duke came out to the truck again, picked up a Louis Quinze sofa, balanced it on his head and shoulder, and picked up another chair with his free hand. "When he came out for another load," Walsh wrote, "I walked over and spoke to him."[2]

Duke had just finished propping *Cheer Up and Smile*, and he had done a bit part as a college youth in the picture, so his hair was cut very short, as they wore it on campus in the late twenties. Unknown to Duke, Walsh was casting for a Western frontier epic, so after talking to Duke for a few minutes and without telling him what part he had in mind, Walsh suggested that Duke let his hair grow for a couple of weeks and then report to his office for a screen test. Without further explanation, the director left.

Duke's remembrance of this part of the story was slightly different from Walsh's. As he recalled, one of the director's assistants, not Walsh himself, approached him while he was unloading the truck and advised him to let his hair grow, saying that Walsh wanted to give him a screen test. This seems a more likely version, as it was, after all, a more momentous occasion for Duke than for Walsh, and Mr. Walsh's recollections were made forty-five years after the fact.

Walsh was in the preproduction stage of *The Big Trail* when he first saw Duke. The film was an epic saga of a group of pioneers who fought the elements, formidable terrain, and hostile Indians on a wagon-train trek along the Oregon Trail from the banks of the Missouri to the Pacific Northwest. It would be filmed on location, and Walsh had assembled an enormous cast (including an authentic Blackfoot Indian tribe) and a fine supporting cast that included Tyrone Power, Sr., Ian Keith, and Tully Marshall. A relatively unknown young actress named Marguerite Churchill had been signed to play the female lead, but Walsh had yet to cast the male lead—the role of Breck Coleman, a frontier scout—and the director was running out of time.

Tom Mix had been Walsh's first choice, but the Western star had committed to another picture. Walsh's next choice was a then-little-known actor named Gary Cooper, who was under contract to Samuel Goldwyn. Cooper seemed eager to do the film, and his agent apparently thought that Goldwyn would be agreeable to a loan-out, for such an ambitious and expensive production would have been a fine showcase for Goldwyn's young actor, but at the last minute, Cooper learned that Goldwyn had cast him in the lead of *The Winning of Barbara Worth* (a Western that established Cooper as a top star), and Walsh was without a prospect. He had tested numerous actors for the lead, but studio boss Winfield Sheehan had turned them all down as unsuitable for the role. So in the last stages of his preproduction schedule, with elaborate logistic plans in motion and a huge cast assembled, Walsh was placing great hope on a young prop man named Duke Morrison.

Two weeks later, Duke reported to Walsh's office and was sent to wardrobe, where he was outfitted in a buckskin shirt and pants. To save time, Walsh ran a quick screen test without sound and showed Sheehan the rushes. The studio boss was impressed with Duke's looks, so Duke was given a second test with a few members of the supporting cast and using sound. Walsh had found Duke's rich baritone voice exactly right for the part, but sound was a new and dreadfully mysterious science in the film industry, and no one knew what magic or mischief the primitive sound equipment might work on one's voice. Walsh let Duke ad lib lines in the second test. However, Sheehan still had reservations; speaking extemporaneously, as Duke had done, gave no clue as to whether he could deliver dramatic lines from a written script with credibility. "He's good," Sheehan told Walsh, "but we'd better be sure."

Walsh coached Duke, emphasizing that he was portraying a rugged plainsman in whose hands a hundred settlers had placed their lives. In his readings, Duke had made a common beginner's mistake by overdramatizing his lines. Walsh told Duke to look directly into the eyes of the people he was addressing and to play the part coolly, but with authority, as though he were on the football field. Fortunately he caught on almost at once.

Sheehan watched the rushes of the third test and said, "He'll do. What did you say his name was?"

"Morrison," Walsh said.

The two men shook hands, relieved that their frustrating search was over. But Sheehan, who made a practice of changing the names of his contract players, was dissatisfied with Duke's name. He thought Duke Morrison a suitable name for a circuit preacher but not for a film actor. According to Walsh, the men retired to Sheehan's office, where the studio boss began jotting names on a note pad. None seemed suitable. While Sheehan continued writing, Walsh pulled a book about the Revolutionary War from a nearby shelf. As he leafed through it, the name Mad Anthony Wayne caught his eye. He showed it to Sheehan, and the executive smiled. He liked the surname Wayne but rejected Anthony and so returned to his note pad, jotting down given names until he finally settled on the name John.

John Wayne it was. Now they had to discuss contract terms. Sheehan wanted to know where Walsh had found their new leading man. Walsh told him that Duke was a prop man on Sheehan's own lot and that he had no agent. Sheehan asked what kind of salary he thought Duke would settle for. Walsh had been a silent screen star himself before losing an eye in an accident and empathized with actors. He suggested that Duke be given several hundred dollars a week. Sheehan was startled by the suggestion, but Walsh pointed out that Duke was the leading man and that several of the actors who would be playing supporting roles in the film were making two or three hundred a week.

Sheehan wouldn't even consider the argument. To his mind, he was giving a mere prop man the opportunity of a lifetime, a chance to star in the most elaborate and expensive film the studio had ever made. Such an opportunity ought to be considered as compensation, as well. And with that thought in mind, he had Duke's contract drawn up at $75 a week.

Duke signed the contract without hesitation. In a time when one could get a complete breakfast for 35¢, a four-course steak dinner in the finest of restaurants for about $1, and a room in the best of hotels for $5 a week, $75 was a lot of money. As for his new name, he would rather have kept his own, but he had been in the business long enough to know that adopting professional names was a common practice.

At least they hadn't rechristened him Marion.

8

THE BIG TRAIL
AND BEYOND

PRINCIPAL photography wasn't scheduled to begin on *The Big Trail* until the late spring of 1930. Meanwhile, the studio prepared its new young contract player, John Wayne, for his starring role as a frontier scout. For several months, Duke was put under the tutorship of veteran stuntman Jack Padgin, who taught him to ride horses and to handle them over the roughest of terrain and under adverse conditions. Padgin also familiarized Duke with the use of the lariat, sidearms, and long guns. Another stuntman, Steve Clemente, taught him how to handle and throw a bowie knife, a vital skill for a frontiersman. Duke enjoyed working with the stuntmen, and he worked eagerly and hard at mastering the skills they taught. It wasn't until he reported to another man named Lumsden Hare that his enthusiasm for the studio's tutorial plan diminished.

When sound came to the motion picture industry, studio bosses realized that many of their silent-screen contract players and stars couldn't speak well enough to be understood, let alone play the wide range of roles expected of them. Some of the players were foreigners who had not bothered to master English. Many were first-generation Americans who spoke with the strong European accents of their parents. Some had Brooklyn accents or

Southern accents or speech impediments or voices that were grating to the ear. To remedy the problem, the studios raced to sign veterans of the legitimate stage (three of Duke's supporting players, Tyrone Power, Sr., Ian Keith, and Tully Marshall, were among those signed) and also hired vocal coaches to salvage whomever they could from the silent-player ranks. Lumsden Hare was among the voice and dialogue coaches Fox signed.

Hare had been a British Shakespearean actor and director, and Duke studied voice and diction three hours a day with him for several weeks. He was undoubtedly a good vocal coach, and Duke learned much about diction and voice projection from him, but Hare apparently couldn't resist supplementing his voice lessons with the theatrical stage techniques of enunciation, movement, and histrionics. To hear Duke tell it, Hare had him mincing around, waving his arms in grand gestures, and rolling his r's like the soft rumble of rising thunder until he could no longer stand it; he had been around motion pictures long enough to know that such grand mannerisms were magnified out of proportion by the big screen. He rebelled and, presumably with Raoul Walsh's aid, escaped the clutches of Lumsden Hare.

That early spring of 1930 was one of the best of times for Duke. Stardom was on the horizon, and marriage to Josie seemed at last within his grasp. His new salary allowed him to date Josie in higher style, and as a contract actor he was put up for membership (probably by George O'Brien) in the Thalians, an organization of young actors and actresses from all studios, who had a beach house at Santa Monica and in whose company Duke and Josie began socializing. Duke's new status as a contract player also enabled him to join the Hollywood Athletic Club, a men's club on Hollywood Boulevard that catered to the movie set. There he dined and swam and worked out with most of the major stars he had admired on the silver screen of the Palace Grand Theatre in Glendale.

While the company was preparing to leave for Yuma, Arizona, the first location set of *The Big Trail*, Duke asked Raoul Walsh if he would cast a friend of his in the picture. Though such requests from stars were routine, Walsh said that Duke made the request humbly, as though he were taking too much liberty in his position. The friend was Ward Bond, and Walsh was so pleased with Bond that he gave him a good part in the film as the wagon-train master and told him to let his whiskers grow so that he'd look suitably grizzly for the role.

The Big Trail was set in 1842 and based on a story by Hal G. Evarts about one of the first mass migrations of pioneers over the Oregon Trail from Independence, Missouri, to Oregon's lush Willamette Valley. Screenwriters Jack Peabody, Marie Boyle, Florence Postal, and Fred Serser wrote a fine scenario, which followed the canvas-covered wagons (called prairie schooners) on their trek to the Pacific Northwest. The wagon train, lined single file and stretching out as far as the eye could see, suffered the dust storms and boiling heat of the prairies and the freezing cold of the snowcapped mountains. In the film, the wagon train stopped by day only for defense against Indian raids and for births and deaths, and left in its two-thousand-mile wake the graves that marked victims of cholera and Sioux Indian arrows.

The production company spared no expense in making the film as historically accurate as possible. *The Big Trail* would be shot on location in five states, and the cast and crew would cover slightly more than two thousand miles in filming it. Close attention was paid to the smallest of details. The film's dozens of prairie schooners, like the originals, were drawn not by horses but by oxen. Even the goods the prairie schooners carried as staples on their trek were researched and depicted in the film: dried and cured meats; 150 pounds of flour; 15 pounds of coffee; 25 pounds each of sugar, baking soda, and salt; spare wagon parts; sundry household goods; Colt revolvers; Sharps and Henry rifles; and ammunition.

The film company's caravan along its two-thousand-mile route must have been as fascinating to behold as had been the original pioneers' seemingly endless stream of prairie schooners. There were busloads of cast and crew members and extras (probably at least 100 persons, for the basic cast numbered 35, and that didn't include dozens of extras; there were also 14 cameramen, 6 assistant directors, and an enormous crew); there were company automobiles carrying the director, some of his aides, and some of the cast; there were trucks carrying camera equipment, reflectors, costumes, props, klieg lights, wind machines, portable gasoline generators, thousands of feet of cable, portable dressing rooms, tents, and food supplies; there were long-bed trucks carrying the prairie schooners; stake-bed trucks for the cattle; enclosed trucks and trailers for the horses; an insulated truck for the raw film stock; sound-recording trucks; a blacksmith truck; a first-aid truck to serve the people and livestock; and even a truck carrying a portable film laboratory, used to "slop test" film footage to ensure that it had good exposure before the company sent it back to Hollywood for processing and moved on to the next location.

As though the logistics of moving such an enormous caravan two thousand miles through five states wasn't challenge enough for director Raoul Walsh, the studio also charged him with making two versions of the film: an English version and a German-language version for the European market. The German version utilized basically the same cast, but the leads were played in German by Marion Lessing and Ed Brendel, who also doubled as extras in the English-language version. To further complicate matters, Walsh had to direct two complete camera crews, for the picture was shot in both conventional 35 millimeter and in 70 millimeter Grandeur film (the forerunner of CinemaScope).

In April of 1930, the cast and crew finally assembled near Yuma, Arizona, where a replica of a frontier settlement had been built. The filming of *The Big Trail* was begun at last. But slowly. The cameras had hardly begun to roll when Duke came down with a case of dysentery so debilitating that he was bedridden and unable to work. Walsh shot the film around him, hoping day by day that he'd soon recover, but by the second week he was behind schedule and told Duke that if he couldn't get back to work he'd have to be replaced in the film. Duke climbed out of his sickbed, twenty pounds lighter and shaky, and went back before the cameras. Then the film's female lead, Marguerite Churchill, developed an extremely bad case of acne that was a constant challenge to her makeup woman and that caused much tension until the rushes revealed that the makeup was effectively covering the blemishes without making her look like a ghost or a painted woman.

Walsh had trouble, too, with some of the legitimate stage actors who were making their first screen appearance. Many of them had never seen a sunrise, let alone been roused from their slumbers and herded to a makeup tent before dawn. A few of them saw Walsh as the devil incarnate, for surely only the embodiment of evil would deliberately provoke them at such ungodly hours. Consequently, they were not prone to sunny dispositions or cooperation.

The original screenwriters had written only a scenario and had fleshed out only the basic plot scenes, for they couldn't possibly have anticipated the opportunities for new action scenes and dialogue that would develop on location. Walsh had been told by the studio to make his own action, and a writer had been assigned to aid him. The writer's first action was to find a bootlegger in Yuma and to lay in a store of booze that would see him through the long trail ahead; then he got drunk and for the most part remained that way for the duration of the shooting. Walsh could have had him replaced, but he was an optimist and apparently thought the drinking binge would end. He was wrong. The writer did have his sober moments, but unfortunately they seldom coincided with the moments Walsh needed him.

The director was inordinately tolerant of drinking because he was known to have a taste for the stuff himself. He also put up with the writer because he was kept busy battling the drinking habits of most of the cast, as well. There was so much drinking during the months of filming that Walsh said the picture ought to have been retitled "The Big Drunk." The heavy drinking was a constant source of anxiety for him, and we gather from his remarks that had the original pioneers put away as much alcohol as his cast, they would never even have found the West, let alone settled it.

Despite such obstacles, the shooting was finally wrapped up in Yuma and the company caravan made its way eight hundred miles north to Sacramento, California, and to the Sacramento River, where they shot all the river footage. The original pioneers had crossed numerous rivers on their journey, including the Snake River, the Green River, and the Powder River; the Sacramento offered a diversity of backgrounds to simulate them all. It had deep, placid areas, where prairie schooners, properly rafted, could be floated across; and it had raging white-water currents that could sweep away schooners, if the script called for such action.

From Sacramento, the company traveled four hundred miles east to St. George, Utah, where Walsh filmed the canyon shots, utilizing the rimrock country of Hurricane Bluffs near Zion National Park. Walsh was behind in his shooting schedule and already over budget, but he was pleased with the filming and particularly pleased with his leading man. Duke proved better in the role than Walsh had hoped. He was certainly the image of a frontier scout, and despite his youth, he had the imposing bearing, deep voice, and commanding presence of a leader of men. Walsh was especially impressed with his horsemanship, and he praised stuntman Jack Padgin, who was on the location shooting as a stunt coordinator, for a job well done in tutoring Duke. Duke handled a horse as though he had been riding all his life, and "his acting," Walsh wrote, "was instinctive, so that he became whatever and whomever he was playing."[1]

Although Walsh was confident that he was getting on film the makings of a fine motion picture, the studio moguls, who were viewing the footage as it was sent back to Hollywood from location, weren't very impressed. Considering the enormous cost to the studio, it's probable that William Fox, Winfield Sheehan, and production chief Sol Wurtzel wouldn't have been satisfied with anything Walsh sent back. The general consensus at the studio seemed to be that they were spending millions for an epic picture and were getting in return what was beginning to look like a moderately budgeted "Western."

The story line was a simple one, and so the onus of delivering extraordinary footage that met the expectations of the studio bosses and was suitable for the wide screen of William Fox's Grandeur Process was squarely on director Raoul Walsh. The early criticism was premature, though, for the Yuma location footage had been expository, introducing and developing the characters and providing background for subsequent action. Even so, Walsh knew that the picture needed more conflict and action than its simple plot engendered. As a sensitive director, he knew also that there was danger in exaggerating spectacle at the expense of plot and character development, and so he was ever alert for situations that would pit man against the elements, that would provide action and character development through conflict. He found one such situation at the Utah location site.

Walsh had already filmed the pioneers crossing desolate flatlands and forging rivers. In Utah, he was shooting the wagon train moving through the canyons of Hurricane Bluffs, when they came to a deep transverse cleft in their path. It formed a seemingly impassable ravine, with a curl of white water below. Ordinarily Walsh would have wrapped the scene and moved to another location, but he was intrigued with the possibility of the pioneers overcoming such an obstacle. He had had coils of stout rope loaded into some of the wagons, and so after conferring with stuntman Jack Padgin, it was decided that they would film the lowering of a few wagons and some of the livestock into the ravine by ropes, and that some of the cast and several of the extras could climb down the rope, hand over hand, thereby representing the overcoming of a seemingly impassable obstacle.

Padgin showed Duke and Ward Bond how to rig the ropes, anchoring them to boulders and sturdy trees along the canyon's rim. By the time they finished the rigging—and finished shooting Duke and others tying the rigging—the sun was directly overhead, eliminating all shadow from the bluffs of the ravine and giving Walsh perfect lighting. Walsh had cameras set up on the rim and down in the ravine, shooting simultaneously as they lowered the first wagon. They made slings for some of the livestock and lowered them, too. Walsh had jotted down a few lines of dialogue for Duke (presumably the writer was indisposed), and he used them, but he also reacted to the events in the scene, making up his own dialogue, and he was very convincing. "I stood and watched him waving his arms and shouting orders," Walsh said, "and wondered where the youthful linebacker [sic] had gone. Instead of a football player, I had a star." And Walsh said later about Duke, "His acting was instinctive . . . he was a natural."[2]

As the last of the wagons to be used in the scene was being lowered, it slipped lopsided in its sling and hung precariously above the ravine floor. It broke away from the slings and went crashing to the bottom of the ravine, broken pieces of it swirling away in the white water. Walsh was ecstatic. Afterward, he staged close-ups of the "pioneers" reacting to the slipping sling and the destruction of one of their prairie schooners, footage that would be intercut with the action when the film was edited. It was a scene that couldn't have been better had it been elaborately staged. Such scenes gave the cast and crew a feeling that they had an extraordinary film in the making.

From St. George, the company moved on to Jackson Hole, Wyoming. Walsh had gotten footage of Indian attacks in the flatlands, but he wanted to stage more Indian skirmishes against the backdrop of Wyoming's beautiful Grand Teton mountain range. He succeeded despite the fact that he failed miserably at keeping the cast, crew, and Indians all sober at the same time.

The company's final stop was about three hundred miles north of Jackson Hole, in Moiese, Montana, about thirty-five miles north of Dixon. Moiese is a small village on the edge of the National Bison Range, home of the largest single herd of buffalo in the nation. The script called for a buffalo stampede, and the studio had arranged with the Department of the Interior to use the buffalo. The company took over an entire hotel in the area and had to rent about a dozen cabins to accommodate the overflow. Walsh put out a call for more Indians, and about forty Blackfoot and Crow answered the call. They all rode spirited multicolored ponies, and Walsh was delighted with them.

The story line called for the wagon train to be stopped by a herd of buffalo being stampeded by Indians. The stampede was supervised by government rangers, who determined how far and over what route the buffalo could be driven. Walsh had cameras set up on both sides of the stampede area and got magnificent footage of the thundering buffalo and the whooping Indians. After the stampede, the Indians returned the buffalo to pasture; the rangers counted them as they did so. All were accounted for, and there had been no injuries to man or beast.

Walsh breathed more than a sigh of relief. The location shooting was finished. There was no need of his throwing the usual wrap-up party, for the picture had been one long party, stretching all the way back to Yuma, Arizona, so the cast and crew just carried on as usual. Duke stopped in at his cabin when they had finished shooting and asked what seemed to the director a rhetorical question. "How did I do, Mr. Walsh?" he said.

"This is your first picture, John," Walsh told him. "This is my eightieth [sic]. I have never directed one before where the action threatened to get out of hand. I guess I should congratulate you and your friend Bond, if only for staying sober." To Duke's mind, the picture should have been retitled "The Big Disillusionment," for none of the hopes it had held for him a few months earlier was realized. When he returned to Hollywood, he learned that the studio had scheduled him for a publicity tour of the East and Midwest to promote the film. Except for the isolated filming locations, he had never been out of California as an adult, and he looked forward to seeing New York City, Philadelphia, Boston, Chicago, and the other cities on his itinerary—particularly while going first-class with expenses paid. Unfortunately, the tour took on a carnival-like aspect that took the joy out of his travels and that he found humiliating.

To begin with, the studio publicity department had fashioned a new biography to go with his new name. The biography and other publicity matter had been sent to the press in advance of his appearances, and Duke had been neither consulted nor informed of the action. According to the releases, he had been born in the West, and among other things had been a football *star* at USC, a Texas Ranger, and it was intimated that the romance depicted in the film between Marguerite Churchill and him was real—a "fact" the publicists thought would draw romantics to the box offices in droves. Duke was very upset with the lies, but was told that the true facts of his life wouldn't get them an inch of newspaper and magazine space; their job, they said, was to generate media and public interest. His job was to cooperate with them.

THE BIG TRAIL AND BEYOND

Fox arranged for Duke's first interview before he went on tour. It was with writer Miriam Hughes and appeared in the December 1930 issue of *Photoplay*. The lead-in was silly—that after being on *The Big Trail* for months, John Wayne longed for a haircut—but as such interviews go, it was interesting. Miss Hughes was impressed with "John's" unaffected manner and opined that since he had worked on both sides of the camera, his chances of remaining unaffected and of not "going Hollywood" were better than those of the youngsters before him who had become stars so quickly.

"I think I've got sense enough," Duke told Miss Hughes, "and that I've seen enough of the other kind to keep myself level-headed. I've heard the prop men and electricians talk about these people who go Hollywood. And I know that nobody, in Hollywood, can lead a life apart. If you don't act right around the sets, they catch on to you at once, and it doesn't pay."

Hughes reported that Duke had been "frightened like a little child in the dark" at the prospect of shooting his first scene as the star of *The Big Trail*. "But Walsh was great to me," Duke told her. "He helped me so much that I even got over that pretty soon."

The interview went well. Miriam Hughes was Hollywood-wise and had liked Duke because he had been himself: shy, unaffected, self-effacing, and honest. But the studio publicist who accompanied him must have swallowed his gum when Duke admitted that he had felt like a frightened child in the dark. He was supposed to be a former Texas Ranger who had, presumably, dropped outlaws dead in their tracks with the blue steel of his icy stare. So afterward the publicists coached Duke on fielding questions from the press, on maintaining the image they had given him. They also gave him short speeches to memorize regarding the film, speeches sprinkled with gross exaggerations that Duke thought would insult the intelligence of those who heard them. Then they took publicity photos of him wearing a dark double-breasted business suit, a white ten-gallon "Tom Mix" hat—with a crown that came to a point—and posed in a knife-throwing stance, knife in hand. Duke thought the outfit and pose truly ridiculous for promoting a frontier story; nobody cared what he thought.

DUKE

When his wardrobe for the tour arrived, he would have settled for the double-breasted business suit. He was given new tan cowboy boots—which he claimed glowed high yellow in direct sunlight—a loud shirt, leather chaps, a ten-gallon hat, a pair of pearl-handled six-guns, and a bowie knife. Duke wanted to wear the outfit he had worn in the film—scuffed boots, worn buckskins, and a flat-crowned Western hat—but that wasn't dressy and showy enough for the publicity people. They assured him that as experts, they knew what they were doing.

As his whirlwind tour progressed through the East, Duke contradicted everything the publicity releases had claimed about him. He didn't do so deliberately; he tried to do the job the studio had sent him to do, but the rehearsed answers the studio had given him for anticipated questions and the lies in his studio biography that he was expected to elaborate on were just too absurd for him to deal with. No, he told them, he hadn't been born on a ranch in Montana; he'd been born in Iowa. No, he hadn't been a Texas Ranger; he'd never even been to Texas. No, he hadn't been a star on the USC football team. No, there had been no romance between Marguerite Churchill and him. The publicist who accompanied Duke apparently sent back reports that didn't please the studio bosses, but there was little they could do but order the publicist to put more pressure on the young star to conform.

For a while, Duke found his appearances at movie houses a little embarrassing, but then he began to enjoy meeting the public, particularly the youngsters, and he began to relax. An incident that took place in New York City, though, brought back the embarrassment full force. Fox had its newsreel cameras on hand in Central Park, where Duke was scheduled for a knife-throwing exhibition. The publicist had arranged to borrow a horse from the city's mounted police detachment, and had Duke make his entrance on horseback. The horse was skittish and hard to control, and when Duke dismounted, the horse jerked the reins from his grip and galloped off across Central Park, the police in hot pursuit. Duke's knife-throwing exhibition was impressive, but it didn't take the edge from the apparent fact that a "cowboy" from the West couldn't even handle a trained city horse. Overall the tour had been a very demoralizing experience, and when it ended in Chicago, Duke got a haircut, put on a business suit, and took the first available train back to California.

Meanwhile, *The Big Trail* was released. Only two theaters, Grauman's Chinese in Hollywood and the Roxy in New York City, were equipped with wide screens for the 70-millimeter version. The rest of the houses showed it in standard 35 millimeter, which detracted a bit from the panoramic views the wide screen offered. Reviews were generally good. The *New York Times*, while not mentioning the cast members, said in its October 25, 1930 review:

> Magnificent panoramic views on an enlarged screen . . . are beheld in the ambitious Fox Grandeur production, *The Big Trail*, which is now holding forth at the Roxy. . . .
>
> Not only do the scenes in this picture elicit admiration for the pioneers, but one senses that the performers . . . had no easy time in emulating what had been accomplished a century ago. . . . Some of the glimpses convey the impression that the mere making of the scenes themselves was filled with risks for those before the camera. *The Big Trail* is a monumental work in which the story is naturally of secondary importance. It is the composition of the scenes that calls forth admiration. . . .

Three days later, the industry publication *Variety* reviewed the West Coast showing of the film and wasn't as kind:

> *The Big Trail* will do a certain business because of its magnitude, but it is not a holdover picture, and it cost around $2,000,000 to produce. Failing to own a kick or a punch, other than scenically, and with no outstanding cast names, *Trail*, as big as it is and 125 minutes long, remains still a "western" of the American pioneer sort, so thoroughly made familiar by those silent epics preceding it. . . .
>
> The narrative has a romance, and John Wayne, a studio property man, was chosen by Mr. Walsh to play the role of Breck Coleman, a trapper who undertakes to officiate as a scout for the wagon train. Mr. Wayne acquits himself with

no little distinction. His performance is pleasingly natural. . . .

No one will find anything against the Walsh direction. . . .

Young Wayne, wholly inexperienced, shows it, but also suggests that he can be built up. He certainly has been given a great start as the lead in a $2,000,000 production. . . .

The consensus of opinion among reviewers was that despite its magnificent production values, the film's predictable, melodramatic story line would keep it from being the huge success necessary to earn back the cost of production. The reviewers were right. *The Big Trail* is considered the definitive film of its genre by some of today's film historians, and it still holds up well as an entertaining film, with some of the most excitingly realistic scenes ever filmed. But it was not a box-office draw. Though it did moderately well in the marketplace, it was a financial disaster and an embarrassment to the studio. After its short run, Fox put it on the shelf and tried to forget it. In a sense, they did the same with its young star, John Wayne. They stopped grooming him for stardom; they stopped the publicity machine, and they no longer tried to cast him in big pictures. He was just another contract player. As for the film, Fox sold off some of its best footage to Republic Studios, who used it as inserts in their B Westerns to add production values.

As *The Big Trail* was dying on the theater circuit, Duke was cast in the lead of a picture called *Girls Demand Excitement*, a film that Duke insisted was thrown together as a cheap vehicle for a bevy of actresses Fox had under contract and didn't know what to do with. Duke played the captain of a men's basketball team in a co-ed college, and the plot centered on a women-versus-men basketball game to determine whether women would be allowed to remain at the college. The film was released in February of 1931 and was, naturally, ignored by critics. Marguerite Churchill, who had co-starred with Duke in *The Big Trail*, had been thrown into the picture too—as a supporting player.

Duke's next film for Fox was *Three Girls Lost*, in which he played opposite another actress whom Fox was grooming for stardom, Loretta Young. Miss Young, who was known off-screen by her true name, Gretchen, had become one of the leading lights in the Thalians and was one of Duke and Josie's best friends, so Duke was happy to be cast opposite her in the film. The cast also included an actor named Paul Fix, who would become very close to Duke and influential in his career.

Three Girls Lost was a cut above Duke's previous effort for Fox, and *Variety* noted: "John Wayne looks as if he'll come along if getting the right stories. Wayne has a fine speaking voice and a pleasing manner." By April 1931, when the film was released, there was no chance that Fox would give him the right stories. They had canceled his contract about four months earlier.

Duke's contract with Fox had been for five years, renewable every six months—at the studio's option—with automatic salary increases at each renewal. So the indications are that he was making at least $200 a week when Fox dropped his option. Duke knew that he could get a job propping, but it was no longer his career goal; he had had more than a taste of acting and the money it could earn him. He had now starred in three motion pictures, and the fact that he had been chosen to star in one of the biggest-budgeted films ever made gave him a certain celebrity around town, despite the fact that the film had failed financially—through no fault of the players in it. So when Duke was let go by Fox, he drove a few blocks to Columbia Studios at Sunset and Gower, where Harry Cohn signed him immediately to a five-year contract, with six-month options, starting at $250 or $300 a week.

The Columbia Pictures Corporation had been formed just five years earlier, in 1926, when Harry Cohn, his brother Jack, and Joe Brandt (all of whom had started producing pictures a few years earlier as CBC Film Sales Corporation) bought the Gower Street property. By the time Duke went to work for them, Columbia, which had begun with a single stage on Gower, had bought out many of the small independent studios along Gower Street, Beachwood Drive, and Sunset Boulevard (called Poverty Row in the business) and had built from them a complete picture-making facility. Under the guidance of the irascible Harry Cohn, Columbia was rapidly becoming one of Hollywood's major studios.

Duke's first Columbia picture was released under the title *Arizona*. Duke portrayed a West Point graduate stationed at an army camp in Arizona, and played opposite silent film star Laura LaPlante. On a day soon after they finished shooting the film, he went to the studio and was stopped at the gate; Harry Cohn had ordered him barred from the premises. Duke was bewildered by Cohn's action. Apparently he called Cohn's office and was told by someone that he could pick up his weekly paycheck at the gate, but that he was to keep away from the studio until Cohn sent for him. No reason was given. It was an astonishing turn of events, for Cohn himself had signed Duke to a contract a few months earlier and had given every indication not only that he had great plans for Duke, but also that he liked him.

After a week or so, he got word that Cohn wanted to see him. Cohn was his usual forceful, blunt, and crude self at the meeting. He claimed to have reports that Duke had been drinking on the set of *Arizona* and that he was frequently seen in the dressing rooms of actresses. He said he didn't want Duke to have anything to do with any actress under contract to Columbia Pictures, on or off the lot. "Keep your fly buttoned up!" Cohn told him. Duke tried to tell him that whoever had given the report was lying, but Cohn ordered him out of his office. The subject was closed.

Duke was mad as hell. He didn't drink on the set, and while he had stopped on occasion to talk to people in their dressing rooms —as everyone did—he didn't hang around them. Cohn's charges were absurd, and Duke didn't like being told what to do with his own time. There was little he could do but fume and wonder who had reason to slander him so. It wasn't until days later, while talking to one of the studio crew, that he learned why Cohn had been so upset with him. The movie mogul had heard that Duke had been carousing and drinking and having a romantic fling with one of the starlets who had appeared in *Arizona*. Cohn had designs on the starlet and he thought Duke was horning in on his property.

It wasn't at all uncommon for actors and actresses to have brief affairs while working together on a picture. Barbara Walters would ask him decades later if he had ever been in love with any of his leading ladies, and Duke replied, "Well, you know, you get a mutual feeling and relationship on occasions with them." When he was at Columbia, Duke was twenty-four, single, and virile. He had now been dating Josephine Saenz, an extremely religious girl, for five years. By all accounts of those who knew Josie, her love for Duke would not be consummated before marriage. He had not been chaste before meeting Josie, and the notion that a man with his appetites would abstain from sex during all the years when he wasn't even sure the day would ever come that he could marry her is simply ridiculous. Duke's problem was that he obviously hadn't known that the starlet at that time was Harry Cohn's flame.

Shortly thereafter, Cohn exercised the studio's option and renewed Duke's contract for another six months, which automatically raised his salary to $350 a week. Duke naturally interpreted this as a sign that Cohn had put the incident out of mind. But he didn't know Harry Cohn; the man could be unreasonably vindictive and devious. Cohn used the option as a weapon, and it didn't take Duke long to realize that Cohn was beating him to his knees with it.

In Duke's next film, *Range Feud*, he was given a supporting role as a young rancher falsely accused of murder. The film starred Buck Jones and Susan Fleming and was reviewed as a "snappy western that fans will go for." Duke's role had been a pivotal one, but having starred in his first four films, playing a supporting role in a low-budget B picture—his first Western—was neither what Duke expected nor what Harry Cohn had intimated he had in store for him.

If there was any question in Duke's mind about Cohn's motivation for casting him in *Range Feud*, it was answered with his next assignment. Cohn knew that Duke had been a USC football player just four years earlier and that he not only took a measure of pride in the fact but that he had hoped for an opportunity to star in a football picture; his next assignment was a college football picture called *The Maker of Men*, which starred Jack Holt,

Richard Cromwell, and Joan Marsh. It did not star or feature John Wayne. He was given only a bit part in the film, as an overbearing heavy. By this time, Duke knew what Harry Cohn was doing. The only question was how long he would keep doing it.

He was given small parts in two Westerns after *Maker of Men.* They were *Texas Cyclone* and *Two Fisted Law.* Both starred Tim McCoy. Then Cohn finally delivered the coup de grace: he had Duke cast in *The Deceiver*, a film starring Ian Keith—who had played a supporting role in Duke's starring vehicle *The Big Trail.* Duke's role in *The Deceiver* didn't require any acting—or even action—on his part; he was cast as a corpse. Then Cohn canceled his contract.

Duke never forgave Harry Cohn.

PART FOUR

PART
FOUR

9

MR. LEVINE OF MASCOT PICTURES

By December of 1931, when Duke was again on the street looking for work, the movie industry had regained a semblance of
balance. The fear and frantic search for talent that had been gen-
erated by the coming of sound had ended. Major studios were
now teeming with actors from the East and with talented youngsters from the performing-arts workshops that the studios had
established. Studio gates were again closed.

The indications are that Duke spent his first week making the
rounds of major-studio casting offices without success. It was an
ironic and bitterly disappointing turn of events. When he had not
aspired to an acting career, Duke was discovered and groomed for
stardom. When the William Fox Studios dropped him, Columbia
had eagerly signed him. And now that he had appeared in more
than a dozen films, had been billed in nine and had starred in
four, the studios didn't want him.

Although Harry Cohn had made slanderous statements about
Duke to executives of at least one other studio, the remarks were
probably not far-reaching or influential enough to have been a
significant factor in Duke's inability to find work. Duke's problem was one of typecasting and background. He was considered a
leading-man type, and the fact that his movie credits weren't ex-

traordinary and that he had been dropped by two studios didn't make him a particularly appealing candidate in studios that already had their complement of leading men. Had he not been quite so young, tall, athletically built, and handsome, the casting people might have put his experience to good use in supporting roles. But in an industry whose celebrities demand that their satellites be gray—or at least shorter and less attractive—Duke was simply too large a presence; he was the type that less physically endowed leading men were loath to have beside them in supporting roles on screen for fear of having scenes, if not pictures, stolen from them.

Either George O'Brien or Paul Fix—or perhaps both of them—convinced Duke that the worst thing an actor with his credits could do was show up in casting offices personally, hat in hand. It gave the impression that he was desperate for work, which made casting people suspicious: why would a young "star" be waiting in line outside a studio's lower-echelon offices unless he was one of those "problem actors," irresponsible, perhaps, or a drunk or a temperamental egotist? What Duke needed, he was told, was someone who could get past the executive secretaries and who could boast of Duke's accomplishments as Duke himself never could. He needed an agent.

It hadn't occurred to him that he was established enough to be of interest to an agent. It was excellent advice, and he took it.

Among the numerous agents in town was one named Leo Morrison, who probably came to Duke's attention owing to their common surname. Morrison had been a booking agent for the Palace Theater in New York City before going west to become a Hollywood press agent and eventually opening his own talent agency. His illustrious clientele included Jean Harlow, Buster Keaton, Francis X. Bushman (for whom Duke had doubled in *Brown of Harvard* while still a USC student), Beatrice Lillie, Spencer Tracy, and, later, Ronald Reagan. Duke stopped in at the agency unannounced one day. He didn't get to meet Leo Morrison, who dealt personally only with the biggest stars under contract to his agency, but he was greeted warmly by Al Kingston, an agent who worked for Morrison. Duke was grateful for the reception; it was the first time in the week or two since he had left Columbia that anyone in the industry had shown interest in him.

Kingston had seen Duke in *The Big Trail* and had liked his performance. And after talking to him for a while, he liked Duke personally, too. What particularly impressed him was Duke's genuine modesty and honesty and the fact that he didn't expect Kingston to work miracles on his behalf. He neither asked nor expected the agency to get him starring roles. Duke told him that he would take any acting job Kingston could get him and that he'd work hard to prove himself worthy of Kingston's efforts.

Before Duke left the office that day, Kingston offered him a contract and Duke signed it, making the Leo Morrison Agency his professional representative for the next seven years. Then Kingston telephoned an independent producer named Nat Levine and made an appointment to take his new client, John Wayne, over to meet him. Levine owned Mascot Pictures, and the meeting the agent had set up with him would radically alter the course of Duke's career.

Nat Levine was a man of enormous energy and drive. He worked fourteen-hour days (except Sundays, when he took a half-day off) and expected the same from the people who worked with him. Levine was one of the few early motion picture producers who began his career in the business end of show business. Most of the others had been tradesmen, dealers, and entrepreneurs in other industries.

He was born Nathaniel Levine in 1900 in New York City, where at age thirteen he got a summer job as an office boy with the Marcus Loew theater chain. He was ambitious and enjoyed the work so much that when it came time for him to start high school, he kept the job and attended night school, taking business courses and shorthand. In time, he became Marcus Loew's personal secretary, and by then the chain was booking silent films along with its usual vaudeville fare.

Levine left the Marcus Loew company in 1919 and became an independent film distributor. The major studios had their own chains of theaters, but there were thousands of small, privately owned theaters that rented films from the independent studios—

and from the majors, when they could afford to do so. Thirty-six regional exchanges evolved (called the States Rights Market) to distribute the products of the small, independent filmmakers in the cities, towns, and villages throughout the country; Levine joined this network, and he continued distributing films for eight years, until he got into movie production himself.

In those days, motion picture companies weren't bankable, as they say in the business. Although the Warner brothers were later backed by a banker in Pasadena, California, and Harry Cohn pulled Columbia Pictures from Poverty Row with the aid of Mario and Amadeo Giannini, who founded what is today the Bank of America, most bankers didn't consider film production a good financial investment. Producers looking for investment capital turned to the film-processing laboratories, which processed their negatives and prints on credit, sometimes offering limited financing. However, the labs were stuck with the often-incomplete footage if the producers went broke, as was often the case. Levine had occasion to buy such footage from the film labs when he made business trips to California, and so kept a film editor and a writer on salary in his New York office to salvage the films for distribution.

Levine's small distribution company turned a very good profit from such ventures, but owing largely to the scarcity of quality films available to him as a distributor, he went into film production himself. In 1927, he moved his operation to Hollywood, taking offices at the Tec-Art Studio on Melrose Avenue, directly across from Paramount Pictures. Over the next ten years, Levine produced thirty feature films under the Mascot logo, including some excellent ones like *Harmony Lane* (the life of songwriter Stephen Foster); *The Marines Are Coming,* starring William Haines and Esther Ralston; *Laughing At Life,* starring Victor McLaglen, Noah Beery, Regis Toomey, and Lois Wilson; *Little Men* (based upon Louisa May Alcott's nineteenth-century novel); and *In Old Santa Fe* (Mascot's only Western), which starred Ken Maynard and introduced a young singer named Gene Autry, whom Levine had brought to Hollywood from Chicago. Levine created the musical Western genre, and Autry was the first true singing cowboy, but despite this fact and the fact that he eventually became half owner and sole manager of Republic Studios, he has been remembered primarily for his serials, or "chapter plays," as they were once called.

The serials were long adventure films (equivalent in length to about three feature-length films) that were divided into twelve to fifteen episodes or chapters. The first chapter was usually three reels long (about thirty minutes running time), to allow for exposition and character introduction and development, and the subsequent eleven to fourteen episodes were two-reelers, with an average running time of about eighteen minutes. The serials played in theaters each week, along with other shorts and features, and were made to appeal primarily to youngsters. Each weekly episode ended with a cliff-hanger, a perilous situation in which the hero or heroine seemed doomed, only to escape (miraculously, more often than not) in the following episode. The serials kept youngsters coming back to the theaters each week, whether or not they found the weekly feature films of interest, and were a boon to theater owners. They were a boon also to Nat Levine, whose only competition in making them was Universal Pictures. But Levine produced them faster and better than Universal, and he became known as the undisputed king of serials.

Levine expanded Mascot each year, and by the time Al Kingston made an appointment to introduce Duke to him, he had taken over the entire second floor of an office building on the corner of Santa Monica Boulevard and Gordon Avenue, which his company of directors, writers, film editors, cinematographers, distribution people, and others was even then outgrowing.

Compared with the major studios, Mascot Pictures was small, but it was a highly efficient first-class operation. Levine paid some stars, like Tom Mix, as much as $5000 a week, and he owned his equipment and budgeted his serials at between $50,000 and $65,000 each—enormous sums in those Depression days. His action-adventure serials were always shot on location, and so he had a fleet of company automobiles, trucks, and buses. The only equipment he didn't own outright was a sound truck he shared with his friend Walt Disney. Disney would keep the sound men on salary six months a year; Levine would pay their salaries the other six months, and they would share their services. It was a very advantageous arrangement for them all.

Nat Levine's first meeting with the young John Wayne and his agent wasn't a particularly momentous occasion for the producer. Kingston called him and told him that he had signed John Wayne; Levine decided to offer Duke a contract even while Kingston was still on the phone. He had seen *The Big Trail*, as almost everyone in the business had, and was surprised to be in a position to get Duke—surprised that he couldn't find work. "When I met him," Levine recalled, "I was impressed with his honesty, his character. You could *believe* him. There was nothing phony about the guy, and that came through on the screen. As an actor, he wasn't the best and he wasn't the worst. He was okay. What helped him more than anything else was his naturalness—along the lines of Spencer Tracy. It wouldn't have surprised me if he had tried to emulate Spencer Tracy."

He signed Duke to a contract within a few days of their meeting. It was an excellent arrangement for Duke, a three-year contract that paid him $100 a week for the first year, $150 a week for the second, and $200 a week for the third. This was considerably less than he had been making at Columbia, but at a time when one in four of the nation's workers was unemployed and when those fortunate enough to have jobs—many of them men with families—were averaging $21 a week, it was a handsome salary. The best part of the arrangement was that Nat Levine's contracts were nonexclusive: he didn't shackle his people as the big studios did. Duke would be on payroll fifty-two weeks a year, but he was required to work for Mascot only six months of each year, usually April through September. He could free-lance during the remaining six months while still drawing his paycheck. As it turned out, Duke had to work only about three months of his first year under contract, and he made far more money while working for Mascot Pictures—and more valuable contacts in the industry—than he could have made in the same period of time while under contract to one of the major studios.

It was at about this time, mid-December 1931, that Duke made a one-reel short for Samuel Bishoff's Tiffany Pictures, which was truly a Poverty Row company. The short was one of a series called *The Voice of Hollywood*, which most film critics agree was one of the most inept series of shorts ever produced. It was a radio-show format; the mythical radio station's call letters were S-T-A-R, and the feature consisted of a guest host introducing people who were billed as Hollywood's brightest stars but who were really either newcomers who were relatively unknown to the moviegoing public or actors who were no longer in demand. Duke hosted number thirteen in the second series, and is said to have introduced Lupe Velez, Gary Cooper, El Brendel, and Jackie Cooper on the twelve-minute reel. Duke was probably paid a few hundred dollars for hosting the show, and we presume that Al Kingston got him the work for quick pocket money.

When Duke signed with Mascot, Levine was in the final preproduction stages for a serial to be called *Shadow of the Eagle*, and he cast Duke in the leading role as Craig McCoy, a skywriting stunt pilot who traveled with a circus. His co-star was Dorothy Gulliver, who would marry Duke in the serial's happy ending.

The plot of the serial was centered on the capturing and unmasking of the arch villain known as the Eagle, who boldly announced his threats to destroy the circus by skywriting them with his dark biplane. The series was shot on location in the Antelope Valley—very close to the Lancaster farm where Duke had moved with his family from Iowa eighteen years earlier—and that first experience in making a Mascot serial was one that Duke would never forget. With Nat Levine's energy and drive, his planning and execution of a film made people like John Ford look indolent. The shooting schedules were so exhausting for the directors that Levine was forced to develop a system to keep from wearing them out.

Shooting a serial of twelve or fifteen episodes was a most difficult job for one director to accomplish, both mentally and physically. Levine devised the method of using two directors on each serial; one would shoot one day and then take a day off while the other shot. To get a conception of what the other director was doing, the one who had been off would see the dailies, so he knew what the action was and how it was being handled.

"I started that system" Levine recalled, "because when we shot our serials, we shot them in twenty-four or twenty-five consecutive days, including Saturdays and Sundays. It was a marathon, a contest, and by the time we finished, these guys were exhausted."

It was on location for *Shadow of the Eagle* that Duke first worked with Enos Edward "Yakima" Canutt. Yak, as he was called, was raised on a ranch in the Northwest Snake River country. He was a former rodeo champion and one of the best stuntmen and stunt coordinators in the movie business. He got his nickname from associating with two rodeo-riding buddies who were from Yakima, Washington, even though he had only visited the city once or twice in his life. He was brought to Hollywood as an actor in 1923 by an independent film producer named Ben Wilson, who had seen some newsreel rodeo footage of him. He continued to do supporting roles in pictures, but he felt more comfortable doing and developing stunts. Nat Levine kept him under contract, and when he wasn't playing bit parts or character roles or doubling as a stuntman, his time was spent developing stunts, and much of the spectacular action that the Mascot serials were known for was the result of Yakima Canutt's efforts. Duke had been introduced to Yak in Levine's office, and they began their long film association with Yak doubling for Duke on a dangerous motorcycle stunt, which Yak had developed. They struck up an immediate, lifelong friendship.

It was soon apparent to Duke that he had made the right move in signing with the Morrison agency. Al Kingston began lining up work for him that kept him busy for the next two years. No sooner had Duke finished *Shadow of the Eagle* than he apparently went straight to Paramount Pictures, where he played a supporting role in a good film titled *Lady and Gent,* starring George Bancroft and Joyce Compton. Duke played a young college graduate who became a professional prizefighter and beat an overconfident seasoned veteran, played by George Bancroft. By film's end, Duke's features are nearly unrecognizable as he becomes a scarfaced, cynical has-been fighter with a misshapen nose and cauliflower ear. This film, which was released in July of 1932, and *The Cowboys*, which was made forty years later, are the only films in which heavy makeup was used to distort Duke's features for realistic effect—the former film when he was playing supporting roles, and the latter one when he was no longer able to play handsome-young-man parts.

From Paramount, Duke went to Warner Brothers, which had taken over First National Studios on Barham Boulevard in Burbank and was releasing films under the banners of Warner Brothers, First National, and Warner Brothers-First National. The market for Westerns had revived, and two Warner Brothers producers, Leon Schlesinger and Sid Rogell, had met with Jack Warner and proposed remaking several of cowboy-star Ken Maynard's silent First National Westerns into sound films, utilizing the action footage from the silent versions. Maynard was still active in films, but he was under contract to Universal and was no longer quite the slim, handsome youth the producers needed to match his old film footage, so they proposed dressing a young actor exactly like Maynard and reshooting the interiors and storyline close-ups, cutting in the splendid silent footage along with sound effects. Of the six proposed pictures, four would be direct remakes of Maynard's late-twenties films, and all would utilize Maynard action footage.

Jack Warner liked the idea because the Maynard silents had been high-budget, quality Westerns, shot at beautiful locations with large casts of extras and with all the trappings that would lend the new films authenticity and high production values. What made the idea even more attractive was Maynard's action footage. Ken Maynard was a superb horseman who had performed some of the most exciting stunts ever filmed. For example, he was the only Western star who could, as he put it, "go under a horse": with his horse at full galloping speed, Maynard could drop out of his saddle and cling to the left side of the horse, making it appear from the opposite side that the horse was riderless; then he would swing beneath the horse's stomach to the right side, from which he swung up into the saddle again. This was a trick he used in his films to "fool" pursuing gunmen into thinking that he had been shot from his saddle and that his horse, a Palomino named Tarzan, was running off and leaving him behind. It was such action, together with the excellent production values, that made the Maynard films most worthy of salvaging.

Al Kingston took Duke to Warner Brothers to test for the role. The producers were delighted with the results, but as the contracts were being drawn up, they had second thoughts. Sid Rogell called Kingston. He was more than a little disturbed. He had heard that Duke was an irresponsible drinker and a studio woman-chaser. Duke and Kingston went back to see Rogell, and Duke explained the origin and the reason behind the rumor, telling Rogell that he was going to close Harry Cohn's mouth for him if Cohn persisted in telling such lies around town. Fortunately, Duke had *Shadow of the Eagle* and Paramount's *Lady and Gent* behind him to prove his responsibility, and Sid Rogell didn't place much value in Harry Cohn's opinions, anyway, so Duke was put under contract to do the Westerns.

The first one was *Haunted Gold*, a remake of Maynard's 1929 silent film *The Phantom City*. Duke played the part of John Mason (he was given the Christian name John in all six of the Warner Westerns), and his co-star was Sheila Terry. They played a couple drawn by a mysterious letter to a ghost town near an abandoned gold mine. The film was shot with eerie lighting, trap doors, sliding panels, and other Gothic trappings, and it was perhaps owing to this questionable genre mix that Warners decided to delay its release until after the next two—more traditional—Westerns were released.

Duke's second film (and the first of the six to be released) was a remake of a 1926 Maynard silent renamed *Ride Him, Cowboy*. It co-starred Ruth Hall, and Duke played the role of John Drury, who, among other things, saves a wild horse from destruction, keeps it as his own, and names it Duke. The horse was used in this and the last four Westerns in the series, receiving billing alternately as "Duke, the wonder horse" and "Duke, the miracle horse."

Duke's Warner Brothers contract was written with a stipulation allowing him to fulfill the tenets of his contract with Nat Levine at Mascot. It is believed that after he completed *Ride Him,*

Cowboy, he went back to Mascot to do a twelve-chapter serial called *The Hurricane Express*. In this serial, Duke again played the part of a pilot, Larry Barker, whose father was killed in a train wreck caused by a villain known as The Wrecker, a master of many disguises bent upon ruining the L & R Railroad, who was played by Conway Tearle. Shirley Gray played Duke's love interest, and Tully Marshall, who supported Duke in *The Big Trail* for Fox and for whom Harry Cohn made Duke double as a corpse in *The Deceiver*, played a supporting role in this film.

Duke had no sooner caught and unmasked The Wrecker than he was back at Warner Brothers to do *The Big Stampede*, in which he played a deputy sheriff, with Noah Beery, Sr., as the villain and Mae Madison providing the romantic interest. Then, in *The Telegraph Trail*, he portrayed U.S. Army scout John Trent, charged with stringing telegraph lines across the Indian plains. Duke brought Yakima Canutt from Mascot to play High Wolf, leader of the Indians. Next came *Somewhere in Sonora*, in which Duke played a rodeo cowboy forced to flee to Mexico. Marceline Day played the woman in his life in this and the previous film, and Duke's friend from his William Fox days, Paul Fix, played a supporting part for the second time in what would be a long association with Duke.

The last Warner Western was *The Man from Monterey*, co-starring Ruth Hall, with whom he did *Ride Him, Cowboy*. John Ford's brother, Francis, played a supporting role in this film.

From Warner Brothers, Duke went over to Universal to do a comedy short called *Hollywood Handicap*, produced by the Thalians, the group he had joined at Fox, and released as a Universal short. Then he went back to Mascot to do his third and last serial for Nat Levine. It was *The Three Musketeers*, which may have been inspired by but was by no means based upon the Alexandre Dumas story of the same name. Duke again plays a pilot, Tom Wayne, who rescues three legionnaires in the Arabian desert. The legionnaire "musketeers" are Francis X. Bushman, Jr.; Raymond Hatton; and Jack Mulhall; and Duke joins their fight against a group of rebels, led by a villain bent upon destroying the French Foreign Legion. The feminine lead is played by Ruth Hall, who had become one of Duke's favorite leading ladies and whom he had apparently recruited from Warner Brothers for the serial.

After finishing *Musketeers*, Duke returned to Warner Brothers to play out the remaining time on his contract. He did a walk-on as a college student, with a few lines directed toward star Dick Powell, in *College Coach*, and he appeared briefly and without lines as a survivor of a plane crash in *Central Airport*. Warners was pleased with Duke's Westerns, which were making money. As a small but temporary star on the lot—he was, after all, under contract to another studio—he was given a good deal of latitude at Warners.

Both of the pictures in which Duke had bit parts were directed by William A. Wellman, whom Duke greatly admired and for whom he no doubt chose to be an extra for the opportunity of working with the director. He liked "Wild Bill" Wellman, and when Duke finally formed his own production company in 1951, he chose Wellman to direct four of the first six films in which he starred, including *The High and the Mighty*.

It was at about this time that Duke did *His Private Secretary* for a small New York production company called Showmen's Pictures. It was a romantic comedy in which Duke played the lead as Dick Wallace, the son of a wealthy businessman who, against his father's wishes, courts and marries the granddaughter of a minister, played by Evelyn Knapp.

Duke finished his Warner Brothers contract with two pictures: *The Life of Jimmy Dolan*, starring Douglas Fairbanks, Jr. (the son of one of Duke's childhood movie idols) and Duke's friend Loretta Young; Mickey Rooney was also in the cast. Duke played a small role as a prizefighter named Smith. In *Baby Face*, starring Barbara Stanwyck and George Brent, he played Jimmy McCoy, an assistant bank manager whom Stanwyck uses and tosses aside in her immoral scramble up the social ladder.

By the time Duke had finished shooting *Baby Face*, Nat Levine had taken over the Mack Sennett Studio in North Hollywood and was subleasing space to other independent film companies. Meanwhile, Duke had signed with Trem Carr and W. Ray Johnston of

Monogram Pictures, an association that would keep him even busier than he had been at Warner Brothers. Before he started work for Monogram, and even before *Baby Face* was released in July of 1933, Duke had married Josephine Saenz.

10

MARRIAGE

SEVEN years had passed since Duke first met Josephine. He worshipped the young socialite and was obsessed with making her his wife. After Josie had finished her secondary education and Duke had found his calling in the movie industry, there were numerous opportune times for setting their wedding date. One of them came in late 1929, when Duke was signed by the William Fox Studio as an actor, given a $2 million picture to launch his career, and groomed for stardom. Then again in late 1930, when Harry Cohn made promises and signed him to a relatively high paying contract, the time must have seemed right to Duke, who was—as always—a paragon of impatience. At the time of his signing a nonexclusive contract with Nat Levine, which allowed him to earn three or four times his salary by free-lancing with Paramount and Warner Brothers, he had another opportunity. But the long-anticipated wedding was neither scheduled nor planned. Clearly the delay was no longer owing to Duke's inability to provide for a wife of Josie's social station; judging from his obsession to marry her and his impatient nature, it's apparent that Josie was having reservations about marrying Duke, even though she loved him.

Duke was no longer the naive young college freshman Josie had fallen in love with, no longer the young man whose only goal was to complete his education so that he might marry her. He hadn't changed appreciably, but he had found another love—acting—and with it a life-style that aggravated Josie's jealous nature. Duke was an attractive and likable man, and when he entered the movie business and was literally surrounded by the kind of feminine beauty Hollywood attracted—stunning young actresses who found him appealing and who, for the most part and by nature, were more bold, more emotionally demonstrative, and less inhibited than most of the young women of their day—the temptation they offered was simply too great for a man of Duke's appetites to resist. Josie finally had just cause for jealousy.

Duke continued drinking, as he had in high school and college, and now he had money, fewer restraints, and lusty drinking buddies like Ward Bond and George O'Brien. He wasn't quite as discreet about his drinking as he was about his sexual liaisons. There's a story, perhaps apocryphal, that at about this time Duke and Ward Bond punched holes with their fists through nearly every door in the Hollywood Athletic Club in a drunken contest of physical strength. True or not, the story exemplifies the kind of behavior that Duke and his drinking pals occasionally indulged in at Hollywood watering holes, behavior that Josephine Saenz and her family no doubt found coarse and shocking.

As the daughter of a wealthy entrepreneur and Central American consul, Josie was raised in a refined atmosphere of elegance and grace. Her world was one of order and harmony, of formal dinner parties for visiting dignitaries. Her home was a gathering place for the Pasadena and San Marino and Santa Barbara social sets and for the Catholic clergy. The only news the Saenz family made was reported in the society pages, and then as now, Josie was listed in the *Southwest Bluebook*, the social register of Southern California. She had friends in the movie business, though. In Hollywood, where gossip seemed to travel with the speed of light, she was aware of Duke's peccadilloes and no doubt made him aware, loudly and clearly, that she knew about them.

Ultimately, though, the tenets of Josie's religion must have caused her the most concern. It would have been a blessing to her and certainly would have eased her mind had Duke been subject to the same tenets—particularly the constraints—by converting to Catholicism. Duke wouldn't entertain the notion for a moment —not even for Josie. He had been raised a Presbyterian and had held a strong belief in God all his life, but he was never a church-goer and had early on rejected the dogma of organized religion. Duke always gave the impression that his God was not without a sense of humor and was not above winking at the foibles of mere mortals, as long as they were kind to one another. He respected the rights of others to believe as they chose, but he demanded the same consideration. He agreed to allow his and Josie's offspring to be raised in the Catholic faith, but he could not find it in himself to embrace Catholic orthodoxy personally. This "liberal" attitude toward religion posed a problem for Josie. To her, mar-riage was an absolutely sacred rite, an eternal bond, and in the later years of their courtship Duke had adopted a life-style that wouldn't have been conducive to a lasting marriage. Duke appar-ently convinced her that things would be different—that as a married man he would change his ways—and on June 24, 1933, Josie became Mrs. Marion Mitchell Morrison. Duke was twenty-six; Josie was twenty-two.

They didn't have the big church wedding that Josie had wanted. As a non-Catholic, Duke couldn't be married before the altar—which was exactly the brand of orthodoxy that he ab-horred. They could have been married in the vestry of a Catholic church, but instead they had a very large and formal wedding in the gardens of the Bel-Air estate owned by actress Loretta Young's mother. The ceremony was conducted by a Catholic priest. Duke was dressed in ascot and tails, Josie in a traditional and exquisite wedding gown. Dr. Saenz gave the bride away, and Duke's brother, Robert, was best man. Among the large assem-blage who toasted the new bride and groom with expensive French champagne were Duke's mother and father and a few of his friends, including Pexy Eckles.

Duke was scheduled to begin work at Monogram Studio shortly after his marriage, so there wasn't much time for a honey-moon. "They took a little time off," Eckles recalled, "then settled into a nice little apartment down near the Hancock Park area before Duke returned to work."

MARRIAGE

Just prior to his marriage, Duke had signed a contract to star in eight Westerns, called Lone Star Pictures, which were produced by Paul Malvern and which were distributed and perhaps partly owned by Monogram Pictures. Monogram rented space at the David O. Selznick Studio in Culver City; it was run by Trem Carr and owned by W. Ray Johnston, who handled distribution from their New York City office. As usual, Al Kingston set the deal for Duke, even though he was no longer Duke's agent.

Kingston had left the Leo Morrison Agency and had formed his own agency by the time Duke had completed his Warner Brothers contract obligations. Duke would have stayed with Kingston but was bound by contract to Morrison, who would neither release him nor find him work; in fact, Duke claimed he couldn't even get Morrison on the phone, so he went to see Al Kingston.

Duke wasn't broke when he went to Kingston; in addition to the money he had saved, he was by then drawing $150 a week on his contract with Mascot Pictures. He wanted and needed work, though; he was planning to marry within weeks and was, as always, impatient and worried that for the first time since he had signed with the Morrison agency, he didn't have a picture or series of pictures he could begin work on.

Although less than half of the pictures Duke had done since starring in *The Big Trail* had been Westerns, the two Westerns he had done for Columbia and the six for Warner Brothers had resulted in his being typecast as a Western actor. Except for a few stars like Dustin Farnam, who had appeared in Westerns after coming to Hollywood from the Broadway stage, Western stars were not considered actors; they were "Western actors" only, and were judged therefore as lacking in the range of acting skills required by feature-film roles.

Nat Levine had employed Duke in three adventure serials—none a Western—and at the time when Duke was running out of work, Nat had begun doing feature films. He was convinced that the Western *features* market was fading—which it was—and even though he was paying Duke a weekly salary and had him under contract for another eighteen months or so, the idea of casting him in one of his feature comedies or musicals or dramas didn't occur to him. He said later that he regretted this lack of foresight.

Al Kingston took Duke to meet Trem Carr and producer Paul Malvern at Monogram in the late spring of 1933, and they signed him to an eight-picture contract, at $2,500 per picture, just prior to his marrying Josie. The Leo Morrison Agency got the ten percent commission on the deal, much to Duke's resentment. Kingston and Duke were casual friends and business associates, and Kingston was bothered by Duke's failure to acknowledge his help by at least offering some token of appreciation. Kingston was aware that he had played a crucial role in Duke's career by putting him back on his feet after Harry Cohn dumped him and when no one else would even talk to him. It's an early instance of Duke's characteristically guileless but nonetheless duplicitous nature.

After Duke and Josie had settled into their apartment, Duke went to work for producer Paul Malvern at Monogram. In his first picture, *Riders of Destiny*, he portrayed Singin' Sandy Saunders, a cowboy who strummed his guitar before battle and sang ballads about how the bad guys' hours were numbered with him on their trail.[1] Cecilia Parker was Duke's romantic interest, and the film also featured George Hayes, who portrayed a character named Denton and who later gained fame among Western buffs as the comic "Gabby" Hayes.

For the next two years, Duke worked exclusively for Paul Malvern at Monogram and made sixteen straight Lone Star Westerns. He would eventually look back on these Monogram years as the best and most enjoyable and most educational of his career—particularly educational: he had often said that one of his most valuable lessons gained in those B pictures was learning to deliver convincingly the long-winded, awkward expositional dialogue that was used in low-budget films in place of additional scenes to develop plot and delineate character. Duke called them "throwaway lines"; they were sometimes absurd in their context, and a challenge that made their mastery an invaluable experience.

The Lone Star Westerns were shot mostly on location and only during Southern California's dry-weather months, so Duke had five or six months off each year. Unlike his previous year at Mascot, when he had worked at other studios between assignments, Duke took the time off. He could afford to do so, for even though it was still the midst of the Great Depression, he was averaging nearly $700 a week from his Monogram and Mascot contracts. He had an added incentive to take time off. He had achieved his first goal in winning the hand of Josephine Saenz, so he relaxed a little and enjoyed the good life with her, the vacations, the society and Hollywood parties, the dining and dancing and sporting events and occasional hunting trips with friends like George O'Brien and Ward Bond, and the trips to Catalina and Mexico aboard John Ford's boat, the *Araner* (by 1933, Ford had allowed Duke back into his fold—at least the periphery of it). The Monogram years were good times for Duke and Josie.

Another reason Duke had more time for the good life was that Al Kingston was no longer hustling work for him. Also, as a "Western actor," he had fewer opportunities for work. This apparently suited Duke fine at first, but in time, his naturally restless nature and his frustration at having been so narrowly typecast began to wear on him.

All Duke's Lone Star Westerns were released between October 1933 and July 1935. Although they were enormously popular in the small independent theaters of the South, the Midwest, and the West, they were critically ignored. They were good B Westerns, though, much better than those of other small companies and far more innovative; some of the techniques developed in them became standard for the Western film genre and were even adopted for use in big-budget epic Westerns. George Hayes and Yakima Canutt (who was also still under contract to Nat Levine at Mascot) were featured in most of the films, and the majority of them were directed by Robert North Bradbury.[2]

The Lone Star Westerns were six-reelers, with a running time of about fifty-five minutes. They were always the second feature on a theater's double bill. Most of the sixteen films had budgets of about $15,000 each and ten- to fifteen-day shooting schedules. They were filmed on locations within a few miles of the studio, around Chatsworth in the west San Fernando Valley, or in the nearby Thousand Oaks and Simi Valley area; as a consequence, they all looked alike scenically, and they looked much like the earlier Westerns of most other small companies, which were filmed in the same areas. The pace and realism of their action footage, however, makes them superior to other B Westerns of their day. Yakima Canutt was responsible for much of this. He not only performed in nearly all of them (usually as the villain), but also devised and coordinated the stunts and doubled for Duke on them.

Before Duke and Yak began working together at Monogram, the barroom brawls and fistfights in Westerns were ridiculous. The stuntmen wrestled, mostly, and in order to avoid serious injury to one another, whatever punches they threw were aimed at arms and shoulders, resulting in what looked about as menacing as a schoolyard fight between two youngsters whose hearts weren't in the battle. Duke and Yak addressed the problem by choreographing their fights and developing what they called the Pass System, whereby one of them would aim with full force at the other's chin and narrowly miss it, while the other went crashing through breakaway tables and the like from the apparent blow. One day director Robert Bradbury was watching them rehearse a fight scene and decided that he could complete the illusion with camera angles. Prior to this, movie fights were shot from the side, the camera at a distance and panning with the action. Bradbury began cutting the action and placing the camera behind the person throwing the punch, so that it was impossible to see that the blows weren't landing. The sound effects of the blows were added later (although for some reason they weren't added to the fights in *Blue Steel* and *The Dawn Rider*).

Duke also insisted on portraying Western heroes as realistically as possible. Most of the Western stars before him had been fighting their barroom brawls by Marquess of Queensberry Rules. While the villains were attacking with broken bottles and chairs, the guys in the white hats were dancing around, throwing jabs, and waiting for the villain to get back on his feet before the fight resumed. Duke insisted on repaying his adversaries in kind; if a villain hit him with a chair, he'd pick up a chair and hit him back, and this, too, added to the realism and action of the Lone Star films and in time became standard practice in Westerns.

The first few pictures of Duke's series paid a handsome return, and Monogram began putting more money into promoting them. The studio even capitalized on Duke's marriage to Josie. When his fifth picture, *Blue Steel*, was released in May of 1934, they sent out press books along with their lobby cards, complete with press-ready ads that theater managers could run in their local newspapers and which read, in part, as follows:

JOHN WAYNE IS ONLY MEMBER OF MOTION PICTURE COLONY IN THE HOLLYWOOD SOCIAL REGISTER

In Hollywood, as in every city in the world, the Social Register is the last word in the judging of those who are to be included and those not to be included in the upper strata of society.

It is only natural that the little book should include the names of many people prominent in the motion picture world, but there is only one name included in this list, of an actor who is the star of western pictures.

That star is John Wayne, who appears on the screen of the _____ Theatre next _____ in *Blue Steel*, a Lone Star Production.

By his marriage in June of last year to pretty Josephine Saenz, his school-day sweetheart, the name of Marion Michael Morrisey [sic] was included in the register of the social elite of Hollywood, for Morrisey [sic] is the real name of this popular favorite of western fans all over the country. . . .

After *Blue Steel*, Duke finished the year by completing the last three films of his eight-picture contract. The series had been such a profitable and enjoyable experience for everyone at Monogram that Duke was signed to do eight more and was given a substantial raise that, together with the automatic $50-a-week raise under his Mascot contract, would bring his following year's earnings to more than $1,000 a week.

DUKE

His new eight-picture contract was cause enough to break out the champagne, but for Duke the crowning event that closed out the year was the addition of another Morrison. On November 23, 1934, Josie gave birth to their first child, a boy, whom they named Michael Anthony Morrison. Duke, who loved children and who had longed for some of his own, had a family at last.

He had proved himself a box-office draw. He rose above the generally predictable scripts and brought a natural sincerity to the roles that make the films credible even by today's standards. Perhaps as a bonus for his good work, the studio launched his new eight-picture contract with a more ambitious project. His first eight had been done from original (and mediocre) scripts, but for the first film of his new contract, the studio purchased the movie rights of James Oliver Curwood's Northwest novel, *The Wolf Hunters*, which the studio retitled *The Trail Beyond* in an apparent effort to keep it from sounding like anything other than a Western. The production values of *The Trail Beyond* are considerably better than those of other Lone Star films. It had a bigger budget and longer production schedule; it had a larger cast of supporting players and extras; it utilized more elaborate stunts, more camera setups and more sophisticated cinematographic techniques; and scenically it offered rivers and lakes and snow-capped mountains. Clearly the production company had gone outside Los Angeles County to film, probably to the Colorado River and to Big Bear Lake, in the San Bernardino Mountains north of Patton, where Duke's paternal grandfather had died.

As *The Trail Beyond* did no better business than the studio's low-budget efforts, the rest of the series were produced with the same cheaper formula that had proved so successful with the first eight pictures. Duke's increased status and influence as the box-office star of the series became increasingly evident. The name John Wayne began appearing on the ads and lobby cards and theater marquees in larger and bolder type than the titles of his pictures, and more of his friends, like Paul Fix, began appearing in them. Even brother Robert benefitted by Duke's clout as the series' star. Robert began getting paid—and getting screen credit as "Robert

Emmett"—for the stories and screenplays, along with Lindsley Parsons, who had written most of the previous screenplays.

By May of 1935, Duke had completed *Paradise Canyon*, the last of the sixteen Lone Star pictures. By the time the last three of the series were ready for market, only one of them was distributed by Monogram; the other two, *The Desert Trail* and *The Dawn Rider*, were distributed by a newly formed company called Republic Studios, for a studio merger had taken place that would again change the course of Duke's career.

11

MR. CARR AND MR. YATES

In the spring of 1935, Herbert Yates scrutinized his accounting ledgers and made a decision that would eventually give enormous impetus to Duke's career; he decided to venture into the production end of filmmaking. As a Wall Street entrepreneur, he had been associated with the movie business almost since its inception on the East Coast, where he had backed a producer or two at a handsome profit. Then in the early twenties, when the business began flourishing in Hollywood, he had done as smart investors do: he looked for the industry's vital spot, the indispensable service that required the least financial risk and investment for the greatest return on his capital, and he found it—film processing. Raw film stock had to be developed and processed; hundreds of prints had to be made from the negatives for distribution to movie theaters throughout the country and Canada and abroad. Without prints of their films, movie producers had no product to market; consequently, although struggling movie producers might sneak out on their landlords, bounce checks on their production crew and actors, and otherwise beg, steal, and borrow to get their motion pictures on film, the film labs had to be paid or the producers were out of business.

So Herbert Yates left his executive position with the American

Tobacco Company and joined Hedwig Laboratories in 1915 to learn the business, and in 1918, he formed Republic Laboratories and took over Eastman Kodak's motion picture labs. In 1926, he bought Rothacker Laboratories in Chicago and then merged all his holdings into Consolidated Film Industries, a company with film labs on both coasts that later became a holding company with diversified interests (including the American Record Company). But Consolidated Film Laboratories was the heart of Consolidated Film Industries, and Yates spared no expense in keeping up with the technological advances in film processing that made his labs second to none. He didn't have big studio accounts (except for RKO), and he didn't need them. Although the movie industry finally evolved into fewer than a dozen major studios, then—as now—hundreds of independent producers and countless small production companies kept his labs operating at full capacity.

Consolidated Film Laboratories continued to prosper through the late twenties and early thirties, but as the business began changing, with smaller studios going broke or, like Columbia Pictures, merging with others to join the ranks of the majors, Yates began examining other investment avenues in the industry. He was particularly interested in Monogram Pictures, which was doing fairly well, and in Mascot, which was doing extremely well. Yates saw, for example, that Nat Levine's Mascot Pictures had developed from a small rented office to Tec-Art to the entire enormous Mack Sennett Studio complex in just six years. The Consolidated ledgers also showed that Levine's line of credit with them had increased from $30,000 in 1927 to nearly a half-million dollars by 1932. It occurred to him that with his investment capital and film laboratories, he might be instrumental in merging several independent and fairly prosperous small companies into a major studio, which he would name Republic Pictures. And so he scheduled meetings with the producers he had in mind and traveled west from his New York City offices to meet with them.

Yates's plan was to form a three-way partnership with W. Ray Johnston and Trem Carr of Monogram, and Nat Levine of Mascot, for he knew nothing about producing films. He proposed a partnership in which Consolidated, Monogram, and Mascot would each have one-third ownership in a newly formed production company. Consolidated would pay a cash settlement to each of the companies in exchange for their participation, their film libraries, their equipment, and their film distribution exchanges. In addition, Consolidated would guarantee full financial backing for the newly formed studio until it reached a certain profit margin on its own, and would also pay each of the partners a weekly salary, beginning at $1,000 a week and escalating each year, presumably in addition to their share of the monies derived from Republic's net.

It was an extraordinary proposition. Yates would remain in New York and would not interfere with production. The former Monogram people would continue to make Westerns and features, and Levine could continue making serials and features, all to be released under the Republic banner.

Levine thanked Yates for the generous offer, but declined. Although Yates's offer was attractive, Levine had always been his own boss, doing what he wanted, when he wanted, and answering to no one. He didn't know whether he could work within the confines of a partnership, no matter how broad the confines. Besides, his company was doing very well and he was enjoying himself; he didn't need partners and could see no advantage to having them. Trem Carr and W. Ray Johnston also shared Levine's feelings regarding autonomy, but they found the Consolidated offer irresistible—the merger would allow them to make bigger pictures without investing their own capital—and so they agreed to go with Consolidated.

Yates was disappointed. Even though he couldn't form the triumvirate he had envisioned—not immediately, anyway—he didn't give up the idea. Meanwhile, in the late spring of 1935, the principals of Consolidated and Monogram formed Republic Pictures in a fifty-fifty partnership deal. Johnston was made president of Republic, in charge of distribution, and he returned to his New York office to coordinate distribution, including the few exchanges Yates had acquired with his small-studio buy-outs. Trem Carr was named vice president in charge of production, and he continued to operate with the members of his now-defunct

Monogram company out of the same rental facility at the David Selznick Studio.

Presumably producer Paul Malvern had sold whatever interest he had had in the Lone Star pictures to Yates, for no sooner had the ink dried on the Republic merger papers than Carr signed Malvern to an eight-picture contract to produce Westerns. Duke was also signed to a new eight-picture deal for considerably more money, and for the first time since he had left Columbia, Duke had solid footing with a highly solvent studio. His future looked promising and secure; Trem Carr was probably the only person in Hollywood who didn't look upon Duke as merely a Western actor. Carr had plans of eventually starring him in features, but in accordance with the merger agreement, he had to continue making Westerns, and the Lone Star formula with John Wayne was a proven money-maker. He had to establish a firm foundation with the new company before he could risk putting Duke in features.

The first Republic production was *Westward Ho* and was released in August of 1935. Duke starred as John Wyatt, along with a supporting cast that included Yakima Canutt. Robert Bradbury directed the picture and Paul Malvern produced it, and like the seven Republic Westerns that followed, it differed from the Lone Star Westerns only in its budget. *Westward Ho* cost the company about $35,000 to produce (three times the cost of the Lone Star pictures), but its production values were no better. The higher salaries Carr paid the production crew and cast explained the increase in costs. The second Republic film, *The New Frontier*, was released six weeks later, and by the time the third film, *The Lawless Range*, was released in November 1935, troubles were beginning to brew at Republic Pictures.

Herbert Yates was a persistent man. He had continued pressing Nat Levine to join the Republic merger, and Levine had continued to refuse him. As the months passed, Levine began having second thoughts. For one thing, he saw that Yates was staying in New York, as he had promised, and was not interfering with Trem Carr's productions. He also saw the possibility of his at last escaping the capital-investment treadmill. Levine had built Mascot by funneling his profits back into the company and expanding it. Aside from the reasonably good salary he gave himself, the only profit he took from Mascot was in 1933, when he paid himself a $72,000 bonus and bought Jean Harlow's Holmby Hills mansion. The idea of selling his company to Republic for what he called "important money" and receiving in addition to a one-third interest in Republic Pictures both the use of operating capital from Consolidated's investment and the autonomy to continue operating as he always had and without interference was too good a deal to pass up.

Levine couldn't recall exactly when he joined Republic; details of the impending merger were reported in the September 19, 1935, issue of Daily *Variety*, though, by which time Levine had completed two features to be released under the Republic banner. He had yet to begin a serial and one feature that were to be released under the Mascot banner, so presumably he joined the merger by mid-November of 1935.

Consolidated put $3 million capital into the venture and assumed Levine's lease on the former Mack Sennett Studio, which in the spring of 1936 became known as Republic Studios. Levine was named chairman of the board, and he brought into the new company numerous contract players, including two who went on to become stars: Gene Autry and Ann Rutherford, both of whom were products of the performing arts workshop Levine had established on his lot.

For two months or so, it was business as usual for both Trem Carr and Nat Levine. They each continued operating from their separate studios and shared their contract players. Each used the invaluable services of Yakima Canutt as a supporting player, stuntman, stunt coordinator, and tutor for Gene Autry and others. Ann Rutherford made her Republic debut playing opposite Duke in *The Oregon Trail* and also appeared with him in *The Lawless Nineties* and in the seventh of his eight-picture deal, *The Lonely Trail*. But the trouble began earlier, when Carr and his former Monogram company moved from Selznick's lot to the Republic lot in the spring of 1936.

With so many features, serials, and Westerns being produced

from the same lot, there was a natural need for someone to be in charge of the overall production. Trem Carr had assumed that he would run the studio; as vice president of the company, he had been put in charge before Levine entered the merger. Perhaps in anticipation of Levine's entry, Carr had taken an unprecedented action in emblazoning his credentials on the title of the first Republic film, which read:

John Wayne

in

WESTWARD HO

Trem Carr: Vice-President in Charge of Production

The action may have been taken in a futile attempt to establish legal precedence rather than to satisfy Carr's ego, as Carr was a very nice, amiable guy and not at all egomaniacal. Like Levine, Carr was an individualist, used to running his own company and answering to no one. When Nat Levine joined the merger and assumed charge of production on the lot, it rankled Carr and was a contributing factor to his eventual split with the company.

All Monogram's Lone Star Westerns had been produced at a cost of between $10,000 and $15,000, including the last, which was released in July of 1935; yet the first film Carr did for Republic, *Westward Ho*, was released only a month later, with roughly the same running time, the same star, and the same crew, but cost three times more than the Monogram production. The cost of Carr's Republic pictures was still reasonably modest, but it was apparent that Carr had rewarded his people for all their lean years with his company, and to the cost-conscious Mr. Yates, Carr must have seemed unreasonably generous with Consolidated's capital. So early on, although Yates wasn't technically interfering with Carr's productions, he was questioning their cost and giving Carr a rough time about them, which Carr regarded as an infringement upon his promised autonomy.

Only the last three of the eight pictures Duke had contracted to do were produced from the Republic lot. Carr was still with the company when *King of the Pecos* was made and released on March 9, 1936, but Nat Levine took over as producer of the last two, *The Lonely Trail* and *Winds of the Wasteland*. By the time *The Lonely Trail* was released on May 25, 1936, Trem Carr had severed his relationship with Republic Pictures.

Carr obviously felt that Herbert Yates had violated the spirit, if not the letter, of their merger agreement by "forcing" him onto Levine's lot and putting Levine in charge of production. In fact, the newly formed Republic Pictures had assumed the lease on the studio, and it was pointless to have Carr's part of the company renting space from Selznick when they had an entire studio of their own in North Hollywood. Carr was also disturbed that Yates hadn't informed him that Levine was named chairman of the board. As an individualist and an executive in the new movie company, Carr found his position intolerable, and his former Monogram company hadn't been on the new lot long when dissension developed between his staff and the former Mascot staff. Levine was troubled by the dissension and felt it unwarranted, but the problem was covert and persistent and insoluble.

There was no power struggle. Although Carr and Johnston had brought less to the merger than had Levine, they were made full and equal partners. Nevertheless, after more than a year in the company and several months on the Republic lot, Trem Carr wanted out. He sold his share of the one-third interest back to Republic for $150,000, and Johnston, who had always been the money man, got $850,000 in the buy-out. Both Yates and Levine put up a half-million on the buy-out, and Republic was now owned by them in equal partnership. Although W. Ray Johnston sold his interest in the studio, he remained with Republic for a while, in charge of distribution.

Trem Carr took his cinematographer, A. J. "Archie" Stout, with him when he left, and while Duke and producer Paul Malvern finished the last two pictures of their contracts with Republic, Carr went to Universal Pictures, where he was signed as a producer and where he was soon joined by both Duke and Paul Malvern.

Duke's Republic contract ended in late May or early June of

1936, when he completed shooting *Winds of the Wasteland*, at which time Republic offered him a long-term contract beginning at $24,000 a year. It was a tempting offer. Republic was a financially solvent studio with great promise. Duke knew Nat Levine, who was now running the studio, and many of Duke's friends, including Yakima Canutt, were now under contract there. His quest for financial security was very much on his mind at the time, for he now had another child to care for: his first daughter, Mary Antonia (called Toni), had been born just four months earlier, on February 26. At about the time of the Republic offer, Trem Carr had made him another offer that he couldn't resist. Carr had signed with Universal to make adventure pictures, none of them a Western and all of them with budgets between $60,000 and $90,000, and he wanted Duke to star in six of them, at a salary of $6,000 per picture.

It didn't take long for Duke to make his decision. Carr's plan was to do all six pictures in twelve to fifteen months, which would earn Duke $36,000. They were B pictures and would get second billing to Universal's big features, but they would play the big theaters of major cities, a market that none of Duke's Mascot, Monogram, or Republic pictures had reached. Most important of all to Duke was the possibility that in starring in six non-Westerns in a row, he might at last lay his "cowboy actor" image to rest, or at least put it in perspective. So he declined Republic's offer and joined Trem Carr and Paul Malvern at Universal.

Duke was out of the saddle for fourteen months. He portrayed a U.S. Coast Guard commander in a melodramatic adventure yarn called *The Sea Spoilers*, which had little to do with the Coast Guard; he was a prizefighter who took on all lumber-camp and mining-town challengers in *Conflict*; he was a traffic manager for a trucking company in a freight-truck-caravan versus freight-train picture called *California Straight Ahead*; he was a newsreel cameraman in *I Cover the War*; a star hockey player in *Idol of the Crowds*; and a South Seas pearl diver in *Adventure's End*, an ironically prophetic title in that it brought an end to his contract and his hopes of being recognized and accepted as a straight actor.

The best that can be said of the six Carr Universal pictures is that they were mediocre, even for B pictures. They weren't good enough in story line or production values to illuminate their star, John Wayne. At least two of them were considered worthy of second billing to the studio's features in New York and other large cities, and so were reviewed, but the movie critics didn't "discover" John Wayne then; neither did they say Duke showed promise if given better stories, as they had said about him during his Fox studio days.

Duke was very disappointed and despondent. Years later, he blamed Trem Carr for failing to capitalize on a splendid opportunity. Judging from the product, Carr had brought a Monogram mentality to the undertaking. Rather than choosing or commissioning scripts on the basis of story line, he had them fashioned to take advantage of whatever standing sets were available on the lot. Even the one screenplay that was not contrived in such a manner, *Conflict*, which was based on Jack London's novel *The Abysmal Brute*, was given the assembly-line treatment. All the films were ground out on five- to seven-day shooting schedules, as though Carr were still producing cheap Westerns. And so a fine opportunity for all involved ended with bitterly disappointing results. Carr remained with Universal and did two more pictures (without Duke) before rejoining W. Ray Johnston, who had revived Monogram, which eventually became United Artists.

By the late fall of 1937, Duke had left Universal and was again back in the saddle, this time for Paramount, where he starred in *Born to the West*, based on Zane Grey's novel of the same title. It was released on December 10, 1937, just five days after the release of Duke's last Universal film, *Adventure's End*. After the Paramount picture, Duke was out of work for seven months—the first and last such totally idle period in his fifty years of filmmaking.[1]

Duke was dissatisfied with the direction his career had taken and with the fact that after seven years of movie acting, he was still not considered an actor by the motion picture community. He couldn't help comparing his career to that of Gary Cooper, who had been cast in a big film, Goldwyn's *The Winning of Barbara Worth*, at the same time Duke got the lead in *The Big Trail*. Coop had become a star with his picture and had risen above the

A photographic portrait of Duke at age five with his younger brother,
Robert.   Springer/Bettmann Film Archive

MARION SEARS MAIR
University of California, Southern Branch. Explosion Staff (4); French Club (2); Parnassian Library Club (3), (4); Girls' Athletic Club (2), (3); Girls' Athletic Association, Swimming Club (4); Hockey Club (4); Basketball Club (4); Soccer Team (4).

ROY NELSON MILLICE *"Lefty"*
University of Southern California. From Lawrence High School, Kansas. Varsity Football (4); Baseball Team (4).

EVA PAULINE MORROW *"Eve"*
Occidental College. Roll Room Representative (3); Honor Pin (2), (3); Three One-Act Plays (4); Parnassian Library Club (4); Glee Club (4).

CHARLES M. MANBERT *"Charlie"*
University of California, Southern Branch. Track (4); Boys' League.

MARION MITCHELL MORRISON *"Duke"*
University of Southern California. Junior Class Representative to Cabinet (3); Vice-President Junior Class (3); President Senior Class (4); Senior Ring Committee (4); Explosion Sport Writer (4); Honor Pin (2); "Dulcy" (3); Southern California Shakesperian Contest (3); Comites (2); "G" Club (3), President (4); Stage Crew (2), (3); Class B Football (1), (2); Varsity Football (3), (4).

VIVIAN NAY *"Viv"*
Pomona College. From Alhambra High School, California. Honor Pin (1); Three One-Act Plays (4); Comites Club (1), (2).

NORMAN L. NELSON *"Normy"*
University of Southern California. Roll Room Representative (2); Variety Show (3), (4); Football Team (2), (4); Band (3), (4); Orchestra (4).

JAMES ARCHIE NEEL, JR. *"Greasy Neel"*
University of Arizona. Secretary Freshman Class (1); Oratorical Committee (1); Sophomore Yell Leader (2); Vice-President Junior Class (3); Junior Dance Committee (3); Junior Yell Leader (3); Senior Ring Committee (4); Senior Dance Committee (4); "Fire Prince" (3); Variety Show (4); Music Club (1), (2), (3), Secretary (2); Glee Club (3), President (4); "G" Club (3), Vice-President (4); Class B Football (2), (3), (4); Class C Basketball (1); Class B Basketball (2), (3), Captain (4); Orchestra (1), (2), (3); School Yell Leader (3), (4).

DOROTHY NORWOOD *"Dot"*
Spanish Club (4); Volley Ball (1); Baseball (2), (3).

HOBERT A. NAIR *"Nair"*
Travel. From Bayard Consolidated High School, Iowa. Welfare Committee Senior Class (4); Boys' League.

A page from Duke's 1925 Glendale High School yearbook showing his true middle name.

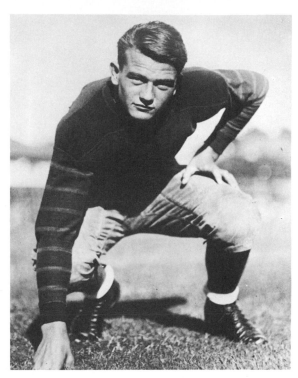

This snapshot of Duke at age eighteen was taken for his 1925 Glendale High School yearbook.

Young Duke Morrison as he looked playing left guard on the University of Southern California freshman team in 1925 and as a substitute on the varsity team the following year.   Springer/Bettmann Film Archive

Duke's childhood home at 224 South Second Street in Winterset, Iowa, as it appears today. The Morrisons moved to this house shortly after Duke's birth in 1907 and lived there until they moved to nearby Earlham in 1910.

© Joe Graham & Company, Winterset, Iowa. Kathy and Randall Lee Collection

He fought for JUSTICE-
Battled for LOVE!

JOHN
WAYNE
IN

THE STAR PACKER

A PAUL MALVERN
PRODUCTION
Written and Directed by
ROBERT N. BRADBURY

A
LONE STAR
WESTERN

Duke was twenty-three and had just been named "John Wayne" when he posed for this photo to promote his first starring film *The Big Trail* (1930).

William Fox Studios
Don Roger Nilsson Collection

An example of the key-art three sheet posters used by small theaters in the 1930s to promote John Wayne Westerns. This was one of many films he did for Lone Star Productions at Monogram Studios.

Robert F. Slatzer Collection

Duke and Marguerite Churchill in a scene from Duke's first starring picture, *The Big Trail* (1930). The picture didn't do well, and it would be another nine years before Duke achieved stardom.

William Fox Studios
Robert F. Slatzer Collection

Following an eight-year court
ship, Duke married his first wife
Josephine Alicia Saenz, on Jun
24, 1933, at the Bel Air home c
actress Loretta Young's mother.
Springer/Bettmann Film Archiv

The certificate of Duke's ma
riage to Josie, written in his ow
hand and in his true nam
Marion Mitchell Morrison, 193

Duke and his second wife, Chata, nightclubbing in the mid-1940s.
Culver Pictures, Inc

Pilar visits Duke on location in Africa for the filming of *Hatari!*, 1962.
Pictorial Parade, Inc.

Duke and Pilar at a social function in the early seventies.
Frank Edwards Fotos International

Studio publicity still of Duke in the 1940s.

Western actor stigma; he was respected as an actor and making far more money than Duke. This fact didn't sit well with Duke, but he didn't want to get out of the movie business. He longed for a break like Cooper had gotten with Goldwyn. It was because of this longing that he stopped making pictures for seven months. He hadn't intended to lay off that long, but that was how it worked out.

In the late spring or early summer of 1937, while Duke was making the Trem Carr pictures at Universal, John Ford invited him for a cruise aboard his boat, the *Araner*, and during the cruise showed him a short story titled "Stage to Lordsburg," which had been written by Earnest Haycox and published in the April 10, 1937, issue of *Colliers* magazine. Ford was so impressed with the story that he bought the screen rights and planned to film it as *Stagecoach*. Ford had bought the rights with the intention of starring Duke in the film, but he didn't mention that fact to Duke. He just had him read it, then asked his opinion of it.

"It's a fine story," Duke said.

"Who do you think would be good as The Ringo Kid?"

"Lloyd Nolan," Duke said.

"Nolan!" Ford shouted. "Duke, you dumb sonofabitch! Don't you think *you* could handle the part?"

"Well, hell yes, Coach. If I had the opportunity."

"You'll have the opportunity," Ford said.

By the time Duke finished his contract at Universal with Carr, Ford's screenwriter, Dudley Nichols, had written the screenplay for *Stagecoach* and Ford, between commitments, was making the rounds of producers, trying to get backing for the film. Duke had taken Paramount's one-picture offer to star in *Born to the West*, but had been advised by Ford not to sign any exclusive or long-term contracts so that he'd be available to do *Stagecoach*. With no other one-picture deals in the offing, he made no other commitments, expecting week by week that Ford would find a producer. Many producers wanted John Ford to direct for them. Many liked the screenplay, too. But nobody wanted John Wayne to play the leading role. They wanted a star.

So from December of 1937 through June of 1938, Duke took a

"vacation" and waited. And waiting was not something he did gracefully or well. There were diversions at first: the anticipation of starring in a feature-length John Ford film, with the prestige and recognition it could bring him; the unstructured time at home with Josie, three-year-old Michael, and Toni, who was just a toddler; browsing through antique stores with Josie to furnish the two-story California-Spanish home they had purchased in Hancock Park a few months earlier, following Toni's birth. But soon the anticipation of working with Ford was replaced by frustration and dejection as one producer after another rejected John Wayne.

Fortunately for Duke, John Ford was in demand as a director and so wasn't forced to do *Stagecoach* with a name actor in order to keep working. It was fortunate, too, that Ford was a contrary and stubborn man; the more that producers opposed the idea of John Wayne portraying The Ringo Kid, the more determined Ford became to use him. In the meantime, Ford had exhausted all avenues in search of a producer, and Duke could afford to wait no longer for his big break. He had to keep active, and as he often put it, he "had to go crawling back to Herbert Yates at Republic Pictures."

PART
FIVE

12
STARDOM

DUKE returned to Republic Studios in June of 1938. He had been away from the lot for two years, and it had changed greatly. Except for Yakima Canutt and a few other craftsmen and contract players, Duke found himself working among strangers, for most of the Monogram and Mascot people were gone; they had been laid off in an austerity move by Herbert Yates. Nat Levine was gone, too. Yates's insistence upon letting personnel go, particularly the Mascot crew, precipitated Levine's departure from Republic while Duke was away. The production costs of Trem Carr's films had drained the new studio's capital, and the films had not drawn well at the box office, which was the primary reason Carr and Johnston had left Republic. Levine's products alone had kept the studio from early bankruptcy. His serials had done well, as always, but what had kept the studio afloat was the enormously popular singing-cowboy genre that Levine had created (starring Gene Autry) and a B-Western series called "The 3 Mesquiteers," to which Levine had bought the rights and which he had brought to Republic in 1936. Nevertheless, Yates demanded that Levine cut from the payroll not only members of Carr's former Monogram crew but members of the Mascot crew as well. It was an unreasonable demand. Most of Levine's crew had been with him since 1927, and they were turning out Republic's only money-making films. The idea of letting them go was unconscionable to Levine—and bad business as well—and he refused to do so; with this, the partners reached an impasse. Yates was adamant. Levine realized that feuding with him would be counterproductive, so he offered Yates his interest in the studio. Yates finally agreed to buy him out, and Levine left the lot, eventually becoming an independent producer at MGM before getting out of the movie business altogether and leaving Hollywood in 1940.

While Yates's austerity demands caused an irreparable split in the partnership, the demands were by no means Levine's only reason for selling out. Herbert Yates knew nothing about the art of making motion pictures, and he couldn't tell a bad screenplay from a good one, but he had become, in Levine's words, a "stage-door Johnny," one who was dazzled by movie stars—particularly the females—and by movie-colony life. It was clear to Levine from such symptoms that Yates was discontented with playing a passive role in movie production, as he had promised to do, and Levine had been his own man too long to work in collaboration, particularly with a partner whose only interest in films was in the glamour they attracted and the money they brought in. So Levine left, and Yates took complete control of the studio, moving his offices from New York to the Republic lot and eventually reorganizing his holdings so that Consolidated Film Industries became a subsidiary of Republic Pictures Corporation. Shortly after Duke returned to the lot, Yates exercised the lease option he had inherited from Levine and bought the studio complex together with the acreage adjoining it.

Duke's remark about having to "crawl back" to Yates and to Republic wasn't a gross exaggeration. Yates had taken umbrage at his leaving Republic to join Trem Carr at Universal when his box-office attraction was sorely needed. Duke had been a good box-office draw in the heartland a couple of years earlier, but Gene Autry's ascendancy as Republic's money-making star and Duke's poor showing at Universal weakened his negotiating position with Yates, and he had to settle for $18,000 a year—$6,000 less than Yates had offered him two years earlier. Yates also tried to sign him for five years, but with the possibility of a Ford film in the offing—and the added prestige the picture might give him —Duke sought and won a concession. He finally agreed to a two-year contract, presumably modeled after his previous Republic contract, a nonexclusive one allowing him to free-lance, but only during certain periods of the year.

Duke's return to the screen under the Republic banner was an embarrassing comedown. He was assigned to replace cowboy actor Bob Livingston as a character named Stoney Brooke in "The 3 Mesquiteers" Western series, which Levine had brought to Republic and which had been created for the screen by Western novelist William Colt MacDonald. Republic had produced sixteen pictures in the series before Duke was assigned to it, and although Duke got top billing in the eight Mesquiteer pictures he did, he had to share the lead in them with two other Mesquiteers, Ray Corrigan, who played Tucson Smith, and Max Terhune, who played Lullaby Joslin. Terhune was a ventriloquist who, with his dummy, Elmer, provided comic relief for the series. He had come West with Gene Autry, but was put in the Mesquiteer series after he and Autry had a falling out.

The series was a strange one for the Western genre, which made it all the more embarrassing for Duke to do. It was set in the West, with all the trappings of the old West, but, as in chapter serials of the day, the action took place during contemporary times, often utilizing automobiles, airplanes, and the like. Besides getting top billing, Duke was featured in the films as the apparent but unofficial leader of the Mesquiteers; he wore a white shirt and hat, setting him off visually from his co-stars, who always wore dark clothing, and his part often called for action independent of the other Mesquiteers. This was small consolation for an actor who had appeared in more than sixty features and who had starred in forty-one of them, but Duke was glad to be working again, even though the product caused discomfort to a man who was trying to establish himself as a serious actor.

Despite its generic mix, the series was very popular among Duke's Western fans. He didn't realize it at the time, but the Mesquiteer series helped reestablish the popularity he had lost during the previous two years and to revive his grass-roots celebrity in the villages, towns, and backroads of the country, particularly among the children of the 1930s. It was this backroad, deep-rooted popularity that eventually established and nurtured his extraordinarily vigorous superstardom.

Duke was back to assembly-line filmmaking at Republic. They had him grind out four of the Mesquiteer films in the first five months. But luck and John Ford were working for him. While Duke was galloping through *Pals of the Saddle, Overland Stage Raiders, Santa Fe Stampede,* and *Red River Range,* John Ford found a producer for *Stagecoach* and began preproduction work on the film.

Walter Wanger was an independent producer working on the United Artists lot at the time. He had one more film to do on his contract there, and he chose to do *Stagecoach.* Like the other producers, Wanger may have had misgivings about casting Duke as The Ringo Kid, but he respected Ford and trusted his judgment. Together he and Ford assembled a fine cast of more than fifty players for the film, including Claire Trevor (who played the female lead and got star billing above Duke), Thomas Mitchell, John Carradine, Donald Meek, and George Bancroft. Ford's brother Francis also had a small part in the picture, as did Yakima Canutt, who portrayed a cavalry scout and also performed the extraordinary stunts for which the picture is noted.

Duke finished *Red River Range* in November 1938 and went to work immediately on *Stagecoach,* which was shot at a dozen locations in California and Arizona. It had been nine years since he had worked with Ford, in *Men Without Women* in the winter of 1929. In all that time, even though Duke and Ford had socialized (Duke and Josie had often taken vacations with Ford and his wife, Mary, aboard the director's yacht), Ford never once offered him a professional boost, not even when he was fired from Fox or when Harry Cohn let him go from Columbia. When Duke wasn't working, Ford ignored him; when he was, Ford constantly criticized his acting and the cheap pictures he was appearing in. One of the director's favorite pastimes was ridiculing Duke in front of others, at his frequent poker parties or on his sets when Duke would drop by to visit. Sometimes on the sets he would look right through Duke, refusing even to acknowledge his presence, let alone help him. Like actor Harry Carey and others before him, Duke languished almost ten years in exile from Ford's "rolling stock company."

Duke and Ford's relationship was a jealous and uneasy one that Duke would look back on with a measure of sentimentality, but which in its prime was regarded with ambivalence by both parties. Duke claimed he never knew why Ford stopped speaking to him for two years or why he didn't employ him for another seven. He was kept and used on the periphery of Ford's clique. When Duke brought Ward Bond to a casting call for *Salute*, Ford saw Bond's potential and immediately admitted him to his inner circle, giving him a better part in the film than he gave Duke. Then in 1930, when director Raoul Walsh "discovered" Duke in Ford's own camp and then, adding insult to injury, cast him in the starring role of a $2 million film, Ford apparently felt betrayed, and so he excommunicated Duke for nearly a decade.

The fact that Duke's star failed to rise after the making of *The Big Trail* didn't elicit sympathy in Ford; the director watched him sink—and apparently took fiendish pleasure in the sinking—before lending him a hand. The deeper he sank, the greater the credit Ford would get for pulling him out and establishing him— or helping to establish him—as a star. This may have been one reason, aside from his late realization that Duke had potential, that Ford wanted him as The Ringo Kid and why he refused to go along with producers who insisted on having a well-known star like Gary Cooper in the role. Ford wanted to be the discoverer of John Wayne, and he couldn't play star-maker with the likes of Cooper. Such pettiness permeated Ford's nature (a trait that was shared by Duke to a lesser extent). For example, when Ford was searching locations for *Stagecoach*, Duke suggested a spot in Arizona he had come across when he was working on a film in the early thirties. It was called Monument Valley, and when Duke accompanied Ford to scout the location, Ford said, "I believe I've discovered a magnificent location for the opening of the film." It irked Duke that Ford took credit for discovering the spot. When Ford mentioned his "discovery" to others, Duke at first contradicted him. But Ford got so angry that Duke finally had to give in to the director's claim or risk excommunication again. Ford had to be the discoverer.

For a good many years, Duke jumped whenever Ford snapped his fingers. He was intimidated by Ford and half convinced by him, too, that he would never amount to anything as an actor without Ford's expert direction. This fact was evidenced by Duke's own comments regarding two Westerns he made ten years apart: *Stagecoach* and *Red River*. Duke often said that *Stagecoach* had established him as a star, but that it was not until he did *Red River* in 1948, under the direction of Howard Hawks, that he proved to himself and others that he could act without John Ford's direction. Owing to Ford's insidious influence and his callously unjust criticism, Duke had been saddled with self-doubt all those years.

Duke reported to work on *Stagecoach* and found that nothing had changed on John Ford sets in the nine years that had passed. The cast and crew of familiar faces were gathered early, as usual, nervously awaiting the director's arrival. Ford's coming would be signaled, as usual, by Danny Borzage, the ever-present accordionist who did bit parts in most of Ford's films and who provided music on the set between takes and in the evenings when on location. Borzage would herald Ford's arrival each morning by playing an Irish medley, beginning with "Bringing in the Sheaves," and Ford would alight from his chauffeur-driven car, stern-faced, as usual, chewing on the stem of his pipe (he later switched to cigars), in rumpled and sometimes soiled clothes that looked as though he had slept in them. He'd always begin the day by inspecting the set and the camera setups and spitting insults at his underlings before settling into his chair, where he'd scowl and brood, usually chewing the corner of his Irish linen handkerchief, especially when he didn't like the way a scene was being played out.

It was evident the first morning on the *Stagecoach* set that Duke would be Ford's whipping boy for the two months it would take to shoot the picture. Ford didn't let up on him for a moment, berating him constantly before the entire cast and crew. Duke couldn't do anything right in Ford's eyes. Ford criticized his acting, his facial expressions, the way he moved, the way he delivered lines—even his walk.

Duke considered *Stagecoach* his chance at escaping the B-Western treadmill, and he worked hard on the film. He roomed with Yakima Canutt on location, and Yak spent many evenings helping him rehearse. Duke did everything he could to please Ford. He was the first man on the set each morning (as he usually was throughout his career), and he always had his and everyone else's lines memorized. He even blocked out and rehearsed his movements before each morning's shooting. But there was no pleasing John Ford. Claire Trevor, Thomas Mitchell, and other cast members recoiled whenever the director shot one of his tirades at Duke; they were embarrassed for him and bewildered by the director's foul moods and tactics. It was often claimed—sometimes publicly by Duke himself—that this was Ford's method for getting the adrenaline flowing in his actors, for keeping them on their toes and heightening their emotions. This rationalization didn't account for the fact that Ford was often just as foul and obnoxious off the set as on.

Duke himself would sometimes have to walk away from Ford to cool off. Yak was sympathetic and a restraining influence on him during the filming of the Ford pictures they did together. After suffering Ford's abuse for a few days on the *Stagecoach* set, Duke finally said of Ford, "I'm going to have to take this bird down!"

"Get in trouble with this guy," Yak said, "and you'll be out of the picture business."

Duke knew—or at least thought—there was truth to Yak's warning; consequently, he never said a disparaging word about Ford in public, but often privately railed against the director for the personal embarrassments and abuses he suffered at his hands. It was not until the 1960s, when Ford had all but retired and had grown distracted, if not mellow, that their personal relationship took on more than a patina of friendship. Even then Duke had ambivalent feelings toward the director. Duke was a pragmatist in business matters, and for this reason above all others he tolerated John Ford's abuse and paid him public tribute. He was grateful for the chance Ford gave him with *Stagecoach*, but as an actor, he was a self-made man, so he wasn't as beholden to Ford for his success as he publicly claimed. Although Duke genuinely admired Ford's work, he also knew that Ford was a man who had to be catered to.

While *Stagecoach* was being edited and scored for release, Duke took a few weeks off and then returned to Republic to complete his series of Mesquiteer films. The series was done in groups of eight films a year, and Duke had four yet to make. Duke had completed *The Night Riders* and was working on *Three Texas Steers* when *Stagecoach* was released in March of 1939. Within ninety days of its release, Duke had completed the other two, *Wyoming Outlaw* and *New Frontier*. These were the last of his Mesquiteer films (Bob Livingston became Stoney Brooke again) and the last B pictures Duke ever had to do.

Stagecoach was an enormous artistic and box-office success. It won the New York Critics' Award for John Ford and Academy Awards for its composers and for Thomas Mitchell as best supporting actor. Duke, Claire Trevor, and the others were given good notices but were not singled out as being extraordinary. They benefitted from appearing in an Academy Award–winning picture, though, and so all of them became bankable and in demand. Duke began getting picture offers from producers who wouldn't have given him an office appointment a few months earlier.

The making of *Stagecoach* coincided with another event that had a marked effect on Duke's career. His seven-year contract with the Leo Morrison Agency finally expired in the spring of 1939, and he signed with another agency. The Morrison agency had done little for him—except take ten percent of his earnings—since Al Kingston had left, and Duke's experience with Leo Morrison makes his accomplishments all the more astonishing; while other rising stars were relying on studio publicity to keep them in the public eye, and on the backing of major studios in getting them good scripts and good directors, and on the good works of their agents, Duke struggled to the top almost singlehanded.

The agent Duke signed with was Charles K. Feldman. Feldman

was an attorney turned agent who had worked in the movie industry while studying law at UCLA. He had even worked as a second-assistant cameraman on one of Ford's pictures, and it's probable that Ford recommended Duke to him.

Charles Feldman was a dynamic and innovative man. After he established his own agency, Famous Artists Corporation, in 1932, he was one of the first agents to take his clients off long-term studio contracts in favor of one-picture deals, getting them two or three times the money for one film that the studios had been paying them for an entire year's work. Actress Irene Dunne, for example, was making $60,000 a year at RKO when Feldman signed her. When her contract with the studio expired, he demanded and got $150,000 a picture for her. He did the same for his other clients, including Claudette Colbert, Tyrone Power, Marlene Dietrich, and George Raft. Feldman was also among the first agents to put package deals together. He'd buy the rights to a book or play, commission one of his writer clients to do a screenplay of it, then sell it to a major studio, with the provision that his producer, director, and actor clients went with the deal. He did this at Universal in 1942 with two of Duke's films, *The Spoilers* and *Pittsburgh*, both of which were written by his screenwriter client Tom Reed, and which, in addition to Duke, co-starred two of his other clients, Marlene Dietrich and Randolph Scott.

Feldman's first order of business on Duke's behalf was renegotiating his Republic contract. Under its original terms, Duke had to appear in whatever films the studio dictated, and he was limited in the time he could have to free-lance at other studios. Duke had interrupted the Mesquiteer series schedule to do *Stagecoach*, which suggests that he had made a special arrangement with Yates for that particular film before signing the Republic contract. There was no such provision for future film offers, and Duke was in the awkward and frustrating position of perhaps having to turn down high-paying outside film offers that might conflict with his B-picture schedule at Republic.

In the spring of 1939, Feldman met with Yates to discuss Duke's career. The agent no doubt pointed out to the producer that Duke's new stardom could be turned to Republic's advantage;

that under Feldman's guidance, Duke could command at least $100,000 per picture from the big studios, which would build his box-office appeal while Yates, having Duke under contract, would have his star's services for a relatively small salary. Ordinarily Feldman would have taken Duke out of Republic, but Duke wasn't yet firmly established, and owing to the specter of insecurity that always haunted him, he probably insisted on signing with the studio as insurance against the possibility of failure in the major-studio marketplace.

There was only a year left on Duke's contract, which put Feldman in a strong bargaining position. If Yates refused to negotiate new terms, he was certain to lose Duke to one of the big studios like Paramount when his contract expired. Aside from Gene Autry (who would soon leave Republic), Yates had no one with the general appeal, box-office clout, and star potential that Duke was rapidly developing. Having a star on the lot under contract would generate money and prestige for Republic, so Yates had much to gain by cooperating with Charles Feldman.

Judging from events that followed—for the exact terms of the new contract aren't known—Yates agreed not to use Duke in B pictures again and to schedule his Republic work around whatever major studio commitments Feldman made for Duke. Duke undoubtedly got a substantial raise, too. In return for these concessions, Duke apparently signed a five-year contract and guaranteed to do at least two pictures a year for Republic, an arrangement that was beneficial for all concerned.

While the new contract was being negotiated and drawn up, Duke went to RKO Radio Pictures, where he did *Allegheny Uprising*, an expensive frontier picture in which he was again teamed with Claire Trevor. It was released eight months after *Stagecoach* and was made to capitalize on the latter's success. Then he went back to his home lot to do the first Republic picture under his new contract, *The Dark Command*. Herbert Yates was willing to invest money to make money with his new star, and he allocated $700,000 to make the picture—the most he had ever spent at that time on any picture. He also signed Claire Trevor for the picture to star once again with Duke, and borrowed Walter Pidgeon from

MGM to give it an added measure of sophistication. He chose Raoul Walsh as director, with whom Duke had worked ten years earlier on *The Big Trail.* Yakima Canutt was made second-unit director and stunt coordinator on the film, and George Hayes was assigned the comedy chores; since working with Duke under Trem Carr, Hayes had let his whiskers grow and had taken the professional name Gabby Hayes, for which he became famous with Western fans. Also in the cast was a rising B-picture star named Roy Rogers, who was being groomed as a replacement for Gene Autry.

After *The Dark Command,* Duke went to work immediately on what was to become one of his favorite films and what was certainly one of the most challenging roles of his career. John Ford had again joined producer Walter Wanger at United Artists, this time to make *The Long Voyage Home,* a screen adaptation of four Eugene O'Neill one-act plays concerning disillusioned seamen aboard a tramp steamer. Ford and Wanger assembled a fine cast for the film, including Academy Award–winner Thomas Mitchell, Barry Fitzgerald, Ian Hunter, John Qualen, and Ward Bond. They again ventured from solid ground in casting Duke in the part of Ole Olsen, an innocent, naive, childlike Swedish sailor who symbolizes for the crew the faith that man is capable of breaking free from the restraints of his condition.

Although Duke's role as Ole Olsen was a subordinate one, it was a key role, and he received top billing as the film's star. His portrayal was remarkable in that it marked the first time he had ever played beyond his usual acting range, and he did so utilizing a passable Scandinavian accent. John Ford deserved much credit for recognizing in Duke many of Olsen's qualities—the innocence, gentleness, and vulnerability—and for drawing out of him a performance few thought him capable of.

The Long Voyage Home made money, and the critics liked it— some raved about it—but moviegoers weren't as enthusiastic; presumably it was too esoteric and stark and naturalistic for the movie audiences of its day. Playwright O'Neill is said to have loved the film, though, and he owned a print of it. Duke often mentioned the film with pride, gratified that even in the mid 1970s university cinema departments thought it worthy of study.

After *Voyage*, Duke went back to Republic to star in *Three Faces West*, a 1930s Dust Bowl drama that was released before *Voyage*. Then he donned a navy lieutenant's uniform at Universal to co-star in *Seven Sinners*, the first of three films he would do with Marlene Dietrich, who was making a strong comeback after several box-office disasters. Following *Seven Sinners*, he returned to Republic, where he portrayed an attorney in both *A Man Betrayed* and *Lady from Louisiana* before being cast by Cecil B. DeMille at Paramount Pictures in *Reap the Wild Wind*.

DeMille was one of the producers Duke had unsuccessfully approached early in his career when things were going badly after the making of *The Big Trail*; consequently, when the influential producer of big-budget epics sought him out to co-star with Ray Milland and Paulette Goddard in his spectacular Technicolor sea story, it was not only a small personal victory for Duke but also a signal to the rest of the movie industry that he had at last arrived.

Reap the Wild Wind was a success. It was also one of DeMille's better films, and Duke acquitted himself well in it—so well, in fact, that Paramount immediately signed him to star in another of their films, *The Shepherd of the Hills*, in which he played Matt Mathews, a young mountaineer moonshiner. *Shepherd* became a hallmark film in Duke's career because it was his first Technicolor release (it preceded *Reap the Wild Wind* in release by eight months) as well as the first time since *The Big Trail* (and the second time in his career) that a major studio had given him both the lead and top billing in an A feature. Ward Bond had a good role in *The Shepherd of the Hills*, as did Duke's old friend Harry Carey, Sr., who played Duke's father in the film and who was a father figure to Duke in private life as well. Carey had been one of Duke's silent-screen idols and was an influence on him both personally and professionally, as was Carey's wife, Olive. The technique Duke often used of pausing in the middle of a line of dialogue, a scene-stealing trick that always drew attention to the speaker and that gave the words more emphasis than a straight delivery would give them, was one he learned from Carey. It was Olive Carey who helped put him back on the trail to superstardom and convinced him that all was not lost after he failed in his attempt to break away from Western pictures at Universal. When Duke lamented his failure to rise above the Western-actor stigma, Olive said to him, "Don't be a damn fool, Duke! The people love you in Westerns. Give the people what they want." Duke, of course, had little choice in the matter at the time, but Olive's observations gave him solace as he took what appeared to be backward steps in his career; at least he was doing what his fans apparently wanted, and Duke was ever conscious of his fans. Throughout his career, he would always respond to movie critics by saying, "Nobody likes my acting but the people."

After completing *The Shepherd of the Hills*, Duke returned to Republic—and to second billing again—portraying a gambler opposite Joan Blondell in *Lady for a Night*, which was considered a woman's picture in its day and a vehicle for Miss Blondell. The film didn't challenge Duke's acting ability, but like the other second-billing films he was doing—and would continue to do with established female stars—it served its purpose, which was to build his credibility and appeal with women moviegoers as a romantic leading man.

Lady for a Night was the last film Duke completed before the United States was drawn into World War II, an event that threatened to interrupt, if not end, the career he was obsessively building on the rocks of his crumbling personal life.

13

WAR AND OTHER SOCIAL DISORDERS

DUKE was thirty-four years old when the United States entered World War II in December 1941. He had four children by then; his second son, Patrick John, had been born July 15, 1939, and his second daughter, Melinda Ann, had been born December 3, 1940. At his age, a married man with four children was exempt from the draft, and although others in the entertainment industry ignored such exemptions by answering the call to arms—including even John Ford, who was twelve years Duke's senior—Duke apparently chose not to enlist. It was a decision that critics sometimes used against him when, in the 1950s, he began publicly questioning the patriotism of other Americans, many of whom had served in the armed forces. It probably bothered Duke to have been among the able-bodied who stayed behind and prospered during the war years, but he did what he could, participating in USO activities and visiting the wounded in hospitals. It was during this time that he first used his celebrity status as a sounding board to lecture others on citizenship. After a ninety-day USO trip to New Guinea, for example, he held a press conference and advised people on the home front about what their loved ones in the service wanted and needed in the way of support from them.

When war was declared, Duke was committed to make several films and was at work on them. Shortly thereafter, he signed with Universal Pictures to do *The Spoilers*, with Marlene Dietrich, then returned to Republic, where he did *In Old California* and his first war film, *Flying Tigers*, before going directly to MGM to star opposite Joan Crawford in his second war film, *Reunion in France*. By that time, the United States had been at war for nearly a year.

Although it was rumored that Duke had tried to enlist but had been turned down because of a broken eardrum and an old shoulder injury, the evidence indicates that he simply exercised his right by law to stay out of the service.[1] Those who later saw John Wayne as the embodiment of superpatriotism couldn't conceive of his *choosing* not to enlist, and so "excuses" were fashioned to conform to their image of him. This was just another example of the kind of claim that Duke publicly ignored but privately discounted by saying, "Hell, *I* didn't say that about me. *They* said that about me!"

Duke's primary reason for remaining a civilian was to attend to his career. He was just on the threshold of stardom when war was declared. Had he entered the armed forces, he would have lost the momentum he had finally developed. With so many of Hollywood's leading men going into the service, he was suddenly very much in demand at all the major studios. It can't be claimed that his rise to stardom was owing to his availability during the war years, but that advantage certainly contributed to it and must have been a factor in his decision. But while the careers of other actors who remained on the home front were eclipsed by the returning stars at war's end, Duke's was not.

Another factor in Duke's decision not to enter military service was, of course, his familial responsibilities. In addition to being the sole provider for Josie and the children, he also contributed to the support of his stepmother, Florence, and her daughter, Nancy. Clyde Morrison had died of a heart attack four years earlier, on March 4, 1937.

It was also during the war years that Duke's marriage to Josie finally failed. Even by the late 1930s, it was evident to all who knew them that theirs was not a happy marriage. At some point after their fourth or fifth year together, they had stopped loving one another—at least Duke had stopped loving Josie. He later said that he didn't know exactly when this happened, but it happened. There were efforts to save the marriage after that, but ultimately their differences were too great and the breach between them became a bitter one. They remained married—Josie because she considered her vows sacred and binding until death, and Duke because of the children, but mostly because Josie refused to divorce him.

To those who had not known Duke during his college days and who had not witnessed his seven-year courtship with Josephine Saenz, theirs seemed a strange mismatch. Duke's friends and drinking buddies, including actors Ward Bond and Grant Withers and Duke's press agent, Beverly Barnett, insisted that he should never have married her. In their decidedly biased view, Josie was incapable of being the kind of wife he needed. They saw her as a woman totally devoted to her church and its charities, to the exclusion of her husband and his needs; a woman with one foot in the spiritual world and the other in the temporal—the bride of Christ and the part-time wife of John Wayne. They hinted that her passions were spiritual only and that she was a cold if not frigid woman who was the worst of all possible mates for their lusty pal. The question of Josie's alleged coldness was raised at a predivorce hearing, and when in defense she pointed out that she had borne Duke four children, Duke is said to have muttered to his press agent, "Yeah, four times in ten years!"[2]

Duke's friends also emphasized that Josephine was a "socialite," intimating that Duke wasn't in her class and that she and her friends looked upon him and his friends as a bunch of rowdy, liquor-swilling, womanizing cowboy actors whom they viewed with disdain. The home Josie kept was equally formidable to Duke's cohorts. Josie, they said, was a cultured woman who furnished their fashionable Hancock Park mansion with antique French furniture and fine paintings and objects d'art that made the place seem more like a museum than a comfortable home. They apparently didn't know that Duke had helped her furnish the place or that he, too, had a taste for antiques and art. They spoke of his fear of breaking the furniture if he sat down on it. It wasn't a place where a guy like Duke could really relax. To make matters worse, Josie often had formal dinner parties for her society friends and for members of the Catholic clergy. Duke would come home tired from the set and be obliged to get out of his comfortable clothes and into a dinner jacket, which, his friends said, he strongly objected to. What he found particularly intolerable were the priests; it seemed to him that priests were always around the house. He never knew how many of them to expect at the dinner table, but there was usually at least one. Duke suspected that the priests were subtly trying to convert him, and he railed against the thought. He was neither for nor against Catholicism; he just didn't like pushy religious people of any denomination.[3]

The man Josie married in 1933 was far removed from the young USC pre-law student she had met and fallen in love with at Balboa in 1926. In those early courtship days, Duke was obsessed with finding a career that would enable him to marry Josie and to raise a family with her; that was all he longed and worked for. Unfortunately, the career he stumbled into not only made the establishment and maintenance of a stable marriage difficult under the best of circumstances but also became an obsessive way of life in itself—and remained so until his death.

The biggest obstacle to success in such show-business marriages are the problems that develop owing to the long absences from home that acting careers necessitate. This was particularly true of Duke's early career, for he was free-lancing in low-budget films for relatively little money, and he had to keep jumping from one film to another without interruption in order to put bread on the table and to keep his career moving. This meant he had to work twelve to fourteen hours a day, often seven days a week, and had to spend weeks at a time on desolate locations away from home. Even if the location sites of those early B pictures had been suitable for Josie to visit (and most weren't), Duke's sunup to sundown schedule wouldn't have made efforts to spend time with him on location worthwhile. In any case, the birth of Michael the year after they were married, followed by the births of the other three children, necessitated Josie's remaining at home.

Duke was away from home more often than not, and Josie had to fashion a life of her own in his absence. She naturally turned to the church and its social activities and charities. With so much time to devote to such work, she became one of the leading lights of the Los Angeles diocese. Because of the children, Josie didn't get out a great deal, and she entertained friends and church associates at home, giving the kind of informal and formal dinner parties she had grown accustomed to as the daughter of a Central American diplomat. So when Duke did return home to relax, the household was often as busy and solidly booked as a movie sound stage. Although he may have preferred a quieter, more settled household, he was often called upon to play host to Josie's society friends and to church dignitaries. It wasn't that Duke felt inferior to Josie's friends, as his friends claimed, or that he was made to feel inferior; it was just that their concerns were not his concerns, and he generally found such gatherings boring. Perhaps because he was bored, or perhaps for spite, or perhaps because he simply wanted to, he began drinking to excess on such occasions. Josie found this repugnant and embarrassing. She thought drinking to excess uncivilized, and she thought Duke disgusting when he was drunk. In time, whenever she planned her clergy dinners, Duke began going off to drink with his cronies. And in time he developed the habit of not coming home afterward; or, and this was perhaps worse for Josie, sometimes he'd come home drunk and leading a party of his friends. Josie thought no more of Duke's friends than he thought of hers.

These, of course, were all symptoms of what Duke considered the primary cause of their incompatibility: an overbearing Catholic influence on Josie. He had wanted and had expected complete devotion from her, but in time he came to the opinion that her devotion and respect for the church were stronger and more important to her than her love for him. He apparently convinced himself of this and felt betrayed, regardless of whether this opinion was well founded. When he found himself trapped in what he believed to be a loveless marriage by the tenets of the very church that he felt had rivaled him for his wife's love, he became defiant and spiteful. He began drinking heavily and seeing other women —and with a clear conscience because he believed Josie had betrayed him.

Duke wasn't sexually promiscuous by nature. A woman had to have more going for her than a pretty face and figure before he was attracted to her. He wasn't comfortable having even brief intimate relationships unless he could convince himself that he was at least half in love. Given his sensitivity and his emotional extremism and the fact that he worked in an industry where on-screen intimacy with extraordinarily beautiful women was routine, he fell in and out of love easily and often. He was by nature capable of loving more than one woman at a time; during the last few years of his stormy marriage to Josie, he was linked romantically with at least half a dozen women, all of them actresses.

During the early years of his marriage, the idea of straying from his vows to Josie would have been unthinkable. But when trouble began brewing at home, there seemed good reason for Josie to give her jealousy full rein. The rumors started in 1938, when he was linked romantically with Claire Trevor while filming *Stagecoach*, and they continued when the two were paired for *Allegheny Uprising* and *The Dark Command*. No evidence supports a romance between Miss Trevor and Duke, but he did have a romantic fling with Norwegian actress Sigrid Gurie, who starred opposite him in *Three Faces West*. Miss Gurie was a sultry and aggressive woman, and Duke found her advances irresistible. Their affair ended only after Duke's agent, Charlie Feldman, introduced him to another of his Scandinavian clients, Danish actress Osa Massen, who never appeared in a film with him but who helped him with the Scandinavian accent he used in *The Long Voyage Home*.

These romantic interests were child's play, though, compared with his encounter with the beguiling Marlene Dietrich, with whom he starred in *Seven Sinners*, *The Spoilers*, and *Pittsburgh*. Dietrich, like Sigrid Gurie, was an exotically charming and extraordinarily aggressive woman who swept Duke off his feet. He was mesmerized by her. She had once had a stormy and much publicized romance with Gary Cooper, and she may have found in Duke the same qualities that had attracted her to Coop. Duke's relationship with her lasted longer than any of the others, and what he found particularly fascinating about her, other than her obvious interest in him, was that she shared many of his interests, including hunting and sailing and fishing. They were inseparable for several months, and the only reason they finally went their separate ways was that Miss Dietrich had other interests and was as obsessive about her career as Duke was about his.

After Dietrich, Duke was linked with others, including Paulette Goddard, with whom he did *Reap the Wild Wind*, and Martha Scott, who starred opposite him in *In Old Oklahoma*. Author Doug Warren, who was a magazine photographer covering Hollywood for Hunter Publications in the forties, recalled being in the Clover Club on the Sunset Strip one night when Duke and Martha Scott came in with another couple. "It was after midnight," Warren recalled, "and both he and Martha Scott were loaded. My job was to cover the night clubs on the strip, so I had my camera with me and asked Duke—I called him Mr. Wayne—if I could take his picture.

" 'You wanna eat that camera?' he asked me, looking at the camera, then to me, then back at the camera.

" 'No,' I said.

" 'Okay, then, put it away and don't point it in my direction, or you'll wind up eating it!' "

Needless to say, Warren didn't point the camera anywhere near Duke that night.

It was widely known that Duke was going out on Josie. Even Josie knew. Her friend actress Loretta Young is the only one who ever publicly alluded to Josie's relationship with Duke, though. She indirectly countered the accusations of Duke's friends that Josie was all but frigid by emphasizing that she was by nature a loving, sensual, and highly passionate woman. She was intelligent and intellectually curious and had a marvelous sense of humor, with, according to Loretta Young, a "beguiling and delightful kind of laughter."

What the evidence points to is not a flaw in Josie's character, evidenced by what Duke would have people believe was religious fanaticism, but rather a flaw in Duke's own personality, a manifestation of the emotional extremism that characterized him all through his life. He went from adoration of Josie to indifference; he simply grew tired of her and wanted out of the relationship. He did this with his second and third wives, too. But Josie was the wife who was hurt most. Owing to the tenets of her religion, she could not remarry unless Duke died, and at age thirty-five she was doomed to spend the rest of her life alone, still wed in spirit to a man who had grown tired of her, had cast her aside, and had gone on to other mates and another family.

Duke was not totally insensitive to her plight, though. There is enough evidence to strongly support the view that he paid a heavy psychic price for his treatment of Josie, that he never forgave himself for what he had done. Decades later, while he was married to his third wife, Pilar, he made a curious remark. He had just had a minor disagreement with his first son, Michael, who had for years been running the family film production company, Batjac, and when Mike left the room, Duke said wistfully, almost as though thinking aloud, "He must still be mad at me for what I did to his mother. I've tried to make it up to him."

What made the remark curious was that Mike had simply disagreed with him over a relatively unimportant business matter that had nothing at all to do with their personal lives. But it apparently seemed to Duke that his son's mere action of disagreeing with him was a deliberate act of retribution for past sins against the family. And it was not. The remark had sprung so obviously from a well of guilt that it brings to mind the self-anger that was always in Duke, bubbling near the surface and threatening.

Could his guilt over Josie have been the source of the self-anger that caused him to strike out at others as he did all his life, often without provocation? There is less than solid footing for suggesting such a cause-and-effect relationship, but it is nonetheless intriguing. Other than the curious disregard he had for his grandfather Morrison, there appears to be nothing in Duke's early life traumatic enough to have caused such self-anger as his failed first marriage and its lasting effect on Josie's life.

The incident that led to the total collapse of Duke and Josie's marriage began in Mexico during the latter part of August 1941. Duke was there with his business manager, Bö Roos, and several of Roos's other actor clients, including Ray Milland, Fred Mac-Murray, and Ward Bond. It was a business-pleasure trip that Roos had organized to look into an investment opportunity his clients might participate in as a group, reportedly an interest in the Churubusco movie studio in Mexico City. At a luncheon given by the studio for Roos's group, actor Don "Red" Barry introduced Duke to a twenty-year-old Mexican woman who, by coincidence, was also named Morrison—Esperanza Diaz Ceballos Morrison—an aspiring actress or would-be actress who was working under her mother's maiden name, Baur, and who only months before had married a Mexico City College student named Eugene Morrison. Esperanza was known to her friends as Chata (Spanish for "Pug-nose"), and she showed more than a little interest in Duke. The attraction was mutual.

Nothing developed between Duke and Chata at the luncheon, but a few nights later, Roos gave a dinner-dance for the Churubusco executives, several local politicians, and several of his Mexican business associates. Chata, too, was invited, perhaps at Duke's urging, and after dancing the night away, she and Duke became inseparable, day and night, for the several days Duke remained in Mexico.

Duke couldn't get Chata out of his mind when he returned to Hollywood. He began corresponding with her, and he may have gone back to Mexico at least once in the following year to see her. Eventually, though, she stopped answering his letters, perhaps because they were both married and she saw no point in continuing the correspondence. Duke became despondent. He had fallen in love with Chata and had apparently even entertained the notion of marrying her, even though she was married and Josie wouldn't give him a divorce. After she stopped writing, he couldn't even get her on the phone. He was drinking heavily one night and making the rounds of the Hollywood watering holes when he ran into Howard Hughes. During the evening, Duke told Hughes of his plight, and the eccentric millionaire offered to help as only Howard Hughes could. He drove Duke out to the Hollywood-Burbank Airport that night, put him in one of his own private planes—which he piloted himself—and flew him to Mexico.

When Hughes brought him back from Mexico, Duke left Josie and took an apartment in West Los Angeles. Shortly thereafter, in early 1943, Chata had her marriage to Eugene Morrison annulled. It was then a question of Duke's getting free from Josie, which at the time seemed highly unlikely; Josie had heard about Chata through her movie-industry friends, just as she had heard about most of Duke's other women. It's doubtful that she took this romance any more seriously than she had the others. She apparently decided to wait it out, feeling, perhaps, that Duke would eventually grow tired of his escapades and ultimately return to her and the children. So on May 2, 1943, rather than suing for divorce, she petitioned the court for a legal separation.

In the meantime, Duke had arranged for Republic Studios to bring Chata to Hollywood for a screen test. It was all a charade, of course; she didn't speak English well, and she wasn't a good actress. Nevertheless, she was put under contract at Republic—to give her an income, and as a favor to Duke. She never made a film for Republic or for anyone else.

Until this point, Duke had acted with relative restraint regarding his extramarital romantic interests. When Josie got a legal separation, however, rather than the divorce Duke had wanted, he was furious. A legal separation could last a lifetime, and with Josie's reputation and standing in the community, Duke could never sue her for divorce. In defiance, he rented a house at 4735 Tyrone Avenue in the nearby San Fernando Valley and moved Chata in with him. It was an outrageously bold act in the 1940s, one that could have caused a scandal and ruined his career had it become widely known that he was living with another woman. Over the next few months, the fact of Duke and Chata's living together apparently convinced Josie that her position was hopeless, and so she finally took the steps necessary to set Duke free.

DUKE

On October 31, 1944, her decision was announced in the *Hollywood Citizen News:*

WIFE WILL SUE JOHN WAYNE

Josephine Morrison, society leader, announced today that she had received permission from the Roman Catholic Church to file suit for divorce from John Wayne, screen star. She said the suit will be filed at once. . . .

Mrs. Morrison said her suit would charge mental cruelty and added that they had reached a property settlement out of court.

"Because of my religion, I regard divorce as a purely civil action in no way affecting the moral status of a marriage," she said in a statement released through her attorney, George M. Breslin. "Divorce, therefore, offers no solution to the personal aspects of my particular marriage problem.

"I am, however, reluctantly accepting the advice of my counsel and am asking a civil divorce from my husband. I have received permission to do this from the proper authorities of my church. It is the only means of clarifying the position of my children, whose interests are of paramount importance."

Josie was granted an interlocutory decree on November 29, 1944, and the divorce became final on Christmas Day, December 25, 1945. Michael was eleven, Toni nine, Patrick six, and Melinda five at the time. Josie was thirty-five and never remarried.

By the time the divorce became final, Duke had been living with Chata for two years. He remained a single man for only three weeks. On January 17, 1946, having just finished co-starring with Claudette Colbert in *Without Reservations,* he married Chata at his mother's church, the Unity Presbyterian in Long Beach, California. Chata's mother came up from Mexico City to attend. Ward Bond was best man, Olive Carey was matron of honor, and the bride was given away by Herbert Yates. In Esperanza Diaz Ceballos Morrison, Duke finally met his match. Their marriage had all the cliff-hanging elements of an old serial or chapter play, one that could have been called "The Perils of John Wayne."

160

14
TALE OF A TIGER

SOME of the actors under Bö Roos's financial management were astonished when Duke married Chata. She had a reputation among them as a "party girl," wild and fiery, who was always out for a good time and who had "slept around" rather shamelessly among a few of the actors and playboys who frequented Acapulco and Mexico City. That Duke consorted with her on the movie-colony playgrounds south of the border was natural, they thought; he was trapped in a bad marriage by his wife's religious tenets. His bringing Chata north to Hollywood and then marrying her was viewed by them as foolish.

How much Duke knew of her reputation isn't known. He knew that she had been the lover of a rising Paramount star who was also a fairly close friend of his at the time. Roos tried to talk him out of the marriage—tactfully, as a "bad investment" for someone who was already saddled with large alimony and child-support payments. Ward Bond tried to talk him into remaining single, too, a state that Bond, a notorious drinker and womanizer, relished and wanted his buddy, Duke, to share with him. Duke couldn't be dissuaded; he was the marrying kind, and he found Chata enchanting.

She was charming. Even Duke's friends and business associates liked her, despite their double-standard reservations about her moral character. Chata wasn't quite as beautiful as Josie, but she had the same physical characteristics. She was a five-foot-six, dark-complexioned brunette with enormous brown eyes; a wide, dazzling smile; and a stunning figure—the physical type Duke had always found irresistible. She was intelligent, fun to be around, and game for anything, from fancy-dress parties to pub crawling, from formal galas to the boxing matches at Hollywood Legion Stadium. She wasn't religious in the orthodox sense (though she had been born a Catholic). Much to Duke's delight, she shared his fondness for drinking and his interest in movie-making. She loved going on film locations with him; she could rough it with the best of them. In fact, she loved going anywhere and doing anything with him. They adored one another. As lovers, they got along wonderfully during the two years they lived together before marriage. As man and wife, though, they fought as often as they loved, and just as intensely.

Insiders said that the first obstacle they faced in their marriage was waiting for them in the doorway of their Tyrone Avenue house when they returned from their honeymoon in Hawaii. It was Chata's mother, Mrs. Ceballos, who had stayed after the wedding to watch over their household while they were away. Duke got along well with his mother-in-law. She had been living alone in Mexico City, and she and Chata had been more like sisters than mother and daughter. When it came time for her return to Mexico, there was much wailing between them at the prospect of being separated by national borders. Duke, caught up in the emotionally charged scene and liking a family around him, agreed that Mrs. Ceballos should stay and share the good life with them —he may even have suggested it himself.

As a lady of leisure in Hollywood, with a maid and a cook in attendance, Chata's mother had little to do but sip cocktails. She sipped a lot of them. Unfortunately, she got belligerent and sometimes cruel when drunk. Often she speculated aloud on the possible consequences of her son-in-law's love scenes with beautiful and desirable actresses: she could not believe that they could be intimate before the cameras, then simply turn their intimacy off. Eventually such talk roused Chata's insecurities and fears and suspicions. Often such talk would turn argumentative, too, and the arguments would sometimes end violently. Chata's mother is said to have struck her on occasion, leaving bruises and once a black eye. Toward the end of their marriage, there were times when Chata would awaken after a drunken night with Duke and accuse him of inflicting injuries she had received from her mother.

Throughout their marriage, Duke had his hands full whenever Chata lost her temper, which was very often. She'd come out swinging at the slightest provocation—or without provocation when drinking—for she had come from a home in which physical violence had apparently been the customary means of settling disputes. In retrospect, Duke often likened life with Chata to shaking two volatile chemicals in a jar. And for the first year or so, his mother-in-law served as the catalyst. Thereafter, it was alcohol.

Just before he married in January, Duke's contract with Republic Pictures finally lapsed and Charles Feldman worked his magic; he negotiated a five-year nonexclusive contract with the studio, under which Duke was required to make only one picture a year, with a guarantee of $150,000 against ten percent of the gross receipts for each picture he made. If his pictures did well at the box office, it was possible for him to gross a quarter of a million dollars or more for each one. Over the next ten years, his average gross from Republic films was better than $200,000 each. To sweeten the contract and keep Duke at Republic, Yates even agreed to let him produce the pictures he starred in.

The new contract marked the beginning of Duke's rise to a position of power in the industry. As a star with considerable influence and as a producer of his own films, he had the power to hire and fire, and he began gathering a group of intimates similar to Ford's rolling stock company. Eventually the group included screenwriter James Edward Grant, stuntmen Chuck Robeson, Yakima Canutt, and Cliff Lyons—the latter two also became second-unit directors—and actors Paul Fix; George O'Brien; Bruce Cabot; Grant Withers; Ward Bond; Jack Pennick; Harry Carey, Sr. and Jr.; Victor McLaglen and his son, Andrew (who eventually became a director); James Arness; boyhood pal Bob Steele; and others.

Duke's growing power, while professionally desirable, adversely affected his marriage. Even though he made only one film during his first year of marriage to Chata, much of the leisure time he would ordinarily have spent with her was taken up with what seemed endless production and business meetings. The executive side of the motion picture business fascinated and challenged him, but Chata found it endlessly boring because she was left to while away lonely hours on the sidelines. Always the compulsive worker, Duke immersed himself in the business of moviemaking, and in time, this caused a great deal of dissension at home.

After the Republic contract was signed, Feldman also negotiated a deal for Duke with RKO Radio Pictures, a three-picture contract at $150,000 per picture. Two years later, Howard Hughes took over the studio, and when Duke completed his contract, Hughes renewed it. In 1950, while Duke was starring in one of Hughes's pet projects, a film called *Jet Pilot*, Hughes, who had been instrumental in Duke and Chata's reunion in Mexico, apparently arranged a tax-shelter deal on a house they had found in Encino, an exclusive area of the south-central San Fernando Valley. It was a rambling, two-story Western-style white clapboard and fieldstone twenty-room mansion, with an enormous living area that included a den, a 1,500-square-foot living room, and servants quarters. There was also a horse-riding ring on the five-acre spread (all surrounded by a high brick wall with an electric gate). It was located in the wooded foothills of the Santa Monica mountain range, which separated Encino from the Bel-Air–Beverly Hills area to the south. RKO reportedly paid a quarter of a million dollars for the place and resold it to Duke for less as part of their picture deal with him. They held the mortgage while he made installment payments at low interest on the reduced sum, considerably lowering his property taxes and requiring no initial cash outlay on his part. Duke added a three-level terraced garden and a bathhouse–swimming pool complex with an upper sundeck after he and Chata moved in.

Three months after he married Chata, Duke went back to work under his new contract at Republic, where he made *Angel and the Badman*. It was his first production effort. It was also the first film he did with screenwriter James Edward Grant, who, like Bruce Cabot, had been part of the hard-drinking, hard-living Errol Flynn entourage and who became one of Duke's closest friends. Grant remained Duke's favorite writer until his death in 1966. In a negative sense, *Angel and the Badman* served as a commercial touchstone for many of Duke's subsequent films. As the first film over which he exercised absolute artistic control (the dream of most actors), it was a learning experience—and a disappointing one.

It wasn't a bad film. Certainly it wasn't a turkey, as Duke would later call such films as *Big Jake* and *McQ*, which he also produced and starred in. *Angel* still holds up well, and it made a little money. However, it wasn't the smash he had hoped for. It received mixed reviews, no special attention, and no awards or even nominations. Duke portrayed Quirt Evans in the film, a notorious gunslinger and former Wyatt Earp deputy who turns pacifist under the influence of a young and beguiling Quaker woman, played by Gail Russell. The film's antiviolence message was a major departure from the traditional code-of-the-West morality themes Duke had played out for more than twenty years. James Grant wrote the screenplay and was given credit for the directing.

It was Grant's first attempt at directing. With Duke's subsequent penchant for directing his directors—of becoming, in essence, the co-director of any film in which he could get his hands on the helm—*Angel and the Badman* is perhaps most noteworthy as Duke's first uncredited co-directing effort. The techniques he had learned from watching Pappy Ford at work are evident, particularly the climactic showdown, a long tracking shot of Duke walking down the main street toward the saloon and calling out the villain, played by Bruce Cabot.

Perhaps the worst that can be said of *Angel and the Badman* is that Duke and Grant were self-indulgent in not editing Grant's dialogue, which tended toward verbosity, particularly in the supporting roles. *Time* magazine gave the film a warm review, praising the gentle handling and refreshing presentation of the Quaker philosophy set against the violent West. Most reviews weren't as warm and were very critical of the directing. Grant took the criticism very hard, and he crawled into a bottle and pulled the cork in after him. He was a heavy drinker in those days, as were most of the members of Duke's stock company, and so it didn't take much to get him off on a binge (he later joined Alcoholics Anonymous and quit drinking).

The making of *Angel and the Badman* was instrumental also in causing the first major breach in Duke and Chata's marriage and in raising Chata's suspicions about Duke's fidelity. The incident took place in 1946, just after they had married, but it wasn't made public until their divorce trial six years later, when Chata alleged that Duke had spent the night with his co-star of *Angel*, actress Gail Russell.

It was revealed during the trial that as producer, Duke gave the traditional wrap-up party when the shooting of the film was completed in early July. The party was held at Eaton's Restaurant, near the Republic studios. Chata had often attended such parties with Duke during the two years they lived together, and she wanted to attend this one, too. Duke wouldn't take her, insisting that it was for cast and crew only, that it would be simply a short, late-afternoon get-together, and that he'd be home in time for dinner. But when he failed to return by ten that night, she called the restaurant and learned that the John Wayne party had ended four hours earlier.

Chata testified that Duke "always drank too much at such parties," and so she became alarmed and called Jewel Silverman, the wife of Duke's production assistant, Al Silverman. Silverman was supposed to have been Duke's chauffeur for the evening. Unlike Duke, Silverman had called home after they left the restaurant and had given his wife a phone number where he could be reached. Chata's alarm turned to suspicion when she learned that the phone number Mrs. Silverman gave her was that of a motel. She became even more suspicious when no one would answer the phone there.

Duke finally returned home at about one in the morning, seven hours after the wrap-up party had ended and presumably too drunk to get his key in the door latch. He said he rang the doorbell and called to Chata. He could hear her and her mother talking, but they wouldn't open the door. So he broke in, shattering a glass panel and reaching through to unlock the door.

Chata claimed that she hadn't heard the doorbell or Duke's calls. She and her mother had heard only the sound of breaking glass, and thinking that a burglar had broken in, she took one of two pistols Duke kept in his nightstand and went to investigate. Fortunately for Duke, Mrs. Ceballos followed closely behind her daughter. "The door was open," Chata testified. "Glass was scattered. I saw somebody lying on the couch. I was just about to shoot him, but my mother grabbed me and said, 'Don't shoot. That's your husband!' He was flopped on the couch. I asked him if he had broken the window. He just mumbled. He was very intoxicated. He couldn't talk. I tried to get him to bed, but he couldn't get up. The smell of alcohol was very strong."

When he sobered, Duke denied that he had taken the actress to a motel and tried to account for the seven hours they had spent together alone. His efforts were fruitless, of course, and the situation was further complicated a few days later when a friend told Chata that Duke had bought Gail Russell an automobile.

In recounting the incident years later, Duke said that he had simply offered to drive Miss Russell home in her own car and that she had accepted. "We were following some friends," he said, "who wanted to stop in a bar for a drink. We lost them in traffic and couldn't find them again. We looked in several bars, then wound up at Carl's café on the beachfront.

"We had some food. I saw some old friends from Glendale who called me 'Marion,' as I was known in grammar school days. An artist did a charcoal drawing of Miss Russell, and I drove her home at about 11:30 P.M. Her mother was there and we talked. I took a cab home about 1 A.M."[1]

Duke told of breaking into his house and of lying down on a seven-foot divan in the living room. "Mrs. Wayne and her mother were in another room," he said. "I could hear them yabba-yabba-

yabba-ing. They came charging in, battling over a .45. They talked a few minutes, then left."[2]

As to the car Chata alleged he gave to the actress, Duke told Chata he had given Miss Russell only a down payment for a car. He told the court that he had gotten Miss Russell on a loan-out from Paramount, and that while he paid Paramount a good sum of money for her services, she received only her regular contract salary from the studio. So he and Jimmy Grant each gave the actress a $500 bonus. "I gave $2,500 in gifts after that picture," he said. "It was my first production effort."

Two years later, Duke brought Gail Russell back to Republic to star opposite him in *Wake of the Red Witch*. They were often seen together away from the studio over the next several months, but always in the company of a third party; even so, it was rumored that if they hadn't been an item while making *Angel* together, they were now playing the game they had been accused of then.

In light of Chata's suspicions regarding Miss Russell, Duke's hiring her again seemed curious if not foolhardy to outsiders. In fact, it was also rumored that even then their marriage was all but on the rocks and that Chata hadn't been faithful to Duke, either. Considering their fiery marriage and the inordinate amount of time they spent apart, it was surprising to their friends that their marriage lasted beyond the third or fourth year. Their attraction to one another was irresistible and, as Duke himself said, volatile —literally so, for given the disposition of each, they were unable to stabilize their relationship. They were drawn to each other when apart, but each coming together was often more an explosive collision than a reunion. And so they loved and they fought. Chata would go home to her mother in Mexico City. Duke would go after her. They'd love and they'd fight again, at home or wherever Duke's work took them.

Chata's mother went back to Mexico City after a year in the Wayne household and usually only returned during the holidays for short visits (with Chata running to her so often, there was little need of her going north). The house was quieter in her absence, but lonelier for Chata. Like Josie, Chata's biggest complaint was Duke's long absences from home and his consuming interest in business matters during those short periods when he was home. In a sense, her plight was worse than Josie's had been. Duke's time was now taken up not only with acting but with producing as well. He produced his own films at Republic *(Angel and the Badman* and *The Fighting Kentuckian)* and became an independent producer with Wayne-Fellows Productions, a partnership he established with former RKO writer-producer Robert Fellows. He decided to go into the independent-production end of the business not only because he found it a challenge but also for insurance—or, as Duke often put it, "for eating money." Now in his mid-forties, it seemed to him that his money-making "handsome leading man" days were numbered and that it could all end abruptly, as he had seen happen to others. He felt that if he could succeed at producing, there'd always be a place for him in the business he loved. But success in film production could be an even greater gamble than acting—and certainly more costly—and so in a sense he was running scared again.

When he wasn't acting for other film companies, then, Duke was either planning films or off with his new partner in South America or Mexico or Hawaii, overseeing such films as *The Bull-fighter and the Lady* (1951), starring Robert Stack, or *Plunder of the Sun* (1952), starring Glenn Ford, or *Big Jim McLain* (1952), the first Wayne-Fellows production in which Duke himself starred. Meanwhile, unlike Josie, Chata had neither children nor a structured social life to occupy her time. She seldom got to go on location anymore. Five of the thirteen films Duke did while he was married to Chata were directed by John Ford, who usually wouldn't allow husbands, wives, or girlfriends on his sets or locations. Duke sometimes took his children, rather than Chata, on the other location shootings. She came to be jealous of them, or at least of the time he spent with them. She resented having to share with anyone what little time he had. And he had little time to spare. In 1948, for example, he spent the months of May and June making John Ford's *Three Godfathers* for MGM, July to early November making *Wake of the Red Witch* for Republic, and then went directly into Ford's *She Wore a Yellow Ribbon* for RKO, which took the remainder of November and December—eight months and three straight pictures, with hardly a day's rest in the six months it took to make the latter two.

To make matters worse for Chata, a series of commercially successful and impressive films, beginning with the September 1948 release of Howard Hawks's *Red River* (co-starring Montgomery Clift), brought Duke to the attention of a larger moviegoing public and put him among the *Motion Picture Herald*'s top ten stars for the year 1949 (a position he maintained for twenty-three of the next twenty-four years). Suddenly he became even more bankable and more in demand.

Duke and Chata did have their good times, of course, their quiet dinners at home and at local restaurants, where they loved to dine; parties and other social events; vacations in Hawaii and Acapulco and South America. Both were hot-tempered and inordinately stubborn, though, and many incidents brought out in their divorce trial gave an impression of what life with the John Waynes could be like in less quiet moments.

There was the time when they were still newlyweds in the Van Nuys house. Chata and the maid were in the laundry room and heard a loud noise and a "rumbling" coming from the back of the house. They went to investigate and found Duke pounding on the back door with a patio table because he had called to Chata for something and she hadn't answered his call.

There was the quiet November afternoon when Duke was playing cards with Chata and one of her friends, Augustina Rojas. The cook served sandwiches made with avocado. Duke hated avocado and thought the cook should have known that, so he cursed Chata and slapped her, making her cry. Mrs. Rojas swore to the truth of the incident in court.

There was the time when Duke stepped from his shower to find that the maid had neglected to put bath towels in his bathroom. He took all the towels from Chata's bathroom (so that she wouldn't have any when she took a shower, he testified) and went storming through the house, cursing Chata and throwing towels in all directions.

And there was the time Duke returned from a stag party at director Budd Boetticher's with a large bite on his neck given to him by a stripteaser the director had hired to entertain at the party. Duke emphasized in court that it had been the only stag party he had attended while married to Chata and that it had been a dull one. He was bitten without his knowledge or consent, he said. Chata wasn't convinced. She went home to mother for a while.

That was one of the things that irked Duke most about Chata. Every time they had a big battle, rather than settling their differences, she'd pack up and fly to Mexico City. Sometimes she'd stay for weeks, and gossip columnists would pester Duke about her absence. Duke usually had to get on the phone and plead with her to come home, or he'd fly down there to effect a reconciliation. He told the court: "Mrs. Wayne made it a practice, the last three years of our marriage, to find every possible excuse to stay away from me."

As an example, he told the court that in 1950 (presumably after the stripper had bitten him on the neck), he returned home from Christmas shopping to find Chata and her mother (who was visiting for the holidays) packed and ready to leave for Mexico City.

"I said, 'Chata, what's this?'"

"She said, 'I'm leaving you.'"

"I said, 'Isn't this sudden—when did you make up your mind? Can't you think it over?'"

"She said, 'I think better in Mexico City.'"

"As we drove to the airport, I pleaded with her to stay, but she said no."

These were the quieter times. Given Duke's work habits and the self-discipline required by the nature of his work, however, it's understandable that he and Chata would really kick up their heels whenever they did have unstructured time. They always overcompensated by drinking too much, of course, and the drinking usually caused complications. They got away so seldom that when they did, Chata never wanted the good times to end or the parties to stop. Duke lamented that they seemed always to be the last couple to leave any party, and much of their fighting was caused by Chata's reluctance—or flat refusal—to leave any place while the drinks were still flowing and the music still playing.

DUKE

Chata fit in at any party, while Duke was often restless and easily bored. He held his liquor better than she, too, and he was often just sober enough to find her drunken antics an embarrassment. When this happened, he'd start barking orders at her, and Chata, not given to following orders even when sober, would become as contrary as he. Neither would back down. The lines would be drawn and the fight would begin.

In court, Chata charged Duke with twenty-two specific counts of mental and physical cruelty. She had been "manhandled" countless times by her husband, she said. Duke countered that he had been "womanhandled," and that the only time he laid a hand on her was when he was holding her arms or feet to ward off her savage attacks. For the most part, witnesses supported his contention, though there were exceptions; Duke was by no means always the innocent victim of their battles.

Numerous incidents that contributed to their breakup were brought out in court, and full-page, blow-by-blow accounts of them were printed by the press.

Although Chata often left Duke for Mexico City, neither of them regarded such long-distance sulking as separations. Their first true separation came in the late fall of 1951, after they returned from Ireland, where Duke had filmed Ford's *The Quiet Man*. Chata had gone to Ireland with him, as had his children, all four of whom had small parts in the picture. They were on vacation in Acapulco following the completion of the film, and they got into a drunken argument. Neither could recall what the argument was about, but both agreed to the particulars of the incident that followed. Duke tried to end the argument by throwing a glass of water in Chata's face. Chata retaliated by dousing Duke with an ice bucket of water, and when she pressed the attack, Duke picked up a bottle of rubbing alcohol and splashed it in her face, momentarily blinding her (and ending the fight). Chata left for Mexico City the next morning, vowing that she was through with Duke forever.

She returned to the United States in January, without seeing Duke, and checked into St. Joseph's Hospital with a respiratory ailment. Gossip columnists got through to her by phone, but she denied a separation. Duke, who was issuing the same denial, sent Chata flowers and notes, called her, and visited her at the hospital. He was so sweet to her, she said, that her resolve not to go back to him again was shaken—that is, until Duke overplayed his hand.

One afternoon he came to see her and broke down, telling her that he realized how horrible he'd been to her and that he loved and needed her and wanted nothing more than the chance once again to prove it.

"He called himself 'a big jerk,' " Chata said, "and he was crying and all upset." Chata was very touched until Bev Barnett, Duke's press agent, walked in and said, "How about it, Duke? Shall I call the reporters?"

"He called Mr. Barnett an idiot and told him to get out because he had come in too soon," Chata testified. "It didn't seem Mr. Wayne cared I was sick after all. I told Mr. Wayne not to see me anymore."

They reconciled two months later. In the first week of May, they went to Hawaii, where Wayne-Fellows was setting up location shooting for *Big Jim McLain*, which starred Duke, Nancy Olson, and James Arness. Naturally there was a round of parties in Honolulu. And naturally, Duke and Chata drank and fought— for the last time.

It began at a party given by the George Vanderbilts. Chata testified that Duke left her stranded at the party and that she had to hitchhike back to the Edgewater Beach Hotel, where they were staying. Duke maintained that he did, indeed, leave the party without her, but that he had no choice. "I pleaded with her to come home with me," he testified, "but she refused. We were making a film in Hawaii and had an early location. I gave up, finally, and went home. At 4 A.M., Mrs. Vanderbilt called and said, 'Duke, please come and get your wife. She's drunk and I can't do a thing with her.' I said: 'Anita, I can't do anything about her, and I told you I had to get up early.' I hung up. An hour later, Mrs. Vanderbilt called again and said: 'Duke, will you come over here and get that bitch out of my house!'

"I said I'd send someone over to pick her up. I went to the

lobby [actually, Duke went down to breakfast with some of the crew members and didn't bother sending anyone to pick Chata up]. The whole crew was there. Suddenly, Mrs. Wayne staggered drunkenly in [she had, indeed, hitchhiked]. Her clothes were stained and disheveled. Her hair was all over her face. She took one look at me and then had a hard time hitting the button for the elevator to take her upstairs."

The battle that initiated their final separation occurred a few nights later, on May 7, 1952. They attended a luau at the home of a sportswear manufacturer, Nat Norfleet, and as usual, Chata didn't want to leave the party. Only this time Duke insisted that she leave with him. It had been raining, and on their way to the car they argued and Duke threw her shawl in the mud and stomped on it. And when they finally got back to the hotel, Chata said that Duke pounded the walls and cursed her and threw two heavy upholstered pillows at her. She caught a plane that night for Los Angeles, and from there went on to Mexico City, where she stayed, flatly refusing to return home.

"I pleaded with her to come back and resume her duties as my wife," Duke testified. "In letters and telephone calls I told her we could not afford to keep up our home unless we used it. I pointed out that the house was something of a front for my career, but that it could not be regarded in this manner if we did not use it."

It was a strange "plea," and hardly Duke's most romantic moment.

They had been separated for several months when Duke finally warned Chata that if she didn't return to him immediately, he'd put the house up for rent. It bugged him to have a mansion on five acres of property, with a maid, a gardener, a cook, and a butler, stand empty while he spent most of his time away on location. When Chata failed to respond to his threat, he leased the property and took a three-bedroom apartment—for her use, in case she returned, he said. Months later, after being gone for nearly a year, Chata decided to take legal action. She returned to California in the spring of 1953 and refused to use the apartment Duke had provided, demanding that he force the tenants out of the house, which she then occupied. Duke had moved to a rented house nearby, at 4031 Longridge Avenue in Sherman Oaks, where he remained.

Chata claimed that she had never wanted a divorce, and this was probably true. But she wasn't yet ready to try a reconciliation, and in late April of 1953, she petitioned the court for separate maintenance. She asked also for temporary alimony pending the separate-maintenance hearing, which was scheduled for October 19. Her request was for a staggering sum: $9,350 a month.

Duke countered her legal moves by contesting the amount of her temporary alimony request and by filing suit for divorce, which he had threatened to do. Chata ignored his action and pressed on with her separate-maintenance suit. Duke advised the court that he had been voluntarily paying Chata $1,100 a month for most of the year they had been separated. He suggested that since he was already paying $1,354 a month for the mortgage and maintenance on the house she was occupying, she could get along well on temporary alimony of $900 a month, not $9000.

It might have been a fairly quick and routine preliminary proceeding had Chata asked a reasonable amount in alimony, but the figures her attorney, Jerome Rosenthal, brought to the hearing made it obvious that Chata thought Duke had more money than he claimed. It was apparent, too, that she believed the more she was granted in temporary alimony, the more she could expect for separate maintenance. So the court had to determine whether or not the amount she demanded was a reasonable portion of Duke's earnings. For a man in Duke's high income bracket, this necessitated not only documentation, but also expert testimony, which took time. Then Chata further complicated matters for Duke by seeking a restraining order to keep him away from her during the six-month wait for her court date. She had to show cause for restraint, and in attempting to do so, she detailed his alleged acts of violence. And so the preliminary hearing dragged on for fifteen court days over a six-week period, becoming increasingly bitter and foreshadowing the possibility of an even more bitter divorce trial.

Chata spent the first ten days detailing the charges against him. Then Duke spent a day answering her charges. "I never at any time during our marriage struck my wife," he told the court in summation. "I will add that many times I had to protect myself from her temper—I call it 'womanhandling.' Many times I had to hold her arms and grab her foot when she was trying to strike or kick me."

When Duke finally stepped from the witness stand late in the afternoon, Chata said for all to hear, "You ought to get an Oscar for that. It was one of your best performances!"

The news media had a field day with the details of her alimony request. Her attorney submitted to the court an itemized breakdown of alleged expenses that astonished everyone, including the judge. It included, among other things: $430 a week for food; $812 a week for personal expenses and entertainment; $227 a week for charities; and even a $145-a-week allowance for her mother. When the judge questioned the veracity of such expense claims, Chata's attorney emphasized that regardless of how the requested alimony would be spent, the sum represented an amount needed to maintain the standard of living Chata had grown accustomed to. It represented also a fair share of her husband's income, the attorney said, and he estimated Duke's monthly income at $45,000.

Duke had no patience with domestic problems and no taste for arguing with Chata in a public forum. He wanted to give her the $9,350 a month and be done with it. Bö Roos and Duke's attorney, Frank Belcher, pointed out to him that the less she got in temporary alimony, the quicker and more likely she would be to reach a reasonable out-of-court property settlement. Presumably they also told him that tactically it was more advantageous to challenge her demands at the preliminary hearing than at the October trial. So Duke went into the hearings with what the newspapers called "a battery of eight managers, accountants, tax experts, and agents" to fight her demands.

As generally happens in such legal proceedings, Duke took the stand with what newsmen called a "hard times story," which was the opposite extreme of Chata's and nearly as absurd. He began by denying that there was any community property, saying, "We spent everything we made during our seven years of marriage."

He claimed to have no savings and only $4,000 in his checking account. He added that his own personal expenses were only $1,360 a month, including $700 a month rental on the Sherman Oaks house he was living in. He said that although he earned a gross of $347,364 the previous year, he netted only $60,000 after expenses and taxes. Finally, he introduced tax statements showing that in 1950 he grossed $392,364, with taxes of $187,258; in 1951, $285,710, with taxes of $125,536; and that he paid $180,239 taxes in 1952.

Duke's attorney told the judge that Duke was paying Josie and the children twenty percent of the first $100,000 of his gross income and ten percent of all income over that amount. He was also paying his agent ten percent and his manager five percent of his gross, with an additional sixteen percent going for fixed business expenses. Considering his client's taxes, alimony payments, and business expenses, the attorney said, Duke would have to gross more than $3 million to net $193,000, and that Chata's yearly alimony demand was for more than half that amount. He concluded that since Duke earned only about ten percent of the hypothetical figure—or $300,000—Chata should receive only ten percent of her demand—or $900 a month temporary alimony.

In the final arguments of the hearing, Chata's attorney charged Duke with "deliberate concealment" to hide his "ample funds." He said that Chata was fighting only for what was due her under the law and that she had been "kept in the dark" regarding her husband's financial affairs because neither Duke nor his bookkeepers would provide the figures she needed for a proper presentation of her case. The books and records that were subpoenaed, he said, were not produced because the firms and corporations having custody moved to quash the summons.

The attorney also charged that even the financial documents presented to the court by Duke's own attorney revealed that his 1950 gross was $230,000 larger than he claimed and that his 1951 gross was $340,000 larger than he claimed. Duke's average net, he said, after taxes, expenses, and alimony, was in excess of $225,000. He said the difference between Duke's claims and his actual gross income was owing to "improper expense deductions" and unreported income.

To support his contention that Duke's accountants were playing fast and loose with figures, Chata's attorney put her on the stand to explain a few of the methods she knew about that he used to conceal income. She testified that RKO had bought their home for them as a tax dodge. She said that Duke had failed to report as income five thousand shares of Republic Pictures stock that he had been given as a bonus. She said that all the expenses of a vacation to Mexico and South America that she and Duke had taken were paid for by RKO in lieu of cash; she said that Duke told her that the studio's publicist accompanied them on the plane so that the trip could be written off as a publicity tour. She told of receiving from Republic Studios $78,000—from 1942 until December of 1952, when Duke left Republic—as spending money "without doing any work for them." She added that the Republic income allowed her to take deductions on some of her expenses. She had used that money to help support her mother, who was ill, she said. (Investigators for Duke's attorney would establish at the divorce trial that Mrs. Ceballos's illness was acute alcoholism, which was the reason she couldn't travel to testify for Chata. The implication was that the disease ran in the family.)

Duke answered most of Chata's charges regarding "concealed income." He said that RKO had loaned him $100,000 at a favorable interest rate to buy their Encino home and that he was repaying the loan from wages he was earning under contract to them. He said that Herbert Yates had given him five thousand shares of Republic stock as a gift, "like a watch," he said, and so the stock wasn't recorded as income on his books. He contended that the South American trip had been a publicity tour and that the studio publicist had worked during the trip.

The preliminary hearing ended on June 4, with the court ordering Duke to continue paying for the mortgage and maintenance of the Encino estate and to continue paying Chata the $1,100 a month he had been paying her voluntarily. Chata had also asked for $35,000 to employ detectives and auditors and other aides to help in preparing her case for October; the judge awarded her only $2,500 for that purpose. The Los Angeles *Times* reported:

> While Mrs. Wayne bit her lips, but otherwise kept her composure at her seat among the spectators, the judge read from the bench the five-page decision which ended the 15-day hearing.
>
> The $1,100 alimony order was on page 1. As soon as the jurist read it, Wayne, also sitting among the spectators, but at the opposite side of the courtroom, relaxed into a wide grin. He kept grinning as he shook hands with his lawyer, Frank B. Belcher.
>
> Wayne was still grinning when he left the courtroom and walked down the corridor, not seeming to mind that he was mobbed by the women spectators, mostly secretaries and stenographers who had taken a few minutes off from their desks in the Hall of Records for a look at the towering actor. Wayne even put his arms around the shoulders of a couple of admirers. . . .

Chata wasn't grinning. It had already been decided that in the event of an unfavorable decision, her attorney would appeal the ruling (he eventually appealed twice). In the meantime, she couldn't accept any of the alimony payments until there was a ruling on her appeal. So while Duke flew off to Mexico to film *Hondo*, taking his sons Patrick and Michael along for company, Chata dug in at their Encino estate and prepared to fight off creditors, who had begun contacting her when Duke filed suit for divorce. When it appeared that Chata was serious about their separation in 1952, Duke had notified Chata's creditors that he would no longer accept responsibility for any future debts incurred by her. Undaunted, Chata got credit in her own name and ran up $16,000 in bills, thinking she could pay them off with her alimony. Most of her creditors honored her plea to wait until after her appeal or until after the divorce trial. But a local market, where she had run up a bill of $2,000 for liquor and groceries, got a judgment on her two weeks after her alimony hearing, and marshals seized her Cadillac. She drove to her appeal hearings in a pickup truck she borrowed from her gardener.

The newspapers loved her new persona. They kept printing pictures of her arriving at the courthouse in "a rubbish truck," dressed in $90 picture hats and $300 raw silk suits. The court, however, finally denied her appeal on September 30.

Meanwhile, two private investigators hired by Chata's attorney to gather evidence against Duke weren't faring any better than Chata. On July 7, newspapers reported that they had been thrown in jail by Mexican officials, who had become suspicious of their activities. The hapless investigators had made the news because Duke had freed them and sent them packing back to the United States. "One of them had an acute attack of appendicitis while in jail," the Los Angeles *Times* quoted Duke as saying. "So I thought I'd return good for evil and get them out of trouble. I managed to get them released from jail today after they signed statements explaining what they were doing."

Duke was loved in Mexico, where he made many of his films and thereby contributed greatly to the local economy. So the private eyes had no sooner hit town and made their first discreet inquiry when the locals notified Duke. When they learned that Duke was displeased with the presence of the intruders, an offer was made to "take care of them" for him, which in that wild and isolated section of Mexico meant that the investigators could disappear from the face of the earth without a trace.

Even though the offer was made as a profound personal compliment to him, Duke was shaken by it and emphasized that he wanted no harm to come to the investigators. He said he didn't want them underfoot, either, and that if they somehow made their way into the local jail, it might keep them from getting into trouble. So they were jailed. Duke was particularly upset that they were being paid with *his* money to spy on him. They might have remained in jail until he finished filming *Hondo* or until the end of his divorce trial had one of them not fallen ill.

Duke finished *Hondo* and returned to Los Angeles on August 4. Chata's attorney tried to get a continuance on the grounds that a lack of court-granted funds had hampered his trial preparations (not to mention the money he wasted on two private eyes), but the judge ordered that the trial begin October 19, as scheduled.

The trial was as explosive as predicted by the local press, but shorter; it lasted just four full court days over a ten-day period. But there was enough rancor in it to last a lifetime. Its opening, though, was like a situation comedy, and it may have been at least partially staged by Chata and her attorney. If so, then Chata, too, should have gotten an Oscar for her performance.

In the weeks before the trial, reporters had asked Chata how she was getting along financially, since at that time she was still having to refuse her alimony payments and had had no apparent income for several months. She told them that she was having to sell her own personal stocks. So she was not without capital—or wealthy friends from whom she could borrow, if necessary—and she certainly didn't have to travel back and forth in a borrowed refuse truck. Still, she continued driving the truck, which represented the financial straits her estranged husband had forced her into, and wearing designer clothes, which represented the past affluence to which she had become accustomed.

Chata entered court nearly an hour late on the opening day of her trial. *The Hollywood Reporter* observed: "Wayne was on time. He appeared annoyed when told that Mrs. Wayne drove the pickup truck to court." The judge was annoyed, too, and sternly rebuked her. Chata blamed the pickup truck for her tardiness. "It is the only means of transportation I have," she said. "It does not go fast, and the traffic was heavy." She apparently found high gear two days later, when she was ten minutes late because a policeman had detained her while giving her a ticket for speeding.

Chata testified for two and a half of the first three days, detailing Duke's alleged physical mistreatment of her and charging that he spent the night with actress Gail Russell. Her charges made headlines, and on the following day, October 21, 1953, Miss Russell gave an interview to gossip columnist Louella Parsons, expressing shock at the charges and denying any "impropriety." The Los Angeles *Examiner* printed the interview, which gave her version of the wrap-up party and the events that followed:

DUKE

Earlier in the day, James Brandt [sic], director and writer, and John Wayne, producer and star of the picture, had surprised me by telling me they were presenting me with approximately $500 because they believed my salary had not been in keeping with the caliber of my work as a feminine lead.

Nothing was ever said about an automobile.

John took me home after the party. He had celebrated too much and apologized to my mother for his condition. He called a taxi. My brother helped him into the taxi and he left about 1 A.M.

The next morning he sent my mother a box of flowers with a note of apology for any inconvenience he might have caused her.

I was contemplating marriage to Guy Madison at the time and was living with my family.

It is upsetting to me that an appearance of impropriety has been placed by some upon the events of that day.

I have instructed my attorney to demand a full and complete retraction under penalty of suit for defamation of character.

Two days later, Duke, who had yet to take the stand, told Aline Mosby of *News Life* that he dreaded having to testify.

What I dislike most is talking about her [Chata]. It doesn't seem right, but there's nothing else I can do.

Sure, I'd like to have settled this out of court. I wanted to, but the price was too much. More than I could afford to pay. You just can't forget about a thing like this, so there is no other course.

I don't think people will blame me for what's happened when all the facts are out. It's what's said before this case is cleared up that hurts.

The things said so far have been in the headlines. By the time I make the denials it'll probably be in small print.

It's a tough spot to be in.

Chata, too, was interviewed before Duke testified. She told Vernon Scott, of *News Life:*

He [Duke] is a hero—one of the most popular stars who ever lived. And it is difficult for anyone to believe that Duke could be anything but 100 percent right. But it is Duke who wants the divorce. I have never wanted a divorce.

When you are very, very much in love, it hurts to be in this position. I tried for a long time to keep our problems to myself. I don't want to hurt his career or position. I know how much it means to him.

The only place I ever said things that might have hurt was in the courtroom. And I said what I had to say there because it is necessary to stand up for your rights.

By the time both interviews were printed, a behind-the-scenes property settlement had already been reached and signed. To clear the way for a ruling in the case, Chata had agreed to amend her complaint from separate maintenance to divorce. The judge was eager to put an end to the sensational headlines by bringing the case to a close, but Duke refused to sign the property settlement unless he was guaranteed his day in court to "clear the names of innocent people" in Chata's testimony. On October 28, he took the stand.

Duke not only contradicted Chata's accusations regarding Gail Russell but also launched a surprise attack. At the preliminary hearing he had testified that most of the time Chata was too intoxicated to run her household and that while she was in Mexico City, she often associated with "other men," even picking up the tab for her escorts at *his* expense. They had been vague accusations, and he hadn't been able to name names. This time he did. He named hotel heir Nick Hilton and said he had heard that Chata had "entertained" a man in his absence but hadn't known the man's identity until his butler, J. Hampton Scott, told him—after Duke and Chata separated—that Hilton had been Chata's houseguest while Duke was away on location. Duke entered as evidence a household memo pad that the butler had given him. The top sheet of the pad was covered with Chata's doodlings, which read: "Chata and Nick," "Esperanza Hilton," "Chata Hilton," and "Mrs. Nick Hilton." Duke added that earlier in their marriage, he had often collected Chata's doodlings because he thought them romantic. "Only then," he added, "it was 'Chata and Duke' and 'Mrs. John Wayne' she doodled."

Duke's attorney asked his reaction upon seeing the doodlings. "I went into the bathroom and threw up!" he said.

Chata then took the stand for a twelve-minute rebuttal. She made no attempt to explain the doodlings, but she said that Hilton had been a guest in her home along with, and at the request of, her friend actress Betsy von Furstenberg, who was Hilton's fiancée at the time. Under questioning by her attorney, Chata testified: "Betsy von Furstenberg was my houseguest. One day she called me from a doctor's office and said Mr. Hilton had been hurt in an accident [he had injured his head and shoulder in an automobile accident]. She said he lived in a hotel by himself and it wouldn't be nice for her to go to his room, so she asked if she could take care of him at my house. I said, 'Fine, yes, as long as you are here to take care of him.' Mr. Hilton remained for a week."

There was no cross-examination and no need of one. Nobody believed that young Nick Hilton was anything more to Chata than an acquaintance, just as nobody really believed all Chata's hangover fantasies of Duke's mistreatment. Dragging Nick Hilton's name into headlines at the eleventh hour, after a property settlement had been reached and signed, and after the judge had already informed Duke and Chata that their divorce would be granted, was the only deliberately contrary action of the proceedings. But it was most characteristic of Duke; he simply had to get even with Chata for bringing Gail Russell's name into court.

The following day, newspaper columnist James Bacon quoted Hilton as saying, "I'm the loser in this fight. This is ridiculous! Everybody leaves out the fact that I was a guest of Betsy von Furstenberg, not Mrs. Wayne. Betsy was my only reason for being in the house, not Chata." His complaint was a valid one; the evening papers bannered his name, but in an effort to recap the trial and detail its conclusion, many of them neglected to mention Miss von Furstenberg or the circumstances of his being in the Wayne house, saying only that Chata had denied the charges.

Within the hour of Chata's rebuttal, the judge granted what

was then a rare "double" interlocutory decree, saying, "In the case of recriminations such as this, the court may grant to each of the parties a divorce. The court finds that this is a case in which it is eminently proper to follow this procedure."

On the afternoon of October 28, 1953, it ended. The exact details of the property settlement were never revealed. Chata filed a "quit claim" relinquishment in Superior Court on all Duke's property, and it's believed that in return she received a cash settlement of $100,000, with the stipulation that another $500,000 and a percentage of Duke's income was to be paid over the following nine years. Chata didn't live to collect it. She returned to Mexico City shortly after the divorce and was found dead of a heart attack in a Mexico City hotel the following year. She apparently had no history of heart trouble, and it was rumored that the fatal attack was, in part, a complication of alcoholism. Chata was thirty-two years old when she died. Her mother is said to have died of alcoholism a few months earlier. A few years later, in 1961, actress Gail Russell died at age thirty-six, also of complications from alcoholism.

Perhaps the best postscript for Chata's tale would be the remarks Duke made during the divorce trial to United Press correspondent Aline Mosby, as reported in *News Life:*

> Maybe the worst part of it [the trial] is that everyone will think that there were no good times or laughs during our marriage. But there were.

PART
SIX

15

SECOND FAMILY

DESPONDENT over his failing marriage, Duke took an opportunity to go south of the border on a combined business-pleasure trip. There he was introduced to a lovely aspiring Latin actress who later was often referred to by the press as a "former Latin film star" but who apparently had appeared in only one film. She was in her early twenties when Duke met her. She was intelligent, and she had a good sense of humor, enormous brown eyes, a dazzling smile, and a stunning figure. She also had an American husband. Duke fell in love with her anyway.

When he returned to the United States, Duke was determined to end his unhappy marriage and to marry the Latin actress, so he moved out of his house. His wife's initial reaction was to petition the court for a legal separation; she didn't want a divorce, but in time, she had no alternative other than to seek one. Meanwhile, Duke arranged a screen test for the Latin actress (although she never again worked in films), and she eventually had her marriage annulled. She also moved to Hollywood and became his constant companion until his divorce was final. Then she married him.

It's a familiar narrative, but what is not familiar about it is that this time the name of the Latin actress was Pilar Palette Weldy.

Pilar's story is so strikingly parallel to Chata's that it sounds like one of those apocryphal tales fashioned to lend a bizarre touch to the John Wayne legend.

DUKE

After Chata left him in Honolulu that May of 1952, Duke completed filming *Big Jim McLain* and then had about ninety days before he was to report in mid-October to Warner Brothers for the making of *Trouble Along the Way*. He spent most of those ninety days in South America, on a tour that is believed to have been arranged by RKO Studios and to have included stopovers in Brazil, Chile, Venezuela, Argentina, and Peru. In addition to swimming, scuba diving, soaking up the sun, and sampling the nightlife, he also made goodwill visits to the distributors of American films in those countries. The tour was arranged via Pan-American Grace Airways, or Panagra, as it was called, and it happened that when he got to Lima, Peru, his assigned host was an American who lived in those parts. His name was Richard J. Weldy, the director of a company called Amazon Adventure Tours and a live-game trapper of rare jungle animals. He also worked part-time as a public relations executive for Panagra.

Weldy got Duke settled into a suite at the Crillon Hotel and then introduced him around and showed him Lima's sights. They took generous samplings of the city's alcoholic spirits and its nightlife together, and they got along like old friends. They had much in common. Both men worked in isolated areas for long stretches of time and so made the most of their infrequent holidays. Like Duke, Weldy was a big man. He was six-foot-two and weighed two hundred pounds, and with his dark hair and blue eyes, he bore a faint resemblance to Duke—enough so that the two could have been mistaken for brothers. Duke admired him and found his knowledge and tales of the jungle fascinating.

After Duke completed his obligatory business in Lima, which included representing RKO as host of a formal dinner given for Peruvian film distributors and other local dignitaries, Weldy took him to Tango Maria, a small tropical tourist resort in central Peru. The resort was being used as a location for a film that was said to have been titled *Sabotage in the Jungle*. Weldy's wife, Pilar, who is said to have been a former Panagra stewardess, had a part in the film, and Weldy introduced her to Duke. On evenings when the film company wasn't shooting, he dined with the

Weldys, and they continued to entertain him when they all returned to Lima, as well.

When Duke left Peru for the United States in late September or early October of 1952, he stopped off at Churubusco Studios in Mexico City, where his Wayne-Fellows company was just beginning to film *Plunder of the Sun*, starring Glenn Ford. Duke's visit was unexpected, and he brought Pilar Weldy with him to make a screen test. Dave Grayson, who was then Glenn Ford's makeup man, was there too, as was Duke's brother, Robert, who was overseeing the production company's Mexico City office, and Duke's partner, Robert Fellows. John Farrow (Mia's father) was directing the picture and also directed Pilar's screen test that day, which she made with Duke.

It was just after returning from Peru and the making of Pilar's screen test that Duke moved from the Encino house, leased it out, and rented another house for himself and an apartment allegedly for Chata. This was five months after he and Chata had separated and only days or weeks after he had met Pilar. He also attempted at this time to effect a property settlement with Chata in order to facilitate legal action, but she refused to return to the United States and did so only after Duke threatened divorce the following spring. Duke, of course, filed for divorce and then left for Mexico to make *Hondo*, while Pilar presumably returned to Peru to arrange for her annulment and to prepare for her permanent move to the United States.

Chata must have heard or suspected that there was another woman in Duke's life at the time. She had been the other woman in Duke and Josie's life, so she knew the pattern—particularly when Duke stopped demanding a reconciliation and moved out of their house. There was no way Chata could have learned the other woman's identity. Her attorney, Jerome Rosenthal, had spoken in court vaguely of people who were "known by description, but not by name," and emphasized the need for "extensive investigation" and "depositions . . . to uncover the facts." It would have been quite an investigation had the detectives picked up Duke's trail in Lima, but they had been restricted by time, lack of funds, and the bars of the Camargo, Mexico, jail.

DUKE

Despite the turmoil and distractions of his private life—or perhaps because of them—Duke worked at a more feverish pace than usual. He finished *Trouble Along the Way* and *Island in the Sky* before his first court date with Chata. Then, between the hearing and the trial, he did *Hondo*. A month after the divorce trial, he did *The High and the Mighty;* then, after a short break, he starred in *The Conqueror* for RKO.

In September of 1954, Duke, Pilar, and Duke's secretary, Mary St. John, went to Hawaii, where Duke starred opposite Lana Turner in the Warner Brothers picture *The Sea Chase*, directed by John Farrow, who had done Pilar's screen test. It was during the shooting of this film, on the morning of November 1, that Duke's divorce from Chata became final. He married Pilar that evening, at the residence of then-territorial governor William Hill, in the Kona district of Hawaii, overlooking Kealakekua Bay. John Farrow gave the bride away, and Mary St. John was the matron of honor. Pilar had just turned twenty-six; Duke was forty-seven.

They had a working honeymoon, for there were five or six weeks' work yet to be done on the interiors at Warner Brothers. It wasn't until just before Christmas that the film was finished and Duke and Pilar could relax and really settle into their Encino estate as man and wife.

Pilar understood Duke's needs and administered to them as well as any wife could. She knew that he was compulsive about his work, but she knew also that unlike many entertainers who are obsessed with their performing selves and who feel alive only when they are performing, Duke was obsessed only with the work and had no concept of himself as a star; he was not driven by self-contained narcissism and had no need or wish to escape into his performing self. Consequently he didn't equate popular adulation with love—and didn't feed upon it—so he had a great capacity to love and be loved, and therefore the warmth of a home and family for bridging the disjunctive elements of his show-business life was absolutely vital to his well-being. Pilar was good at establishing and maintaining the continuity he needed. She continued to do so for eighteen years, until she, too, was finally worn down by the almost impossible task of being Duke's wife.

SECOND FAMILY

They were deeply in love for the first fifteen years or so. Pilar traveled with him wherever he went—to Japan, Hong Kong, England, France, Italy, Mexico, Africa (twice), and, of course, to locations in the United States. Duke was never happier than when he had his wife or other family members or friends with him on location—preferably his wife, naturally. While at first such visits were no doubt exciting and diverting for a new wife—location shoots did have their entertaining moments—it was essentially a gypsy life: traveling from one location to another; living out of suitcases in wayside and often dilapidated motels, hotels, or rented houses; having no place on the sets and no part in the activities and feeling like an encumbrance and being terribly bored watching the same scene being shot again and again and again; or staying back at the lodging alone, sunup to sundown, always a stranger to the area and always waiting for Duke to return—often he'd be exhausted and have little time to share before having to retire in preparation for the next morning's sunup call, seven days a week; and more often than not, sharing him with others who talked only of moviemaking. It wasn't a glamorous life; it was an immensely boring existence, particularly for a nonparticipant. Small wonder that Duke wanted a wife there for diversion, and small wonder that a wife would rather have been anywhere but there.

Pilar's travels with Duke were finally (and perhaps mercifully) curtailed by the birth and necessity of caring for their three children: Aissa, born March 31, 1956; John Ethan, born February 22, 1962; and Marisa Carmela, born February 22, 1966. (Aissa's birth was preceded by the birth of Duke's first grandchild, a son born to Toni and Donald LaCava.) Pilar traveled with him until Aissa's birth. Aissa was conceived during the time *The Searchers* was filmed, the Ford film in which Duke played Ethan Edwards, the fictional character after whom John Ethan was later named. Aissa was only four months old when Duke began his next film, *The Wings of Eagles*, so Pilar missed the location shooting of that film. She had no intention of going to his next location, either—to North Africa, where he filmed *Legend of the Lost*—for Aissa was only a year old at the time. But Duke missed her and the baby so much that when he was wrapping up the location shooting to go to Italy, where the interiors would be shot in Rome's Cinecitta Studios, he sent Pilar a cryptic cable that said, "Come over right away," and that she interpreted as urgent. The African location was so isolated that she had no way of contacting him immediately, and thinking him ill (he had injured his foot and was temporarily on crutches), she flew to Africa, a journey that took her the better part of three days in those prejet times. Presumably she stopped off at Rome to get Aissa settled in with her nurse before going on to the location. When she finally arrived in Africa, Duke met her, obviously in robust health, and she asked why he had had her come all that way on such short notice and in such a hurry. Duke is said to have replied enthusiastically, "Wait till you see the sunsets!" She wasn't quite as enthusiastic as he about the location, where she said he had to sprinkle water on the dirt floor of their hut to keep the dust down.

Their three weeks in Rome compensated for the dirt floors, but that one trip had been quite enough of traveling with the baby as far as Pilar was concerned, and so a few months later, when Duke was scheduled to go to Kyoto, Japan, to film *The Barbarian and the Geisha*, she chose instead to remain at home with Aissa. As it turned out, both would have found a long trip to Asia far less debilitating and traumatic than their stay at home.

On January 14, 1958, while Duke was still filming in Japan, Pilar was awakened at three A.M. by their dog, a dachshund named Blackie, who was bounding around on her bed and barking frantically. She awoke to find the fireplace wall of her master bedroom ablaze and the entire second floor clouded with smoke. Pilar grabbed Aissa and made her way downstairs, where she woke her maids, Consuela and Angelica Saldana, and put them in charge of the baby while she went back upstairs to the master bedroom with a fire extinguisher. It was so smoky that she could neither see nor breathe well enough to fight the blaze, so she opened most of the upstairs windows to clear the smoke. As firemen later told her, it was the worst thing she could have done; the draft created by the open windows admitted more oxygen and fanned the flames, and she burned her arm trying to fight the blaze before she was driven back by the heat and out of the house entirely.

The fire department had already been called by Mrs. Webb Overlander, the wife of Duke's makeup man, whose house adjoined Duke's six-acre property. After calling the fire department, Mrs. Overlander ran toward the Wayne house. "Flames were shooting out all over the second floor," she told newsmen. "It was like an explosion. I was afraid they were all trapped in there. Then I saw Mrs. Wayne with the baby and the maids coming out of the kitchen area on the ground floor."

Since the house was located in the fire-prone wooded mountain section of the San Fernando Valley, seven fire companies responded to the alarm and battled the blaze until sunrise. By the time they got the fire under control, the walls and charred skeleton of the roof were all that remained of the second floor. The fire was believed to have been caused by a faulty gas jet in the fireplace; the damage was estimated at $75,000.

Pilar's first act upon leaving the house was to call Duke and tell him of the fire. Then her doctor, Delmar Mitchelson, treated her burns and gave her a sedative. The next day she sent Duke a cable, which read: "How do you like one-story houses? Love, Pilar." Blackie, the dachshund, was credited by the press with saving the lives of Pilar and Aissa and perhaps the lives of the maids as well. Duke instructed Pilar to give Blackie all the steaks he could eat.

Pilar stayed with the LaCavas, who lived nearby, for thirteen days; then she and Aissa flew to Honolulu to meet Duke upon his return from Japan. They took a brief vacation there before returning home and renting another place until their own could be restored.

The Waynes took advantage of the restoration work by making alterations they had always wanted, including the addition of a movie-projection studio, where they could screen films; however, there were rumors that their marriage might not last long enough for them to see the house completely restored. On Saturday, September 6, the day after they had begun moving back into the house, Duke confirmed the rumors, saying that he would move back in while the house was still being worked on, but that Pilar and the baby would take an apartment. It was the same old refrain, but with a different wife. "The going has been pretty rough for us," Duke told reporters, "because of my picture schedule and the fact that I'm all wrapped up in my career. Sometimes I'm gone for three or four months at a stretch when I make a picture on foreign location. We are not actually separated yet, but it appears definite that we will be. Pilar and I can't seem to get an understanding between us any more. I don't know whether the separation will lead to divorce. It's too early to tell just yet."[1]

His remarks made it obvious that if it came to a choice between cutting back on his work and breaking up his marriage, the marriage would have to go. But cooler heads prevailed. The following Monday the Los Angeles *Times* announced that Duke and Pilar had reconciled and settled into the Encino house together. "It was just a small argument," Pilar told the *Times*. "We're back together now and in our new house. It was a hot day and we were moving . . . well, I'm Latin and I sometimes explode, you know."

Even more emotionally disruptive than the fire and their first major fight were the developments of the following May (1959), when columnist Louella Parsons revealed that Duke and Pilar were expecting again. Duke was very happy and said he hoped the baby would be a Christmas present. But exactly a week later, he announced sadly that they had lost the baby through miscarriage. It was a great emotional loss for them both, but they were thankful that Pilar had suffered no ill effects physically, and she recovered at home.

The twenty-month period in which the fire, the miscarriage, and the near-separation occurred was the rockiest that Duke and Pilar faced in their marriage—except for their ultimate separation, of course. For the next twelve to fourteen years, their relationship was stable. Unlike Chata, Pilar accepted and was not at all jealous of Duke's first four children, and the family grew closer. At first, they had full reunions, particularly around the holidays, but as Pat and Mike and Toni and Melinda increased the size of their own families (Duke had twenty-one grandchildren by 1979), they began having to visit in shifts. Of course, Duke and Pilar added two more to the Wayne clan, with Ethan, as he was called, and Marisa.

It was around the time of Ethan's birth in 1962 that Duke indulged himself with the purchase of his most prized possession. He loved the sea and had a number of boats over the years, including a speedboat called *Apache*, then a larger one he named *Isthmus*, then the 73-foot yacht *Nor'wester*. They weren't big enough for him, though, and he finally bought a 136-foot converted U.S. minesweeper of wood construction, which was said to have seen action during the last six months of World War II. Duke bought the boat from Seattle lumber baron and tug company owner Max Wyman after he and Pilar had taken a cruise with the Wymans and another couple aboard it. Wyman had converted the boat to a pleasure cruiser in 1961 and had named her *Wild Goose II*, after his cook's small sailboat, *Wild Goose*. Duke rechristened her simply *Wild Goose* after he purchased her, and a couple of years later, he customized the vessel, which included raising the ceilings of the bridge, salon, and master stateroom to accommodate his height.

The *Wild Goose* was quite an impressive vessel. In addition to the pilothouse, it had a master stateroom and guest stateroom on the top deck; two staterooms, a galley, a head, and a large salon on the main deck; and two afterstaterooms (for the crew), a head with shower, a storage cabin, a walk-in freezer, and an engine room below deck. The master stateroom had a seven-foot-square bed, a color TV, and a luxurious bathroom (or head) with an enclosed tub. The main salon had a wet bar, a wood-burning fireplace, a motion picture projector and screen, a teleprinter that received UPI, AP, and weather bureau reports, custom-upholstered lounge furniture, and a large game table. There was an enclosed dining room that seated eight off the galley, and the galley was equipped with two propane gas stoves, a microwave oven, and two refrigerators. The boat was also equipped with a cast-iron barbeque, a washer-dryer, a liquor locker and wine cellar, and, of course, state-of-the-art navigational aids. To run the vessel, Duke kept a year-round crew of four to six, including a skipper, an engineer, a cook, a steward, and sometimes two deck-hands. When he wasn't using the boat, he chartered it, together with its crew.

Duke got away on the boat often. He always tried to take her out for a full month at least once a year, mostly for vacations with Pilar and the children to Mexico. Whenever possible, he also used it for his work. He even sailed across the Atlantic to Spain when he filmed *Circus World* there from September 1963 to February 1964. Often he sailed it to Seattle, where he also used it while making *McQ* in 1973. He kept the boat for sixteen years, finally selling her in 1978, shortly before his death, after the Internal Revenue Service made changes in the tax laws that disallowed his writing the boat off as a business expense.

In 1965, Duke and Pilar sold their Encino estate to the daughter of Walt Disney and moved to Newport Beach, seventy miles south of Hollywood, to a house right on the bay and with a view of Balboa. Duke had misgivings about moving so far from his work, and would later grumble that he had moved there only because Pilar loved the area and its social life. In fact, he loved it too. When they found a place on Bayshore Drive, which had its own jetty on the bay, the idea of having the *Wild Goose* anchored only a few minutes' drive from his home greatly influenced his decision to settle there, and they contracted to have the elegant, custom four-bedroom house remodeled, with the den and living area rebuilt along the lines of their Encino place.

They moved from the Encino estate before the remodeling at Newport was completed. They put their furniture and belongings in storage and tried living on the *Wild Goose* in Newport Bay, which they thought would be fun. That arrangement lasted only three or four weeks; Ethan was just three then, and since Pilar couldn't let him out of her sight for fear of his falling overboard, they took a hotel bungalow in Newport until the remodeling was nearly finished.

Between the time they had put the Encino estate up for sale and had contracted to remodel the house at Newport, Pilar learned that she was pregnant again. She was thirty-eight and Duke was fifty-nine, and an addition to the family had not been expected. They moved into the new house just a few months before the baby was due. Having lost one baby when she was younger, Pilar wanted to take no chances with this one, and she insisted upon being attended by her regular San Fernando Valley physician, Dr. Delmar Mitchelson, necessitating periodic 140-mile round trips to see the doctor. Duke thought such an arrangement a little inconvenient, but he wanted Pilar to feel secure and he didn't object strongly. When she told him that she also wanted to have the baby in Encino, at West Valley Hospital, because she was familiar with the facility and the staff, he put his foot down. He had visions of her delivering the baby in the family car, en route. Pilar insisted, though, and Duke told her that she'd have to get someone else to drive her there, because he flatly refused to do so. Period. Of course, when the time came, he drove.

Despite his wish to be present for the blessed event, under the circumstances Pilar had chosen, he would not have been overly distressed had nature taken the matter out of his province and ushered in the newborn early, while he was on location. He went off to Arizona to film *El Dorado*, with Robert Mitchum, James Caan, and Edward Asner, which shot from early October 1965 to early February 1966. But when he returned, he saw that Pilar had not cooperated at all; she was still carrying the baby. The interiors for *El Dorado* were done at Paramount, and so upon his return, he commuted back and forth each day. One evening when he came home from the studio, Pilar informed him that during her visit to Dr. Mitchelson's that day in Encino, the doctor had strongly suggested that she check into the hospital immediately; she could go into labor at any moment, the doctor had said. Instead of checking into the hospital and calling home with instructions for her household help, Pilar had driven back down to Newport in order to make the arrangements personally and to pack some things for her hospital stay. She had been through all this before and knew that the labor would not begin quite as soon as the doctor suggested that it could.

One can't appreciate how truly courageous Pilar was in even consenting to let Duke drive her to the hospital unless one ever saw him drive. One of the world's worst drivers, he always drove like a bat out of hell, impulsively, gas pedal to the floor. He used brakes only as a last resort. Still, they arrived at the hospital safely, and Marisa, too, arrived in due time, all six pounds fourteen ounces of her.

Life at the Wayne household on Bayshore Drive returned to normal for the next six years or so. But as all of the children were enrolled in school and began having friends and school activities and social lives of their own, Pilar's movements were restricted and, like Josie before her, she developed interests that Duke didn't share. He complained most often about tennis; it required a great deal of time and dedication of the enthusiast, and there was a separate social life that developed among the followers of the game, as well. While Duke was happy that Pilar was active with a life and interests apart from his, he was at the same time unhappy, jealous of the time and attention those interests seemed —in his opinion—to take away from *him*. She began traveling with him less frequently and visiting him on location less frequently. Like Josie, she couldn't just switch off her personal life on demand. She had an existence apart from what he conceived the role of Mrs. John Wayne to be. Not only could he not resign himself to that fact, he also deeply resented it.

Duke truly thought Pilar's acceptance in Newport society was predicated almost solely on her celebrity as Mrs. John Wayne, and he felt that she should therefore *be* Mrs. John Wayne, that she should plan her life around his. It infuriated him when he'd ask her—usually on impulse at the last minute—to accompany him on a business trip, for example, and she would refuse because of a previous commitment to a social function or a tennis tournament. He adored Pilar, but unless she doted on him in a slavish manner, unless she subordinated her identity to his and lived only to serve him, then, in his opinion, they simply could not get an understanding between them.

Presumably Pilar had hoped that Duke would finally slow down at Newport Beach and enjoy the fruits of his labor. She wasn't asking him to stop but rather to stop running, to stroll the rest of the way at a pace that would permit him to enjoy where he was and who he was and what he had. Intellectually he knew that there were more important things in his life than work. That knowledge, though, caused him more anguish and frustration; he knew better, but he couldn't do better. Clearly he was a driven man, driven by some deep-seated emotional fear and need that operated apart from and in spite of knowledge and conscious effort. So, for all the experiential lessons and for all the soul-searching he had done—even at death's door—he was in his mid-sixties and running as hard as ever and apparently still looking over his shoulder at what he perceived to be the specter of poverty close on his heels. He was a multimillionaire by then, but he truly did not see himself as financially secure. It was impossible for him to slow down; it was impossible for Pilar to keep up with him.

They would eventually separate. She couldn't share his compulsions. She wasn't driven by whatever furies were chasing him. She couldn't even imagine such furies, let alone understand the need and drive to escape them. No one could; they were beyond imagining.

16

PRELUDE

IT'S clear that penuriousness was not at the root of Duke's compulsion to work. What drove him was apparently an unreasonable fear that his fortunes could—and probably would—somehow collapse. There were times during his career when his fear of financial failure did have a substantial basis. This was particularly true in 1960, after his production company completed a film project he had been working on for almost ten years. The film was *The Alamo*. It was the most expensive motion picture ever made to that date, and one of the most ambitious. Duke had become so obsessed with the film that he broke old ties, severed business relationships, and nearly went bankrupt making it.

The cause of his obsession was that he considered the story of the Alamo not only good historical film fare but also—and primarily—propaganda for the West's cold war against international communism. The film was to be his personal contribution to what he and many ultraconservatives were calling Americanism; thus he thought it his patriotic duty to make the film, which he hoped would be inspirational and would remind Communists that Americans would fight to their death for the cause of freedom.

The film was based on just such a fight to the death in the Texan war of independence against Mexico. In December of 1835, a small group of Texan insurgents, including the legendary frontiersmen David Crockett and James Bowie and led by Colonel William Barret Travis, occupied a sleepy Mexican settlement known as San Antonio de Bexar (known today as San Antonio, Texas). Two months later, a Mexican force of 4,000 soldiers, commanded by General Antonio López de Santa Anna (a despot whom the Mexican people later overthrew and drove into exile), arrived on the outskirts of the settlement, and the Travis garrison, numbering only 155 men, withdrew to a small former Franciscan mission known as the Alamo and used it as a fortress against the attacking Mexican forces. It was a delaying tactic, used to keep Santa Anna's army occupied so that General Sam Houston, the leader of the Texan army, would have time to muster sufficient forces to oppose Santa Anna.

The Mexican Army's siege on the Alamo began on February 23, 1836, but Santa Anna withheld an all-out attack until his artillery arrived. Meanwhile the Texans were reinforced by 32 men on March 1, and the 187-man garrison withstood the Mexican attacks until March 6, when Santa Anna's soldiers breached the Alamo walls and annihilated the Texans in savage hand-to-hand fighting. The only Texans to survive were three women, two children, and a young black slave. Later the Texan Army, led by Sam Houston, used the battle cry "Remember the Alamo!" as inspiration in defeating Santa Anna's forces (and capturing Santa Anna) at San Jacinto, thereby winning the Texans their independence.

That the Texans lost the battle made the story of the Alamo all the more effective for Duke's purposes, for by their courage, they showed that freedom was not only worth fighting for but worth dying for as well. And on January 11, 1960, just three weeks after Duke finished shooting the film—and nine months before it was ready for release—he was quoted in *The Hollywood Reporter* as saying, ". . . The growing defeatist attitude in the Cold War imposed on us by the Soviet [sic] is a disgrace. . . . They are trying to defeat us by breaking our spirit and morale. America—the true, legendary, heroic America—fears no bullying nation. The real American is ready to die for his freedom and the sovereignty of his country. . . . I just finished making *The Alamo*, and I'm not dragging that subject in by the heels at this point. . . . I'm proud to have played a part in bringing this film to the world . . . which shows the world the sort of spirit and indomitable will for freedom that I think still dominates the thinking of Americans. . . ."

Duke had begun beating the drum for *The Alamo* almost a year before the film was even ready for release. It was such sincere but nevertheless overbearing and didactic patriotic fervor that eventually mired the film in controversy and caused him the bitterest disappointment of his career—financially, artistically, and philosophically.

It was in the late 1940s, while he was still at Republic Studios, that the idea of doing a film based on the battle of the Alamo first occurred to him. The idea took root not only as a result of his interest in American history but also as a manifestation of his political activism, which had begun at this time. Herbert Yates was most solicitous of Duke's project interests in those days— particularly after he was nominated for an Academy Award for his portrayal of Stryker in *Sands of Iwo Jima* in 1950, the only Oscar nomination a Republic picture ever received—so he encouraged Duke's plan to produce *The Alamo*. After Duke formed his own production company with Bob Fellows and wanted *The Alamo* to be their production, with Republic's backing and distribution, Yates's enthusiasm cooled considerably.

Duke had made a number of financial investments in Panama, which included a partnership in a shrimp business with former Panamanian ambassador to Great Britain Roberto Tito Arias (the husband of British ballerina Dame Margot Fonteyn). With his connections in that country, he scouted locations there and found an area that was similar in terrain to old San Antonio, with an airstrip nearby, which was vital to the production. He began making plans to film there, which would have cost him $2 million less than making the picture in the United States.

Duke had a showdown with Yates regarding *The Alamo* just after he finished working in *The Quiet Man* in August 1951. He and Bob Fellows were determined to produce the film, and they had been wining and dining wealthy Texans in order to raise the money needed to do it. Their budget then was about $3 million.

Yates wanted Duke to reconsider; he wanted him to let Republic produce the film, and on a drastically reduced budget. Yates was preparing for an extended business trip to New York City at the time of the meeting. He wanted Duke to think the deal over. But Yates had apparently put him off for several years, and Duke had no intention of delaying the project any further. He gave Yates an ultimatum: make a decision before leaving for New York, or he would be moved off the Republic lot by the time Yates returned.

Yates didn't take the matter seriously; he thought Duke was bluffing. They had had a fine relationship, and Yates knew that Duke often lost his temper and said things, only to recant after he cooled down. He told Duke to be patient and to consider his offer until he returned from New York. As he had warned, Duke had moved his office off the lot by the time Yates returned, and *The Quiet Man*, which had been shot from June to August, 1951, was his last film for Republic.

By 1952, the major studios were beginning to abandon their old contract player system and were starting to hire actors and actresses as they were needed, on a free-lance basis. The studios had also come to accept, grudgingly, the practice of distributing films for independent and star-owned production companies. Humphrey Bogart was among the first of the film stars to form his own production company (Santana, in 1947), while he was still under contract to Warner Brothers. It was Warner Brothers that offered Duke a marvelous deal when he left Republic. Duke had been among Hollywood's top ten box-office draws for three years by then; in fact, he had been number one in 1950 and 1951, and Jack Warner offered him an astonishingly generous arrangement. He guaranteed to finance and distribute ten of the Wayne-Fellows pictures (within a specified budget, which precluded making a high-budget film like *The Alamo*), if Duke agreed to star in several Warner Brothers productions, for which he would be given at least $150,000 per picture plus ten percent of the gross receipts. Duke was undoubtedly disappointed that Jack Warner wouldn't work *The Alamo* into the arrangement, but the deal was too good to pass up.

The films he starred in for Warners were undistinguished, but his own company's productions made money for the studio. Besides *Plunder of the Sun*, starring Glenn Ford, Duke's company produced, among others, *Ring of Fear*, starring Pat O'Brien; *Track of the Cat*, starring Robert Mitchum; *Goodbye, My Lady*, with Walter Brennan, Phil Harris, and Sidney Poitier; *Seven Men from Now*, starring Randolph Scott and Lee Marvin, and featuring Gail Russell in an attempted comeback role; *Gun the Man Down*, starring James Arness and Angie Dickinson (Andy McLaglen's first picture as a full director); and *Man in a Vault*, with Anita Ekberg and William Campbell, which McLaglen also directed.

Ironically, Duke was a last-minute replacement in what turned out to be two of Wayne-Fellows's most successful films. Glenn Ford was set to star in *Hondo* for them, but the actor turned the project down because he didn't want to work with director John Farrow again (with whom he had worked in *Plunder*), so Duke took Ford's role. *Hondo* was a big commercial success and Duke later needled Ford by saying, "Gee, Glenn, thanks for turning down *Hondo*." Three months later, the Wayne-Fellows organization tried to get Spencer Tracy (whom Duke greatly admired) for *The High and the Mighty*. Tracy considered the role but finally turned it down. Duke's second choice was Humphrey Bogart, but Bogie wanted $500,000 to do the film, so Duke stepped into the role himself. Claire Trevor, his leading lady from *Stagecoach*, got an Oscar nomination for her role in the picture, as did actress Jan Sterling, though neither won. *The High and the Mighty* was an enormous success and is still making money for Duke's company, Batjac (now operated by Mike Wayne), in television rentals, as is *Hondo*.

Duke followed *The High and the Mighty* with what most critics and fans consider his worst film: RKO's *The Conqueror*, in which he attempted to portray Temujin, better known as Genghis Khan. He played opposite Susan Hayward, who was equally miscast—and even more absurd in her role—as his Tartar princess lover, Bortai. RKO publicists claimed that Duke had seen the Genghis Khan script at the studio and had demanded to do the picture. Perhaps, in this instance, there was more than a grain of truth to a publicity story; certainly no one connected with the project would have thought of or sought John Wayne to play the menacing Mongol. According to writer Oscar Millard, who did the screenplay, Duke apparently promised actor-turned-director Dick Powell that he'd work hard on the film—particularly to overcome his Midwestern drawl.

Not since he played Ole Olsen in *The Long Voyage Home* had Duke attempted to step so far out of character. But in *Voyage*, he had had John Ford directing and screenwriter Dudley Nichols's tasteful handling of playwright Eugene O'Neill's material to work with. He didn't have much to work with in *The Conqueror*. Screenwriter Millard later admitted that he and his agent had conned their way into the project, which Millard viewed as an "Eastern" Western with swords instead of six-guns. The Howard Hughes organization got so excited about the concept, however, that they decided to put $6 million into the picture and to get Marlon Brando on loan-out from Fox to star in it. Caught up with their enthusiasm, Millard decided to write the screenplay in what he described as "stylized, slightly archaic English," which, he said, was a mistake that he never repeated. The story he had hastily put together was, in his words, "nothing more than a tarted-up Western," and he said he had thought the formal language would give it a "certain cachet."

Before the loan-out deal with Fox could be consummated, however, Millard says that Marlon Brando got himself suspended (in those days, contract players were suspended without pay whenever they refused to do any film assigned to them, no matter how bad the film), and Duke, who still owed RKO one or two pictures, was signed to star as Genghis Khan. Upon hearing of this, Millard expressed doubt to director Powell about Duke's ability to handle the archaic English, but the director assured him that Duke had promised to work on the lines with a coach and a tape recorder.

"At our first meeting for a run-through [probably in early May of 1954], Wayne was genial, complimentary and drunk," Millard recalled. "He dozed off after the first few pages and there was no more talk of his working on the dialogue." Millard suspected that Duke never looked at the script again until the day before the shooting was to begin, at which time Duke called him at home and complained about the dialogue, saying he couldn't read the lines. Millard told him that he should have said something sooner, that to change the style of his dialogue, he'd have to change the style of the entire script, and there wasn't time for that. He said that Duke muttered an expletive and hung up.[1]

It's highly unlikely that Duke had not gone over his script meticulously and often, which was his custom. The most likely reason for his contacting Millard at the last minute is that Jimmy Grant, who sometimes secretly doctored Duke's scripts, might not have been immediately available or might have finally given up in frustration at the impossible task. Grant had a natural talent for writing dialogue that Duke was comfortable with, and so Duke made a habit of bringing him into his projects—officially if possible, secretly if necessary. Grant usually rewrote Duke's dialogue so that it was substantially unchanged but phrased in a manner that more nearly approximated his natural speech patterns. Then Duke would memorize the new lines and deliver them on camera. Directors rarely objected to these apparent "improvisations," because in most instances the lines were good, natural, played well, and, more important, that was the way their superstar apparently wanted to say them.

One of the few times Duke was caught—or challenged—using Grant's secret rewrites was on the film *Trouble Along the Way*, which had been co-authored by the film's director, Melville Shavelson. When Duke first read the script, he told Shavelson that he liked the story and would star in the picture, but that he felt the script needed polishing and he knew just the writer for the job: James Edward Grant. Shavelson flatly refused to hire Grant or to let anyone change his script, but Duke signed to do the picture anyway, and when he began "improvising" his lines, Shavelson rightly suspected that Grant was at work behind the scenes. Shavelson is said to have countered by bringing in phony revisions, which Grant would then rewrite, and then Shavelson would shoot from the original script instead, making Grant's lines, which Duke had memorized, useless. As a result, the set of *Trouble Along the Way* was emotionally charged and thundered with confrontations between Duke and Shavelson until the picture was completed. Shavelson could not be intimidated.

During the shooting of *The Conqueror* at St. George, Utah, Millard spent a weekend on location making changes in the dialogue —at Powell's request and, no doubt, owing to his star's insistence. Millard implied that there was a good deal of tension on the set, saying that when he arrived, the company had just narrowly missed being washed away in a flash flood and that Duke had been drunk for three days. He added that it was unusual for Duke to drink so heavily while working, a fair and accurate observation.

There was a meeting of minds on location, and Millard did effect dialogue changes on Duke's behalf that he said made at least one scene play better. The film was a very expensive flop, and when Howard Hughes sold RKO and its film library a few years later, he mercifully withheld two films from sale—both John Wayne pictures: *Jet Pilot* and *The Conqueror*. Hughes personally fussed with *Jet Pilot* for seven years prior to releasing it in October 1957. By then it was hopelessly outdated and it bombed spectacularly; the film had Hughes's personal stamp on it and was such an embarrassment to him that he yanked it from distribution and shelved it to preclude its ever being shown again. He didn't have the same personal involvement with *The Conqueror*, but presumably he didn't want to be haunted by a multimillion-dollar flop projected on wide screen for all to see. Whether he took Duke's embarrassment over the film into account, too, isn't known, but Duke benefitted from the eccentric billionaire's action.

The Conqueror was a visually spectacular film; its production values were excellent. It was shot in CinemaScope, with breathtaking action footage staged by second-unit director Cliff Lyons (who would later work on *The Alamo*), but the miscasting of the leads and their use of the rather inept dialogue made it ridiculous. Susan Hayward was no help at all to Duke or to the picture. Though she was supposed to be fighting and fleeing across the sweltering Gobi Desert, she refused to be photographed in disarray. She had one cinematographer fired for filming her with the sun glinting on her nose. In one scene, she is chased on horseback across the desert by Genghis Khan and is finally unhorsed by him, flopping into the sand; she emerges with pancake makeup, eye shadow, and lipstick unsmudged, and with her meticulously brushed Hollywood coiffure in place—looking very much, in fact, as though she's ready for a luncheon in the Polo Lounge of the Beverly Hills Hotel. At the end of this scene, Duke is supposed to have said to her, "I take you for wife!" But Millard contends that instead he "drawled, 'Ah take yer fer wife.'" That reading, he says, "provoked a titter heard round the world."[2]

British film historian Allen Eyles has noted that Duke made a passable-looking Genghis Khan, but that "his voice was so quintessentially American that his interpretation is doomed from the start, especially when called upon to utter the stilted clichés of Oscar Millard's script." As an example of Millard's penchant for clichés, Eyles described one scene in which Duke was called upon to paraphrase the line, "You're beautiful when you're angry," a line all too familiar to anyone who has seen more than one Hollywood movie. In the scene, Susan Hayward stands in the blazing desert sun, perfectly made up and coiffured and wearing what appears to be a silver brocaded evening gown and boots. She swings a sword at Duke's head and misses, falling to her hands and knees in the sand. Duke scoops her into his arms and is supposed to say, "You are beautiful in your wrath," then exit into his tent with her. The line would be bad enough to cause groans from an audience no matter how it was delivered, but Duke made it worse. We doubted Millard's recollection of Duke's saying, "Ah take yer fer wife," thinking it clouded by his obvious dislike of the John Wayne image, if not of Duke himself. Duke spoke English well. He didn't usually drop his *g*'s in informal conversation, as many interviewers quoted him as doing. He knew grammar and corrected it in others, and so it's doubtful that he fractured the language quite as badly as Millard remembered. In the scene just described, though, he did, indeed, look into Susan Hayward's eyes and say, with that characteristic cadence that impressionists love to emulate, "Yer beau-ta-ful in yer wrath."

It's small wonder that he got drunk on the set of *The Conqueror.*

Given the circumstances, it took great courage for him to sober up at all during the filming of that picture. Duke must have been as unsure of himself in that film as he had ever been in his career. The mystery is why he committed to do it at all, let alone talk Dick Powell into letting him play the part. Presumably he did it for the money and to complete his commitment to RKO, for at the time, he had just gone through a costly divorce, was reorganizing his own production company, was planning to marry Pilar in a few months, was trying to raise money to do *The Alamo*, and, as always, *had* to keep busy. No doubt he thought he could handle the part of Genghis Khan. He had successfully altered his quintessential American drawl to play Ole Olsen, a Swede. What passed as archaic English should have been easier for him to master than Swedish dialect. But it wasn't. It appears that he let the affected dialogue undermine his confidence, as evidenced by his performance.

It is in St. George, Utah, the location site for *The Conqueror*, that an inordinate number of residents have reportedly developed numerous forms of cancer. It has been suggested that the high incidence of the disease may be owing to contamination from nuclear tests conducted during the early fifties in the desert nearby—the same desert that the cast and crew of *The Conqueror* used in the late summer of 1954 to simulate the Gobi Desert. Several members of that company have since died of cancer: Duke, director Dick Powell, actor Pedro Armendariz, and actresses Susan Hayward and Agnes Moorehead. However, there are about fifty members of the company who didn't die from the disease and many who are still around, including scriptwriter Millard and Duke's sons Mike, who had a small part in the picture, and Pat, who was at the location for ten weeks.

It was just after filming *The High and the Mighty* (and during the filming of *The Conqueror*) that Duke and Robert Fellows began phasing out their association as producers. It was an amiable parting. Duke liked Fellows but said that Bob had never really brought much to their partnership. In light of Duke's obsession with making a picture about the Alamo, Fellows was not at all averse to severing their business relationship; the budget proposals for the picture were growing by the millions as the years passed, but Duke couldn't be dissuaded from his quest, even though people like John Ford cautioned him about making his directorial debut with such a massive undertaking. Bob Fellows was reportedly against the idea and didn't want to be around when it materialized.

Meanwhile Duke formed a new and wholly owned production company and named it Batjac, after the Batjack Trading Company in his 1949 film *Wake of the Red Witch*. His first film under the Batjac banner was *Blood Alley*, in which he starred with Lauren Bacall. Then, as his production company produced seven films without him—before undertaking *The Alamo*—Duke continued working for the major studios, which could pay him more than he could afford to pay himself through Batjac. Like Bogart, who ranked well below him as a box-office draw, Duke was now getting a half-million dollars or more per picture. He did several good films during this period, most notably Ford's *The Searchers* and, to a lesser extent, *The Horse Soldiers*, which he did with William Holden. His need for money to help finance Batjac and the making of *The Alamo* was probably the moving force that caused him to break from his tried and true stereotypical roles and to do forgettable films like *The Conqueror* and *I Married a Woman*, a George Gobel comedy produced by RKO in which Duke played himself in a cameo role as a henpecked movie star whose wife complains that all he ever thinks about is making motion pictures! Another eminently forgettable film he did at this time was *The Barbarian and the Geisha*, a nineteenth-century period picture in which he portrayed Townsend Harris, America's first consul general to Japan.

The Barbarian and the Geisha was filmed entirely in Japan (it was during the filming of this picture that Duke's Encino house caught fire). Duke got a then-record-breaking $700,000 for the fourteen weeks he spent making the picture, but owing to his battles with director John Huston, it seemed to him longer than fourteen weeks. The project had started on an upbeat note. The star and director had never worked together, and each seemed enthusiastic to do so. At a news conference announcing the initiation of the project, which was then called *The Townsend Harris Story*, Huston said of the Harris part, "Only one man is right for him and that's John Wayne. I want to send Duke's gigantic form into the exotic world that was the Japanese empire in the 1800s. Imagine! The massive figure, with his bluff innocence and naïveté, with his edges rough, moving among these minute people. Who better to symbolize the big, awkward United States of one hundred years ago? Duke's our man."[3]

That sounded pretty good. But it soon became painfully clear that the star and the director had different interpretations of how the gigantic form should move through such an exotic world. As the shooting progressed, Duke began to fear for his image. Huston ignored Duke's suggestion that his right and not his left profile be photographed. Then, for a fight scene, he brought in a tiny judo master who threw Duke's gigantic form all over the set, and Duke is said to have wondered darkly what John Wayne fans would think about that. Huston thought it was delightful.

Duke was not delighted. When he saw the early rushes, he complained that the portrayal didn't suit his screen image. "Huston has me walking through a series of Japanese pastels," he said. "Hell, my fans expect me to be tall in the saddle. Usually I gain a director's confidence, but when I go up to Huston's room and ask what's coming up for the day, he sighs and points out the window. 'Duke, just look at that view. Isn't it magnificent?' "[4]

The director and star were not on speaking terms when the picture was wrapped. Duke called Huston the slowest director he had ever worked with. Huston, when asked about their rumored feud, told newsmen, "Suppose you just say that there is no great meeting of souls." Later Huston fought with the studio brass over the way the picture was being edited. He was overruled, and when he left the country to direct another film, Duke exercised his considerable influence as the picture's $700,000 star by cutting scenes and reshooting and adding others. Huston had indeed had Duke moving rough and awkward against the pastel subtleties of a nineteenth-century Oriental culture. It was, as the director had envisioned it, a quiet film, with the simple imagery of a fine Japanese print and with the focus, economy, and understated profundity of haiku. The director was mad as hell when, during the filming, he was notified that the studio had changed the title from *The Townsend Harris Story* to *The Barbarian and the Geisha*. The title change reflected what the studio ultimately expected: a fast-moving commercial vehicle in the studio-mill tradition. Their star had obviously agreed with them. So Huston, who had been very happy with the film as he had shot it, said, ". . . a man I have no great esteem for, John Wayne, took over, shot scenes I hadn't planned and took out others I liked, in short changed completely the picture, which I now disown."[5]

Years later, Huston was kinder when referring to the matter. "John Wayne apparently took over [postproduction on *Geisha*] after I left. He pulled a lot of weight at Fox, so the studio went along with his demands for changes. . . . When I finally saw it [the film], I was aghast. A number of scenes had been reshot, at Wayne's insistence, simply because he didn't like the way he looked in the original version. By the time the studio finished hacking up the picture according to Wayne's instructions, it was a complete mess. My friend Buddy Adler [head of production at Fox] put up with all this. I would have taken legal steps to have my name removed from the picture, but learned that Adler was terminally ill with a brain tumor. Bringing suit under such circumstances was unthinkable."[6]

Duke once remarked that he had tried to get along with Huston, that he had wanted the director to accept him, "But," he added, "he hated my guts." He said also that he saw Townsend Harris as a "real he-man," but that Huston had made the character "weak and effete." In short, Duke found in John Huston a director who, when pushed, pushed back and who tried unsuccessfully to get Duke to play beyond his image. Twenty years later, still petulant, Duke grumbled about the director: "Without Bogart, Huston never did a good film." He had obviously not taken into account Huston's work on such films as *The Red Badge of Courage* and *The Asphalt Jungle*.

In 1956, Duke ended his splendid association with Warner Brothers. According to him, there were too many people at the studio who thought he and Batjac had too good a deal; there was talk of renegotiating for an arrangement more favorable to the studio, so Duke went shopping for another distributor and eventually signed with United Artists. Probably Warners' unwillingness to consider financing any part of *The Alamo* had something to do with Duke's leaving them, for his deal with United Artists wasn't nearly as good as the one Warner Brothers would probably have given him through renegotiation. Although the United Artists deal provided no participation in box-office receipts, it did provide him more latitude as a producer and, most important of all, the studio agreed to put up two and a half million dollars toward production of *The Alamo*. That was incentive enough for him to sign with them.

In between and sometimes during the making of his pictures from 1952 to 1959, Duke and members of his company had been working on various phases of the Alamo project. His biggest setback had been his split with Herbert Yates, for Duke had apparently gotten commitments for backing from wealthy Texans contingent upon Republic's participation and distribution, even though he had planned to shoot the film in Panama. Duke claimed that Yates had had contact with the Texas backers and left them with the impression that the film was to be shot in Texas, which would have cost him a million or two more than he had budgeted for. When he left Republic, he had to renegotiate with his backers. This time the Texans apparently insisted that the film be shot in their state, and so the project had to be set aside while Duke tried to raise the additional money he'd need to make the film there. Meanwhile his film budget had to be adjusted yearly, due to inflation; the longer it took him to raise the funds, the more it cost, and the more it cost, the more he had to scratch for funds.

The biggest problem he faced was in getting major-studio distribution. Most studios saw potential in a film based on the battle of the Alamo; most thought it good business to employ the nation's top box-office draw; and most were willing—some even expressed eagerness—to produce such an epic. To ensure the film's financial success, all wanted Duke to star in the picture and none wanted him to direct it. Duke was a movie star, not a director, and the thought of giving him a multimillion-dollar epic for a learning experience seemed an absurdity to them.

The film was Duke's dream, though, and he knew that in such a collaborative medium, his dream would take the exact form he envisioned only if he maintained absolute control over the making of it. He had to produce and direct. And those two difficult and time-consuming tasks precluded his starring in it as well. It was simply too enormous a project for that. He had always intended to be in the film, but only in a small cameo role as General Sam Houston.

Duke had become a dream merchant trying to peddle his wares to hardheaded businessmen. His was not a sound investment opportunity. Even so, on the strength of his celebrity and personality and convictions alone, he raised a few million. It took time, though, and the price kept rising as time passed. Then came his break from Warner Brothers and his deal with United Artists, and the dream was beginning to materialize at last.

Batjac could produce the film and Duke could direct, but there were two conditions to the studio's offer: first, Batjac had to match United Artists' investment, which meant that the three-year-old company had to come up with $2,500,000; second, the studio insisted that Duke play a starring role in the film. By now the budget had risen from its original $3 million to almost $8 million. The studio's offer covered about one third of that. It was the best offer he had received—very close to his own terms—and he took it.

The signing of the United Artists deal freed another $2 million that had been pledged by his Texas business contacts, and within months—by August 1957—ground was broken for the construction of the location sets. Batjac's art director, Alfred Ybarra, had thoroughly researched the small, mid-nineteenth-century settlement of San Antonio de Bexar and had designed what was considered a fairly accurate replica of it from drawings, plans, and written descriptions. San Antonio de Bexar is said to have comprised several dozen adobe buildings, a central plaza, and, of course, the Alamo, which was faithfully reproduced from the original, still standing in the city of San Antonio, Texas. Duke had leased a site about 120 miles west of San Antonio: 400 acres of a 22,000-acre ranch near Brackettville, Texas belonging to J. T. "Happy" Shahan.

The replica of San Antonio de Bexar wouldn't be simply a movie set with false fronts to be used only for external establishing shots; it would be an inhabitable town, with some buildings totally finished, inside and out. That wasn't Duke's original intent, and it's one of the reasons the picture went so far over its (adjusted again) $10 million budget. The construction of the town was a colossal and costly error. "The production manager made a bad mistake," Duke said. "When we first went down [to Brackett-ville], we planned to use ordinary false-front sets for the town and the shell of the Alamo. Then we figured the cost of trailers to house actors and crew and got around to the idea of putting up buildings instead.

"We put dressing rooms in some buildings, used others for warehouses. So we came up with something we hadn't intended, and before we got through we'd built a town."[7]

It was an enormous project that took a few days short of two years to complete. It's still standing today and is marked on maps as Alamo Village, a tourist attraction.

Duke sent a twenty-man construction team from Hollywood to supervise the hundreds of cement workers, bricklayers, brick-makers, plasterers, carpenters, electricians, plumbers, and general construction workers who built the town. According to Batjac's press releases, twelve million adobe bricks were used in the construction, as were a million square feet of lumber, 200,000 feet of construction steel, 125,000 square feet of concrete flooring, and 30,000 square feet of Spanish tile. A river was needed for the picture, so several wells were dug that produced 25,000 gallons of water daily. The water was also filtered and piped throughout the location site. Corrals were built for hundreds of horses, mules, and cattle. The publicity releases claimed that 1,500 horses, 400 mules, and at least 100 head of longhorn cattle were bought, leased, or borrowed for the picture.

Even though the shooting would take only eighty-four days, it was an isolated location and Duke made it a comfortable one for the three-hundred-member regular cast and crew and for the hundreds of extras. Rather than providing the usual portable toilets used on such locations, he had modern toilet and shower facilities installed, including five miles of sewage lines. He had $75,000 worth of portable air conditioners installed in the interior sets and dressing rooms. There were ten miles of underground electronic and phone cables. There was a small army of chefs, waiters, and kitchen help supplying three meals a day for at least three hundred people, and thousands of lunches for the extras. Fourteen miles of asphalt roads were laid to carry the heavy trucks of building supplies, set furnishings, movie equipment, livestock, tons of food, and daily buses of extras. A four-thousand-foot airstrip was built to accommodate the twin-engine planes used to fly the exposed film to Dallas to be processed and returned the following day for screening. The planes were also used to fly cast and crew members to Dallas or Houston on their days off.

Nate Edwards, Duke's production manager, and George Coleman, who had been Duke's driver captain since they worked together at Republic, were charged with handling the logistics and ensuring that everything ran smoothly. Coleman, in particular, did a remarkable job and, as usual, alienated everyone in the process. He was incredibly loyal to Duke, and he usually carried out his duties efficiently and within or below budget. Almost everyone looked upon him as a destructive fellow—abrasive, gross, and backbiting. He was a man of no apparent redeeming qualities. Someone once told Duke that he considered Coleman a sonofabitch, and Duke said, "Sure he's a sonofabitch, but he's *my* sonofabitch!"

The Alamo Village was finished at a cost of $1.5 million, which helped push the film's final cost to $12 million. Duke had scrambled for more money as expenses mounted; he had asked United Artists for additional funds, but the studio executives turned him down, claiming they simply didn't have it to invest. Duke reportedly added at least another half-million dollars of his own money to finish the project.

During the two years that the village was under construction,

Duke did *Legend of the Lost* in Africa, *The Barbarian and the Geisha* in Japan, *Rio Bravo* in Arizona, and *The Horse Soldiers* in Louisiana, all the while monitoring developments at the construction site, conferring with his office, and making hundreds of long-distance decisions as day-to-day problems arose. As costs mounted, he dispatched Batjac publicist Jim Henaghan on fund-raising junkets. Henaghan, who had been a reporter for newspapers and *Daily Variety* and a columnist for *The Hollywood Reporter,* had good contacts in the industry. He was working as a motion-picture story developer for producer-agent Charles Feldman when Duke met him. He went to work for Batjac at about the time Duke signed with United Artists, and he worked almost exclusively on the Alamo project, developing presentations and acting as Duke's personal representative.

Finally the village was completed. Heavy equipment was trucked out, and the army of construction workers and laborers was replaced by a small company of maintenance people. The corrals were filled with livestock, and tons of feed had been brought in. Trucks rumbled in loaded with movie equipment, generators, miles of cable, lights, reflectors, props, set dressings, kitchen equipment, refrigeration units, hundreds of costumes, and tons of food. Then the Hollywood bit players began arriving in Brackettville and the surrounding communities, where they were quartered. It was claimed that nearly four thousand people were ultimately involved in the production. Certainly there were hundreds and hundreds of extras in the big battle scenes. Casting people had begun placing newspaper ads and putting up help-wanted posters and hiring extras three months before production began; they were recruited from four counties to make up Santa Anna's army.

The crew arrived in Brackettville. And the main cast arrived, most of them staying at the Fort Clark Hotel, where Duke and Pilar had taken a suite.

Then came that long-awaited dawn, the awakening after a ten-year dream, the morning he would begin recording it on film. Duke awoke in a strange hotel bed in a small southwest Texas cattle town. He awoke with the realization that ten miles north of him, in a $1.5 million nineteenth-century adobe town he had built on someone else's property with someone else's money, in the middle of nowhere, several hundred people were preparing for his arrival, awaiting his orders. Hundreds of others would be coming and going in shifts over the next few months, all of them on his payroll. Stars like Laurence Harvey and Richard Widmark and Linda Cristal and Richard Boone would be awaiting his direction. Thirty other actors and actresses and hundreds of extras would move only when and where and how he told them to. What was at stake was all his own money and another $9 million dollars he had borrowed. What happened over the next eighty-four days could be wonderful or disastrous.

It had to be at once one of the happiest and most terrifying moments of Marion Mitchell Morrison's life.

17

CONSUMMATION

On Tuesday morning, September 22, 1959, the 321 members of the cast and crew gathered in the plaza of Alamo Village to begin the first day's shooting and to hear a prayer. Father Peter Rogers, of St. Mary's Church in San Antonio, had driven more than two hours that morning to give the benediction. *Variety* called it a "box-office prayer" and noted it as "Something veteran film men say they had never seen done in all of Hollywood history." Father Rogers prayed that the film be not only "the world's outstanding production" but also a "tribute to the spirit" of the men who had built the real Alamo mission and to those who had lived and died there. It was apparently Duke's eldest son Mike who suggested that his friend Father Rogers bless the village and the work about to begin there. Duke didn't object; if ever one of his projects needed a prayer, it was this one.

After the benediction, the first scene to be shot was set up and lighted. Duke called for quiet, then said, "action" and "speak," and his obsession began taking form. At United Artists' insistence, he had taken one of the leading roles—the smallest of them —portraying Davy Crockett. He had signed Richard Widmark to play James Bowie, Laurence Harvey as Colonel William Barret Travis, and Richard Boone as General Sam Houston. As usual, there were friends before the cameras, too. Olive Carey had a part, as did Chuck Robertson, who doubled as a stuntman, and

Jack Pennick, among others. Pennick was also charged with drilling the Mexican extras, who would represent Santa Anna's army in the battle scenes. There were old friends conspicuous by their absence, as well. Ward Bond was busy with his successful TV series, *Wagon Train*, and Duke's old drinking buddy actor Grant Withers had committed suicide six months earlier.

The shoot was a family affair, too. Pilar was there for moral support and to take care of three-year-old Aissa, who made her film debut in the picture. Mike, who had portrayed one of the children in *The Quiet Man* seven years earlier (along with his brother Pat and sisters Melinda and Toni) and who had been billed as a Mongol guard in *The Conqueror*, worked with his dad this time as an associate producer; he had the business head in the family and had gone into the production end of filmmaking after college. Pat Wayne, the only one of the Wayne children to become a professional actor, portrayed Captain James Butler Bonham in the film.

Considering its complexities, the filming went remarkably well. There was tension between Duke and Richard Widmark, but it was controlled. Widmark had irritated Duke before the shooting even started. Duke had taken an ad in the trade papers announcing the signing of "Dick Widmark" and welcoming him aboard. It was good publicity for Widmark and an unnecessary expense for Duke, but instead of thanking him for the ad, Widmark told him pointedly, "My name is *Richard*, not Dick!" To which Duke is said to have replied—after a slow and silent burn —"I'll remember that *if* I ever take another ad, *Richard.*" The incident set the prevailing cool tone of their working relationship.

John Ford threatened to throw the shoot into turmoil, too. He showed up on the third or fourth week of shooting and had been on the set only hours before he began making directorial suggestions and even ordering some of the crew about. He couldn't stand being on a movie set and seeing things not done exactly *his* way (Duke was like him in this respect). Duke got him off the set by asking him to direct some second-unit footage that was apparently never used in the picture.[1]

CONSUMMATION

While Duke handled what could have been an explosive situation with Ford, the stress of his undertaking was manifest in his break with Jim Henaghan during the filming. Duke had great affection and regard for Henaghan. Whenever Duke was away on location or vacation, Henaghan wrote to him frequently, keeping him abreast of the goings-on at Batjac and in the industry. The letters were written with such wit and humor that Duke eagerly anticipated receiving them. They were drinking and poker buddies, too, and Henaghan worked tirelessly, often on his own time, raising cash for the Alamo project. Aside from his Batjac salary as a publicist, Henaghan alleged that Duke had promised him a finder's fee of $100,000 and a small percentage of the picture's gross for the backers he was instrumental in getting and for his constant travels, meetings, and conferences as Duke's personal representative during the several years it took to put the Alamo project together. It was presumably these alleged promises—or a misunderstanding about them—that led to their falling out.

During the shooting, Henaghan got drunk in Brackettville and made a derogatory remark or two about Duke, remarks that were quickly relayed to Duke. Duke sent for him, but Henaghan told the messenger that if Duke wanted to see him, he knew where he could find him. According to one insider, a confrontation finally did take place, one that was witnessed by several people, including Pilar and actor Laurence Harvey. Both Duke and Henaghan had been drinking, and they had a heated altercation. Henaghan made the tactical error of using foul language. He could have said almost anything to Duke in private, but Duke considered such verbal abuse in front of witnesses a blow to his dignity. Although Duke routinely used foul language himself, he was intolerant of others doing so with women present. He took a swing at Henaghan, missed him, and accidentally knocked Laurence Harvey through a window (evidently Harvey wasn't seriously injured). Henaghan was fired (and replaced by publicist Russell Birdwell) and later filed suit, reportedly claiming that Duke had paid, or was intending to pay him, only $9,000 of the $100,000 he had been promised. The suit was settled out of court for an undisclosed amount.

DUKE

The filming was also clouded by a tragic occurrence. Two of the many extras who were flown in from Hollywood to take part in the film were a thirty-two-year-old actor named Chester Harvey Smith and his twenty-seven-year-old girlfriend, an actress known as Le Jeanne Ethridge, who was billed in the film as Le Jeanne Guye. Both were members of the same Hollywood repertory group and, owing to the overcrowded conditions created by the influx of personnel for the filming, both were billeted with several other extras in a bunkhouse in Spofford, Texas, a rail-junction town of about 250 residents twenty miles south of Brackettville. During the filming, Le Jeanne evidently acquitted herself so well in her brief scenes as an extra that she came to the attention of someone in the Batjac organization and her role in the film was expanded, giving her a small part (as an unnamed woman) and a raise in salary from $75 to $350 a week. As a member of the cast, she was also assigned living quarters closer by, in Brackettville.

Le Jeanne went back to Spofford to get her clothes, and while she was packing to leave the bunkhouse, her boyfriend stabbed her to death. The details of the case were never made public, for Smith's preliminary hearing and arraignment were closed. As president of Batjac and Le Jeanne's employer at the time, Duke was subpoenaed to testify briefly at the hearing, but there was no jury trial; Smith pleaded guilty and was sentenced to twenty years in prison.

On December 15, 1959, eighty-four days after the shooting had begun, and fourteen days behind schedule, Duke wrapped the last scene of *The Alamo* and headed for home, leaving cinematographer William Clothier and second-unit director Cliff Lyons behind to complete a week of pickup shots. He had hardly set foot back in California when he began touting the picture as exemplary of the kind of films Hollywood *ought* to be making to show the world what the American people are *really* like—uncompromising and indomitable in their determination to remain free. It was evident that his passion for the message he wanted to send the world hadn't been spent in the making of the picture. Not content with simply promoting his own film, he launched attacks against what he called "certain quarters of Hollywood" who, in his opinion, were "splashing garbage" on the screen. "It is giving the world a false, nasty impression of us," he said, "and it isn't doing our own people any good, either. I don't like to see the Hollywood bloodstream polluted with perversion, and immoral and amoral nuances."

Among the examples he cited were the screen adaptations of Nevil Shute's novel *On the Beach*, which dealt with the consequences of an atomic holocaust—a subject Duke said contributed to our defeatist attitude in the cold war—and of Tennessee Williams's *Suddenly Last Summer*, which he said was "too disgusting" to discuss. "Ten or fifteen years ago," he said, "audiences went to pictures to see men behaving like men. Today there are too many neurotic roles. It's the Tennessee Williams effect both on Broadway and in the movies. Williams and a lot of other writers go far afield to find American men who are extreme cases. They aren't representative of the average man in this country, but they give the impression that we are a nation of weaklings who can't keep up with the pressures of modern living." He added that a motion picture ought to be, in his view, "a universal instrument at once entertaining peoples and encouraging them to work toward a better world, a freer world."[2]

While Duke was thumping the drum for his picture—and alienating those "certain quarters in Hollywood" by thumping *them* in the process—Russell Birdwell, who had been the publicist for *Gone With the Wind* and other films, was gearing up to amplify Duke's polemic in an unprecedented manner: he launched the film's ad campaign on the windy tails of the 1960 presidential primary campaign. He began three months before the film's release by taking a $152,000 ad—a four-color, three-page gatefold—in the July 4, 1960, issue of *Life* magazine. The ad compared the words and motivations of Alamo heroes Bowie, Crockett, and Travis with those of the 1960 presidential candidates. The implication was that the frontiersmen had acted and spoken from deep convictions, while the two soon-to-be-selected presidential nominees were suspect. The ad pictured the battle-torn Alamo and asked rhetorical questions about the presidential candidates:

DUKE

Who has written his speeches? Who—or what board of ghost-writing strategists—has fashioned the phrases, molded the thoughts, designed the delivery, authored the image, staged the presentation, put the political show on the road to win the large number of votes? Who is the actor reading the script?

There were no ghostwriters at the Alamo. Only men.

The ad was signed by Duke, Birdwell, and Jimmy Grant. It was presumptuous and insidious, in that it appeared to be a non-partisan challenge even though many knew that Duke had always been an ardent supporter of Richard Nixon, who, as Vice President, was assured the Republican nomination.

Birdwell scored another dubious first two weeks before the film's premier when his organization issued a press release on *The Alamo*. Such releases are customary; they usually run from a few to a dozen pages or so and list cast and production credits and background information for columnists, reviewers, and film exhibitors. The *Alamo* release was something else: it ran 173 pages, weighed more than two pounds, and, according to *Daily Variety*, it was distributed "to some 10,000 columnists, government officials, opinion makers, libraries, schools, and exhibitors." And the publicity blitz had only just begun.

The Alamo finally premiered on Monday, October 24, 1960, at Woodlawn Theater in San Antonio—just a few blocks from the real Alamo—following three days of festivities attended by Texas Governor Price Daniel, Duke, and five of the film's cast: Richard Boone, Pat Wayne, Frankie Avalon, Linda Cristal, and Chill Wills. There was also a press conference (the San Antonio Press Club greeted out-of-state news people with a banner that read: "Welcome, foreign press").

The festivities leading up to the film's premier included a parade, a cake fashioned into a thirty-foot-long replica of the Alamo, a fiesta ("A Night in Old San Antonio"), a frontier breakfast outside the Alamo, a symphony of "The Alamo Suite," conducted by Dmitri Tiomkin, a "Texas Under Six Flags" luncheon (the six flags being, in order, those of Spain, Mexico, France, the

CONSUMMATION

Texas Republic, the Confederacy, and the United States), and local university awards were given to Grant for his screenplay and
to Tiomkin for his musical score. Then there was the screening of
the three-hour-and-twelve-minute film, with one intermission
(the film was later cut by half an hour for general distribution).

It wasn't a bad film. It wasn't a great film, either. John Ford
paid tribute to it in *Look* magazine (two months before the film
premiered) as "the greatest picture I've ever seen. It will last forever—run forever—for all peoples, all families, everywhere." No
doubt there were those who suspected that he was being his usual
perversely sardonic self, but director George Stevens joined him
in lavish praise: "When the roll call of the great ones is made, *The
Alamo* will be among those few by which the films of the future
will be measured . . . it is a modern classic."

When *Newsweek* got a chance to see what all the drum-beating
was about, it said of *The Alamo:* ". . . its own place in history will
probably be that of the most lavish B picture ever made . . . 'B'
for banal." And a week later, *Time* reported: "*The Alamo* is the
biggest Western [sic] ever made. Wayne and company have not
quite managed to make it the worst."

For John Ford to have called *The Alamo* the greatest film he'd
ever seen was absurd; such fulsome praise is baffling and may in
fact have hurt the film—as the overblown publicity campaign
surely did—by raising expectations among moviegoers that no
film could satisfy. The film was not a "modern classic," either,
nor was it "banal" or anywhere near the worst of Westerns. The
consensus of critical opinion was that it had its moments—some
of them outstanding ones, particularly the battle scenes in the last
third of the movie—but that the first two thirds moved at such a
leisurely pace (even after a half-hour was cut) that it bordered on
tedium, a problem compounded by a plethora of preachy
speeches written by James Grant but with the feel of Duke's
heavy-handed influence. Duke was given good marks as the film's
producer—it was an impressive accomplishment—but his direction was looked upon by most as only adequate, which was very
disappointing to him at the time.

One of the reasons he had insisted on directing the film—aside from his need to control it—was his conviction that he would have to turn director soon to stay in the business. In numerous interviews, he suggested that owing to his age (he was fifty-three then), his days as a leading man were numbered and that he *had* to direct, for producing didn't offer the artistic fulfillment he needed as an outlet.

Duke and his publicist muffled their thundering publicity machine while *The Alamo* made its fall 1960 premier and play dates. Then, when it came time for the Academy Awards, they went a little crazy. *The Alamo* was nominated for several Oscars: best picture, best musical score, best sound, best supporting actor (Chill Wills, as Beekeeper), and best color cinematography (William Clothier). Duke was understandably disappointed not to have been nominated for best director. He also thought that Jimmy Grant was deserving of a nomination. His disappointment was assuaged by the best-picture nomination, which he felt not only vindicated him in the eyes of all the scoffers who had turned their backs on him and his obsession—including some of the critics—but also promised additional millions in revenue if the picture should win. So anyone who thought that the flag-waving Fourth of July ad in *Life* was the nadir of *The Alamo* publicity campaign was wrong; there were new records in bad taste to be set.

In early March of 1961, five weeks before the Oscars would be awarded, Duke and the Birdwell organization took a full-page ad in the trade papers to answer a local film critic who had given the picture an unfavorable review. Then full-page ads were taken showing the battered Alamo, and above it, in large type, the ad read:

WHAT WILL OSCAR SAY TO THE WORLD THIS YEAR?

This ad was followed by another, which said above the film's title: IT'S UP TO OSCAR! Then, when a *Variety* reporter asked Duke how he thought his film would do in the Oscar race, he replied, "This is not the first time the Alamo has been the underdog. We need defenders today just as they did 125 years ago this month."

Duke's remark finally prompted entertainment editor Dick Williams of the Los Angeles *Mirror* to devote a complete column

Claire Trevor and Duke in a scene from *Stagecoach* (1939), the film that established Duke as a star. Springer/Bettmann Film Archive

On-screen in *Pittsburgh* (1942), Marlene Dietrich and two suitors: Randolph
Scott and John Wayne; off-screen La Dietrich had eyes only for Duke, and the
attraction was mutual. R. R. Stuart Collection (Grayson Collection)

Duke and Lauren Bacall on the set of *Blood Alley* (1955), which was produced by his own company, Batjac. Springer/Bettmann Film Archive

Duke visits with son Patrick (back to camera) and director John Ford (in sunglasses) on the set of Patrick's first major film, *The Long Gray Line*, on location at West Point, 1955. Culver Pictures

Duke and Richard Widmark talk between takes at Alamo Village, which Duke's company, Batjac, built to film *The Alamo* (1960).

Springer/Bettmann Film Archive

Princess Margaret presents Duke with a silver-inlaid saddle at the London premiere of *The Alamo*, October 27, 1960.　　　UPI/The Bettmann Archive

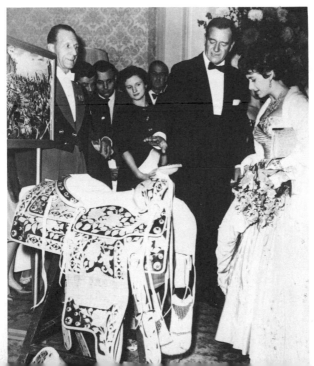

Duke and director John Huston on a set for *The Barbarian and the Geisha* in Japan, 1958.
London Daily Express/Pictorial Parade

Duke and Jimmy Stewart in a scene from *The Man Who Shot Liberty Valance* (1962).
Springer/Bettmann Film Archive

Director Otto Preminger coaches Duke for an upcoming scene on the set of *In Harm's Way* (1965). It was only weeks after the completion of this film that Duke discovered he had lung cancer. Dave Grayson Collection

Duke on location for *The Green Berets* in 1968. Springer/Bettmann Film Archive

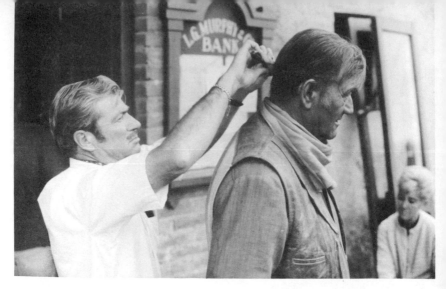

Dave Grayson prepping Duke's hair for *War Wagon* on location in Durango, Mexico.

Duke as "Rooster" Cogburn on location in *True Grit*, for which he won the Academy Award for best actor.

Duke and Katharine Hepburn on the Deschutes River at Bend, Oregon, for the filming of *Rooster Cogburn,* fall 1974.   The Bettmann Archive

Duke in his last public appearance, a few months before his death.

to the film company's questionable promotion practices, which read in part:

> The members of the Academy of Motion Picture Arts and Sciences are being subjected to one of the most persistent pressure campaigns this year I have seen since I started covering the Oscar show 13 years ago.
>
> Almost daily in their customary reading material—the Hollywood trade papers, *Daily Variety* and *The Hollywood Reporter*—the voters are being hit with full-page ads. . . .
>
> The implication is unmistakable. Oscar voters are being appealed to on a patriotic basis. The impression is left that one's proud sense of Americanism may be suspected [sic] if one does not vote for *The Alamo.*
>
> This is grossly unfair. Obviously, one can be the most ardent of American patriots and still think *The Alamo* was a mediocre movie. But you'd never infer this from the advertising barrage being laid down by Russell Birdwell, John Wayne's promotion majordomo. . . . Some Academy officials are deeply concerned, but they don't speak publicly about it. . . .
>
> Wayne obviously takes his own advertisements seriously. I wonder how many other Academy voters will also?[3]

Birdwell responded by placing ads critical of Williams's inferences, and Duke wrote a letter to the editor of the Los Angeles *Times* saying that he was "sickened" by the "belittling" of the critics. Then actor Chill Wills, obviously caught up in Duke's enthusiasm and rhetoric, put his own publicist to work placing ads promoting his nomination as best supporting actor.

Though neither Duke nor Birdwell had anything to do with Wills's ads, it was obvious that Wills was playing a variation on the theme they had chosen for the ad campaign. One ad named all the big stars Wills had supported in his years as an actor. Another quoted testimonials from Texans. Then he took a two-page spread listing hundreds of Academy members, saying, "Win, lose, or draw, You're still my cousins, and I love you all." This prompted Groucho Marx to take an ad saying, "Dear Mr. Chill

Wills: I am delighted to be your cousin, but I voted for Sal Mineo." Which, in turn, prompted satirist Mort Sahl to suggest that a new Oscar category be created and that an Oscar be awarded to Groucho for "Best Ad" in an Academy Award nomination campaign.

Meanwhile Duke and Birdwell placed a series of ads quoting the fulsome testimonials of directors John Ford and George Stevens, among others. The production company of *Exodus* (which was also nominated for best picture) ran an ad imploring Academy members: "Judge the picture—not the ads."

Then Chill Wills touched bottom, putting the Alamo company on the defensive and probably alienating everyone in the industry. He ran a picture of the entire *Alamo* cast, gathered before the real Alamo, along with the message: "We of *The Alamo* cast are praying harder—than the real Texans prayed for their lives in the Alamo—for Chill Wills to win the Oscar. . . . Cousin Chill's acting was great.—your Alamo Cousins." *Variety* refused to take the ad, but *The Hollywood Reporter* printed it.

It was an outrageous ad, and a sobering one for the Batjac-Birdwell bunch; they met to discuss it. Duke was incensed. It was decided that the ad couldn't be ignored, so Duke took an ad in both the *Reporter* and *Variety*, saying, in part: "I wish to state that Chill Wills' ad . . . 'We of *The Alamo* cast are praying harder . . .' is an untrue and reprehensible claim. . . . I refrain from using stronger language because I am sure his intentions were not as bad as his taste."

The last volleys were fired by writer Joe Hyams and director Billy Wilder. Hyams wrote in the Los Angeles *Times* that in light of Duke's advertising excesses, he was in no position to censure Wills for bad taste. Wilder, who directed *The Apartment* (which won the best-picture Oscar) satirized both Wills and Duke when, accepting the Screen Writers of America award for best picture, he closed his remarks by saying, "Keep praying, cousins! We hope Oscar will say the right thing this year."

The Alamo won only one Oscar—for best sound. *The Apartment* won for best picture; Peter Ustinov won for best supporting actor (in *Spartacus);* color cinematographer Russell Matty took an

CONSUMMATION

Oscar for *Spartacus;* the best song was "Never on Sunday"; and
the best score was for *Exodus.* Columnist Dick Williams had
pointed out even before the voting: "One of the incongruities of
the entire *Alamo* furor is this: it won a nomination as best picture,
yet it did not win a nomination for best actor or actress, best
director or best screenplay—all key elements in insuring the
perfection of any top picture."[4]

The film didn't go unnoticed. Neither could it have been considered a bomb or totally unsuccessful. It had, after all, been one
of only five films nominated for best picture by the Academy.
And even before the awards ceremony, it had been given the
Thomas Alva Edison Award for "the best film serving the national interests" and the Western Heritage Award as "the most
outstanding film of 1960." It proved popular with moviegoers,
too; they spent $8 million to see it in its first year of distribution
—an enormous box-office gross in those days. But it wasn't
enough. There's a rule of thumb among moviemakers that a film
isn't a great financial success unless it grosses three times its cost.
Applying that rule, *The Alamo* would have had to gross $36 mil-
lion.

In time, all the backers of the film were paid back from film
rentals and by Duke, who had to sell his interest in the picture to
United Artists to do so. He never recovered his own investment,
which was at least $3 million, or the $4 million he estimated he
lost in potential earnings during all the time he put into the project. Meanwhile, when his attention was finally drawn from his
obsession, he looked around and found his financial world in
shambles.

He had had an inkling of his financial straits when, with costs
of production mounting, he is said to have dug into his own pockets for more production money and to have come up empty-
handed. His cash-flow problems so stunned him that he fired his
business manager, Bö Roos. It was a bitter irony for Roos, who
had repeatedly cautioned him about the film project—about his
extravagance and about the inadvisability of investing his own
capital in it. In fact, perhaps because he sensed that Duke's judgment was being clouded by his obsession, Roos was against *The*

231

Alamo almost from its onset. That alone may have sealed his fate with Duke; if you were against that project, you were against Duke.

Years later, Duke would often tell of the time in 1960 when, after being a successful film actor for thirty-five years and thinking he had assets of about $6 million, he suddenly discovered that he was all but broke; he said, in fact, that he *was* broke but that he didn't change his life-style. He wouldn't mention names, he said, but his managers had enjoyed his money more than he. There is evidence that another manager, at a later time, did indeed mishandle his funds; Duke told us that he lost $17 million due to the manager's malfeasance. The Roos matter was quite different. Roos guided the fortunes of several Hollywood millionaires, and evidently guided them well, but there was little he could do for a client in the grips of an obsession who insisted on funding his obsession with his own capital.

The obsession exerted its toll. Shortly after the film was completed, Duke learned that United Artists had had the money all along that he had needed late in the production, but had decided not to risk any more on the project. Duke broke off with them for lying to him. He had also broken with Republic and Herbert Yates over the film. He had ended his friendship with Jim Henaghan and Bö Roos, too, and had alienated many people in the industry. He had burned a lot of bridges behind him and had gone broke in the process.

18

THE APOSTLE OF PATRIOTISM

DUKE'S *Alamo* ads and statements regarding the Soviets were instruments by which he first made his patriotic sentiments known to the general public; in essence, the John Wayne political image was projected from Hollywood in a fuzzy, out-of-focus manner.

John Wayne as political enigma was a media creation. He was, after all, nothing more than a movie star who spent most of his waking moments thinking about or making movies or going about his daily life just as everyone else does. He read his newspaper and tried to keep abreast of the swirl of current events. He subscribed to the newsletters and house organs that most nearly reflected and reinforced his own viewpoints and concerns. He was curious and intelligent. He had opinions on almost every subject and enjoyed expressing them, and he had a public forum in which to express them. His opinions were trumpeted by major newspapers and periodicals and by the broadcast media across the nation and sometimes around the world. Yet he was no better informed than his doctor or gardener; maybe less informed, for he hated politics and so reacted emotionally and didn't often bring his intellect to bear on the subject. Because he was so often asked about and so widely quoted on political matters, many assumed that a high degree of political sophistication lay behind his pronouncements. Mostly it wasn't so. The fact is, his sometimes bluntly outrageous and always entertaining remarks were good copy on slow-news days. In this sense, he was used by the media; he knew it and anguished over it, but he took the bait each time it was dangled before him.

It was the media, too, that fostered the image of John Wayne as a right-wing extremist and as a spokesman for the ultraconservative point of view. So pervasive was this media practice that even today the name John Wayne is thought synonymous with ultraconservatism. Yet he was neither a right-wing extremist nor a spokesman for them. He was a freethinker in the literal sense of the term: he formed his opinions independent of political and religious authority—and sometimes, unfortunately, independent of thought. As with other mortals, he often articulated gut reactions, which were hard to retract once they had been broadcast by the media. Still, they were his own opinions and not necessarily those of church or state. He distrusted government and religious dogma, saying, "I think government is the natural enemy of the individual, but it's a necessary evil, like, say, motion-picture agents."[1]

The political label that most nearly fit him was that of conservative Republican. He liked to think of himself as a Jeffersonian liberal, subscribing to the principle that that government is best which governs least. He was a fiscal conservative, but he supported many social programs, including welfare—though he thought the welfare system should be reformed to demand work by those who were able to do so. His moderate bent was evidenced in numerous actions. When conservatives sponsored and funded an initiative to ban pornography in California in the mid-1970s (Proposition 18), Duke made radio and television spots to defeat the initiative. He did so because he was against censorship. In the late 1970s, when the Carter administration was meeting stiff opposition in its ultimately successful efforts to return the Panama Canal to the Panamanians (the canal had been in possession of the United States under a perpetual sovereign grant since 1904), Duke publicly supported the Administration—even against his friend Governor Ronald Reagan—and was harshly criticized by conservatives and ultraconservatives for doing so.

Duke's association with the ultraconservative wing of the Republican party was not one of allegiance but of alliance. It coincided with his political awakening in the mid-1940s, when he became aware of American-Communist recruitment activities within the movie colony and was introduced to the concept of an international Communist conspiracy to destroy capitalism and to establish world communism. As a consequence, Duke became a fervent anti-Communist, and in time, his fervor turned passionate and fanatical and then phobic. It was as a reactionary anti-Communist and not as a subscriber to the ultraconservative philosophy that he found himself in association with right-wing extremists and came to be identified with them.

Duke claimed to have been somewhere to the left of political center when he entered the university in 1925. He often said that his two years at USC—and presumably his associations with the offspring of the city's influential capitalists in that bastion of conservatism—gave him additional political perspective that, together with what he called his "life experiences," tempered his political outlook and made him less "radical." In 1971 he said that he had been a socialist when he entered the university. He told others that he had been a "radical," and emphasized that a youngster's college years are a time for radicalism, but that if the youngster came away from the university with degree in hand and radical views unchanged, then he or she had failed in the educational process. More often than not he told interviewers that he had been a "liberal" and that he still considered himself a liberal, which he defined as one who considers all sides of an issue before making a judgment independent of others. To draw inferences regarding his political philosophy from such proclamations required more than a heaping measure of presumption, for he often used the terms "liberal," "radical," and "socialist" interchangeably, and whatever his political views had been prior to his "enlightenment," they seem to have been revised in light of the Communist menace shortly after the end of World War II.

When the cold war between the Communist and free-world

nations began, with it came what Duke may have considered his second chance to serve his country and the cause of freedom. In late 1948, he was asked to serve as president of the Motion Picture Alliance for the Preservation of American Ideals, a movie-colony organization that had been formed to root out Communists within the industry even before the House Un-American Activities Committee (HUAC) focused its attention on Hollywood.

The Alliance had been formed in 1944 by a small group of movie people who had become alarmed at the inroads the American Communist party had made within the industry. Among the most active of the Alliance's founding members were producer James McGuinness, West Coast union boss Roy Brewer, screenwriter Morrie Ryskind, and actor Adolphe Menjou. Menjou, who was known for his dapper-sophisticate roles on screen, was apparently well versed in theoretical Communist and Marxist literature and was the group's self-appointed expert: "I'm a witch-hunter and a Red-baiter," he boasted, "and I've read about a hundred and fifty books on Communism."

The Alliance met at first in the homes of its members. Duke came into contact with the group through Ward Bond, who took him to one of the meetings at a private residence. But as its membership grew, largely owing to the HUAC focus on Hollywood and to the increased national anti-Communist sentiment over the Korean conflict, they acquired offices and had to hold their annual meetings in Hollywood's American Legion auditorium, where they drew audiences of a thousand or more. By this time, influential Hollywood gossip columnist Hedda Hopper was among the Alliance's officers, and among the twenty-nine-member executive committee were Ward Bond, Cliff Lyons, John Ford, Clark Gable, Gary Cooper, Robert Taylor, Pat O'Brien, and Herbert Yates. Duke's screenwriter buddy Jimmy Grant became an Alliance member, too.

Duke watched the Alliance grow, but he wasn't very active in it until he was asked to serve as its president. Even then he hesitated because he was away on location so much of the time. Many of his friends warned against his becoming involved as an officer in the Alliance; they thought that his taking such a prominent position could adversely affect his career.

When the Soviets lowered the Iron Curtain and reactivated the Comintern (an organization established in 1919 at Moscow to spread Communism and which was dissolved during the war to gain Allied trust), their actions made it clear that they intended to resume their drive to spread Marxian socialism throughout the world; therefore, the American Communist party was again assigned the task of overthrowing the capitalist system in order to establish a dictatorship of the proletariat. President Harry Truman and Congress took measures to counter such Communist activities. The Party couldn't be outlawed, but steps were taken to keep Communists out of sensitive positions, out of the government, trade unions, and the like. Communism was finally labeled subversive, and some of those who had drifted with the political ebb and flow or who had innocently fallen into it were suddenly caught in the undertow.

In 1947, members of the House Un-American Activities Committee (HUAC), which had been established by the United States House of Representatives in 1938, turned their attention to the performing arts in both New York City and Hollywood and found active, Party-directed cells. It found, too, movie moguls and movie actors who gave the Committee names of people they suspected of being Communists or Communist sympathizers or whose politics were questionably leftist. The Committee also found the Motion Picture Alliance for the Preservation of American Ideals; it had been functioning for three years, and it was a rich source of names, which it gave to the HUAC along with other information. The HUAC issued subpoenas, took testimony, and gathered more names. Those who agreed in advance to "cooperate" with the Committee—which was HUAC parlance for a willingness to "name names"—were seen as "friendly" witnesses; those who indicated that they would refuse to cooperate were labeled unfriendly. A good deal of publicity was garnered by the Committee when ten of the Hollywood people, mostly screenwriters, who were called to testify refused to cooperate and were found in contempt; most of them served time in jail and were thereafter blacklisted, though a few of them did find "black market" jobs using pseudonyms, and one of them even won an Academy Award under his pseudonym and couldn't show up at the ceremonies to claim it.

It was evident even before the "unfriendly ten" were called to testify that those who were willing to cooperate were being "tried by publicity." They were presumed guilty and were jeopardizing their careers and the careers and social standing of anyone they named. One would admit, for example, to having contributed money, or to having joined, or to having allowed his or her name to be used, or to have raised funds for worthy causes like the Theater Arts Committee or the Hollywood Anti-Nazi League or the Hollywood Democratic Committee or, during the war, The Committe for Yugoslav Relief, only to find that the HUAC considered these and dozens of other legitimate organizations like the National Council of Arts, Sciences, and Professions to be Communist "front organizations." A connection with any of the organizations for any reason made one subject to the onus of guilt by association. If one named others who were seen at meetings of such organizations or who were known to have contributed money or time or the use of their name, these others, too, were likely to be called before the public hearings of the HUAC and their careers and community standing—as well as that of their family members—jeopardized also.

Those who were subpoenaed were asked if they had ever attended a Communist cell meeting and, if so, to name others who had been in attendance. What was particularly insidious about this line of questioning was the fact that committee members were aware that Communist recruiters used to invite unsuspecting motion-picture acquaintances to parties at private residences without telling them that they were Communist cell recruitment parties. So by admitting to having attended such a party, they were suspect, and by naming others in attendance, the others were liable to be called before the Committee. Ironically, many years after the HUAC "trials," Duke himself admitted to having been duped into attending one of those recruitment parties. And there, but for the grace of someone who may have refused to cooperate with the Committee, could have gone John Wayne himself.

The Alliance was formed by honorable people of both parties. John Ford, for example, was a Roosevelt Democrat and a member of the executive committee. They were alarmed by a problem within their industry and banded together to do something about it. They were in a good position to do so, too, for they drew their membership from all phases of the industry and therefore, as a unit, had enormous influence, power, and considerable intelligence-gathering potential. There were Communists within the industry. The Alliance, as a whole, was in a unique position to know exactly who and where they were.

When the HUAC opened fact-finding hearings on the West Coast in late 1947 for the purpose of looking into Communist infiltration in the motion picture industry, many of the film colony's luminaries volunteered to testify before the Committee. In addition to movie moguls Jack Warner and Louis B. Mayer and Screen Actors Guild activist Ronald Reagan (who was a Democrat in those days), the Alliance was also well represented at the hearings by director Sam Wood (a past president of the Alliance) and actors Robert Taylor (who was then the Alliance's president-elect), Gary Cooper, and Adolphe Menjou (both members of the executive committee). All denied that the industry was infested with Communists, but it was generally agreed that Communists made up about one percent of the industry's work force and that they were a very well organized group. Using pre-war estimates of the industry's population, that would put the number of active Communists in Hollywood at roughly three hundred.

By the time the HUAC again publicly turned its attention to Hollywood in late 1950 (having taken three years to complete its background work), most if not all of the known Communists were gone from the industry, as guest columnist Ronald Reagan had announced in Victor Riesel's syndicated column in July of 1951. The credit must go almost exclusively to the Alliance, with a little help—mostly shadow support—from the HUAC. Duke often said that the Alliance had been ineffective until the Committee took an interest in Hollywood. Then it had no problem in purging the Communists with the HUAC apparently looming behind them. Duke later said of the Alliance:

> Our organization was just a group of motion-picture people on the right side, not leftists and not Commies. I was the president for a couple of years [actually three]. There was no blacklist at that time, as some people said. That was a lot of horseshit. Later on, when Congress passed some laws making it possible to take a stand against these people, we were asked about Communists in the industry. So we gave them the facts as we knew them. That's all. The only thing our side did that was anywhere near blacklisting was just running a lot of people out of the business.[2]

Not having a blacklist was simply a matter of semantics with Duke. He could interpret the term literally and truthfully say: there was no blacklist. Whether the names of Communists or suspected Communists were put on a list or named one at a time, technically avoiding a "list," the result was the same. If the Alliance named someone as a Communist, then he or she was let go and would find all other industry doors closed. If the HUAC wanted the cooperation of a potentially unfriendly screenwriter or director or producer or actor, when one of that person's films was due out, then a hint from the Alliance of possible boycott or distribution problems and the like might well make the individual eager to testify. Of course, the Alliance had no official connection with the HUAC, but the effect was the same.

Had the story ended here, the Alliance membership could have been unreservedly proud of their accomplishments—and some of the more radical members were anyway. But years later, Duke would look back on the Alliance days in somber reflection, not with pride but with "no regrets" at having driven "certain" people out of the business. His ambivalence was understandable, for the small core of right-wing extremists who controlled the Alliance extended their purge to include innocent people—some say hundreds of them—whom they regarded as undesirable—mostly non-Communist liberals. Industry people stopped talking politics in public for a long time. For the sake of one's career, some didn't consider it safe to admit even to being a Democrat.

There were people in the industry who had either joined the Communist party or had been associated with it in some manner during the late thirties, when they had become aware of the dictatorial fascist movements in Europe during the Spanish Civil War, even though the United States was officially neutral; like Winston Churchill, who was being ridiculed by his peers for his alarmist views toward the fascist menace, some Americans wanted to oppose fascism, neutrality or not, and their only means of doing so was through organizations like the Hollywood Anti-Nazi League. Some of these would later be named.

There were people, too, who joined the Communist party in the twenties because it was chic and intellectual and diverting to do so, and rather entertaining and quaint to be associated with such impassioned philosophical and lively "Bohemians." Some of these would later be named.

There were even more who weren't totally obsessed with themselves and their careers and who had genuine interest in the welfare of others less fortunate than they. These were the joiners and fund-raisers, the contributors of their names and their time to what seemed to them worthy causes. They probably thought of themselves as humanitarians, but, depending on one's point of view, they could have been thought bleeding-heart liberals or misguided or naive or even foolish. Whatever they were, they were surely not active Communists and were certainly not bent on overthrowing their government. Yet they also would be named.

The misguiding lights of the Alliance made no fine distinctions. They purged the non-Communists whom they suspected of being sympathetic to the Communists just as ruthlessly as they purged the Communists themselves. There was a very stubborn element within the group that was intent on ruining anyone who didn't believe exactly as they did. Even Duke ran afoul of the misguiding lights once; he made the mistake of seeming to "go soft" on communism in the infamous Larry Parks episode.

After Larry Parks gained a measure of fame for his portrayal of

Al Jolson in *The Jolson Story*, he admitted that he had once belonged to the Communist party, though he had broken from the Party ten years earlier. His honesty in admitting that he had erred was used against him, and in an effort to save his career, he agreed to testify before the HUAC in 1947, though he wasn't called before the Committee until 1951. As president of the Alliance, Duke was asked by the press what he thought of Parks's decision to testify. He told them that he thought "young Parks should be commended for his decision" to cooperate fully with the HUAC and that "he needs our support."

Hedda Hopper vehemently and publicly disagreed with her senior officer, humiliating Duke. At an Alliance meeting shortly after Duke had talked to the press about Parks, she berated him for offering "sympathy to a Communist" at a time when our boys in the armed forces were dying at the hands of Communists in Korea. More than a decade later, Duke was still talking about the incident. "In she came, very dramatic," he said. "Oh, I love her, but. . . . She gave me fifteen minutes of the roughest go—our boys dying in Korea and the whole bit. And I had to take it."[3]

Parks appeared before the Committee and cooperated fully with them, but he was not welcomed back into the "fellowship of loyal Americans." His career was ruined. Later it was said that he didn't have much potential anyway (the same could have been said for young John Wayne early in his career), but in fact Parks had gained popular acclaim in *The Jolson Story* and was making a film at MGM, *Love Is Better Than Ever*, with Elizabeth Taylor, when he was called before the Committee; he was billed above Miss Taylor, and major studios didn't give top billing to actors they thought had no box-office potential. Parks spent his remaining years as a building contractor, building houses in the Los Angeles area.

Owing to the nature of the Alliance's operations, not much is known about its internal workings. It had offices at 159 South Beverly Drive in Beverly Hills, from which it furnished the HUAC with names of suspected Communists, issued press releases, circulated anti-Communist brochures, and engaged in such foolhardy activities as initiating and backing a proposition to register all Communists living in Los Angeles. Its daily work was diversified and was done in the offices of its individual members. Only one behind-closed-doors incident has been recorded.

The scene was Bö Roos's office, where Duke had agreed to meet with Carl Foreman, a fine screenwriter who had written *High Noon*, among other scripts. Foreman said he was "on the list" at the time of the meeting and so was out of work. A press-agent friend of his had been seen talking to him in public, and so the Alliance was going to punish the agent by taking away all his clients. Foreman was meeting with Duke on behalf of the press agent. It was a Saturday morning and it was obvious that Duke had been drinking, but he was by no means drunk. They were alone and equally uncomfortable, "like two teenagers in a whorehouse," Foreman said. Duke was courteous and charming, and "for openers," Foreman said, "old Duke magnanimously agreed to let my errant friend off the hook." Then Duke got down to the main reason he had taken his Saturday morning off to meet with the screenwriter: he wanted to help him make a political comeback. "All that was required were a few public confessions," Foreman said, "complete with breast-beating and a reasonable amount of informing on old friends, passing acquaintances, or absolute strangers, for that matter. Just a little cooperation, that was all, and I'd be working again."

Foreman said no, and Duke told him that if that was his final decision, then he'd never work in films again. It was a pity, Duke told him, because he didn't think Foreman was a "Commie bastard, really, just a dupe." Foreman told Duke that he might go abroad to make films, and Duke told him that the "blacklist" would follow him overseas if his passport wasn't revoked. "Then he reeled off names of a dozen others who would soon be unable to leave the home of the brave and the land of the free," Foreman said. "And you know, it all came true . . . he sure had a lot of inside information then."[4]

Carl Foreman did go to England, where he settled and raised a family and made his mark in the British film industry—he even worked on a project with one of Duke's idols, Sir Winston Churchill. It is surprising that Foreman had so much compassion for a man who had almost single-handedly driven him out of Holly-wood and out of his native country (as Duke readily admitted) in order to pursue his career. "For my part," Foreman said, "I have a strange, rather corrupt affection for old Duke, despite everything, and that covers a slice of territory large enough to contain the corpses of more than three hundred careers. I have always liked him on the big screen. . . ."

What prompted Foreman's remarks was Duke's appearance on a British television talk show. "There he was, that marvelous granite Mount Rushmore face . . . scaring the hell out of poor [talk-show host] Mike Parkinson and graveling, 'What about Carl Foreman? I'll tell you about Carl Foreman and his rotten old *High Noon!*'" It had been twenty-two years since Foreman had written the screenplay, and Duke was still steaming about it. Duke once said of the picture: "Everybody says *High Noon* is a great picture because Tiomkin [an Alliance member] wrote some great music for it and because Gary Cooper [an Alliance member] and Grace Kelly were in it. . . . It's the most un-American thing I've ever seen in my whole life. The last thing in the picture is ole Coop putting the United States marshal's badge under his foot and stepping on it. I'll never regret having helped run Foreman out of this country."[5]

And there he was in 1974 on British television, still fuming over *High Noon* and still misrepresenting it: "Here's this church," Duke told the British television viewers, "supposed to be an American church, and all the women are sitting on one side of the aisle, and all the men on the other. What kind of an American church is that? And all the women are telling the men to get out there and fight those killers, and all the men are afraid. What kind of Western town is that? And then at the end, there's this sheriff [marshal], he takes off his badge and steps on it and grinds it into the ground. What kind of sheriff is that?"[6]

As Foreman later pointed out, he had not written a synagogue into the old Western town, nor had the marshal ground his badge into the dirt with his boot (he dropped it to the ground, though). Foreman suggested that, "as we used to say in the real old West," Duke had "disremembered" much of what had actually happened in the film. And he noted that Duke had apparently disremembered the Academy Awards ceremony in which, on national television, Duke had presented his friend Gary Cooper the Oscar for his performance in *High Noon* and had done so by saying, "Why can't I find me a scriptwriter to write me a part like the one that got you this? Good sportsmanship is okay as far as it goes, but when I leave here I'm going to get hold of my agent and damn well make him find me a writer who can write me a picture like *High Noon*. . . ."⁷ That was in 1952, and Foreman was looking for work in England at the time.

Duke had developed such "an impressive persona of rocklike sincerity," Foreman said, that even *he* was more than half convinced for a moment that what Duke had said about the picture was factual, even though it wasn't. But he pointed out other things that Duke had disremembered over the years, and added, "Well, they say that when a man starts growing old, the first faculty to go, or is it the second (I forget which), is the memory. . . . For example, International Who's Who says he was born on the twenty-fourth of June, 1924. . . ."⁸ The implication was that Duke had allowed seventeen years to be shaved off his real age. A minor point, it would seem.

During the London shoot for *Brannigan*, a crew member discovered Foreman's remarks in an article written by Foreman for the British magazine *Punch*, and brought it to Duke's attention. Duke read it immediately. Besides Foreman's saying in the article that he had been blacklisted, that his press-agent friend had faced ruin by the Alliance for merely speaking to him in public, that Duke had told him during their private meeting that he would never work in Hollywood again, and that Duke had praised *High Noon* in his Oscar-presentation speech, Foreman outlined for British readers the awful consequences of the Alliance and the HUAC's practices and charged that nobody could work in Hollywood during those days unless his or her "Americanism" was passed upon by Duke or Hedda Hopper or union boss Roy Brewer or Ward Bond (actually Foreman called him "Ward 'The Hangman' Bond, who could smell a Commie-Jew a mile away").

Duke read the article and grew very quiet and reflective. Finally he said, "One dishonest note in the article for sure: I've never lied about my age."

It was during the *Brannigan* shoot in July of 1974 that the Watergate scandal broke. Duke never wavered in his support of Nixon during the stormy days that followed; he blamed those around Nixon. A British television crew came to the Manor House, where Duke was staying, and taped a short film of him to be shown at a Republican rally back in the United States. In his taped address, Duke referred only in passing to Watergate being wrong, but he went on to praise the Republican party and to attack the American press; the gist of his attack was that the Founding Fathers had created three branches of government, not four, meaning the press. Duke also made reference to then-Attorney-General John Mitchell being "convicted" by the press. Later, a crew member suggested that he should have said "charged" rather than "convicted." Duke looked at the man coolly for a moment, then bellowed, *"Convicted!"*

After Duke finished his last term as president of the Alliance, he continued to be an active member of the group. He even carried the Alliance banner once as a producer. His first Wayne-Fellows film, which he began shooting two months after he left office, was *Big Jim McLain*, which he was working on when he parted with Chata. The film is noteworthy only because it's so professionally inept—a rarity for Duke. He allowed his patriotic emotions to override his judgment and expertise both behind and before the camera. The picture was made from a screen story by Richard English, an Alliance member who was said to have specialized in the writing of anti-Communist movies. English collaborated with HUAC investigator William Wheeler on the story, which was supposed to have been based very loosely on Wheeler's experiences as a Committee investigator in Hawaii. And, of course, Jimmy Grant—also an Alliance member—had a hand in the final fashioning of the script.

What made *Big Jim McLain* so incredible was that it was nothing more than a gangster film, with the HUAC investigators as the good guys and the Communists as the gangsters. Duke and James Arness portrayed the Committee investigators whose task was to break up a Communist ring. The film made no attempt to deal with the Communist ideology or subversive movement. The only ideologist in the film (a college professor) was also an active spy, sending microfilm to the Soviet Union. The rest of the Communists were terrorist thugs who broke all manner of laws, betrayed each other (there's no honor among Commies), and murdered Duke's partner, Mal Baxter (Arness). Duke is left to fight the entire cutthroat gang single-handed. He does, but he's an honorable real American, and so he refuses to hit one Commie because he's short. In the end, the Commie ringleader invokes the Fifth Amendment and goes free, but Duke wins a nurse, played by Nancy Olson. His emotional involvement simply precluded his making a good film.

The last haunting refrain from the old Alliance camp was sounded for *The Alamo* in 1960 by screenwriter Borden Chase. Chase had been a founding member of the Alliance and one of its moderates, he claimed, along with Duke. He said of Duke's magnum opus, "When *The Alamo* was coming out, the word of mouth on it was that it was a dog. This was created by the Communists to get at Wayne. Then there were bad reviews inspired by the Communists." In Chase's opinion, the Communists were trying to get even with Duke for what he had done to them as president of the Alliance. Duke agreed that this might have happened. "Well," he said, "there's a little truth in everything you hear. The Alliance thing was used pretty strongly against me in those days."⁹

The Motion Picture Alliance had withered to nothing by 1960. By then, Duke had turned his full attention back to moviemaking, with only an occasional foray into conventional politics. He had become politically active as a Republican at about the time he joined the Alliance. Before that, he is said to have been a Roosevelt Democrat, but it's doubtful that he voted for Truman, though he admired him. He had made a trip to the Midwest in support of Senator Robert Taft in the late forties or early fifties. He supported young Richard Nixon in his campaign for the House of Representatives in the late 1940s. Then when Nixon gained celebrity as an anti-Communist on the HUAC, culminating in the celebrated Alger Hiss perjury trial, and made a bid for the United States Senate, he had no stronger supporter than John Wayne. Duke then supported the Eisenhower-Nixon ticket and was later bitterly disappointed when Nixon lost the presidency to John Kennedy.

He became a great admirer of Senator Barry Goldwater, too. In fact, Goldwater was one of three public figures whom Duke most admired—the others being General Douglas MacArthur and Sir Winston Churchill. When Goldwater ran against Lyndon Johnson, Duke supported him. Johnson campaigned on the promise that he wouldn't send "American boys to fight Asian boys' battles." When he won the election and sent American soldiers to Vietnam, Duke was furious. Not because Johnson made a larger commitment to Vietnam, but because he had done what Goldwater told the people he would do if elected and was apparently defeated for. Duke was sure Goldwater would have made an allout effort in Vietnam, as Johnson wasn't prepared to do. He disregarded the fact that by electing Johnson, the people had apparently voted against American involvement there; this was the Communist menace again, an imperative, not a choice, and a matter of patriotism, not politics.

He made *The Green Berets*, and admitted it was a propaganda film. He believed it was for a just cause. Duke baffled a lot of people with non sequiturs about Vietnam because he always got hotly emotional about the subject. At rock bottom was a belief he often expressed when he had control of his Irish temper and when he was engaged in quiet discussion: "If we're going to send even one man to die," he'd say, "we ought to make it an all-out conflict." To Duke it was clear: we *had* sent that man, and so he made an all-out effort to honor that man in the only way he could —by making a film tribute to him and by using his celebrity to support him—and to hell with his political critics and with the politicians who wouldn't finish what they had begun.

When former Alabama governor George Wallace was running for president on the American Independent Party ticket in 1968, his representatives approached Duke about the possibility of his joining Wallace on the ticket as the vice-presidential candidate.

Duke declined, saying he had no interest in political office. But soon afterward, it was widely rumored that he had accepted the offer, and the wire services found him in Montrose, Colorado, where he was on location filming *True Grit*. They reached the film's publicist, who in turn relayed the rumor to Duke, asking whether he wanted to make a public statement. "Tell them the rumor's bullshit!" Duke said, and dismissed the subject. The next day he learned that his one-word reply had been relayed to the wire services verbatim, and he was furious. He collared the publicist. "What the hell did you go and tell them *that* for?" he demanded.

"Because that's what you told me to tell them," the publicist said.

"Well, for chrissakes!" Duke roared. "Couldn't you have cleaned the statement up a little bit?"

When Richard Nixon made the biggest political comeback in American history and became president of the United States, Duke was able to stomach politics again for a while. In fact, he took advantage of the situation; Nixon recently revealed that while he was in office, Duke asked him to intercede with the Internal Revenue Service on his behalf (as did the Reverend Billy Graham). Apparently Duke thought the IRS was paying him undue attention. Nixon intimated that he took care of the matter. Duke had remained his staunch supporter even after Nixon lost his first bid for the presidency and followed this with a losing bid for the governorship of his home state. Then, after his comeback, he was roundly criticized by ultraconservatives as being too moderate. Duke always came to his defense.

He wore his Vietnam POW bracelet and watched that war become increasingly controversial. He was totally frustrated by My Lai, which he objected to being called a "massacre." The North Vietnamese were doing worse things to us and to the South Vietnamese, he said.

The vice president of the United States resigned his office in disgrace with a nolo contendere plea to the charges of accepting bribes earlier in his political career. Duke had said of him only months before: "The men that give me faith in my country are fellows like Spiro Agnew."

And then Richard Nixon resigned. Duke couldn't believe that Nixon hadn't destroyed those Oval Office tapes. He was doing a Bob Hope sports special the night the damning taped evidence was revealed, and he said privately to Howard Cosell, who was also on the show, "I feel betrayed."

When Gerald Ford assumed office and pardoned Nixon, Duke said nothing to his fellow workers. He had fallen silent on the subject of Nixon.

Not everything he believed in was falling away. There was Ronald Reagan.

Duke and Reagan had known each other since the thirties, but they had led very different life-styles and didn't associate much until the late 1940s and early 1950s, when they were allied against a common enemy—Communist infiltration of the Hollywood trade unions. Duke was president of the Alliance and Reagan was president of the Screen Actors Guild at the time.

They were in the same camp in 1964, too, when they both supported Barry Goldwater and when Reagan came to political prominence with his stirring campaign speeches for Goldwater. Duke was filming *The War Wagon* in Durango, Mexico, with Kirk Douglas when Reagan challenged Pat Brown for the governorship of California. Duke and Douglas had a friendly political rivalry going. Douglas took time out from the filming to tape a television promo for Pat Brown, whom he was supporting. Duke had planned to do one for Reagan later, but to get even with Douglas, he stopped the filming, too, to make a promo for Reagan. Duke had great admiration for Reagan and often said he thought he'd make a good president. He didn't live quite long enough to see the day.

Duke liked Jimmy Carter, too. Naturally, he didn't vote for him, but he attended his inauguration and told Carter that he was a member of the loyal opposition, "with the emphasis," he said, "on the *loyal.*" He thought President Carter a very personable man, and he was deeply touched when the President visited him in the hospital just prior to his death.

In time, Duke began speaking of Nixon again. Privately he had kept in touch with the Nixons. He thought Pat Nixon a great lady, and he marveled at the way she had stood by her husband and had stood up to all that had happened. When Pat was hospitalized with a stroke, Duke sent her a telegram wishing her well and calling her "one of the greatest ladies of our time."

Columnist William F. Buckley, Jr., wrote an article critical of Nixon for visiting China after he had resigned from office. Duke inferred that Buckley felt Nixon's visit as a fallen leader was demeaning to the Presidency. Duke disagreed and thought Buckley too hard on Nixon; by then he had come to believe that Nixon had done what any politician would have done in his place.

And that's why he hated politics.

19

VALLEY OF THE SHADOW

THE first half of the 1960s was the most crucial period Duke had ever faced. It was a time, ironically, when he had at last gained solid footing where the going had been most precarious—his marriage—even as the other avenues of his life began crumbling beneath him, causing him to stumble and then to fall.

He was fifty-two years old when he finished making *The Alamo*, a film that can be viewed as a manifestation not only of his patriotic fervor but also of his mid-life crisis. He had begun to think of himself as too old to be a dashing leading man anymore. He knew he lacked the dramatic range to handle the meaty, mature roles that would be left to a man of his approaching years.

During this period, his friends were leaving him. There had been the suicide of Grant Withers, one of his dearest of drinking buddies from the Fox days of the 1930s. For a short time, Withers had been the husband of Duke and Josie's closest friend, actress Loretta Young. His death wasn't entirely unexpected; he was an incurable alcoholic, and Duke had spent tens of thousands of dollars in an effort to save him from himself. But he slipped away.

Then there was his dearest friend, Ward Bond, whose sudden and unexpected death from a heart attack in November of 1960 shook Duke profoundly. Bond was only two years older than

Duke and was at the pinnacle of his career, with the popular television series called *Wagon Train*. The last episode Bond did of that series was a reunion of sorts; John Ford directed it, and Duke played a cameo role in it, disguised in a beard as General William Tecumseh Sherman. Duke had done the show as a lark and was billed in the cast credits as Michael Morris. That last episode aired three weeks after he had helped carry Bond to his grave.

Less than six months later, Duke's respected publicist and friend Bev Barnette died. In the same year, Gary Cooper died of cancer and Duke's close friend and Panamanian business partner, Tony Arias (who was Aissa's godfather), died in a plane crash. Before that dark half-decade was over, Jimmy Grant fell ill with cancer, which would be terminal.

His own age was bothering him, too. He began having trouble controlling his weight, a problem that would plague him the rest of his life, and there were those wrinkles and rolls and sagging flesh. Duke wasn't a vain man, but his face was his fortune.

His financial fortune had slipped away, too, and his losses weren't restricted to those he had suffered in making *The Alamo*. Bö Roos had involved him in an Acapulco hotel that wasn't paying off and in a six-story, fifty-four-room hotel in nearby Culver City that was losing money (he finally gave the hotel to the YMCA in 1967). There were other business investments that were going sour, as well. He had invested half a million dollars with the Arias brothers—Tony, Tito, and presumably Gilberto—in a Panamanian shrimp boat fleet that had captured seventy percent of the shrimping business in Panama before Tony's death—and before the Arias family fell out of political favor. The business failed without Tony's guidance. One of Duke's business investments with Roberto Tito Arias even brought him to the attention of the Panamanian police and government.

Duke had apparently invested $525,000 with Tito to start a much-needed ship repair business on the Panama Canal, but shortly thereafter, Tito became embroiled in a political feud with Panama's new president, Ernesto de la Guardia, who, upon assuming office, had removed Tito as ambassador to Great Britain and brother Gilberto from his position as finance minister. At about the time Duke was preparing to shoot *The Alamo*, Panama was "trembling with rumors of revolution and invasion"[1] and Tito Arias was apparently involved in the plot. Some of the Panamanian newspapers had been comparing in size and determination the Panamanian rebel force in the Veraguas mountains with the Sierra Maestra guerrillas of Fidel Castro. But the American press reported that the mountain rebel force consisted of just four self-appointed officers and three soldiers, although another thirty armed men were said to have landed on the Caribbean coast.

The strange incident involved playboy Tito Arias, his ballerina wife, Dame Margot Fonteyn, and an English actress, and as *Newsweek* reported, "Underneath this comic-opera surface lay a real if apparently not very realistic plot."[2]

While looking for Tito, the Panamanian police and national guardsmen apprehended Dame Margot and detained her for twenty-four hours. They had to release her for lack of evidence, and she immediately fled to England. Meanwhile Tito had taken refuge in the Brazilian embassy in Panama and had left behind a traveling bag containing a letter from Duke and a memorandum indicating that Tito had received from Duke the sum of $525,000. The bag also contained letters that seemed to implicate Dame Margot and British actress Judy Tetham in the plot.

The presence of Duke's letter and money memo along with the letter from Miss Tetham raised suspicions about Duke among Panamanian government officials. When news of his letter and memo was released to the press, Duke told reporters that he was in business with Tito and that the money was a business investment. Nothing more came of the plot, or of the ship-repair service, and the incident was soon forgotten. There was a grim postscript to the story, though. Later Tito Arias was shot by a political rival and rendered paralyzed for life. Duke often visited him while in England, where Tito retired with his wife.

It was into such ventures—hotels, oil wells, mines, shrimp boats, a Mexico City company that included among its holdings a fleet of taxi cabs and rental cars, and motion picture productions —that Duke drained his capital. He had invested perhaps six or seven million dollars of it, including the more than three million he reportedly put into the *Alamo* project alone. The failure of that film to make a quick return on his investment caused extraordinary complications. The financial toll of the *Alamo* project undermined his hopes for a directing career. The instrument by which he could have gone on profitably with directing was through his own company, Batjac. But Batjac was in such deep financial trouble after *The Alamo* that it had to suspend production for almost three years. In order to make the enormous sums of money needed to get himself and his company back on solid financial footing, he had to concentrate on acting and to modify his screen persona to compensate for his limitations as an actor.

On paper, he was broke, but he had an incomparable asset: he was still among the top ten box-office draws in the business, though he had dropped to tenth place in the 1960 poll (after dropping out of the top ten for the first time in a decade two years earlier). He still had more than a million dollars coming on his Twentieth Century-Fox contract, too, and he set out to rebuild his financial base while at the same time overhauling his screen image in keeping with his advancing years.

His first film after *The Alamo* was a comedy, *North to Alaska*, which he made in 1960 with Ernie Kovacs and Stewart Granger, and in which he played a middle-aged inveterate-bachelor gold miner, very set in his ways, who had struck it rich with his partner and who had a deep distrust of women and of marriage. *Alaska* was followed in 1961 by *The Comancheros*, with Lee Marvin and Stuart Whitman, also for Fox. It was evident that Duke's influence at Fox hadn't waned since he had reworked Huston's *The Barbarian and the Geisha* in 1958, which had been the first film of his three-picture contract with them. He made *Comancheros* a family-and-friends affair, employing in the cast his son Pat, his daughter Aissa, his buddies Bruce Cabot and Bob Steele, and even his personal masseur, Ralph Volke, along with other solid players, including Jack Elam and Edgar Buchanan. Jimmy Grant co-wrote the screenplay, and Duke and Cliff Lyons often substituted for director Michael Curtiz, who fell ill during the filming and who died shortly after it was completed. Duke had total control of *The Comancheros*, and it is remarkable in that it further delineates the image he had begun to develop a year earlier in *North to Alaska*. Through his choice of material and with the aid of Jimmy Grant, he created a new and complex screen image that ensured him a place in motion pictures—not as an aging character actor but as an older leading man. In many respects, his new image was a re-creation of himself, set in fictional worlds where the lines between good and evil, right and wrong were clearly defined and widely separated. It was this new image that firmly established him as a national institution and an ageless international superstar and that eventually won him an Academy Award. It was the John Wayne image, the one by which he would come to be identified and remembered the world over.

He portrayed a man named Jake Cutter in *The Comancheros*, a widower and captain in the Texas Rangers who is very much a product of his rip-snorting, hell-raising past, a man who, rather than sinking gently into middle age, is being dragged there by time and against his will, bellowing and kicking. Although far from perfect, he has more good in him than bad. He gives the impression of having mellowed philosophically; his years have brought him a gentle wisdom and a keen appreciation for mortal foolishness. Owing to his hard experience, he's unbending in his adherence to traditional values: independence, honesty, dependability, and courage. He's a man whose word and handshake are his bond and who demands the same of others.

Duke steps into the background in *The Comancheros* and for the first time in his career leaves the main love interest to the youngsters, played by Stuart Whitman and Ina Balin. In the end, though, Duke wins the affection not of the young beauty but of the older blond widow.

Ten months lapsed between the making of *Alaska* in August 1960 and *The Comancheros* in June 1961. Duke spent some of that time promoting *The Alamo*, which had just been released, and he moved from tenth to fourth place in the *Motion Picture Herald*'s poll. Usually he would never have taken quite so much time between pictures, but by then he could afford to do so, for it was during this period that he signed a nonexclusive multipicture $6 million contract with Paramount Pictures. To get him, Paramount had agreed to advance most of the $6 million when he signed the contract, and so he took additional time off to shore up his sagging finances and to revitalize Batjac. It was at about this time (1961) that he also purchased his yacht, *Wild Goose*, and anchored her at Newport Beach.

Less than a month after he finished *Comancheros*, he was at work on his first Paramount release, a John Ford film, *The Man Who Shot Liberty Valance*, co-starring James Stewart and featuring Lee Marvin. He followed this by doing *Hatari* in Africa, also a Paramount release, and then doing cameos in two star-studded films, each with several segments and each segment handled by a different director. The first one he did (though it was released second) was *How the West Was Won*, an MGM release and the first dramatic film made for Cinerama. He played General William Sherman—as he had for Ward Bond's *Wagon Train* a year earlier—and he was again directed by John Ford. The second epic, for Twentieth Century-Fox, was Darryl Zanuck's *The Longest Day*, depicting the Allied invasion of Europe on June 6, 1944. Duke played the part of Lieutenant Colonel Benjamin Vandervoort, and it was on this picture that he got even with Zanuck. He liked Zanuck, but a year earlier, Zanuck had publicly criticized the products of star-owned production companies and had humiliated Duke by singling out him and *The Alamo* as being typical of the stars' disastrous attempts at making their own motion pictures. Duke had answered him in the press by saying that *The Alamo* was making money and that he needn't worry about "poor ol' John Wayne." He was still mad, and when Zanuck tried to get him as a replacement for Bill Holden, who had originally been cast in the part, Duke refused. Darryl Zanuck wasn't a man who took no for an answer, though, and he kept after Duke.

Such cameos required only a few days' work, and other stars were being paid about $30,000 plus expenses for their participation. Duke finally told the movie mogul that he'd do the part, but his price was $200,000. To his amazement, Zanuck agreed. Later Duke said he felt a little sorry that he had charged Zanuck so much, but he couldn't resist getting even with him.

Duke's next Paramount release was the last film he did with

director John Ford. It was *Donovan's Reef,* a comedy that was filmed on the island of Lauai in Hawaii, with family members Pat and Aissa Wayne taking part along with the usual Ford-Wayne regulars and with a supporting cast that included Jack Warden, Cesar Romero, and Dorothy Lamour. The film co-starred Lee Marvin, with whom Duke had worked in *North to Alaska, The Comancheros,* and *The Man Who Shot Liberty Valence.* Jimmy Grant co-authored the script along with Ford's favorite writer, Frank Nugent. It was, in essence, a "vacation" location shoot, where old friends and family members got together to have a good time and to make a movie while they were at it. The story itself was a loosely woven Irish-American yarn, stitched together rather crudely with broad gags. Duke portrayed Michael Donovan, owner of the bar from which the film took its name, and Marvin played his friendly antagonist, Boats Gilhooley, with whom he shared such quaint traditions as celebrating their common birthday each year by meeting at the bar, drinking, shaking hands, and then trying to knock each other senseless—along with any innocent patrons who were unfortunate enough to be in the bar at the time.

It was during the making of this film that Ford, who had by now given up heavy drinking, plotted unsuccessfully to keep Duke and Lee Marvin apart when they weren't filming, for they had a penchant for getting roaring drunk together and raising hell, just as Donovan and Gilhooley did on screen.

One night Duke came back to his hotel smashed, and a little man who happened to be in the hotel lobby at the time approached Duke and told him that he resented him. His wife had always loved Duke, the little man said. Duke picked him up off the floor and bellowed into his face, "I haven't even *met* your wife!" Later Duke accosted a group of Catholic priests and launched a verbal tirade against the Catholic Church. The priests took his criticism good-naturedly, and in repentance, Duke made a donation on the spot to the Catholic Church. There were other such incidents involving both Duke and Marvin, and presumably the cantankerous Mr. Ford couldn't stand seeing the boys having the kind of rip-roaring good times that he used to enjoy on location during his own hard-drinking days.

Duke's Hawaiian "vacation" film was followed by *McLintock!*, the film with which Batjac reentered the marketplace two years and ten months after the company had stumbled out of Alamo Village with barely enough funds to maintain payroll. To follow the grim Alamo story, the company chose a Western comedy that was very much a friends-and-family effort. Jimmy Grant wrote the story and screenplay. Young Mike Wayne, who turned twenty-nine during the filming, made his debut as a full producer with this film. Duke's brother, Bob, was production supervisor. Andy McLaglen directed. Maureen O'Hara repeated a role similar to the one she had played in *The Quiet Man*, and Yvonne De Carlo also co-starred. Pat Wayne headed a supporting cast of twenty-six players, which included Aissa, Chill Wills (forgiven for his *Alamo*-ad trespasses), Edgar Buchanan, Bruce Cabot, Bob Steele, and other Batjac regulars. Conspicuous by his absence was Duke's friend and Batjac contract player James Arness. Like Ward Bond before him, Arness was starring in his own very popular television series, *Gunsmoke*. The series had first been offered to Duke, but he turned it down and recommended Arness.

After *McLintock!*, Duke somehow let himself be talked into playing a cameo role in the United Artists release *The Greatest Story Ever Told*, which was the life of Jesus. Duke played a centurion who leads Christ to his crucifixion and who has only one speaking line: "Truly, this was the Son of God." A then-relatively unknown actor, Max von Sydow, portrayed Jesus, and when he and Duke appear on screen together, superstar John Wayne, by his mere out-of-context presence, steals the scenes from Jesus. Truly, it was an absurd casting idea. The incongruous portrayal led to a great Hollywood anecdote. When Duke first delivered the line, "Truly, this was the Son of God," director George Stevens is said to have cut the action and to have said to Duke, "You're referring to the Son of God here, Duke. You've got to deliver the line with a little more awe." Duke agreed, and on the next take, he said, "Aw, truly this was the Son of God." It never happened, but even Duke had to admit that it was a great story.

DUKE

In late June of 1964, four months after he returned from making *Circus World* in Spain, Duke was back in Hawaii again, this time filming *In Harm's Way* with Kirk Douglas and Patricia Neal. It was on this picture that he began having bad coughing spells that interfered with his work before the camera. The cough had developed even before he had done *Circus World*, and it had been irritating, but not troublesome. At first, Duke thought he had caught a slight cold or that it was symptomatic of a new allergy, for he was allergic to such things as facial tissue and most theatrical makeup. When the cough persisted, though, he decided that it was a cigarette cough, and he tried to cut down on his smoking. He was a compulsive smoker. He smoked a popular brand of unfiltered cigarettes and liked them so much that he did magazine ads for the tobacco company. Two years earlier, author Dean Jennings had observed in an interview with Duke:

> As he talked, frequently cussing and using the same grim drawl that has cowed badmen from Fort Dodge to Tombstone, he compulsively lighted one cigarette after another. "So maybe it's six months off the end of my life," he said, opening the day's fifth pack, "but they're not going to kill me."[3]

He had smoked three to five packages of cigarettes a day since the 1930s, and so he wasn't very successful in his efforts to cut down on them. Pilar was along on location and became concerned. She made him promise to visit Scripps Clinic in La Jolla for his annual physical when the picture wrapped. He said he would, but he didn't say it with a great deal of conviction. He had been too busy to take his annual physical that year. He ruled out the possibility of there being anything seriously wrong with his lungs, though; he had just had a chest X-ray along with the routine physical examination required of all stars by their production-company insurance carriers before he began work on *In Harm's Way*. Such physicals are cursory, but Duke thought that if there had been anything seriously wrong, it would have been found on his X-ray. So he took cough syrup and went on working and smoking.

The picture was completed in early September, and the Waynes returned to their Encino place, where Duke began getting involved with his business ventures and made plans to take Pilar and the children on a cruise, sure that a little rest and ocean air would clear up his cough. Pilar reminded him that he had promised to make an appointment with Scripps. He didn't want to take the time off for it, but she literally nagged him into the medical clinic, and in so doing, she undoubtedly saved his life.

Duke checked into the clinic, where he stayed for the several days that were required to complete the numerous lab tests that are necessary for a thorough physical examination. It was found that he had a cancerous growth on the lower lobe of his left lung. It was a large tumor, and he was told later that his chance of survival was only one in twenty. Years later, he recalled to Dave Grayson—with more than a little irritation—how he had been informed that he had cancer. They had taken X-rays of his chest and then had sent him back for more X-rays during the course of his physical.

"I already had a chest X-ray taken a few months ago for *Harm's Way*," he told the radiologist.

"Yes, I know. We have it," the radiologist said.

"Then why all these X-rays?" Duke asked.

"We're trying to determine how far it's gone."

"How far *what's* gone?" Duke said. "You mean I've got cancer?"

"Yes," the radiologist said, "you have cancer."

Duke said the radiologist's words struck him "like a blow to the belly with a baseball bat." He intimated that there were more humane ways of telling a patient that he has a terminal disease than doing so when he is most vulnerable to shock—in a stark and cold X-ray lab, with the patient uncomfortable and all but naked in an open-in-the-back smock, and informing him with an almost cool, off-handed throwaway line: "We're trying to determine how far it's gone."

When his doctor did talk to him before he left the clinic, Duke was shaken by his urgency. He was told that he had to be operated on immediately, and the clinic arranged for Dr. John Jones of Good Samaritan Hospital in Los Angeles to perform the surgery. Jones was considered a specialist in the surgical removal of cancer, and was known by reputation to Duke.

Duke had driven down the Pacific coast to the clinic alone, and so he had a good deal of time to think on his drive back. He said that his primary concern was for his family—not so much for his older children, who were grown and could take care of themselves, but for Aissa, who was only eight, and for John Ethan, who was only two. He worried, too, about the possibility of being an invalid and a burden to his family. He worried about how he could break the news to Pilar. He had called her from the clinic and told her that there was nothing seriously wrong with him— that he had something called Valley Fever, which the doctor's didn't know much about. He told her that because it would have been too cruel to deliver such shocking news by phone, too impersonal. There was also his mother. She wouldn't even watch the last half of *The Alamo* because Duke died on screen. He didn't know how he could tell her.

Pilar took the news bravely and didn't lose her composure until after the operation, when she was overwhelmed with relief and with the shock of what could have been. Brother Robert broke the news to their mother, who didn't take it well at all. Michael managed to bear up well, as did Patrick, although he couldn't quite manage to hide his shock. Melinda and Toni were reduced to tears. Aissa and John Ethan were too young to tell.

Duke entered Good Samaritan Hospital on September 16. The cancer was so large—about the size of a golf ball, or, as Duke often described it, "the size of a baby's fist"—that Dr. Jones had to go in through Duke's back to ensure getting any tentacles that might have grown from the tumor. He made a U-shape incision about twenty inches long that went from Duke's chest, under his left arm, and to his back. Then he removed a rib and the lower half of Duke's left lung. He got all the cancer, and it hadn't spread.

Duke seemed to be recovering well for the first few days, but then complications set in. He had trouble breathing—he later said that his windpipe had been twisted when he had been sewn up after the surgery—and he began swelling. His face swelled so much that one could barely see his eyes. One eyelid swelled to the size of a golf ball. His neck swelled to twice its normal size. The doctors couldn't bring the edema under control. His entire body began swelling to alarming proportions, and it was decided that another operation was vital. And six days after his initial operation, he was sent back to surgery, which was successful. Duke later said that the surgery to remove his lung had not been half as worrisome as the second operation. When he began swelling uncontrollably, he thought sure his kidneys had failed and that he was dying.

Meanwhile, only a few insiders knew that Duke had cancer. It was decided that admitting it publicly would be bad for his image. The news media were told that he had entered the hospital to surgically correct an old ankle injury. When complications developed, making his hospital stay far longer than anticipated, the family announced through Michael that Duke had suffered a "setback from a respiratory ailment" that had been brought on by his inactivity during treatment of the ankle injury (a complication that Michael himself had suffered only a few months earlier following an automobile accident in which his uncle Robert and others in the car had also been badly injured). "The doctors removed an obstruction from his chest," Michael told reporters, "and he is feeling fine now." Few in Hollywood really believed the reports. There were rumors of cancer, but very few knew for sure.

Duke was released from the hospital on October 8 and was told to rest for six months to promote proper healing. He was too impatient a man for that, though, and his recuperative powers were astonishing. Within a few weeks, he was up and pacing restlessly around the house, tired of television and reading and inactivity. He did some of his recuperating in Mexican waters aboard the *Wild Goose*, and by December, he was feeling physically fit again, but he was mentally troubled. The press had not been told the truth about his illness, and that fact weighed heavily on him. There was still a stigma about cancer in the mid-sixties, and there were those around him who questioned whether knowledge of the illness would affect his box-office appeal. Many writers have suggested that Duke and his family were trying to protect his "macho" image—a term that Duke detested. That simply wasn't true. The question that bothered Duke and his advisers was this: if people knew that he had had cancer, would his image on the screen be a constant reminder of the disease and cause them to avoid his movies because of it? It was a legitimate question, and no one knew the answer. But what the public didn't know wouldn't hurt his image, and that had seemed the safest course.

As Pilar later pointed out to the press, technically neither she nor Duke lied to the press about his condition. She said that members of the media had asked, "Does he have cancer?" She said that she and Duke had replied no with a clear conscience, for Dr. Jones had assured them that he had removed all the cancer. "Fortunately," she said, "no one ever asked us if he had had cancer."

Duke pointed out that he had been heavily sedated when the press was misled and that by the time he was able to speak for himself, the damage had been done. But the decision bothered him, and he spoke to his doctors about it. They apparently advised him that there was no better image than John Wayne beating cancer. So four days after Christmas, he called a press conference at his Encino home and announced that he had had a showdown with what he called "the big C" and had won. "I was saved by early detection," he told the press. "Movie image or not, I think I should tell my story so that other people can be saved by getting annual checkups."

He also told the press that he was feeling fine. And he proved it when six days later—and just fourteen weeks after he had had a rib and half a lung removed, a twisted windpipe, and two major operations—he was in the mountains of Mexico, near Durango, filming *The Sons of Katie Elder*, a Western, with Dean Martin and Earl Holliman.

20

TRUE GRIT

MEMBERS of the press from all quarters of the world gathered in the mountains near Durango, Mexico, that first week in January, 1965. Duke's motion-picture sets were always open to journalists, and usually a few of them showed up at each of his shootings, no matter how desolate or isolated the location sites. This time they turned out in droves to watch him work on *The Sons of Katie Elder*. They followed him from one location to another as the shooting progressed—from Saltillo to Chupaderos to Casa Blanca to other sites along Mexico's Northern Plateau that had no names, and finally to the Churubusco Studios in Mexico City, where the interiors were shot. They followed him and reported his every move. On this occasion, their reports were filed not only with their entertainment editors but also with their features editors.

Just fourteen weeks earlier, John Wayne had ridden through the valley of the shadow of death, and now he emerged before them—high in the mountains of Mexico—riding like the wind on horseback, throwing "stage" punches and reeling from those he received, getting soaked to the skin in an icy mountain stream. He was fifty-seven years old and had been felled by cancer only weeks before, and there he was before them, tall as ever in the saddle.

It was a wonderful human interest story. It was the stuff that legends are made of. Only this time it was true and was unfolding before the eyes of the journalists who had gathered there to see for themselves—exactly as Duke had planned for them to do. He had waited not only until he himself knew that he was surefooted and strong enough to get back in the saddle, but also for the moment when he could *demonstrate* that fact.

The Sons of Katie Elder was a typical hard-hitting, hard-riding John Wayne Western, filmed on location in rugged terrain. The action alone that was required of him would have been test enough of his one lung's capability of supplying the oxygen necessary to maintain his strength and endurance so soon after his two operations and after weeks of almost total inactivity during his convalescence. He had an additional handicap. The locations had been scouted and chosen and the logistics set in motion long before his cancer was detected. On January 4, he began working again, under the close scrutiny of the press, and at location sites as much as eight thousand feet above sea level, in rarefied air that sapped the strength and endurance and taxed both lungs in the healthiest and fittest members of the company.

"I know I came back too soon," he told reporters, "but I had to. I can't stand being idle. I have to work." Pilar knew that he wasn't feeling his best. She also knew that once he was committed, he would push himself hard, and so in his second week of shooting, she briefly visited the location. It was the first time she had ever left the children at home to be with him—Aissa was in school and John Ethan too young for such a rugged trip—but she was worried. She knew how compulsive he was about his work. She knew that he had too much to prove—to himself, to his co-workers, and to the journalists gathered there. She knew that he would sooner be carried off the mountain in a box than not give the picture his best effort.

She needn't have worried, and she didn't have to stay long. If there had been any doubt in her mind before, she must have come to the realization then that work was Duke's benison; he thrived on it. Work was therapy for him, and he seemed to get stronger by the day.

To those who watched, there seemed little change in him. He grimaced noticeably whenever he pulled himself into the saddle;

he had to mount a horse, in his words, "like a tenderfoot," because doing so put great stress on his left arm and side. An oxygen inhalator was kept nearby, and he often used it before and after his strenuous scenes. He had quit smoking and had taken to chewing tobacco—as he had done during football season in college. He told reporters to stand clear whenever he spit; the chewing part was easy, he said, but after forty years without practice, he was a little rusty on the straight-spitting part.

He spent a good deal of time between takes joking with the press. He was witty and sometimes corny, showboating for them. There was one scene in which he was knocked into a river while fighting. It had to be done in close-up for effect, so a double couldn't be used. The water was cold, and the scene took the better part of a day to shoot. Once, between takes, he took some vitamin-C tablets to help guard against catching cold; he washed them down with a long pull from a jug of mescal, a 120-proof liquor known in those parts as *La Gasolina*. He shook off the heat and shock of the powerful drink and thundered, "Goddamn! I'm the stuff men are made of!" He was joking, of course, but he was making a point, too. His trainer and masseur, Ralph Volke, who had been with him for more than a decade and who had once been a prizefighter before going to work for Duke, wasn't very subtle either, telling all who would listen, "Duke's got his punch back. It's the hardest right-hand punch I've ever seen." It made great copy. John Wayne had, indeed, "licked the big C" and had come through the valley undaunted, if not unscarred, spitting tobacco juice, swigging *La Gasolina*, and doing his own stunts, as active and strong as ever.

The picture was wrapped in March, and within two months, Duke and Pilar had sold their Encino mansion and moved to Newport Beach. Duke had undergone several checkups after his surgery, but he had learned his lesson about the need for annual physicals, and so in May, as his family was settling into their new house, he went back to Scripps for a three-day medical checkup and was found in good health.

In July, with the paint hardly dry in his newly remodeled den, Duke was on his way to Rome for the filming of *Cast a Giant*

DUKE

Shadow, with Kirk Douglas, Frank Sinatra, Angie Dickinson, and Yul Brynner. The film was based on the biography of Colonel David "Mickey" Marcus, the American officer who helped organize the Israeli army to defend its newly established nation at the end of the British Mandate. The story had been brought to Duke's attention by writer-director Melville Shavelson, with whom Duke had fought (over Jimmy Grant's secret rewrites of Shavelson's script) during the making of *Trouble Along the Way* in 1952. As with most people who had had run-ins with Duke, Shavelson figured he had heard the last of him after that film's bitter battles. To his surprise, Duke wrote him a warm letter a few years later, complimenting him on one of his productions. So when Shavelson bought the film rights to the Marcus biography and was having trouble getting interest in backing and distribution for it, he took it to Duke. The John Wayne name was bankable. Duke was too old to play the lead—Kirk Douglas would be signed for that—but Shavelson hoped to get Duke interested in a supporting cameo role and thereby to attract backers. Duke liked the idea and agreed not only to appear in the film but also to co-produce it. With Duke aboard, the Mirisch brothers, who had a distribution contract with United Artists, also joined the production team. Shavelson wrote the script, directed the picture, and co-produced it with Mike Wayne.

Most of the film had already been shot in Israel when Duke reported to Rome's Cinecitta Studios in July or August to shoot his scenes. He and Shavelson got along very well. Perhaps to compensate for their conflict on the earlier film, Duke didn't try to direct the director. As Shavelson recalled later, Duke was always the first actor on the set—and he "blasted" those who were late—always knew his lines, and played the script exactly as it was written. The only problem on the film was one that sent Duke to the hospital.

One scene called for him to leap from a jeep and wrestle with Kirk Douglas. He injured himself in the leap and was rushed to the hospital on October 14. When hospital officials refused to comment on his condition, wire services reported that he had been admitted for "an undisclosed ailment" and grimly noted that when he had been hospitalized a year earlier with cancer, the information had been withheld from the public for three months. The implication of the news release was obvious, and the story was prominently featured in newspapers throughout the world. Duke's injury had nothing to do with his previous illness, though. Doctors thought at first that he might have slipped a disc, but the injury was soon diagnosed as a pulled muscle, and he was back before the cameras after a few days' hospital rest. Upon his release, he told newsmen that he had been more "irritated [at the jeep] than injured. Hell," he said, "to get even with a horse after a fall you can give it a swat on the rump. But what can you do with a jeep? Pull off its tail pipe?"

He finished his scenes for *Cast a Giant Shadow* in October, and then had only a week or so at home before beginning *El Dorado,* a Western with Robert Mitchum and James Caan, which was filmed on location in Arizona and at Paramount until January 1966. Finally, eight months after Pilar and the children had moved into their new home, Duke, too, had a few months to enjoy it and to oversee the remodeling of the *Wild Goose.* It was during this period, on February 22, that their last child, Marisa, was born.

Duke enjoyed being at home with his family—relaxing, screening films he had missed while on location, occasionally accepting some of the countless dinner and cocktail party invitations they received. And he enjoyed his afternoons at the clubhouse of the Big Canyon Country Club, having lunch and drinks and playing bridge or poker or backgammon with friends. It wasn't work, however, and he felt like a caged animal when he wasn't working. It must have become disconcertingly clear to Pilar that the crisis of a near-fatal illness had done nothing to alter his priorities or to change his life-style.

In June, he took a three-week tour of South Vietnam, primarily to get a feel of the place and what was happening there, in preparation for the eventual filming of his production *The Green Berets.* He toured numerous bases, telling the marines and soldiers, "I'm not here to entertain. I can't sing and dance, but I can sure shake a lot of hands." He did, and he signed hundreds of autographs. His visit made news back in the United States on two occasions: once on June 21, when a Vietcong sniper had taken a few shots in his direction while he was signing autographs at a marine base. Naturally, it was reported that he was "nearly hit" by the sniper's fire, an inaccurate account that he corrected when he returned, saying that contrary to reports, he had been in no real danger and hadn't even known they were under fire. The sniper's bullets kicked up dirt within fifty feet of him and the cluster of marines who had gathered around him for autographs. The second news story was the result of a press conference he held at the Universal Studios commissary upon his return. He took the occasion to expound on the threat of international communism and his opposition to admitting Red China to the United Nations.

In September, Duke was back in Durango, Mexico, shooting *The War Wagon*, with Kirk Douglas, Bruce Dern, Keenan Wynn, and the Batjac regulars. He had enjoyed working with Douglas on *In Harm's Way*, and as co-producer of *Cast a Giant Shadow* had insisted that Douglas be given the lead in that film. He was convinced that he and Douglas made an interesting combination on film, that they had, in his words, "a dynamic quality" that he thought worked well. Duke's always steady and laid-back manner was nicely complemented by Kirk Douglas's volatile, crackling performances.

The War Wagon was written by Clair Huffaker, who had co-written *The Comancheros* with Jimmy Grant (Grant had died of cancer in February, and Duke was now using various writers, but none would replace Grant as a friend). Huffaker, like Grant, had a flair for humor, and it was in this film that a much-quoted exchange of dialogue took place when two outlaws try to gun down Duke and Douglas and are beaten to the draw by them. The characters portrayed by Duke and Douglas coolly eye the bodies of the fallen outlaws for a moment.

"Mine hit the ground first," Douglas said.
"Mine was taller," said Duke.

By this time, Duke had completed his $6 million contract with Paramount and was asking (and getting from other studios) $1 million per picture, plus a percentage of the profits and of the television rights. Paramount didn't want to meet such a price, so Duke made a two-picture deal with Universal. *The War Wagon* was the first of those two pictures, and *The Green Berets* was to be the second, but Universal was having second thoughts—probably after seeing the script. Duke made an appointment to meet with one of the studio's top executives about the matter and was informed at the meeting that there was so much controversy about Vietnam that the studio thought a film on the subject might be more trouble than it was worth as a business venture. They had decided not to back the film. Duke obviously disagreed with their view and told the executive so, but it was their studio and there was nothing he could do about their decision.

He eventually made a distribution deal with Warner Brothers-Seven Arts for *The Green Berets* and shot the film at Fort Benning, Georgia, from August to early December 1967. Mike Wayne produced it and Pat had a role in it. Duke directed and starred in it with David Janssen, Jim Hutton, and Aldo Ray. It was one of those projects that was fraught with dissension from its onset and that had Batjac personnel running for cover most of the time—not from the simulated shell fire and other war-film pyrotechnics of the special-effects crew, but from Duke's temperamental incendiary volleys, which he fired in all directions and usually at the wrong targets.

To begin with, it was a picture that Duke was passionate about, and this alone was enough to have the Batjac bunch scrambling for helmets and flak jackets. It got off to a bad start when two studios turned the project down. When the show did get underway, the Pentagon didn't offer the kind of cooperation it had customarily given to producers of war films in the past, which Duke found both incredible and odious. This disappointment was followed by the arrival at Fort Benning of veteran director Mervyn Le Roy, whom the studio sent as an "adviser" to look after its interests and to oversee Duke's work, as though they didn't fully trust his directorial judgment. This did nothing to sweeten his disposition. Le Roy was a diplomat, though, and a respected old acquaintance, and Duke got along well with him.

The dissension didn't end with the completion of the film. *The Green Berets* bore little resemblance to the Robin Moore novel from which it was adapted, and it was roundly denounced by film critics. Even New York *Times* critic Renata Adler, who was not given to strident criticism, wrote a devastating review, saying, in effect, that it was not only an absurdly incredible oversimplification of the Vietnam conflict, but a perverse one. She wrote, in part:

> What is sick, what is an outrage and a travesty, is that while it is meant to be an argument against war opposition . . . it seems so totally impervious to any of the questions that it raises. It is so full of its own caricature of patriotism that it cannot even find the right things to falsify. . . .[1]

The critics were right about the film. It was as inept as *Big Jim McLain*. What they failed to realize—or at least failed to address—was the fact that in Duke's mind, *The Green Berets* was not a film about Vietnam. It was a film about the international Communist conspiracy. Like the real conflict, it just happened to be set in Vietnam among the Vietnamese, whose national problems, like personal problems, were insignificant if not irrelevant to that greater evil. Like the concept he had introduced in his early Westerns of using the villain's own tactics against him, Duke was convinced that the battle against the menace of international communism couldn't be fought by the Marquess of Queensberry Rules.

There was a lot of political fallout from the film. Duke spent months defending the making of it, and then when everything seemed to quiet down, a United States congressman raised the issue over whether the Army had charged enough for its help in making the film. Duke called him "a publicity seeker." The congressman fired some statistics at him. Duke shot back statistics of his own, and that issue, too, eventually died.

Meanwhile, American moviegoers ignored the critics. *The Green Berets* earned back its $8 million production cost in its first three months of release. Meanwhile, too, Duke had done two more films. One was *Hellfighters*, with Katharine Ross, Jim Hutton, and Vera Miles, which was based loosely on the life of Texas "Red" Adair, the oil-field fire expert. It was this film that Universal took in lieu of *The Green Berets*. The second film was *True Grit*, and Duke's performance in it made critics forget all about *The Green Berets*.

Duke read Charles Portis's novel, *True Grit*, in galley proofs, which had been sent to movie agents and producers prior to the book's publication. The story is about a boozy, one-eyed deputy U.S. marshal named Reuben J. "Rooster" Cogburn, who wears an eye patch and who is hired by a young girl to track down her father's murderer. Rooster makes his living collecting rewards offered for the capture of outlaws—and collecting any whiskey in their possession when captured. He's a man who "loves to pull a cork," as his landlady observes, but encased in that slovenly carcass is a being who places great value on his dignity, as one humorous incident attests: on his trek to catch the murderer, he pauses to take a long drink from his whiskey bottle and falls off his horse while doing so—without spilling a drop. While lying where he has fallen, he surveys the area with his one good eye and declares it a suitable spot to make camp for the night, as though this was the method by which he always chose his campsites.

Duke loved the story and bid $300,000 for the movie rights. He wanted to make it a Batjac production. But producer Hal Wallis outbid him (by very little, Duke later found out). Duke wasted no time in letting Wallis know that he wanted to play the part of Rooster. Wallis, who was an independent producer at Paramount, couldn't have been more delighted. He had produced Duke's "comeback" film, *The Sons of Katie Elder*, which Henry Hathaway had directed for him. He signed Duke and Hathaway again for *True Grit*, along with a fine supporting cast that included Glen Campbell, Kim Darby, Robert Duvall, Dennis Hopper, and Strother Martin.

During the preproduction stage of the film, author Charles Portis had sent Wallis a photograph of what he thought Rooster should look like. It was a picture of a man about Duke's age (Duke was sixty-one then), with a black eye patch and a full mustache. Wallis apparently thought the conception worthy of consideration; presumably a sot like Rooster, who spent most of his time on the trail pursuing outlaws, would not be very well groomed or clean-shaven. He showed the photographic suggestion to Duke, who immediately vetoed the idea. "For crissakes!" he said. "With a mustache *and* an eye patch, how the fuck are they going to see *me?*"

When Duke read the shooting script, which was written by Marguerite Roberts, he was even more excited at the prospect of playing Rooster. He said it was the best script he had ever read. Duke's characterization of Rooster, however, was taken straight from the book, which he said he followed scrupulously. "Rooster was the kind of marshal never portrayed on screen before," he said, "an old, sloppy-looking, disreputable, one-eyed sonofabitch who used every trick, fair or foul, to get his man. And that's the way I played him." Duke had no idea that he'd get an Academy Award nomination for his portrayal, much less the Oscar. He had played older, disreputable types before—though with less humor —such as Tom Dunson in *Red River*. And he hadn't been nominated for that fine film, so he had no reason to expect *True Grit* to fare any better.

The locations were shot around Montrose, Colorado, and Mammoth Lakes, California. The shooting went fairly well. Duke got along fine with Glen Campbell, whom he liked. Kim Darby, who played the fourteen-year-old Mattie Ross in the film, seemed to have arrived predisposed to disliking him—at least that was how it seemed to Duke—and so their relationship was rather cool. Robert Duvall arrived prepared to do battle with the director. Duvall was to play the main heavy in the film, an outlaw named Ned Pepper. Presumably he had heard that Hathaway could be tough on actors, even cruel to them, and he had decided not to let him get the upper hand. When they were about to shoot the scene in which Rooster takes on Pepper and his gang, Hathaway made his first directorial suggestion to Duvall.

"Fuck you, Henry," Duvall said to him.

"You talking to *me*, son?" Hathaway said, eyeing Duvall coolly.

"Yeah, I'm talking to *you.*"

"You're talking to the *director?*"

"Yeah," Duvall said, "I'm *talking* to you."

"I'm your director."

"So you're my director. So what?" Duvall said.

It was one of those psychological confrontations that grew and grew, each man putting the other on notice that he wouldn't be pushed around. Finally Hathaway said, "All right, son, we'll do it your way. We've gotta get it done."

Duke stood watching the confrontation, saying nothing. "I was just waiting," he said later. "If Duvall had put a hand on the old man, I'd have sent him sprawling across the goddamn field!" Duvall was tough, but Hathaway was seventy years old then, and it's doubtful that the actor would have laid a hand on him. The irony was that "the old man" Duke talked about was only nine years older than Duke himself and that Duke had treated directors just as badly—or worse—and would continue to do so. His relationship with the director went back twenty-eight years; Hathaway had first directed him in *The Shepherd of the Hills* in 1941, and so Duke had a nostalgic affection for this particular director that the young Duvall didn't share.

Two months after *True Grit* was wrapped, Duke was working on location in Durango, Mexico, and Baton Rouge, Louisiana, with Rock Hudson on *The Undefeated.* It was his eighth film in the four years since his cancer operation, and it apparently became clear to Pilar that although Duke had been given a new lease on life, he wasn't sharing much of it with his family. He was just turning sixty-two and was away most of the time and had three more films in the planning stages. Finally she visited the Durango location, where they had a showdown of sorts and an argument that caused her to leave for California. Duke said nothing, but he couldn't keep the tears from his eyes as Dave Grayson made him up for his last scene.

On his return to California, Duke took Pilar and the children on the first extended vacation they had taken together since his operation. They cruised aboard the *Wild Goose* for nearly two months, then visited their enormous cattle ranch in Arizona.

DUKE

There is little doubt that the vacation was an effort on Duke's part to make up for his constant absences from home. Even so, Pilar had little choice than to fashion a social life of her own apart from his, for he continued to average making two pictures a year, taking him away from home two or three months at a time, and when he did return, he was seldom at home; he had to keep busy, occupied.

Duke's next film, *Chisum*, was a Batjac production and was filmed in Durango with Forrest Tucker and Christopher George. He was working on this film when he received news of his Academy Award nomination for his performance in *True Grit*. He had already been given the Golden Globe Award for his performance, but it had been twenty years since his only other Academy Award nomination—for *Sands of Iwo Jima*, in 1949—and he was delighted to be one of the five nominees. "Whether or not I win an Oscar," he told reporters, "I'm proud of the performance . . . it sure is nice to do a piece of work people seem to like. . . ."

The Oscar competition this time was even more formidable than it had been when he lost twenty years earlier and had remarked facetiously to the press, "You can't eat awards, nor, more to the point, *drink* 'em." He was not unaware that in some quarters he was the sentimental favorite, as a man with forty years in the business and who had made an incredible comeback from cancer. He genuinely thought his politics would nullify that apparent edge: "I'm aware I'm unpopular in the industry because my political philosophy is different from the prevailing attitude," he said. He also figured he had little chance because this time there were four solid dramatic actors in contention who he thought would get most of the Academy votes. Both Dustin Hoffman and Jon Voight were nominated for their performances in *Midnight Cowboy* (a film that Duke hated and cited as exemplary of the "garbage" Hollywood was throwing on the screen), but he thought the Oscar would go to either Peter O'Toole for his performance in *The Lion in Winter* or to Richard Burton for *Anne of the Thousand Days*, each of whom was due because each had been nominated previously—three and five times, respectively—without winning.

Duke said he'd like to win an Oscar, but he was happy just being nominated again and in such company, though he did think his performance in *True Grit* was a solid one and that it contained a scene or two as good as anything he had ever done on film.

In the meantime, he had eagerly looked forward to his next film, *Rio Lobo*, in which he was reunited with director Howard Hawks and second-unit director Yakima Canutt; in fact, it was said that he had agreed to do the film (a Howard Hawks production) without seeing the script and on the basis of Hawks's and Yak's participation. His elation at the prospect was blunted when, just as he was to begin filming, his mother died in Long Beach on February 17, 1970, from heart failure. Although her death had not come as a total surprise (she had been in failing health with a heart condition), it didn't lessen the pain for him.

He had little time for mourning. The cast and crew of *Rio Lobo* had already assembled at Old Tucson, Arizona, a "frontier" town that had been built especially for the making of Western films, and he flew there immediately after his mother's funeral. The atmosphere on the set was naturally somber.

On Monday, April 13, about three weeks after they had begun filming, Duke and Dave Grayson took two days' leave from the production to return to Hollywood, where Duke was to be one of the emcees for the 42nd Academy Awards Presentation show. Duke took Bungalow 3 on the grounds of the Beverly Hills Hotel, next to the Richard Burtons (Elizabeth Taylor was Mrs. Burton then), and Pilar came up from Newport for the occasion. Duke and Elizabeth Taylor attended rehearsals the following morning —each had parts in the Awards show—and then returned to the hotel to prepare for the gala evening. Grayson accompanied Duke to the Dorothy Chandler Pavilion that evening. Duke had to be there early for a television run-through and to be made up. The show would be broadcast around the world live, via satellite. Pilar and the children followed later and took their seats in the audience, next to a seat reserved for Duke. After he completed his portion of the ceremony, he sat in the audience with Pilar to watch the rest of the show.

It was Barbra Streisand who read the names of nominees for

best actor, then opened the envelope: ". . . and the winner is
. . . John Wayne!"

Duke climbed the steps to the stage quickly, his eyes brimming
with tears. He was a sentimental man, and he was easily moved to
tears by beauty, sadness, or such touching moments as this, when
members of the Academy from all phases of the motion picture
business honored him not only for his performance in *True Grit*
but for the body of his work as well.

He stood brushing tears from his eyes for a moment, then said,
"Wow! If I'd known that, I'd have put that patch on thirty-five
years earlier." His acceptance speech was short:

> Ladies and gentlemen, I'm no stranger to this podium. I've
> come up here and picked up these beautiful golden men be-
> fore, but always for friends. One night I picked up two: one
> for Admiral John Ford and one for our beloved Gary Cooper.
> I was very clever and witty that night—the envy of, even,
> Bob Hope. But tonight I don't feel very clever, very witty. I
> feel very grateful, very humble, and I owe thanks to many,
> many people. I want to thank the members of the Academy.
> To all you people who are watching on television, thank you
> for taking such a warm interest in our glorious industry.
> Good night.

He had to go back on location the following morning. Grayson,
who had stayed home with his family in the Hollywood hills
nearby, went over to Duke's hotel bungalow at eight in the morning. They would return to Old Tucson together. Duke wasn't
ready when he arrived. It was one of the few times Grayson had
ever had to wait for him. When Duke finally emerged, he was
happy and smiling and still half drunk. He and Pilar and the
Burtons had celebrated through the night.

As usual, Duke was the first one on the set the next morning.
As a joke, he grabbed a broom on his way out of the trailer, and
when he stepped outside, he waved the broom and shouted,
"Where do I start?" But it was *he* who was surprised. Before him
was a ten-foot-high cardboard replica of Oscar (wearing a black
eye patch) and a banner that read: *We Love Ya, Duke*. Assembled

before the Oscar was the entire cast and crew of *Rio Lobo*—forty people or so—all wearing black eye patches—including Duke's horse.

The *Rio Lobo* company moved to the CBS Studios (on the old Republic Studios lot) in June to do the interiors and to wrap the film. Pilar didn't join Duke, and he stayed alone at the nearby Sportman's Lodge. He hinted to Grayson that he was having marriage problems. "The trouble I'm having now," he said, "is from letting my wife develop a social life of her own in Newport Beach."

About six weeks after finishing *Rio Lobo*, Duke was again stunned by a death in the family. His brother Robert died on July 25 at St. Joseph's Hospital, Burbank, of cancer. He was fifty-eight and was survived by his widow, Patricia. They had had no children. Robert's death had been quick and unexpected and had come just four months after their mother's death. Duke took it very badly. He was now the last of the Iowa Morrisons. He had brought Robert into the movie business with him when he was under contract to Republic. Robert had been a lifeguard in Long Beach at the time. He had never shown much interest in the movie business, but he had looked after Duke's interests as best he could and he had enjoyed the Hollywood life-style. Like his father, nothing bothered Robert much. He was easygoing and almost unflappable.

In accordance with his wishes, Robert was given a nonreligious funeral service at the Scovern Funeral Home in Glendale and was cremated. He and Duke both hated traditional Christian funereal practices; they thought them barbaric. Both had expressed wishes to be cremated and for their friends and family to have something like a wake after the services and reminisce about the good times. Duke wept uncontrollably at the funeral. On reflection, he had apparently found Robert's life less fulfilling than he would have wanted for his kid brother. He expressed the wish that he had bought Robert a hardware store—or had even left him a lifeguard —apparently thinking that such a life would have been more meaningful to him than the movie business had been. But Robert had lived an easy and prosperous life, thanks to Duke, and had apparently enjoyed it to the end.

In October, Duke went back to Durango and filmed *Big Jake* with the Batjac bunch. Eight-year-old John Ethan portrayed his son, Little Jake McCandles, in the film. Then on April 5, 1971, after a four-month break, Duke began filming *The Cowboys*, a Warner Brothers release, with Roscoe Lee Browne and Bruce Dern. Mark Rydell produced and directed the picture. The location site for *The Cowboys* was the San Cristobal ranch near Santa Fe, New Mexico, and Pagosa Springs, Colorado, isolated spots that, for Duke, lacked the comfortable familiarity of Durango. On the locations, he seemed to grow more withdrawn and lonely. He had his good friends like Chick Iverson and Ed Smart, who visited most of his locations, but he needed his family. Robert and his mother were now gone, and he and Pilar were growing more estranged.

Once, while they were shooting on a makeshift sound stage in New Mexico, Duke called to Grayson, who was a distance away, talking to someone, and didn't hear him. Duke got mad, picked up a chair, and threw it across the sound stage, accidentally striking Grayson on the arm with it. Grayson was enraged. Witnesses said later that his complexion went ashen when he realized that Duke had hit him with the chair. He charged toward Duke. "What the hell did you do that for?" he shouted.

"Well, I *called* you, damnit!" Duke said. "And you deliberately ignored me!"

"Like hell I did," Grayson said. "You know better than that! If I'd *heard* you, I'd have come!"

It was a tense moment, but Duke broke the tension by joking. "Kiss me," he said.

"If you do that a thousand more times, you're off the show," Grayson said.

Duke apologized to him for three days.

Such angry outbursts weren't particularly unusual for Duke, of course. He often kicked things and threw things and slammed things down for emphasis. He was tough to work with. He often shouted abusively during such temper tantrums, which is the rea-

son those who didn't know him very well—and some who did—
gave him a wide path or tried to avoid him whenever possible.

"He had fascinating, contrary qualities," Grayson said. "He
was a humble man, without great vanity, but he never wanted to
look bad before others. So there he was, calling me, and I wasn't
answering. Everybody on the sound stage was watching to see
what he would do about it. In effect, his image was exposed. He
felt suddenly undignified, and what better way to regain his image than with a macho action like throwing a chair clear across a
sound stage? Afterward, everyone was privately telling me what
they would have done in my place: they would have belted him or
sued him. They wouldn't have, of course. In an apologetic mood,
Duke was like a big, vulnerable kid, charming and ingratiating.
He couldn't hold a grudge against anyone for long, and those who
really knew him couldn't hold a grudge against him, either."

In July, the company returned to the Burbank Studios to complete the film. Duke had gone down to Newport before reporting
to the studio, and he returned very depressed. Things weren't
going well for him at home. One day he came into makeup drunk.
It was the only time Grayson had ever seen him drink while
working. He showed up for makeup this morning with tears
brimming in his eyes and making no attempt to hide them or his
drinking. He phoned his lawyer and discussed a separate maintenance settlement, and he said of his marriage, "Well, this is the
end."

After a few days, he seemed to have adjusted to the inevitable.
There had been one exterior sequence shot at Pagosa Springs that
had yet to be finished and that everyone connected with the film
had dreaded broaching with him. The script had called for
Duke's character, Wil Andersen, to have a bloody fight with the
film's lead heavy, a character known as Long Hair, portrayed by
Bruce Dern. Duke's character was killed in the scene, and it was
the bloodiest sequence ever made in a John Wayne Western. Mark
Rydell had talked to Grayson a couple of times about the fact that
the script called for a bloody scene and that someone should talk
to Duke about it. A fake broken nose had been fashioned for
Bruce Dern to wear in the scene and throughout the rest of the

picture, and he would be realistically bloodied for the scene. Duke had always opposed such graphic depictions in his films, and neither Mark Rydell nor anyone else had wanted to face Duke with the fact that he, too, had to be scarred up and bloodied. The script called for such a violent scene that it would have been unrealistic for Duke's character to remain unmarked.

On the morning that part of the scene was to be filmed—closeups and the part in which he was to be shot would be filmed later at the studio—Grayson got a call from Rydell, who wanted to see him. He went over to the director's trailer, where several members of the production company had gathered. Again, the problem was raised about "mutilating" Duke.

"Look, Mark," Grayson said, "I can do it if Duke permits me to. But it'll take four makeup men."

"Why four makeup men?" Rydell asked.

"Three are gonna have to hold him down."

That got a laugh, but an uneasy one. The problem remained. Duke could make life miserable on a set over what seemed the most trivial of matters. Now the director wanted him to compromise his beliefs—that graphic violence, like graphic sex, should be left to the imagination. And everyone knew that Duke's reaction to such a suggestion could be volcanic. Finally stunt director Buzz Henry volunteered to talk to Duke about it. He followed Grayson back to Duke's trailer, said hello to Duke and made smalltalk, but then left without saying a word about the upcoming scene.

Nobody wanted to face Duke about it, so Grayson finally said, "Look, Duke, they want me to mutilate you for this scene, and nobody wants to tell you." Then he stepped back, figuring Duke would probably stand up like a shot and run his head through the top of the trailer. But Duke just said, "Bullshit! You know I don't believe in that stuff." Then he paused for a moment, and added, "Well, all right. Go ahead and put the stuff on." It had been as simple as that. He personally didn't like such scenes, but times had changed and he knew that moviegoers expected such realism, whether he liked it or not—although he hated and wouldn't tolerate the extreme, "bodies opening up and liver flying out at you," he'd say. That, to him, was gratuitous and sick.

Grayson had Polaroids of the makeup job he had done at Pagosa Springs so that he could match it for the sequence to be shot on the sound stage, where a forest had been built to match the one on location. That was the day Duke showed up for makeup pleasantly drunk. Grayson duplicated the wounds on his face and slopped the stage blood over his shirt front to match the photograph. Duke looked at himself in the mirror, dripping with stage blood. "For crissakes," he said sarcastically, "why don't you put a little *more* blood on me?"

"I can't," Grayson said. "You drank it."

He went out and did the scene with Bruce Dern drunk, and really enjoyed himself. He entertained the entire company between takes, cutting up, joking. He was very loose and relaxed, and enormously witty and funny that day.

Duke followed *The Cowboys* with a cameo apppearance as a smiling face (in Bob Hope's nightmare) in *Cancel My Reservation*, and finished 1972 with two Batjac Westerns, both filmed in Durango: *The Train Robbers*, with Ann-Margret, and *Cahill, United States Marshal*, with George Kennedy. Both were formula John Wayne Westerns—the last of them he did—and neither measured up to *The Cowboys*, which had been a good film. Duke liked Ann-Margret and enjoyed working with her.

Duke had turned down the lead in *Dirty Harry*, which had become a box-office smash with Clint Eastwood, in order to continue making Westerns, but by 1973, the interest in Westerns had declined and he, too, turned to the increasingly popular police-story genre with the Batjac co-production of *McQ*, with Eddie Albert, Colleen Dewhurst, Clu Gulager, and Diana Muldaur. The film's story line wasn't particularly good, and Duke knew it, but his presence—playing a detective for the first time in his fifty-year movie career—and a fine supporting cast and refreshing location made it a palatable film, despite its loosely organized construction. *McQ* was filmed on location in Seattle, Washington, where Duke had many friends, and he sailed the *Wild Goose* up there and anchored her in the Seattle Yacht Club, which had been her home before he bought her from Max Wyman more than ten years earlier. It was Duke's intention to live on the yacht while he was filming, but he also rented a house for the ten-week stay.

It was while working on *McQ* that he established a relationship with the new love of his life, his new secretary, Pat Stacy. Mary St. John, his secretary of more than twenty-five years, was making arrangements to retire with her husband and was grooming Pat to replace her. Mary had hired Pat while Duke was in Durango filming *The Train Robbers*, and Pat had worked for Batjac for almost a month before she even met Duke. She worked for him as Mary's assistant for a full year before *McQ* was filmed. Had it not been for these facts, one might have sworn that Duke himself had chosen Pat. She was a thirty-two-year-old divorcée, a Southern belle from Louisiana, petite, dark-complexioned, intelligent, with a good sense of humor, large brown eyes, a dazzling smile, and a nice figure. She hadn't been scheduled to go to Seattle, but shortly before the filming was to begin, in the first week of June 1973, Mary St. John hurt her shoulder and couldn't make the trip.

Pat was assigned a small cabin below deck on the *Wild Goose*. Everyone liked her. She was warm and friendly and totally unaffected, and like a child in a toy shop on the sets—wide-eyed and enthusiastic about moviemaking. Her enthusiasm was contagious. Duke saw her in a new light in Seattle. He was despondent over his failing marriage, and he looked up and there she was: small, with large brown eyes, a dazzling smile, and a nice figure. The chemistry and circumstances were right. Their attraction was mutual, and it wasn't long before they were sharing his master stateroom aboard the yacht, under cover of darkness. They were very discreet, but the intimacy they soon developed made their attraction to one another noticeable to the cast and crew. It would be ten months, though, before Duke would commit himself entirely to the relationship.

McQ wrapped in August, and shortly thereafter, Duke and Pilar separated. Pilar made the announcement to the press in November. Under their separate-maintenance agreement, she had taken a house in the Big Canyon section of Newport Beach, not far from the Bayshore Drive house, where Duke remained. Duke went back East in November to present an award to artist Norman Rockwell and to receive one himself, and when he returned to Newport the first week in December, Pilar had moved.

In mid-January 1974, Duke again went back East to accept an award, this one at Harvard University, in Cambridge, Massachusetts. It wasn't an honorary degree, for the invitation didn't come from the university itself but from the staff of its satirical publication, *The Harvard Lampoon:* it was the Brass Balls Award, presented to him for his "machismo" and for his "penchant for hitting people in the mouth." He had been "dared" by the *Lampoon* staff to preview *McQ* at Harvard, and he accepted. As a gag, the organizers had him chauffeured into Harvard Square atop an armored personnel carrier, and he was pelted with snowballs (some of which, he claimed, contained a little iron) all along the way. Once inside the auditorium, he was given a splendid introduction. "We all know what John Wayne stands for," the speaker said, "but we invited him anyway." Then, before the film was screened, Duke was submitted to a half-hour of questioning from the audience. Grayson felt a slight hostility from the audience at first—no doubt because most expected a big, unschooled cowboy —but the hostility was soon dispelled as Duke took the questions in stride and in the spirit with which they were tendered:

QUESTION: Where'd you get that phony toupee?

DUKE: It's *not* phony. It's *real* hair. It's not *my* hair, but it's real.

QUESTION: Has President Nixon ever given you suggestions for your movies?

DUKE: No. They've all been successful.

QUESTION: Do you look at yourself as the fulfillment of the American dream?

DUKE: I don't look at myself any more than I have to.

QUESTION: What have you done with the Watergate tapes?

DUKE: If anyone's taping this show, I hope it's a Democrat; a Republican would surely lose it.

DUKE

The audience was so obviously surprised—and delighted—with Duke's humor that he was given a standing ovation when the question-and-answer period ended. The screening of the film followed, then a formal dinner-dance, with lots of drinking. Duke couldn't have enjoyed himself more.

The following June Duke was in London to make another detective movie, *Brannigan*, produced by Jules Levy and Arthur Gardner. Mike Wayne was the executive producer, and the filming was done on location in London, with the interiors shot at Shepperton Studios. Pat Stacy was along.

It was in London that Duke and Pat's relationship fully developed. Duke rented a beautiful Victorian mansion on Cheyne Walk, just off the Thames, where he and Pat settled for the duration of the picture. About halfway through the shooting, though, Pilar called to tell Duke that she was bringing the children to London for a visit. Pat moved out of the house and into the Penta Hotel during Pilar's relatively short visit.

When Mike Wayne learned of his father's developing relationship with Pat, he seemed annoyed—particularly when Pat and Duke slipped away to Ireland on a long weekend without telling anyone they were going. They just disappeared, and Mike had apparently worried about them. Pilar showed up in London shortly thereafter; she had heard about the trip to Ireland, and some, including Pat, wondered if she had come to London to effect a reconciliation. As had happened when he was married to Josie and to Chata, Duke had found another woman who shared his interests and who was willing to give up her own identity to share his. It was in London that Pilar must have come to the full realization that Duke would not compromise, would not stop running, would not retire with his yacht and his millions and enjoy his twilight years with her and the children. In Duke's eyes, Pilar had abandoned him by becoming someone other than the person he had married. Whether they would divorce would be left to her; he would seek no divorce, partly for the sake of the children, but mostly because he was turning sixty-seven and considered himself too old to begin again. When Pilar left London, they were through. Pat Stacy moved back to the Cheyne Walk mansion.

They finished shooting *Brannigan* in August, and there was the usual wrap-up party for the cast and crew. Duke had been his usual irascible and contrary self to members of the British film crew, but they were a forgiving bunch and liked "Big John," as they called him. At the end of the filming, they presented him with gifts, and they lined up for his autograph and for mementoes. It had been a relatively pleasant shoot. Duke had been in better spirits than usual, owing largely to his diverting excursions to Paris and Ireland with Pat. He even got along with the director, Douglas Hickox.

Within two weeks of their return to the United States, Duke and Pat were on their way up the Pacific coast for the filming of *Rooster Cogburn*, at Grant's Pass and Bend, Oregon. *Rooster* was an original screenplay fashioned by Martin Julian for producer Hal Wallis to capitalize on the success of *True Grit*. It wasn't a sequel but another adventure of the boozy, one-eyed character created by novelist Charles Portis. Stuart Millar directed—or tried to— and Duke's co-star was the incomparable Katharine Hepburn.

Duke and Kate Hepburn had been making movies in Hollywood for half a century, but they had never met—that is, until Miss Hepburn happened to be in London when Duke was making *Brannigan* and she stopped by during the shooting (in Piccadilly Circus) to introduce herself. They had great respect for one another, and just before the filming was to begin, Duke told the Batjac bunch, "I can't take my anger out on her, so I'll have to take it out on you guys." As it turned out, he took his anger out on everyone, but mostly on the director and the assistant director. At times there was so much bad blood between him and Millar that Hal Wallis told Duke if they didn't stop fighting he'd have to replace the director.

"Do you want me to fire him?" Wallis asked.

"Of course I don't want you to fire him," Duke said.

Nevertheless, that didn't keep Duke from making Millar's life miserable throughout the shooting.

He got along well with Katharine Hepburn, but she was a

shrewd judge of character and had him figured out almost immediately. On one of the first shooting days, Millar was in his trailer and, as an afterthought, sent his assistant out to tell Duke something with regard to an upcoming scene. Duke blew up. "Have the director come out here and tell me himself!" he boomed. "Tell him to stop directing us from his goddamned trailer!"

"Look, I'm just the messenger," the assistant said.

"Oh, yeah?" Duke said. "Then give him my *message!*"

Between takes, Miss Hepburn came into Duke's trailer. "You're wasting your energies getting mad at the wrong people," she said. "And what good does it do taking it out on a person who's merely conveying a message? Have you seen where they're setting up for the next shot? Down the road, where there are no *trees*, no perspective! Now *that's* something to get angry about!"

"Then why don't *you* get angry and tell them?" Duke said.

"Me?" she said. "Not me. I'm a pussycat."

"How Machiavellian," Duke said of her when she left the trailer.

One morning he had flowers sent to Miss Hepburn. Later that day, they had a slight difference of opinion about how a particular scene should be played. Finally she stared into his unpatched eye and said, "You want your flowers back?" He had to laugh.

Later he said that the only direction and comments that helped him during the scene were the ones that came from her. They got along very well, on the set and off. She was known for being all business on a picture and for rarely socializing, but she did attend two informal dinner parties during the shooting—one at the producer's rented place, and one at Duke's. Years later, she wrote a perceptive little essay about Duke for *TV Guide*, which was printed September 17, 1977, during the week that *Rooster Cogburn* made its first run on network television. Among other things she wrote of him:

A face alive with humor . . . and a sharp wit. Dangerous when roused. . . . Funny. Outrageous. Spoiled. Self-indulgent. Tough. Full of charm. Knows it. Uses it. Disregards it. . . .

John Ethan and Marisa and Dave Grayson's son, Bruce, visited the location during the shooting. On one of his afternoons off, Duke decided to teach Marisa how to swing a golf club. They were in the backyard of the house he had rented. Marisa was only eight, and they were using one of the irons. Duke stood behind her but didn't step back far enough, and he caught the iron fully in the eye. It stunned him and he momentarily lost consciousness. His eyebrow was cut and his eye swelled and turned a bluish purple. Fortunately, his eye wasn't permanently injured, and it was fortunate, too, that the club had caught him in the left eye, which is the one that "Rooster" wore the patch over.

After the accident, Duke received an affectionate and humorous letter from Melinda, his youngest daughter by Josie. "Lucky Marisa," she wrote, and she went on to tell Duke that Marisa had done exactly what the rest of his children had been wanting to do to him for years.

The film was completed by December. It had been a particularly rough one for Duke, coming as it had with only a couple of weeks' rest after shooting *Brannigan* in London. It had been a physically rough regimen, too. The location at Bend was 3,500 feet above sea level, with rigorous scenes reminiscent of *The African Queen* in Bend's Deschutes River. He had had to use his oxygen inhalator because of the altitude. The shooting schedule had been thoughtfully arranged to accommodate both its aging stars, with many afternoons or mornings or even days off. But rather than resting, he had done a lot of drinking and playing and had often shown up for work not having slept at all the night before, which made him even more impatient and ill-tempered than usual.

His parting with Kate Hepburn had been with the hope that they might get together again soon for a sequel to *Rooster*. The producer spoke of it and apparently some ideas were roughed out for such a picture, but when *Rooster* failed to create much excitement at the box office, nothing came of the idea.

After seven straight months of work, Duke took an entire year off, from December of 1974 to January of 1976. It was one of the longest periods in almost fifty years that he had ever gone without making a film. He did with Pat Stacy what Pilar had been trying to get him to do: he traveled and loafed—well, as near to loafing as he was capable of. He tended to his business matters and made several television appearances—the opening of the John Wayne Tennis Club in Newport Beach, which was covered by *ABC's Wide World of Sports;* Bob Hope's twenty-fifth anniversary show on NBC; a guest appearance on a Don Rickles show; a Howard Cosell interview; an appearance with Frank Sinatra, Bing Crosby, and Bob Hope; and the like. In late March of 1975, he accepted an invitation from the Academy to present Howard Hawks with a special Oscar, and in October, he attended an important dinner: Emperor Hirohito visited Los Angeles and was asked if he had any special requests. The emperor said he wanted to see two things: Disneyland and John Wayne; so Duke attended a banquet given in the emperor's honor, and the emperor got his wish. The occasion made Duke mad as hell, though. He was seated so far from Hirohito that he could barely see him, and the emperor had to go looking for *him* so that the introduction he had requested could be made. The politicians and Los Angeles socialites had all the choice seats.

Pat Stacy moved to Newport that year, staying in a trailer home that Duke had kept for his masseur (Duke later rented the house across the street for Pat; she didn't stay at his place because Aissa, Marisa, and John Ethan often stayed with their dad). She and Duke became inseparable, frequenting the Big Canyon Country Club for lunches and afternoons of cards and backgammon, and sailing to Catalina aboard the *Wild Goose.* In November, they went to his ranch in Arizona for the annual bull sale, an event that he tried to make each year. They rang in the New Year aboard the *Wild Goose* in Mexican waters before returning, finally, to do a picture. There had been a few conferences at his Bayshore Drive home that fall with director Don Siegel on the script of a motion picture to be called *The Shootist.* It was to be his last motion picture.

PART SEVEN

21

THE SHOOTIST—1976

IT was in mid-January, on location in Carson City, Nevada, to shoot the opening scenes of *The Shootist*, that Dave Grayson suddenly realized how old-looking Duke had grown. Even his nose had changed shape; it had grown wider and more bulbous. This realization had come to him early one morning when they were in Duke's suite at the Ormsby Hotel.

He was carrying too much weight, of course. He was up to 265 pounds and was on a salt-free diet, trying to get down to his usual 235 pounds and complaining bitterly about the blandness of the food he was having to eat. That didn't help his disposition. It wasn't the added weight that was making him look older. It was as though an entire decade had gathered like an ocean wave and swept over him all at once.

He turned from the mirror and began putting on his coat and Stetson. Grayson had his own coat on and was closing his makeup case when Duke opened the door to the corridor and turned back to him. "You don't have to go," he said. "They probably won't start shooting on schedule, anyway."

"I'd like to," Grayson said, following him into the corridor and pulling the door closed behind him.

Duke walked ahead, toward the elevator. "Suit yourself," he said.

They said nothing more in the elevator or in the lobby. Duke walked quickly, eyes straight ahead, ignoring the few early-morning arrivals who were startled to see John Wayne striding across the lobby of their Carson City hotel. There was a car waiting at the curb. He nodded to the driver, who opened the door, and he got into the car, taking his Stetson off and resting it on his lap. Grayson got into the backseat, and the driver eased the car from the curb. They drove in silence toward the base of the snow-capped Sierras; the location had been set up just a few miles from town. The streets were still slippery that early in the morning, so the young driver was cautious, but when they finally got out on the open road and he didn't speed up appreciably, Duke got impatient. "You're not going to drive like this all the way out there, are you? *Twenty-five* miles an hour?"

The driver said nothing, but speeded up to about forty-five. Duke turned his attention from the speedometer to the Sierras; he commented on their beauty, but said nothing more. Finally they came to an area where the road made a bend, and they could see the crew off to the side, several hundred yards from the main highway and dwarfed by the magnificent mountains behind them. The driver pulled off the road and eased the car to a stop. Between them and the crew lay a dirt field that sloped gently downhill, rough and deeply rutted with the now-frozen tracks of the film crew's heavy-equipment trucks. It wasn't impassable or dangerous for an automobile, but it was uneven terrain and would be a jarring ride and one that the driver had apparently been told not to make.

"Drive down to the edge of the activity," Duke said.

"They said I'm not supposed to do that, Mr.—"

Duke cut him off, shouting, "Between you and me damnit, I've got a bad *pump* and this car is for *my* convenience! Now, forget what they told you and drive me down there!"

The startled driver did as he was told. It was the first time Grayson had heard anything about Duke's having a bad heart. He had blurted it out in an explosion of anger, out of embarrassment that he found walking a few hundred yards too exerting in Carson City's rarefied 4,600-foot altitude. When the driver finally stopped the car near the crew, Duke climbed out, put on his

Stetson, took a deep breath of the cold mountain air, and the anger was gone.

Director Don Siegel stopped talking to the camera crew for a moment and called out a cheerful greeting, but Duke only nodded, studying the set, taking in every detail, occasionally nodding to a few familiar faces, who kept their distance. Someone brought him a large styrofoam cup of steaming coffee. He stood by himself on the periphery of the set, cradling the cup in his hands to warm them, hands now mottled with liver spots. His only consolation at the moment was that in less than two weeks, the company would be back at the Burbank Studios, where the rest of the picture would be shot on the Western street of the back lot and on a couple of sound stages, at an altitude that did not affect his breathing and sap his strength.

The picture had gotten off to a rocky start with Duke. Producer Mike Frankovich had purchased the film rights to Glendon Swarthout's novel *The Shootist* and had commissioned Scott Hale and the novelist's son, Miles, to do the screen adaptation. Owing to the subject matter, Duke would have seemed the obvious choice to play the part of John Bernard Books, an aging gunfighter dying of cancer. However, the film was first offered to Paul Newman, who turned it down. Then it was offered to George C. Scott, but Scott had read the book and apparently refused to sign for the part unless the script was written in a manner more faithful to the novelist's handling of the story, which was realistic and very earthy. Although the fact wasn't highly publicized in the industry, the role was also turned down by Charles Bronson, Gene Hackman, and Clint Eastwood before it was finally offered to Duke.

Finally, in August of 1975, *Daily Variety* columnist Army Archerd announced that John Wayne was set to play the lead in *The Shootist*, which would be a Mike Frankovich–William Self production, in association with Dino De Laurentiis and Paramount Pictures. Duke asked for and got script approval, and his opinion of the script was the opposite of George C. Scott's. Duke considered even the "sanitized" version of the script (which Scott had objected to) "dirty and vulgar," and so there followed numerous script conferences with director Don Siegel at Duke's home in Newport Beach before Duke finally approved the script. Duke and Siegel got along fairly well during their script conferences, but once the cameras began rolling, the amiability ended. Siegel was a good director and only a few years younger than Duke; he was not a man who would yield to anyone. Of course, Duke was Duke.

The supporting cast was a good one that included Jimmy Stewart, Lauren Bacall, Ron Howard, and Richard Boone. Signing Duke for the lead had automatically solved a problem that the production company would otherwise have had to work on. It had to be established that the protagonist had been a gunfighter all his life, and so with the use of film clips and still photographs from Duke's old Westerns, they were able to show the progression of time, to show Books at various stages of his life, from youth to the age he had attained by the time the story opens. This montage was followed by the first scene, in which the protagonist, John Bernard Books, dressed in a greatcoat and grown old and sick and heavy in the saddle, rides through the muffled stillness of the snowcapped mountains. He is stopped momentarily by a would-be robber, whom he wounds and leaves behind, presumably to contemplate his wayward ways. The shootist then moves on to slip quietly into a peaceful town nestled in the mountain's flanks, where he will eventually learn from the town's doctor (played by Jimmy Stewart) that he's dying of cancer. It was this first scene that the movie company was waiting to shoot in early January on the outskirts of Carson City.

As the sky began to lighten, Duke got ready for the first shot. Siegel, all bundled against the cold, was standing near the camera talking to director of cinematography Bruce Surtees, and Duke finally walked over and conferred with them before mounting his horse and riding off to his mark, a lonely figure of a man, large and riding tall as he always did, yet looking small and insignificant against the mountains.

The rest of the day was spent doing retakes of the scene. Once, while he was waiting for another setup, Duke noticed that a stranger was shooting the still photographs that would be used for publicity and other purposes by the production company. He had requested that photographer Dave Sutton be assigned to the picture; he always used Sutton whenever possible because he was an excellent photographer and a friend who knew what photographs *not* to take. For example, Duke hated to have photographs taken of him getting his makeup touched up with a powder puff, considering such candid views unflattering, unmanly, and not in keeping with his image. It was just such views—contrasting the man and the image—that photographers found most truthful and intriguing. Dave Sutton took such photographs himself, but Duke knew that Sutton would not let them get out of hand.

Duke asked Siegel where Sutton was and learned that the director hadn't known of Duke's request. Siegel said that Al Horowitz, who was in charge of publicity for the picture, had hired the still photographer. The fact that his request had either not reached Horowitz or had been ignored by him irritated Duke, and after a few heated words, it was decided that Sutton would be summoned immediately to Carson City.

Duke was in a far better mood the next day. Sutton had replaced the stranger, and the gray skies had cleared; there were no more weather delays in the filming, and with everyone concentrating on the work at hand, there was much less friction and tension on the set. The calm lasted only a day, though. At 7:15 the following morning, Grayson went up to Duke's suite to make him up, but there was no answer to his knock, so he went to Pat Stacy's adjoining suite, and she let him in. Grayson walked through Pat's suite and through the open doorway that connected her living quarters with Duke's. He got only a few steps into Duke's suite when he realized that Duke and Siegel were having a meeting. "For crissake, Dave," Duke roared at him, "didn't you hear me say to *stay out?*"

Grayson retreated to Stacy's suite and waited there for the meeting to end—though it was more a shouting match than a meeting. Duke yelled, and occasionally Siegel would yell back at him. After a short while, Siegel left and Duke appeared in the adjoining doorway and motioned Grayson in. "Okay, it's all clear," he said, taking a seat before the dressing table in his room.

"I didn't mean to butt in," Grayson said. "I really didn't hear you yell at me."

"No matter," Duke said. Then Duke added, "They always resent you when you start making suggestions."

After a few minutes, Duke said in a less heated and quieter tone, "Siegel's trying to get back at me. I just read the riot act to him."

"About what?" Grayson said.

"The damned script," Duke said. "I told Siegel at our meetings in Newport, for crissakes, that I was against having Books dying of cancer of the *bladder!* That was one of my *main* objections. *Bladder* sounds so damned ugly and unmanly. We settled for cancer of the prostate, but they didn't change the script as they agreed, and I had to make an issue of it."

Just as Grayson was finishing up, Duke again muttered something about Siegel's trying to get even with him. Grayson had no idea what Duke thought the director was trying to get even with him for, although he guessed that Duke had made script changes and directorial suggestions that Siegel might not have totally agreed with. In an attempt to make Duke feel better, Grayson said, "You know, Duke, Siegel's got a reputation as a better-than-average director. Maybe he didn't realize how important the change was to you. Or maybe he just forgot."

"I've contributed more than a small share to this script," Duke said. "There were many production story conferences down in Newport with Siegel and Scott Hale. Probably Frankovich thinks Siegel and Hale did the whole thing themselves, but a lot of this script is mine. So why did Siegel tell the press, 'I know Wayne eats directors, but I'll give him indigestion'?"

The filming that day was a little more harmonious. Duke and Siegel did have a quiet confrontation or two regarding Siegel's direction, but otherwise things went smoothly. That evening, though, Siegel didn't help matters. The cast and crew were screening footage that had been taken of Bacall the previous day, and when the lights came up, Siegel got to his feet and said for everyone's benefit, "It's terrific! Wayne and I did a hell of a job of directing." Siegel got a laugh, but Duke wasn't at the screening.

On the set the following day, Duke happened to see a Polaroid photo Dave Sutton had taken of him. It was simply a continuity photo of Duke wearing his toupee and without a hat, taken only for Grayson's reference, but it had been shot quickly and in front of the house used for exteriors in the film. Duke, no doubt mad about something else, exploded when he saw the Polaroid. "Where's Sutton?" he roared. "He's got the damned *roof* growing out of my head in this still!" Sutton was too far away to hear Duke, but word was passed along that Duke wanted to see him. And, of course, those who passed the word edged over Duke's way to watch the fireworks—anything for diversion on a movie set.

Sutton appeared within a minute or so, wondering what Duke wanted. But before he could even ask, Duke shouted, "You little sonofabitch! I have to bust my ass getting you this job, and you can't even shoot a damned *still!*" Sutton knew that Duke had a high opinion of his work. He knew, too, that the Polaroid wasn't important and wasn't, in fact, what was really bothering Duke. It was just another example of Duke's misdirected anger, and so Sutton eventually kidded Duke out of his snit, saying something like, "Let me see that photo again. By God, you're right, Duke. That is a roof. I thought it was the point on your head!" Those who didn't know Duke well would have been astonished at such a seemingly impertinent remark from a subordinate, but people who worked closely with him, like Sutton and Grayson, knew his moods, knew that he didn't consider himself anointed, and knew, too, that Duke not only expected such banter but sometimes encouraged it as a means of breaking tension.

Within the next day or two, the conflict between Siegel and Duke got worse and broke into the open. Duke made directorial suggestions, and Siegel had obviously had enough of them. During one such encounter, Duke made a suggestion for a shot and Siegel exploded, demeaning Duke in front of the entire cast and crew. This humiliated Duke and he stormed off the set. "If Siegel ever does that again," he said, "I'm gonna let him have it—no holds barred!"

Producer Mike Frankovich became alarmed about Duke and

Siegel's confrontations. Siegel was complaining—with justification—that Duke wouldn't allow him to direct freely, and even director of cinematography Bruce Surtees was complaining that Duke was stifling his creativity. Frankovich realized that such bickering was counterproductive, and he finally put out the word that if it didn't stop, he'd have to replace the director. This wasn't a matter of the producer siding with the star; it was just good business. Whenever a director and a star reach an impasse once they're into the actual shooting of a picture, the director usually goes, regardless of who is at fault. To replace a star would require time and the refilming of all footage in which the replaced star appeared, at great cost.

Much to Duke's embarrassment, the stories of his run-ins with director Stuart Millar on *Rooster* had spread through the industry. After such recent and widely known battles, the thought of Siegel being replaced on the film because of him was a sobering one for Duke. "Hell," he said, "there are a lot of directors I've never interfered with, like Doug Hickox on *Brannigan* and John Sturges on *McQ.* But after my trouble with Millar, if Siegel got fired I'd get all the blame. They'd say I can't work with directors anymore, and I can't have that."

Duke no doubt discussed the problem with Frankovich and probably assured the producer that he'd go at least halfway to patch up his differences with Siegel. To ensure that the cast and crew got the message, too, he waited until their last night at Carson City, and after a screening of the previous day's rushes, he made a point of praising the scenes.

The entire company moved from Carson City to the Burbank Studios the fourth week in January. Paramount had rented space to complete the film there, on Sound Stage 14 and on the Western street of the studio's back lot. The sound stage contained the interiors: the boardinghouse that was run by the widow Rogers and her son, Gillom, portrayed by Lauren Bacall and Ron Howard; the livery stable; the doctor's office; a barbershop; and other sets, including the ornate Metropole Saloon, with its sixty-foot-long bar. A thousand yards of medium-gauge trolley track were laid for the town's horse-drawn trolley, an authentic one that had once been used as a shuttle between El Paso, Texas, and Juárez, Mexico. In the film, after the shootist disposes of the horse and saddle he can no longer use, he takes the trolley from his boardinghouse to the Metropole Saloon, where he has arranged for a shoot-out with an old rival, played by Richard Boone; thus he dies quickly by the gun rather than slowly from the cancer that Dr. Hostetler, played by Jimmy Stewart, has diagnosed as terminal.

Duke and Pat Stacy settled into the Oakwood Garden apartments in Burbank, a few minutes' drive from the studio, and stayed there for the duration of the shooting, going down to Newport Beach only when time allowed. Duke felt better and could breathe easier once they were out of the mountains, and the filming went smoothly for the first couple of weeks on the lot. He got along well with the other members of the cast. He had worked with Bacall on *Blood Alley* and with Richard Boone on *Big Jake*, and he liked them both. He particularly liked Ron Howard, whom he considered one of the best young actors he had ever worked with. Richard Boone never drew a sober breath during the filming, but he made his calls on time, knew his lines, and did his job. Duke said nothing about Boone's drinking.

Duke had worked with Jimmy Stewart on *The Man Who Shot Liberty Valance*, and he admired him. Stewart kept to himself on the set and didn't socialize. Some thought him aloof; he wore a hearing aid, and sound stages are enormous and hollow, with bad acoustics, so he probably had great difficulty hearing. It was only natural that he would avoid getting into conversations. His problem was evident during the filming of his scene in the doctor's office with Duke. Both actors muffed their lines badly and on so many takes that the director finally asked them to try harder. "If you want the scene done better," Duke joked, though half seriously, "you'd better get yourself a couple of better actors." Later he commented in private that Stewart knew his lines but apparently couldn't hear his cues.

There was an obvious effort on Duke's part to keep his temper under control and to get along with the director during the first two weeks in Burbank. He played chess with him between takes and even sided with him on one occasion. Siegel had asked Bacall if she'd report early, ready to work at 8:30 instead of her usual 9:00 call, and Bacall had reportedly told him it was impossible. "If she were working for my company and was asked to report at a certain time," Duke said, "then she'd do it or I'd know the reason why!"

The truce between Duke and Siegel didn't last long. Duke grew more irritable as the filming progressed. His accountant had just finished an audit of his finances and had found that he didn't have as much money as he thought. He was irritated, too, by the diet he was on and the struggle he was having to get his weight down. He was on diuretics, too, because he was retaining too much fluid. One day Grayson looked into the cabinet in Duke's dressing room where he kept the toupees and found a couple of empty glass jars. "What the hell is this?" Grayson said.

"I'm on these damn water pills," Duke said, "and I gotta piss *somewhere*. The toilets are five minutes away."

"Well, just don't piss on the wigs," Grayson said.

The trailers and motor homes of stars were usually parked on the sound stages or just outside them to be used as dressing rooms and lounges. They were status symbols, too: the bigger the star, the larger and more luxurious the motor home, complete with shower and toilet facilities. *The Shootist* sound stage, however, was so crowded with sets that the production company was compelled to use small, vintage trailers without toilet facilities, and so Duke used the jars.

Duke usually used an Apollo motor home, which had shower and toilet facilities, but it was comparatively small and far from luxurious. He was always hitting his head on things and cursing. Grayson found it difficult to do his job in such crowded quarters and with such bad light, and he often complained to Duke, telling him that he deserved a motor home that wasn't built for midgets. Duke always agreed, but he was easily satisfied and he'd forget all about the idea moments later. For years, the Batjac bunch talked about getting him a larger one or having one custom built to accommodate his height, but the idea never got beyond the talking stage. "Hell," Duke said, "if they ever did build me one, they'd probably lease it out to another actor!" He made the statement sardonically, but with admiration, too. Mike Wayne ran a cost-efficient operation, and Duke was thankful for that and left Batjac entirely in Mike's hands. "If he'd been old enough to manage my business interests from the start," Duke said, "I'd never have had money problems."

Fighting on *The Shootist* broke into the open again about mid-February, when Duke got into a shouting match with cinematographer Bruce Surtees and Siegel. Duke came out to do a scene after viewing the rushes with Frankovich and apparently said something about Surtees's camera work. Surtees said he was tired of Duke's trying to tell him how to do his job.

"Somebody has to," Duke said. "You made my face blue and gray!"

"We wouldn't have that problem if you weren't using that damned red makeup!" Surtees said.

They argued for a moment, then Duke dragged Siegel into the argument, charging the director with lack of direction. "If you'd shut up," Siegel told him, "I could direct!" All three shouted at one another until Duke walked off the set. Frankovich joined him, putting his arm on his shoulder and talking privately with him before going over and having a quiet conversation with Siegel as well. Duke cooled down quickly, as usual, and went back to the set, but between takes, he walked around the sound stage muttering about Siegel, "That bastard couldn't get out of a trolley car with both doors open."

Complaining to Duke about his makeup had been a tactical error on Surtees's part, even though he had good reason to do so. Duke was sick of such complaints. He got them on almost every picture he did. He had grown accustomed to a certain kind of makeup ever since his black-and-white film days. It was nonallergenic and a dark tan, and he insisted on using it even for pictures shot in color. It was a perfect makeup for his skin and complexion, and he knew it, but it did create technical problems that could have been avoided had he used a more natural color. Grayson once talked him into trying different shades of makeup, which Duke predicted wouldn't work for him as well as the dark tan, and when Grayson saw the rushes, he had to agree that Duke was right. Unfortunately, unless the cameraman adjusted his camera to balance the red, which could be done, everyone else in the film looked pale or even washed out by comparison, and the color would have to be adjusted in the print-developing process, which could also be done. Still, cameramen and directors were always trying to get him to use a makeup with less red, and Duke always refused. It was his position that skin tones could and should be balanced to the star's makeup, and he was right; but it was a bothersome process. It was apparently Duke's anger about Surtees not correcting the color in the camera—making Duke look bad in the rushes and no doubt prompting Frankovich to get after him about the makeup problem—that sparked the blowup after an uneasy truce.

Eventually Frankovich, too, complained to Grayson about Duke's makeup, explaining that it made Duke appear too red and Bacall too pale. Grayson told him that he was powerless to do anything about the matter. "Duke likes his makeup that way," he told Frankovich, "so you'll have to speak to *him* about it." Later Frankovich told Grayson that he had broached the subject with Duke.

"What did he say?" Grayson asked.

Frankovich laughed. "He told me to get lost."

Duke continued to argue with Siegel, and the director was upset and perplexed. He was talking to screenwriter Scott Hale one evening in the studio parking lot when Grayson came out to his car, which was parked nearby.

"What's bothering Duke?" Siegel asked Grayson. "Why does he attack everybody? You, me, the wardrobe people—everybody. What's the reason?"

"The best answer I've been given to that question," Grayson said, "was from Ralph Volke: don't try to figure it out. In all the years I've been with Duke, I've been unable to."

"I don't know how you put up with it," Siegel said. "He never lets up!"

"I know," Grayson said. "But somehow, despite his temper and abusiveness, there's something basically lovable about the guy. I just can't take his attacks seriously, and I don't feel threatened by them."

"I do like him," Siegel said. "I appreciate his creativity, his suggestions, and I think he's a good actor, too. But his temper tantrums are disruptive."

"I don't pay much attention to his ranting and raving," Grayson said. "I realize that's easier said than done, but his anger is really superficial—and impersonal. Nobody's exempt from it."

Siegel agreed.

After his conversation with Grayson, Siegel became a little more tolerant of Duke's outbursts, and Duke's attention was turned to other irritants on the set. He railed against a famous German still photographer who was visiting the set as the director's guest and had innocently taken a picture of Grayson powdering Duke's face. He roared at the noise of the air traffic from nearby Hollywood-Burbank Airport. He roared louder a few weeks before the filming ended, when one of the supermarket tabloids published a front-page exposé of his romance with Pat Stacy. The tabloid, which was notorious for its use of innuendo and its practice of inventing quotes to support its stories, claimed Duke had said of Stacy, "She's the only girl for me," and claimed Stacy had said of him, "He's my man." Of course, neither Pat nor Duke had said anything of the sort; neither had they talked to anyone connected with the tabloid. But that didn't stop Duke from accusing Stacy of collaborating with the paper. After all, he noted, they had *quoted* her, so she must have talked to them. He seemed to have overlooked the fact that the tabloid had quoted him, too.

There had been the usual phony stories about a romance between Duke and his leading lady, Lauren Bacall, too. And a day or so after the Duke-Stacy exposé appeared, Bacall greeted Duke on the set with a kidding reference to her and Duke's alleged romance. "Yeah," Duke said, "and *now* the bastards have me in love with my *secretary!*" And he went on to tell Bacall the details of the tabloid article, as though it were no more true than the articles alleging a romance between him and Bacall. He really didn't care who knew of their romance, but he didn't want it distorted and exploited. What had apparently bothered him most about the story was that it had claimed Pat was in her early twenties—ten years younger than she actually was—and Duke thought it made him look like a cradle snatcher.

In March, before the film was finished, Duke was stricken with influenza and went home to Newport Beach to recuperate. He hated to hold up production, though, so he returned after only three days' rest, which proved to be a mistake. He soon suffered a relapse, and the company had to close down production for another week. Ordinarily he would have worked through such an illness, but he no longer had the stamina, and with only one lung, he was very afraid of catching pneumonia. He followed his doctor's advice the second time and didn't resume filming until the doctor let him return.

The picture was wrapped the first week in April. At the wrap-up party, the crew lined up for Duke's autograph. "He was the most charismatic actor I've ever known," Grayson said. "He was really quite irresistible. In spite of everything he'd done to alienate some on that picture, they still all wanted his autograph—and these were blasé professionals, not fans. It was quite astonishing, and unprecedented in my thirty years' experience in the business."

It was to be Duke's last wrap-up party, but of course he didn't know that. As usual, he left early. He didn't say good-bye. He just slipped off quietly. Like his experience on *Rooster Cogburn*, the making of *The Shootist* hadn't been pleasant for him. The shooting had had its lighter moments, of course, some laughs and clowning around, but he hadn't felt well and had missed days due to sickness. It just wasn't like old times. He had lived all his professional life for the joy of working, and he was now finding more anguish than joy. That realization had to be devastating to him. For one thing, he was losing his confidence in himself—losing control of his body—and he was angry with himself for that. He questioned the ability of others, like directors Millar and Siegel, even more than usual and probably more for his own perceived shortcomings than for theirs. His last few films hadn't done very well at the box office. He had slipped from the *Motion Picture Herald*'s top-ten list for the second year in a row after dominating the poll for a quarter of a century. And that depressed him. He found consolation in his being voted Actor of the Year in the second annual People's Choice Awards during the filming of *The Shootist*, though. He accepted the award in person and was in high spirits when he reported to the set the next day and received congratulations from the cast and crew.

Duke's problem now was simply age. To paraphrase him, he hadn't become champion by making drawing-room comedies. He made action films. Like an aging heavyweight champion who is suddenly faced with defeat at the hands of an opponent he could have dispatched easily and quickly in his youth, he had suddenly lost his punch and stamina. The making of *Rooster Cogburn* had taken a great deal out of him; it had been as psychologically and physically debilitating as any film he had ever done. The effort had exhausted him. He had labored through it only with great determination and with the aid of his oxygen inhalator. He had even injured his knee doing the raft scene and had had to undergo surgery on it when he returned to Newport Beach. And for a while, he got around only with the aid of a walker and then a cane. When the champion of action pictures looked up from his work on *The Shootist*, his sixty-ninth birthday was less than six weeks away.

22

FELLED AGAIN

DUKE flew into Philadelphia, Pennsylvania, on July 6 by private jet from Cody, Wyoming, where he had appeared as grand marshal in a Fourth of July parade celebrating the nation's bicentennial. The festivities had included a premiere of *The Shootist*. Duke had wanted the picture to be released later, in the fall. He didn't think that a film about a man dying of cancer was the kind of diverting entertainment that drew audiences into theaters during summer-vacation season. Paramount didn't agree, and just ninety days after the picture was wrapped, they rushed it into release. That they did so with comparatively little advertising irritated him. He thought the studio had devoted most of its attention and resources to an enormously expensive remake of *King Kong* and assumed that John Wayne's name on theater marquees was enough to ensure its success, even in summer. He had no such illusions, though, and when it was suggested that he make a short eight-day tour to promote the film during its opening play dates in four cities, he eagerly agreed.

Duke looked good—better than he had looked while making *The Shootist* three months earlier. He and Pat had taken a short vacation in Mexican waters aboard the *Wild Goose* immediately after the picture was wrapped, and he had obviously benefited from the rest, although his voice was still raspy and he still suffered occasionally from shortness of breath.

FELLED AGAIN

Their small entourage settled into suites on the twenty-first floor of the old midtown Regal Hotel in Philadelphia for a two-day stay. A bar had been set up in Duke's suite, where everyone, including visitors, gathered. Grayson hadn't been to Philadelphia in years, so he took the opportunity to get in touch with an old friend, Dr. Victor Satinsky, while he was there. Satinsky was a prominent heart surgeon. Grayson invited him up to the hotel to meet Duke. It was strictly a social occasion, with lots of drinking and storytelling, but Duke eventually got around to discussing his breathing problem with the doctor. Nothing came of the discussion, though. Judging from the angry remark he had made to the driver on location in Carson City, Duke knew or strongly suspected that his shortness of breath was owing to a heart condition, yet he did nothing more about it than mention it casually to a doctor at a cocktail party. He seems to have told no one else of his suspicion, not even Pat Stacy. Grayson wouldn't have known about it himself had not Duke lost his temper in Carson City and blurted it out.

After the Philadelphia premiere of *The Shootist*, an elaborate luncheon was given for the press and Duke made the rounds of each table, chatting with news people and answering questions. He also made an appearance on the popular Mike Douglas network television program, and then he and Pat attended a formal ball given for Queen Elizabeth, who was visiting the United States at the time. From Philadelphia, they went on to Atlanta, Georgia, for two days, and from there they flew to Dallas, Texas, the last stop of their tour. *The Shootist* was generally well received by movie critics, but as Duke had predicted, it was largely overlooked by the public, and he was frustrated that there was nothing more he could do to promote a film that he thought deserving of more attention and far better marketing treatment than it had received.

With no film projects in the offing, Duke concentrated on his numerous other business interests when he returned home from the tour. Most of his efforts were devoted to Deco Industries (an acronym for Duke Engineering Company), which was based on Jamboree Road in Newport Beach. Deco had developed a process for synthesizing oil not only from coal and oil shale but from old tires as well; in fact, the process yielded an extremely high grade oil and other useful by-products from tires, and Duke was enthusiastic enough about it to travel extensively to Europe and the Far East promoting the process. Much to his dismay and frustration, he couldn't get his own government interested in the process, even though he had spent months of his time and energy in an effort to do so and even though he had found interest abroad.

Along with his own projects, he also became a spokesman for a company that mined and marketed an aluminum silicate compound called Product 76, which had numerous uses but was particularly effective as a mine sealant when sprayed in thick, cementlike layers on mine walls to hold down the concentration of methane and radon gases in coal and uranium mines. Duke traveled extensively in 1976 for the company, visiting mines, talking to miners, and pitching Product 76.

He thoroughly enjoyed his role as pitchman, for he believed in the product and he had a particular fondness for mines and mining. He had invested in mining ventures all over the world for more than forty years, and he owned mining property in central and northern California. As with his numerous oil well investments, none of the mines ever paid off—indeed, he probably lost millions of dollars on them over the decades—but he had a prospector's fever and fascination, and someone had only to mention casually a mining venture to have Duke scrambling for his checkbook. It's doubtful that he used the services of investment counselors or brokers. He invested on impulse, and his investment portfolio—if one could dignify his holdings with such a term—looked like something assembled by the Mad Hatter. There were two exceptions: his movie company, Batjac, which was skillfully managed by Mike Wayne, and his multimillion-dollar Arizona Ranch Properties, Inc., a corporation holding interests in Arizona cattle and cotton ranches, including Red Eye Farms, Rio Bravo Ranches, Buckshot Farms, 26-Bar Ranch, and the John Wayne Cattle Company, as well as the largest privately owned cattle feedlot in the United States. Most of his Arizona holdings were brilliantly managed by his friend Louis Johnson. At his death, Duke's interest in the Arizona ranch properties alone was worth more than $6 million.

To supplement his income and to keep active, Duke also signed to do a series of television commercials, the first he had ever done —if one doesn't take into account television appearances he made in the 1960s to promote a "hair restorer" called Hair Trigger. In the fall of 1976, he signed with Bristol Myers to promote their headache remedy, Datril 500. He was paid handsomely for the commercials and given a degree of control over their production, but not enough control to suit him. The first series was filmed at Duke's suggestion in Monument Valley that fall; the last of them was filmed in April 1977. When John Wayne said about the product, "It's strong medicine," people believed him; he could have made a good living making commercials, for he had great credibility, but he found the medium too restrictive and the experience unnerving. The ad agency people knew how to sell a product, and they drove him crazy with their seemingly arbitrary "rules" about what the public would or would not like him to say and do in his commercials. He locked horns with the film crew on almost every detail during the filming. By the time he had fulfilled his commitment, he wanted nothing more to do with the making of television commercials.

Duke also made guest appearances on several television specials that fall, but the highlight for him was a fund-raiser given by Variety Clubs International in his name to build a children's cancer wing in a Miami hospital, a wing that was named after him. The show was an "All-Star Tribute to John Wayne" and was taped at the Burbank Studios on November 6 for broadcast on the ABC television network later that month. It was a black-tie, wine-and-cheese testimonial, hosted by Frank Sinatra and attended by hundreds of film and television personalities. Among those who entertained or gave testimonials were his former co-stars Maureen O'Hara, Claire Trevor Bren, Jimmy Stewart, Lee Marvin, Glen Campbell, Angie Dickinson, and Ron Howard. Duke was seated at the central table with all seven of his children during the show—Pilar and Josie were not in attendance, of course, and Pat Stacy was given a table nearby. Duke made a very funny entrance, walking through a breakaway wall when announced, and at the end of the show, when he was given time to say a few words, he broke everyone up by saying, "Tonight you made an old man and an actor very happy." He paused, looked over at Sinatra, and added, "You *are* happy, aren't you, Frank?"

In December of 1976, Duke entered Hoag Hospital in Newport Beach for corrective prostate surgery. It wasn't a serious operation, but it was necessary and he had put it off for a long time. He was home before Christmas and feeling fine. He was still recuperating at home in late January 1977 when he received an invitation to attend President-elect Jimmy Carter's inauguration and to speak at the preinaugural gala at Kennedy Center in Washington, D.C. Duke was more shocked (and honored) by this invitation than he had been by the one from Harvard, which he had considered a bastion of Eastern liberalism. Carter was a John Wayne fan, and the invitation had been offered at his special request.

At his gala appearance, Duke spoke briefly and sincerely and with electrifying impact. The three-hour show was studded with stars like Paul Newman (whose acting and intelligence Duke greatly admired), Joanne Woodward, Shirley MacLaine, Bette Davis, Linda Ronstadt, Chevy Chase, and dozens of others, many of whom had supported Carter in his bid for election against President Gerald Ford. Duke's appearance in their midst was a stunning curiosity; as everyone knew, he had supported Ronald Reagan's unsuccessful attempt to gain the Republican party's nomination over Ford in 1976.

Pat Stacy recalled that after the show, she and Duke entered a room in which a receiving line had been formed to meet President-elect Carter and Vice President–elect Walter Mondale. When Carter and Mondale saw Duke enter, they excused themselves from their own receiving line and crossed the room to him, thanking him for participating in the gala.[1]

Duke continued working on his other business matters during the early part of 1977 and read movie scripts with the hope of getting back into films. He felt he could ill afford to do any more formula Westerns or detective stories, though, and he could find nothing extraordinary in the screenplays that were being sent to him. But in the meantime, he had an opportunity to get more active in television. In June, the ABC television network made him an offer he couldn't refuse: a two-year, $3 million contract to do just six television specials and to guest on a few of the network's variety shows. A few months later, he was offered another television commercial contract by California-based Great Western Savings, a multibillion-dollar savings and loan company. Duke flatly refused the contract, but Mike Wayne was a friend of one of Great Western's executives, and he interceded, eventually working out a deal that his father found acceptable. Duke signed a three-year contract for a reported $1 million plus, and he was given more artistic control by Great Western than he had been given in his previous series of commercials.

His experience with Great Western was a happy and rewarding one. A very small crew filmed the first series on the ranch of Duke's friend Chick Iverson, at Grant's Pass, Oregon, on October 29, 1977. The commercials were so effective and popular that by the time the second series was filmed, the first series had won numerous regional and national awards and had drawn in new depositors in unprecedented numbers. The budgets for the commercials were increased, and the film crew grew from several people to forty.

Duke kept busy with his television commitments and commercials, but he kept searching for a movie property to do, and he finally found a story he liked, a novel by Buddy Atkinson titled *Beau John*, a 1920s story set in Kentucky. He optioned the movie rights through Batjac and talked a good deal about commissioning a screenplay and making the film (with Ron Howard, he hoped). But it sat on the shelf and never got beyond the talking stage. His commercial and network television commitments kept him fairly busy, of course, but that wouldn't have slowed him down in the past; the desire and need to do another film were there, but his health was deteriorating and he simply lacked the drive and strength to initiate the project. Nevertheless, *Beau John* served him well. Although he gained a degree of satisfaction from his television commercials and appearances, they weren't his work; films were his work and his life, and the *Beau John* project gave him hope, something to live and plan for.

By early March of 1978, Duke was a very sick man. His voice was unrecognizable and almost gone, which troubled him even more than his weakened condition did, for he couldn't work at all without his voice. Consultations with a Beverly Hills voice specialist did him no good, and he became terribly depressed and irritable. He was also bloated from fluid retention, and his weight was up to 250 pounds. It took all the stamina and determination he could muster to attend the American Film Institute's tribute to Henry Fonda; he dragged himself to the award ceremony only out of loyalty to his old friend.

By mid-March, his physical condition was so bad that he entered Hoag Hospital for an angiogram. It was discovered that he had a defective mitral valve in his heart. There was no question that an operation was necessary; the question was whether he was strong enough to survive the trauma of open-heart surgery. It was finally decided that he should see a specialist at Massachusetts General Hospital in Boston, and on October 30 he flew there by private jet and was admitted for several days of testing.

The doctors at Massachusetts General didn't want to operate; they thought the risk factor too great. But Duke was appalled by the prospect of remaining a semi-invalid. When the doctor cited the "risk factor" as his reason for not wanting to undertake the surgery, Duke threatened to jump from the hospital window if he didn't. "Measure your risk factor for that!" he told the doctor.[2]

He went into surgery on the morning of April 3. Besides Pat Stacy, several of his close friends, his sons Patrick and Michael, and his daughters Toni, Melinda, and Aissa gathered in Boston for the vigil. He was on the operating table for twelve hours as his defective mitral valve was replaced with one taken from the heart of a pig. The operation was a complete success, and on April 27, he was released from the hospital and on his way back to Newport Beach by private jet.

He had round-the-clock nurses at Newport for a while, but his recovery was so swift and complete that within three weeks of his return home, he taped a segment at his Newport Beach home for Bob Hope's seventy-fifth birthday television special. He looked great. He had lost about thirty pounds, had recovered his strength, and his voice had returned to normal. He looked and sounded like John Wayne again. He also began talking again about doing *Beau John* and planning to catch up on his ABC and Great Western commitments, but before he had fully recovered— during the first week of June and only five weeks after he had left the hospital—he fell ill with hepatitis and was down again for another six weeks. He spent some of his recovery period with Pat aboard the *Wild Goose* off Catalina Island.

By August, he was back on his feet and back at work. He spent a week taping a General Electric hundredth anniversary special for ABC with Elizabeth Taylor, Henry Fonda, Lucille Ball, and Michael Landon, and then he did another series of commercials for Great Western. During the making of the commercials, he began losing his voice again, and in late September or early October, he suddenly began having severe stomach pains. He suspected he had cancer again, but apparently said nothing to Pat Stacy or his family about his suspicions. Pat tried to get him to see his doctor, but Duke dismissed the idea, saying he couldn't go running to the doctor every time he had a pain. On October 5, however, he made out a new will, with a provision in it for Pat.

In the first week of November, he went East with Pat; his driver, Barney Fotheringham and Dave Grayson to colonial Williamsburg, Virginia, to tape a Perry Como Christmas special. When Grayson was making him up, Duke told him of his stomach pains. "I hope it isn't the big C," Duke said. He could no longer drink liquor, and he was eating mostly fruit. Even the smell of food made him sick.

Grayson saw him again two weeks later, on Sunday, November 19, at Warner Brothers, where he taped the Variety Clubs International tribute to Jimmy Stewart. He was having dreadful stomach pains and had apparently been undergoing tests to determine the cause. He told Grayson that he couldn't pass barium into his liver and that while no diagnosis had been made, it was suspected that the problem might be his gall bladder. "I hope I don't have cancer again," he said. "If these pains are from an ulcer, I'll be happy. I couldn't take another operation again." Despite his illness, Duke made an effort to enjoy himself at the Stewart tribute. A few days later, it was determined that he needed a gall bladder operation, but he put it off for seven weeks.

On Christmas Day, Grayson called Duke to wish him a merry Christmas, and asked how he was feeling. Duke was very worried. "I'm losing a pound a day," he said, "and I can eat only porridge. I think I've got cancer again."

Grayson was shocked by the statement and by Duke's grave tone of voice. It was an awkward moment, and Grayson didn't know what to say. "I'm sure it's probably just your gall bladder or an ulcer," he said.

Duke seemed to ignore Grayson's remarks. "Well, you can't win them all," he said.

On January 8 and 9, 1979, Barbara Walters taped an interview with Duke at his Bayshore Drive home and aboard the *Wild Goose* as part of her tenth special, to be aired on March 13. Miss Walters knew, of course, that Duke had had a lung removed in 1964 and open-heart surgery nine months before the interview, but she didn't know that he was sick again or that he had finally made arrangements to enter the hospital for gall bladder surgery the day after their interview. He carried the interview off well, looking and acting as though he were in perfect physical shape and giving the viewers no hint of his pain or his fear that he again had cancer.

WALTERS: What's your idea of a very good day?

DUKE: Well, getting up in the morning, being still here. That's . . . far as I'm concerned, that's reached a point now . . . I've had enough experience to know that if I open my eyes and look outside, and it's a nice foggy day, it's great. If it's a sunny day, it's beautiful.

WALTERS: If it's *any* kind of day, it's okay, huh?

DUKE: If I'm there.

* * *

WALTERS: Is there a woman in your life now?

DUKE: Well, I have a very deep affection for Miss Stacy. She's young and wonderful and has made my life very comforting. And very exciting at times. She likes to travel and likes the things that I like to do. And I have a very pleasant life with her.

* * *

WALTERS: Off-camera, off-screen, do you like you?

DUKE: I'm crazy about me. I just want to be around for a long time.

WALTERS: To enjoy you. At this point in your life, having faced illness—I guess having faced the prospect of death—are you, do you have a philosophy, or do you have a point of view that you think kind of sums up your thinking today?

DUKE: Listen, I spoke to the Man up there on many occasions and I have what I've always had: deep faith that there is a Supreme Being. There has to be, you know, it's just . . . to me, that's just a normal thing—to have that kind of faith. The fact that He's let me stick around a little longer, or *She's* let me stick around a little longer certainly goes great with me, and I want to hang around as long as I'm healthy and not in anybody's way.

WALTERS: Do you fear death?

DUKE: I don't look forward to it because, you know, I don't care what faith you have; maybe He isn't the kind of father that I've been to my children. Maybe He's a little different; maybe He won't be as nice to me as I think He will. But I think He will.

WALTERS: Has it been a good life?

DUKE: Great for me.

WALTERS: Any regrets?

DUKE: Great for me. Ah, here and there, probably.

WALTERS: If you had it all to do over again, would you—

DUKE: I'd do it the same way.

WALTERS: The same way. Stick around for a while longer, will you?

DUKE: I sure want to.

He entered the UCLA Medical Center the following day. And after the usual preparation and tests, he went into surgery two days later, on Friday, January 12. All his children gathered at the hospital with Pat Stacy and waited. The operation should have taken two or three hours at most, but there was no word to the family for three hours, then four. Finally a doctor was sent up to their ninth-floor waiting room to tell them that Duke was still on the operating table and that he had a cancerous stomach; the entire stomach, together with associated lymph nodes, had to be removed. The operation took nine and a half hours. A new stomach was fashioned from the upper intestine and attached to the esophagus.

The good news was that Duke pulled through the operation well and was out of intensive care three days later. The bad news was that lab tests taken on the lymphoid tissue revealed that the cancer had spread, and the metastasis was so general that further surgery would have been futile. Duke would have to undergo radiation treatments. The family was told that radiation had often proved effective in bringing about remission in such cases.

On February 10, four weeks after he had entered UCLA Medical Center, Duke was home recuperating and undergoing his treatments at Hoag Hospital. He was down to about 180 pounds and fighting to gain weight. Despite the radiation treatments, which were making him nauseous and frustrated and irritable, he was able to eat once again, but he had little interest in food and had to force himself to eat what little he could in order to get his weight and strength back. He continued losing weight. It was an ominous sign, and he knew it and agonized over it.

He had been invited by the Academy of Motion Picture Arts and Sciences to present the Oscar for best picture on Academy Awards night, and he decided to accept the invitation. He didn't feel up to it, but there were rumors in the industry that he was down again and dying, and he felt a great need to prove the rumors wrong. His clothes no longer fit him, so he had a tuxedo made for the occasion. He was failing fast, though, and it was questionable whether he'd have strength enough to make the appearance when the time came. There was a good deal of speculation within the industry that he wouldn't.

On Monday, April 9, the day of the Academy Awards ceremony, Dave Grayson was working on a picture that was filming on location in the San Fernando Valley when he received phone calls from both Pat Stacy and Mike Wayne informing him that Duke would appear to present the award and asking him to make Duke up for the occasion. It was clearly a last-minute decision, and that evening Grayson went to the Los Angeles Bonaventure Hotel, where Duke had taken a suite to prepare for his appearance at the Music Center, from which the awards ceremony would be televised. Grayson arrived at the hotel about six P.M., but Duke was resting and so he didn't go up to his suite. Grayson, Pat, Barney Fotheringham, and thirteen-year-old Marisa went down to a coffee shop for a sandwich. A little later, and in private, Barney tried to prepare Grayson so that he wouldn't be shocked by Duke's appearance; Grayson had talked to Duke by phone but hadn't seen him for almost five months. Barney told him that Duke didn't look well and that he had lost about fifty pounds.

At seven thirty, Grayson was summoned to Duke's suite. Duke was waiting for him, seated in a chair without his shirt or toupee. Nothing Barney told him could have prepared him for what he saw. He was shocked, but tried not to show it. Duke laughed when he entered the suite. "I thought I'd shock you," he said. Grayson felt he had to be honest. "You do look thin, Duke," he said. It was, as Grayson recalls, a colossal understatement, and he was being kind. Duke was pale and had wasted away to half his chest size. And the indelible "tattoo" on his lower chest that was used to mark the focus of his radiation treatments was a dreadful reminder of what he was going through. His face had shrunk to half its normal size, too. Grayson was shaken and deeply touched, but he went about his business as usual. Duke hadn't lost his sense of humor. As Grayson opened his makeup case, Duke looked at himself in the mirror and said jokingly, "I'm looking so damn good, Dave, I don't think I need any makeup."

When he was made up, and wearing his toupee and newly tailored tux, he looked quite handsome—as trim-looking as he had been in youth. They went over to the Music Center, where Duke was given the VIP room, which he shared with Cary Grant. Pat, Grayson, and Marisa were with them. Grant was charming. He talked to Marisa about his own thirteen-year-old daughter. There was a single rose on the table, and Grant gave it to Marisa.

A steady stream of celebrities filed through the room, asking for Duke's autograph. As usual, Duke didn't sit down at all. He seemed his old self, moving around the room, signing autographs for famous people, joking. He mentioned aloud that he'd like a drink (he was able to drink again since his operation), and Cary Grant rushed out and got him one. There was a television monitor in the room, and Duke occasionally watched the show as it progressed. It wasn't progressing fast enough for Duke, though. It went on and on, and he finally began to get impatient. "I'll never get on at this rate," he said. As he watched, Steve Lawrence —who ordinarily performed with his wife, Eydie Gorme—was teamed with Sammy Davis, Jr., and they were doing a long medley of songs. Duke, who knew and liked them both, said, "I recognize Steve Lawrence, but Eydie doesn't look at all like she used to."

When he was finally announced and went out to present an Oscar to the producers of *The Deer Hunter*, Duke was given a standing ovation and was very moved by the reception. "That's just about the only medicine a fellow would ever need," he said. "Believe me when I tell you I'm mighty pleased that I can amble down here tonight. Oscar and I have something in common. Oscar came to the Hollywood scene in 1928. So did I. We're both a little weatherbeaten, but we're still here and plan to be around a whole lot longer. . . ."

The Academy Awards show was Duke's last public appearance. Nine days later, on Wednesday, April 18, he was rushed to Hoag Hospital with what was eventually diagnosed as pneumonia. He responded to treatment well and was ambulatory within three days and home again by the following Wednesday. The cancer and side effects from the radiation treatment were ravaging, however, and he became sicker and weaker and more depressed. Pat Stacy revealed later that while Duke was confined to Hoag those seven days, he had asked his son Patrick to bring him his .38 pistol. Like John Books in *The Shootist*, the time had come when he no longer wanted to suffer through the kind of life he was leading. Patrick had naturally refused to get the gun, so Duke made the same request of Pat Stacy the following day, telling her, "I want to blow my brains out."[3] He railed against her when she, too, refused his request. Duke apparently thought the doctors at Hoag were keeping something about his condition from him and that he might not leave the hospital alive. But when he was discharged on Wednesday, April 25, he said no more about killing himself.

His friends kept him occupied for the next few days. He received countless phone calls. Maureen O'Hara came to visit for a day, and Duke was so cheered by her presence that she was encouraged to stay for three days, and she did. Claire Trevor Bren and her husband, Milton, stopped by one afternoon, too, as did Yakima Canutt, whom Duke invited out to discuss some ideas for Great Western commercials—Duke still talked of work even though he couldn't actually do it.

On the evening of May 1, Duke doubled over with excruciating abdominal pain and Pat drove him to Hoag Hospital. X-rays revealed an intestinal blockage, and he was immediately taken to UCLA Medical Center, where he was operated on the following morning. An intestinal bypass was performed and tissue samples were taken. It was several days before the lab studies on the tissues were completed. Meanwhile Duke was moved from intensive care to a private room the following day. More people than he had strength to see wanted to visit him, so for the most part, only his family and closest friends were allowed. President Carter visited him on the fifth. Over the next few days, he was visited by Jimmy Stewart, producer Paul Keys, Frank and Barbara Sinatra, Archbishop Marcus McGrath of Panama, who was the brother of two of Duke's Panamanian friends, and director Henry Hathaway.

Several days after his operation, the lab tests were completed; cancer had spread throughout his body. On May 11, the doctors began giving him immunotherapy, a then relatively new treatment that entailed injecting chemicals to stimulate the body's own immune system. Radiation hadn't worked, and while immunotherapy had been modestly successful in the treatment only of small cancers in their early developmental stages, each individual's immune system responded differently, and so doctors thought it worth a try. The therapy did no good, though, and by the end of the month it was discontinued.

Duke's seventy-second birthday was on May 26, but he had such a bad day that he was given an injection of morphine and he slept through it. He was feeling better the following afternoon; Pat and his children brought in a birthday cake and presents, and sang "Happy Birthday" in an effort to cheer him. He did as good an acting job as he could under the circumstances, but he had neither the strength to open his presents nor the interest in doing so, and they were sent down to Newport Beach unopened. There was one gift that did lift his spirits, though. On May 3, Representative Morris Udall and Senator Barry Goldwater sponsored a bill to mint a special gold medal to honor him. President Carter supported the legislation, and it was approved unanimously by the Senate. Maureen O'Hara and Elizabeth Taylor testified before a House subcommittee on May 21, urging passage of the special legislation. Tearfully Miss O'Hara said, "Please let us show him our appreciation and love. He is a hero, and there are so few left." The subcommittee approved the measure that afternoon. Such legislation had been enacted only eighty-three times; congressional medals had been given to such Americans as George Washington, Thomas Edison, Robert Frost, the Wright brothers, Dr. Jonas Salk, and Robert Kennedy. Duke's was the eighty-fourth such medal. It bore a landscape of Monument Valley on the back and his portrait on the front, with an inscription suggested by Maureen O'Hara: "John Wayne, American." He never lived to see the medal, but he was proud to know that he was being so honored.

Duke had been given occasional morphine injections for pain since he first entered the hospital, but on May 29, they began administering morphine intravenously. X-rays had shown that his intestines were almost totally blocked by adhesions. He had only days to live. One of the doctors told Pat Stacy, "I think we should just leave him alone now."[4]

On June 5, he was taken off intravenous nourishment. To have left him on it would have prolonged his agony and increased his pain. Duke had fought the disease as long as he had strength. He had insisted on taking short daily walks in the corridor even into the third week in May—at first on his own, and then, as his strength left him, leaning on Patrick and Michael for support.

On June 8, he drifted in and out of a comatose state throughout the day, and it was thought that it would be his last. He spent the entire day of June 9 in a coma. As so often happens in such cases, he suddenly came out of it at about nine that night, bright and alert and feeling no pain. Fortunately Pat Stacy and all the children were there. He joked with them and laughed and asked to watch television with them for a while, which he did. He recognized everyone and seemed to know where he was, but the time element was apparently out of sync for him, and he kept talking as though he were still making television appearances and films. He remained alert and seemingly lucid for about three hours. Then, about midnight, he slipped into a coma again and remained that way for the rest of the next day and night. On the morning of June 11, while Pat was waiting for the morning nurse to come on duty and was standing at Duke's bedside, he suddenly opened his eyes for a few minutes, staring blankly, and Pat asked him if he recognized her.

"Of course I know who you are," Duke said. "You're my girl. I love you."[5]

They were apparently his last words. He sank into a coma again and never regained consciousness. He died at 5:23 P.M. that evening of June 11, and was officially pronounced dead at 5:30. He was survived by Josie and Pilar, by his seven children, and by twenty-one grandchildren.

Michael Wayne made the funeral arrangements. The body of Charlie Chaplin had been exhumed and held for ransom a year or so earlier, and it was presumably with this fact in mind that Mike took elaborate security precautions. Round-the-clock guards were assigned to Duke's body. The mortician, Joseph O'Connor, was sworn to secrecy. Duke's body was taken from the hospital to the Laguna Hills Mortuary, a few miles southeast of Newport Beach, before his death was announced later that night. Even the flowers for his funeral were ordered in someone else's name—that of son-in-law Gregory Muñoz, Melinda's husband.

The Los Angeles County Board of Supervisors ordered the flags of all county buildings flown at half-mast until after Duke's funeral. His death made headlines across the nation and in many countries abroad. Tributes were paid to him in the press by statesmen and entertainers alike, but none expressed the sentiments of his fans better than President Jimmy Carter, who said, "He was bigger than life. In an age of few heroes, he was the genuine article. But he was more than a hero; he was a symbol of many of the qualities that made America great. The ruggedness, the tough independence, the sense of personal courage—on and off screen—reflected the best of our national character."

He was given a Catholic funeral at 5:45 A.M. on June 15 at Our Lady Queen of Angels parish in Newport Beach. Archbishop McGrath conducted the mass. The time and place of the funeral were kept secret. Only the family and a few of Duke's intimate friends attended; none of his celebrity friends was invited. He was buried at Pacific View Memorial Park in Newport Beach, in a plot overlooking the Pacific. Two graves were dug in preparation for his burial. After he was buried in one of them and the mourners had left to gather at Pilar's home for a breakfast reception, the flowers that had covered his grave were moved to the mound of the freshly dug and empty grave—to deceive potential vandals or others who, it was feared, might disturb his final resting place.

According to Duke's will and probate papers, he left an estate that was ultimately valued at more than $17 million. Batjac went to his son Michael, who continues to operate the company. The will provided a generous income for Josie and the means to administer his separate-maintenance agreement with Pilar. Pat Stacy was left $30,000, and Mary St. John was given $10,000. The remainder was divided equally among his seven children.

Duke's Catholic funeral and burial raises questions that are impossible to disregard. Three days after his death—and a day before his funeral—it was publicly revealed that he had converted to Catholicism. The news story alleged that on Saturday, June 9, he was suffering great pain and that his son Patrick had asked if he wanted to see a priest. Duke is said to have replied that he thought it a good idea; a priest was immediately summoned, and he was baptized. According to eyewitnesses, however, he was in a coma the entire day that he is alleged to have converted.[6]

His burial was puzzling, too. Duke hated funerals and found burial rites "medieval and primitive." When he was in his midsixties, he said, "I'd prefer to be cremated—anything rather than be buried in a box."[7] He also talked of having his ashes strewn in the sea between Newport Beach and Catalina Island. He made no such provision in his will, however, and today he lies buried in a box by the sea.

At this writing—five years after his death—Duke's grave is still unmarked. Fans from the world over who visit the cemetery and who bring flowers for his grave are told to leave them at the base of the cemetery's flagpole. On orders from the family, the cemetery attendants may not reveal the location of Duke's grave.

In a sense, the disposition of his remains is not important. Marion Mitchell Morrison lies in an unmarked grave by the sea, but to his fans the world over, John Wayne lives.

NOTES AND REFERENCES

CHAPTER 1

From the recollections of Dave Grayson, Robert Slatzer and Wilson S. Hong.

CHAPTER 2

1. Kendall Williams and Sue McKean, a John Wayne Genealogy. The research of this genealogical study of the Morrison family formed the basis of an article by Lisa Ray Clewer in *Roundup* (published by Great Western Savings). Marion Morrison sustained a gunshot wound to his head and one across his nose and below his eye. A conical-ball slug was still embedded in the top of his head—and maggots had infested the wound—when he reached the hospital.

2. Several biographers have assumed that Clyde was a pharmacist, and one claimed him a graduate of Simpson College at Indianola, Iowa. According to Simpson's registrar, Miriam B. Jenkins, there's no record of Clyde ever attending Simpson. In fact, there's no evidence that Clyde spent more time in college than his one semester at Iowa State. All indications are that he was a pharmacist's clerk, not a pharmacist; he may have worked as a lay pharmacist in Iowa, for this was before strict regulation of pharmaceutical dispensaries.

3. Katheryne Smith Dansforth, narrative of a holograph letter filed with the Madison County Historical Society, Winterset, Iowa, by a friend of hers. Until this narrative was filed in 1976, the location of the

house of Duke's birth had been in dispute. Katheryne Smith, at age sixteen, had been close to Molly Morrison; her parents, Chris and Jesse Smith, were among Clyde and Molly's first friends in Winterset. Katheryne's mother, Jesse V. Smith, was a medical doctor and helped deliver scores of Winterset residents. Although no record exists of Molly Morrison's attending physician, it was most likely her friend Dr. Jesse V. Smith. The narrative from Katheryne's friend says, in part, ". . . I still have Kate's [Katheryne's] letter saying she definitely knew [that the house at 214 East Court Avenue was the one in which John Wayne was born], in fact went to that house and held the infant in her arms the day he was born. Kate's letter states she is positive her mother delivered the baby, or she would not have heard the news so early in the morning. . . ." The house on Court was razed, and a larger one now stands in its place.

4. The Second Street house still stands, and is open to the public from May through October. It's occupied by the Winterset Chamber of Commerce and was officially dedicated the "John Wayne House" in a ceremony held during Winterset's annual Covered Bridge Festival in 1982. The Chamber uses one room of the house as an office, and has furnished the kitchen and parlor with period furniture of Clyde and Molly's day. The fourth room is used to display photographs and exhibits relating to Duke's movie career.

5. Maurice Zolotow, *Shooting Star, A Biography of John Wayne* (New York: Simon & Schuster, 1974).

6. Ibid.

CHAPTER 4

1. James Gregory, an interview with Duke, *Photoplay*, November 1972. Duke is quoted as saying about his family's move from Iowa to California: "His [Dad's] father, who lived out there [California], had suggested that he ought to go out in the desert and homestead, which he did." Duke was referring to his paternal grandfather, Marion Mitchell Morrison.

2. An interview, *Playboy*, May 1971. Duke is quoted as saying about movie people changing his name: "My real name, Marion Michael Morrison, didn't sound American enough for them. . . ."

3. Mrs. Esther Guzman told us in 1983 that she had been on the Glendale High School staff for thirty years and that "the arrangement with Mr. Wayne" had long been in effect when she joined the staff.

4. James Gregory, op. cit.

NOTES AND REFERENCES

CHAPTER 5

1. Robert W. Waste, Glendale *News Press*, February 9, 1973; reprinted June 12, 1979.

2. Glendale *Evening News*, March 9, 1920.

3. Previous biographers have claimed that Clyde owned or had an interest in a business or two in Glendale; his contemporaries say he did not. City directories of the period indicate no business interests and list him as a druggist in the employ of others.

4. Mrs. Ellen Perry, a native Glendalian and feature writer for the Glendale *News Press*, interviewed many of Clyde and Molly's contemporaries in the 1970s; the interviewees didn't wish to be quoted, but their general impressions were corroborated by others we interviewed.

5. These general impressions of Clyde and Molly are derived from interviews with two of their contemporaries, both of whom requested anonymity.

6. Pexy Eckles had reservations about our quoting him at length; he felt our doing so might seem to exaggerate his role in Duke's life. For this reason, he had refused interviews with other biographers. "I don't want the impression given that I was Duke's *only* friend or that we palled around together constantly," he told us. "Certainly Duke was one of my closest friends, and I was one of his. But we each had other close friends, and we each had separate groups of friends in addition to our mutual friends."

7. Maurice Zolotow, *Shooting Star, A Biography of John Wayne* (New York: Simon & Schuster, 1974).

8. Ibid.

9. James Gregory, an interview, *Photoplay*, November 1972.

10. Ibid.

11. Norman Nelson, Glendale *News Press*, June 12, 1979. An uncredited interview with Nelson, who was Duke's former classmate.

12. James Gregory, *Photoplay*, November 1972.

13. Mrs. Barbara Boyd, Special Collections Librarian, Glendale Public Library.

14. Maurice Zolotow, *Shooting Star*.

15. Ibid.

NOTES AND REFERENCES

16. Mr. Vic Pallos, Director of Public Information, Glendale Unified School District, recalled seeing a copy of the remembrances, which have since been misplaced or lost.

17. Al Ames, Glendale *News Press.*

CHAPTER 6

1. Zolotow, *Shooting Star.*

CHAPTER 7

1. At least one biographer has claimed that Duke had learned his famous rolling-gait walk from Yakima Canutt. Western film historian Colin Momber pointed out to us that Duke's distinctive walk was evident in the films he made before meeting Canutt. We asked Pexy Eckles, and he said Duke always walked like that, even as a youngster. "I'll tell where he got it," Pexy said. "He came by it naturally; his father, Clyde, walked exactly like that, too."

2. Raoul Walsh, *Each Man In His Time* (New York: Farrar, Straus and Giroux, 1974).

CHAPTER 8

1. Walsh, *Each Man In His Time.*
2. Ibid.

CHAPTER 10

1. Duke's previous biographers have proclaimed *Riders of Destiny* the first singing-cowboy film and Duke the first singing cowboy. One claimed he sang in the film; others that Smith Ballew dubbed his voice. Colin Momber of London, England, a Western film historian, told us that Duke "sang" in four Westerns: *Riders of Destiny* and *The Man From Utah,* both dubbed by Jack Kirk, and *Westward Ho* and *The Lawless Range,* which were dubbed by Glenn Strange. Other cowboy stars had sung in films before Duke appeared as Singing Sandy—Ken Maynard, for example, in *Mountain Justice* and *Fargo Express*—but none of the stars was a singer and none of the films could be considered in the singing-cowboy genre. The first singing cowboy was Gene Autry, whom Nat Levine brought to Hollywood from Chicago and with whom Levine established the genre.

2. Contrary to the claims of many biographers, Robert North Bradbury was not the father of cowboy actor Bob Steele. Steele was the

screen name of Duke's boyhood friend Bob Bradbury; his father was William Bradbury and was not related to the director of Duke's Lone Star Pictures.

CHAPTER 11

1. One biographer claimed that Duke tried to give up acting during this period and that he tried his hand and failed at being a stockbroker, a realtor, and a professional prizefighter. There is no truth to the claims.

CHAPTER 13

1. A biographer claimed that Duke tried three times to enlist and that he flew to Washington, D.C., in an effort to join John Ford's naval unit, but that an old football injury precluded his being accepted. The biographer had interviewed Duke, but did not claim that Duke told him this and did not cite the source. This is the same biographer, however, who claimed Duke quit acting to become a prizefighter, and other such nonsense. A source very close to the Batjac organization told us that he, too, had heard that Duke had been rejected for service because of a broken eardrum and a bad shoulder. Had there been any truth to the claims, however, Duke would surely have made it known; he was scrupulously honest about such matters. But he made no such claim.

2. Zolotow, *Shooting Star.*

3. This, of course, is Duke's side of the story, as related by friends. While it apparently contained a grain of truth, it's a biased and no doubt exaggerated view. The late Sylvia Picker McGraw, who was under contract to William Fox Studios when Duke was there in 1930 and who had known him ever since, told us that Duke said the reason his marriage to Josie failed was, in his words, "Because I was up to my ass in Catholics."

CHAPTER 14

1. Los Angeles *Examiner*, October 29, 1953.
2. Ibid.

CHAPTER 15

1. Los Angeles *Examiner*, September 7, 1958.

NOTES AND REFERENCES

CHAPTER 16

1. Oscar Millard, Los Angeles *Times* Calendar section, June 28, 1981.

2. Ibid.

3. Axel Madsen, *John Huston* New York: Doubleday & Company, Garden City, 1978.

4. Ibid.

5. Ibid.

6. John Huston, *An Open Book* New York: Knopf, 1980.

7. Chicago Tribune-New York News Syndicate, October 24, 1960.

CHAPTER 17

1. Writers and industry people have speculated that Ford's arrival on location was an embarrassment to Duke because it raised the question of whether Ford was the guiding light behind the filming of *The Alamo*. No one who understands the complexity of a director's role in preparation for filming such an epic would seriously entertain this notion. As *The Hollywood Reporter* announced several months before the filming, Ford had agreed to direct the scenes in which Duke appeared; that's why he was in Brackettville. Later Ford remarked that he had gotten good second-unit footage, but that it had been cut from the film; some inferred he said this to cover his real reason for being there. It wasn't.

2. *The Hollywood Reporter*, January 11, 1960.

3. Dick Williams, Los Angeles *Mirror*, March 20, 1960.

4. Ibid.

CHAPTER 18

1. Dean Jennings, *Saturday Evening Post*, October 27, 1962.

2. *Playboy*, uncredited interview, May 1971.

3. Jennings, op. cit.

4. Carl Foreman, *Punch*, August 14, 1974. An article written on the occasion of Duke's London visit to film *Brannigan*.

5. Ibid.

6. *Playboy*, op. cit.

7. Foreman, *Punch*, op. cit.

NOTES AND REFERENCES

8. Ibid.
9. *Playboy*, op. cit.

CHAPTER 19

1. *Newsweek*, May 4, 1959.
2. Ibid.
3. Jennings, *Saturday Evening Post*, October 27, 1952.

CHAPTER 20

1. Ranata Adler, New York *Times*, June 20, 1968.

CHAPTER 22

1. Pat Stacy, *Duke, a Love Story* New York: Atheneum, 1983.
2. Ibid.
3. Ibid.
4. Ibid.
5. Ibid.
6. A hospital employee who was in a position to know but who asked not to be named told us that Duke was no longer in control of his faculties on June 8 and was in a coma on June 9, when it is alleged that he converted. Pat Stacy's memoirs (cited previously) corroborate this; Stacy does not dispute Duke's conversion but fails to mention at what date or time it occurred. She was at Duke's side throughout his final days, however, and meticulously details each day. According to her, Duke was "unconscious" the entire day of June 9, and he didn't regain consciousness until late that night, when he spent three apparently lucid hours with his family before sinking again into coma.
7. Mike Tomkies, *Duke, the Story of John Wayne* Chicago: Henry Regnery Company, 1971.

FILMOGRAPHY

DUKE appeared in 153 feature-length films, 3 serials of 12 chapters each, and numerous shorts, documentaries, commercials, and promotional and industrial films. The following is a chronological listing of his major films, together with release dates and abbreviated credits.

Brown of Harvard (MGM, 1925). Cast: William Haines; Jack Conway; Francis X. Bushman, Jr.; Mary Brian. Duke cited this as his first appearance on film, a collegiate football picture in which he doubled on the playing field for Francis X. Bushman, Jr. Pexy Eckles was an extra in grandstand scenes. Neither received billing.

Bardelays the Magnificent (MGM, 1926). Cast: John Gilbert; others unknown. Duke's participation in this film has been heretofore unknown. Pexy Eckles recalled it during our interview with him. Duke portrayed one of several spear-carrying guards gathered around a gallows where Gilbert was to be hanged. Pexy doubled for Gilbert; neither he nor Duke was billed.

The Drop Kick (First National, 1927). Dir., Millard Webb. Cast: Richard Barthelmess, Barbara Kent, Dorothy Revier. Duke and Pexy were grandstand extras in this football picture; neither received billing.

Hangman's House (William Fox Studios, 1928). Dir., John Ford. Cast: Victor McLaglen, June Collyer, Hobart Bosworth. Duke got his first close-up in this film as a racetrack spectator; he was unbilled.

Words and Music (William Fox Studios, 1929). Dir., James Tinling; prod., Chandler Sprague. Cast: Lois Moran, David Percy, Helen Twelvetrees, William Orlamond. Duke received his first screen credit in this college musical; he was billed as Duke Morrison. Another bit-part player named Ward Bond became his closest friend.

Salute (William Fox Studios, 1929). Dir., John Ford. Cast: George O'Brien, Helen Chandler, Stepin Fetchit, Joyce Compton. An Army-Navy football rivalry film. Duke played a bit part as a naval cadet on and off the football field. He was billed as Duke Morrison.

Men Without Women (William Fox Studios, 1930). Dir., John Ford. Cast: Kenneth MacKenna, Paul Page, Frank Albertson. Story of a disabled submarine trapped on the ocean floor. Duke has a small part as a sailor relaying messages between the commanding officer and the rescue divers.

A Rough Romance (William Fox Studio, 1930). Dir., A. F. Erickson. Cast: George O'Brien, Helen Chandler, Antonio Moreno, Eddie Borden. Duke has a few lines in this outdoor adventure, filmed in the Oregon forests; billed as Duke Morrison.

Cheer Up and Smile (William Fox Studio, 1930). Dir., Sidney Lanfield. Cast: Arthur Lake, Dixie Lee, Whispering Jack Smith. Duke played a college student in this campus musical comedy; billed as Duke Morrison.

The Big Trail (William Fox Studio, 1930). Dir., Raoul Walsh. Cast: John Wayne, Marguerite Churchill, El Brendel, Tully Marshall, Tyrone Power, Sr. Duke's first starring role and his first appearance and billing as John Wayne. A pioneer trek on the Oregon Trail, from Missouri to Oregon.

Girls Demand Excitement (William Fox Studio, 1931). Dir., Seymour Felix. Cast: Virginia Cherrill, John Wayne, Marguerite Churchill, Helen Jerome Eddy. Another collegiate story; Duke plays a college student, leading the men in an effort to get female students out of the student body.

FILMOGRAPHY

Three Girls Lost (William Fox Studio, 1931). Dir., Stanley Lanfield. Cast: Loretta Young, John Wayne, Lew Cody, Joyce Compton. Comedy-drama about a trio of girls in the big city who get involved with racketeers.

Men Are Like That, also released earlier under the title *Arizona* (Columbia, 1931). Dir., George B. Seitz. Cast: Laura LaPlante, John Wayne, June Clyde, Forrest Stanley. Duke plays a young army officer falsely accused of making romantic advances toward the wife of his commanding officer. It was while making this film that Duke became persona non grata with studio mogul Harry Cohn for making romantic advances toward an actress Cohn himself had designs on. (British title: *The Virtuous Wife.*)

The Deceiver (Columbia, 1931). Dir., Louis King. Cast: Lloyd Hughes, Dorothy Sebastian, Ian Keith, John Wayne. Duke doubled as Ian Keith's corpse in this film, a consequence of his falling out with Harry Cohn.

Range Feud (Columbia, 1931). Dir., D. Ross Lederman. Cast: Buck Jones, John Wayne, Susan Fleming, Ed LeSaint. Duke plays a young rancher falsely accused of murder.

Maker of Men (Columbia, 1931). Dir., Edward Sedgwick. Cast: Jack Holt, Richard Cromwell, Joan Marsh, John Wayne. Duke plays an antagonist in this college football picture. It was his last film for Harry Cohn and for Columbia, although two films he had done prior to this were released later.

The Voice of Hollywood, number 13 (Tiffany, 1932). Dir., Mark D'Agostino. Cast: John Wayne, George Bancroft, El Brendel, Jackie Cooper, Gary Cooper, and Lupe Velez. Duke was the emcee for this twelve-minute short.

Shadow of the Eagle (Mascot, 1932). Dir., Ford Beebe; prod., Nat Levine. Cast: John Wayne, Dorothy Gulliver, Yakima Canutt. In his first twelve-chapter serial, Duke played a skywriting carnival stunt pilot who pursues and eventually apprehends and unmasks The Eagle, a villain who writes his evil intentions in the sky before carrying them out.

Texas Cyclone (Columbia, 1932). Dir., D. Ross Lederman. Cast: Tim McCoy, Shirley Grey, Wheeler Oakman, John Wayne. Story of a former rancher (Tim McCoy) who suffers from amnesia and regains his memory at film's end; Duke is his sidekick and has very few lines in the film.

Two Fisted Law (Columbia, 1932). Dir., D. Ross Lederman. Cast: Tim McCoy, Alice Day, Tully Marshall, John Wayne. McCoy plays a rancher who is cheated out of his ranch and eventually regains it; Duke is his sidekick.

Lady and Gent (Paramount, 1932). Dir., Stephen Roberts. Cast: George Bancroft, Wynne Gibson, Charles Starrett, James Gleason, John Wayne. Duke plays a young prizefighter who, by film's end, is a scarred has-been.

The Hurricane Express (Mascot, 1932). Dirs., Armand Schaefer and J. P. McGowan; prod., Nat Levine. Cast: John Wayne, Shirley Grey, Tully Marshall, Conway Tearle. Duke plays an airline pilot who chases and finally captures a villain known as The Wrecker in this twelve-chapter serial about the rivalry between the airlines and the railroad.

The Hollywood Handicap (The Thalians Club–Universal, 1932). Dir., Charles Lamount; prod., Bryan Foy. Cast: John Wayne, Anita Stewart, Bert Wheeler, Tully Marshall, Dickie Moore. Duke was a guest in this two-reel comedy, which was one of a series produced by the Thalians, of which he was a member.

Ride Him Cowboy (Warner Brothers, 1932). Dir., Fred Allen; prod., Leon Schlesinger. Cast: John Wayne, Ruth Hall, Harry Gribbon, Henry B. Walthall. In this remake of a Ken Maynard film, utilizing Maynard trick-riding footage, Duke tames "Duke, the Devil Horse" and hunts down a murderer. (British title: *The Hawk.*)

The Big Stampede (Warner Brothers, 1932). Dir., Tenny Wright; prod., Leon Schlesinger. Cast: John Wayne, Noah Beery, Mae Madison, Luis Alberni. Another Maynard remake. Duke plays a sheriff who brings a ruthless cattle rustler to justice.

Haunted Gold (Warner Bros., 1932). Dir., Mack V. Wright; prod., Leon Schlesinger. Cast: John Wayne, Sheila Terry, Erville Alderson, Harry Woods. A remake of the Maynard film *Phantom City;* Duke battles the Phantom for an abandoned gold mine.

FILMOGRAPHY

The Telegraph Trail (Warner Bros., 1933). Dir., Tenny Wright; prod., Leon Schlesinger. Cast: John Wayne, Marceline Day, Frank McHugh, Yakima Canutt. A remake of Maynard's *The Raiders.* Duke plays a government scout who clears the way for the stringing of telegraph wire across the plains.

The Three Musketeers (Mascot, 1933). Dirs., Armand Schaefer and Colbert Clark; prod., Nat Levine. Cast: John Wayne, Ruth Hall, Jack Mulhall, Francis X. Bushman, Jr. This serial was inspired by the Dumas story. Duke again portrays a flyer who saves three legionnaires from a band of rebels led by the mysterious El Shasta and helps the legionnaires defeat them. In 1946, the footage was edited and released by Favorite Films as a feature called *Desert Command,* as were many of Levine's serials.

Central Airport (Warner Bros., 1933). Dir., William A. Wellman. Cast: Richard Barthelmess, Sally Eilers, Tom Brown, John Wayne. Duke had only a nonspeaking bit part in this as an injured co-pilot in an aircraft downed at sea.

Somewhere in Sonora (Warner Bros., 1933). Dir., Mack V. Wright; prod., Leon Schlesinger. Cast: John Wayne, Henry B. Walthall, Shirley Palmer, J. P. McGowan. Another Maynard remake in which Duke is a cowboy who goes south of the border, foils a plot to rob a silver mine, and saves a kidnapped boy.

His Private Secretary (Showmen's Pictures, 1933). Dir., Philip H. Whitman. Cast: John Wayne, Evalyn Knapp, Alec B. Francis, Reginald Barlow. A contemporary film in which Duke plays a skirt-chasing rich man's son who courts and marries a minister's granddaughter against his father's will.

The Life of Jimmy Dolan (Warner Bros., 1933). Dir., Archie Mayo. Cast: Douglas Fairbanks, Jr.; Loretta Young; Fifi D'Orsay; Mickey Rooney. Duke has a small part in this fight film; he plays a boxer who is killed in the ring.

Baby Face (Warner Bros., 1933). Dir., Alfred E. Green. Cast: Barbara Stanwyck, George Brent, Donald Cook, John Wayne. Duke plays one of the men Barbara Stanwyck uses and tosses aside in her ruthless social climb. (British title: *The Kid's Last Fight.*)

The Man From Monterey (Warner Bros., 1933). Dir., Mack V. Wright; prod., Leon Schlesinger. Cast: John Wayne, Ruth Hall, Luis Alberni, Francis Ford. Duke plays a U.S. Cavalry officer who goes to Monterey on a mission to ensure that the Mexican landholders register their Spanish land grants.

Riders of Destiny (Monogram, 1933). Dir., R. N. Bradbury; prod., Paul Malvern. Cast: John Wayne, Cecelia Parker, George Hayes, Forrest Taylor. Duke is an undercover agent sent from Washington, D.C., to a small Western town to investigate water rights problems among the ranchers.

College Coach (Warner Bros., 1933). Dir., William A. Wellman. Cast: Pat O'Brien, Ann Dvorak, Dick Powell, Hugh Herbert. Duke has only one line in this college football film. (British title: *Football Coach.)*

Sagebrush Trail (Monogram, 1933). Dir., Armand Schaefer; prod., Paul Malvern. Cast: John Wayne, Nancy Shubert, Lane Chandler, Yakima Canutt. Duke plays a cowboy wrongly accused of murder. He escapes from jail and finds the real killer.

The Lucky Texan (Monogram, 1934). Dir., R. N. Bradbury; prod., Paul Malvern. Cast: John Wayne, Barbara Sheldon, George Hayes, Yakima Canutt. Duke plays a young college graduate who goes West and discovers gold. Action is provided by two claim jumpers.

West of the Divide (Monogram, 1934). Dir., R. N. Bradbury; prod., Paul Malvern. Cast: John Wayne, Virginia Browne Faire, Lloyd Whitlock, George Hayes. Duke plays a cowboy who, as a child, was left for dead beside the body of his murdered father. He hunts the murderer, finds him, and in the process, finds his missing brother and a wife.

Blue Steel (Monogram, 1934). Dir., R. N. Bradbury; prod., Paul Malvern. Cast: John Wayne, Eleanor Hunt, George Hayes, Yakima Canutt. Duke plays a U.S. marshal who saves the townspeople from a gang of outlaws who are trying to swindle them out of property that contains a gold mine.

The Man From Utah (Monogram, 1934). Dir., R. N. Bradbury; prod., Paul Malvern. Cast: John Wayne, Polly Ann Young,

FILMOGRAPHY

George Hayes, Yakima Canutt. Duke plays a cowboy who deals with a gang of outlaws bent on exploiting a rodeo and who wins the judge's daughter.

Randy Rides Alone (Monogram, 1934). Dir., Harry Fraser; prod., Paul Malvern. Cast: John Wayne, Alberta Vaughn, George Hayes, Earl Dwire. Duke plays a cowboy accused of murder and jailed; he's set free by the sympathetic young heroine and finds the real murderer.

The Star Packer (Monogram, 1934). Dir., R. N. Bradbury; prod., Paul Malvern. Cast: John Wayne, Verna Hillie, George Hayes, Earl Dwire. Duke plays a cowboy who takes a job as sheriff to rid the town of outlaws led by a man known only as the Shadow.

The Trail Beyond (Monogram, 1934). Dir., R. N. Bradbury; prod., Paul Malvern. Cast: John Wayne; Verna Hillie; Noah Beery, Sr.; Noah Beery, Jr. A contemporary setting in which Duke dons a three-piece suit for the opening scenes before he searches the Pacific Northwest for a missing girl. He finds the girl and a gold mine.

The Lawless Frontier (Monogram, 1934). Dir., R. N. Bradbury; prod., Paul Malvern. Cast: John Wayne, Sheila Terry, George Hayes, Earl Dwire. Duke plays a man who avenges his parents' death at the hands of a Mexican outlaw.

'Neath Arizona Skies (Monogram, 1934). Dir., Harry Fraser; prod., Paul Malvern. Cast: John Wayne, Sheila Terry, Jay Wilset (Buffalo Bill, Jr.), Shirley Rickert. Duke plays the guardian of a girl who is heir to rich oil land and whose father is missing. He saves the girl from outlaw predators and finds her father.

Texas Terror (Monogram, 1935). Dir., R. N. Bradbury; prod., Paul Malvern. Cast: John Wayne, Lucille Brown, LeRoy Mason, George Hayes. Duke plays a sheriff who gives up his badge because he thinks he's killed his best friend; he helps the dead man's sister and later learns he wasn't responsible for the death.

Rainbow Valley (Monogram, 1935). Dir., R. N. Bradbury; prod., Paul Malvern. Cast: same as *Texas Terror*. Duke plays a government agent working undercover as a convict who stops a band of outlaws from taking rich gold mine property from the towns-people.

The Desert Trail (Monogram, 1935). Dir., Cullen Lewis; prod., Paul Malvern. Cast: John Wayne, Mary Kornman, Paul Fix, Edward Chandler. Duke plays a rodeo star wrongly suspected of commit-ting a holdup who clears himself.

The Dawn Rider (Monogram, 1935). Dir., R. N. Bradbury; prod., Paul Malvern. Cast: John Wayne, Marion Burns, Reed Howes, Yakima Canutt. Duke plays a young cowboy on the trail of an outlaw who robbed an express office and killed his father.

Paradise Canyon (Monogram, 1935). Dir., Carl Pierson; prod., Paul Malvern. Cast: lead players same as *The Dawn Rider*. Duke again plays a government undercover agent, this time after a gang of counterfeiters on the Mexican border.

Westward Ho (Republic, 1935). Dir., R. N. Bradbury; prod., Paul Malvern. Cast: John Wayne; Sheila Mannors (later, Sheila Bromley); Frank McGlynn, Jr.; Jack Curtis. Duke plays a man whose parents were killed by a band of outlaws in his youth and whose brother was kidnapped by them. Now the leader of a vigi-lante group, Duke accompanies a group of pioneers on their trek West and encounters the outlaw gang—and his brother—along the way, avenging his parents' murder. This was his first film under the Republic banner, and the beginning of a long associa-tion with Herbert Yates.

The New Frontier (Republic, 1935). Dir., Carl Pierson; prod., Paul Malvern. Cast: John Wayne, Muriel Evans, Murdoch MacQuar-rie, Alan Cavan. Duke again plays a man out to avenge his fa-ther's murder.

The Lawless Range (Republic, 1935). Dir., R. N. Bradbury; prod., Trem Carr. Cast: John Wayne, Sheila Mannors, Earl Dwire, Frank McGlynn, Jr. Duke is again an undercover agent who's sent to investigate mysterious cattle rustlings and discovers that they are a cover to drive ranchers off land that contains a hidden gold mine.

The Oregon Trail (Republic, 1936). Dir., Scott Pembroke; prod., Paul Malvern. Cast: John Wayne, Ann Rutherford, E. H. Calvert,

Yakima Canutt. Duke plays an Army captain who searches for his father, who disappeared while leading a supply train along the Oregon Trail.

The Lawless Nineties (Republic, 1936). Dir., Joseph Kane. Cast: John Wayne, Ann Rutherford, Harry Woods, George Hayes. Duke is an undercover agent assigned to break up an outlaw gang.

King of the Pecos (Republic, 1936). Dir., Joseph Kane. Cast: John Wayne, Muriel Evans, Cy Kendall, Jack Clifford. Once again Duke plays a man avenging the murder of his parents. This time he uses law books (he's a law student) and a six-gun to bring the villain to justice.

The Lonely Trail (Republic, 1936). Dir., Joseph Kane; prod., Nat Levine. Cast: John Wayne, Ann Rutherford, Cy Kendall, Bob Kortman. Duke plays a young Texas rancher who, shortly after the Civil War, is asked by the governor to rid the territory of plundering carpetbaggers.

Winds of the Wasteland (Republic, 1936). Dir., Mack V. Wright; prod., Nat Levine. Cast: John Wayne, Phyllis Fraser, Douglas Cosgrove, Yakima Canutt. Duke and Yakima Canutt play former Pony Express riders who successfully compete for a government contract to haul the U.S. mail. Duke left Republic for a while shortly after completing this film.

The Sea Spoilers (Universal, 1936). Dir., Frank Strayer; prod., Trem Carr. Cast: John Wayne, Nan Grey, William Bakewell, Fuzzy Knight. Duke plays the commander of a U.S. Coast Guard cutter who breaks up a smuggling ring.

Conflict (Universal, 1936). Dir., David Howard; prod., Trem Carr. Cast: John Wayne, Jean Rogers, Tommy Bupp, Eddie Borden, Ward Bond. Duke plays an itinerant worker who's handy with his fists and takes on a local tough for money, fully intending to throw the fight. Meanwhile, he falls in love with a woman reporter, saves a young boy from drowning, goes straight, and defeats the tough guy.

California Straight Ahead (Universal, 1937). Dir., Arthur Lubin; prod., Trem Carr. Cast: John Wayne, Louise Latimer, Robert McWade, Tully Marshall. Duke plays a school-bus driver turned truck-company manager who leads a caravan of his trucks in a race with a freight train to deliver aircraft parts to the Pacific coast.

I Cover the War (Universal, 1937). Dir., Arthur Lubin; prod., Trem Carr. Cast: John Wayne, Gwen Gaze, Don Barclay, Pat Somerset. Duke plays a newsreel cameraman who covers an uprising against the British in North Africa.

Idol of the Crowds (Universal, 1937). Dir., Arthur Lubin; prod., Trem Carr. Cast: John Wayne, Sheila Bromley, Charles Brokaw. Duke plays a professional hockey player who refuses to cooperate with local gamblers to throw a game. He hides out until the championship game, then emerges to help his team win.

Adventure's End (Universal, 1937). Dir., Arthur Lubin; prod., Trem Carr. Cast: John Wayne, Diana Gibson, Montagu Love, Maurice Black. A South Pacific yarn in which Duke plays a pearl diver who gets involved with a mutiny aboard ship and who marries the ship captain's daughter.

Born to the West (Paramount, 1937). Dir., Charles Barton. Cast: John Wayne, Marsha Hunt, Johnny Mack Brown, Monte Blue. Duke plays a Western drifter who's put in charge of a cattle drive and eventually proves himself worthy of the attentions of the ranch owner's daughter. The film was later reissued as *Hell Town*.

Pals of the Saddle (Republic, 1938). Dir., George Sherman. Cast: John Wayne, Ray Corrigan, Max Terhune, Doreen McKay. This is the first of the "Three Mesquiteers" series, which were set in contemporary times but with all the Western trappings. In this one, Duke leads the Mesquiteers against foreign spies who are smuggling a chemical compound out of the country via Mexico for nefarious purposes.

Overland Stage Raiders (Republic, 1938). Dir., George Sherman. Cast: John Wayne, Ray Corrigan, Max Terhune, Louise Brooks. Duke and the other Mesquiteers buy an airplane in order to carry gold out of a remote mining area, thereby thwarting hijackers who have been intercepting trucks carrying the gold.

Santa Fe Stampede (Republic, 1938). Dir., George Sherman. Cast: John Wayne, Ray Corrigan, Max Terhune, William Farnum. The

Mesquiteers try to aid a friend who has struck gold, but the friend is killed and Duke is jailed for the murder until his two sidekicks apprehend the real killer.

Red River Range (Republic, 1938). Dir., George Sherman. Cast: John Wayne, Ray Corrigan, Max Terhune, Polly Moran. The governor enlists the Mesquiteers to break up a ring of cattle rustlers.

Stagecoach (United Artists, 1939). Dir., John Ford; prod., Walter Wanger. Cast: Claire Trevor, John Wayne, John Carradine, Thomas Mitchell. This is the film that established Duke's stardom. He plays The Ringo Kid, who has escaped from jail to avenge the death of his brother and father and whose work is done for him by a marshal who sets him free.

The Night Riders (Republic, 1939). Dir., George Sherman. Cast: John Wayne, Ray Corrigan, Max Terhune, Doreen McKay. The Three Mesquiteers expose the true identity of a man posing as a Spanish don who uses a forged land grant to tyrannize local settlers.

Three Texas Steers (Republic, 1939). Dir., George Sherman. Cast: John Wayne, Ray Corrigan, Max Terhune, Carole Landis. The Three Mesquiteers help a young woman who had inherited a ranch and a circus and who is being victimized by outlaws who try to sabotage the circus and take the ranch. (British title: *Danger Rides the Range.*)

Wyoming Outlaw (Republic, 1939). Dir., George Sherman. Cast: John Wayne, Ray Corrigan, Raymond Hatton, Donald Barry. The Mesquiteers take on a crooked politician who is selling state and federal work contracts to destitute farmers.

New Frontier (Republic, 1939). Dir., George Sherman. Cast: John Wayne, Ray Corrigan, Raymond Hatton, Phylis Isley (later Jennifer Jones). The Mesquiteers aid settlers who have been swindled in a land deal. (Television title: *Frontier Horizon.*) This was Duke's last Mesquiteers film.

Allegheny Uprising (RKO, 1939). Dir., William Seiter; prod., P. J. Wolfson. Cast: Claire Trevor, John Wayne, George Sanders, Brian Donlevy. Duke plays a frontiersman during pre-Revolutionary times who takes the law in his own hands by combatting traders who are supplying guns and liquor to the Indians. (British title: *The First Rebel.*)

The Dark Command (Republic, 1940). Dir., Raoul Walsh. Cast: Claire Trevor, John Wayne, Walter Pidgeon, Roy Rogers. Duke plays a traveling dentist's helper whose job is to pick fights and loosen teeth, sending his victims to the dentist's chair, until he falls in love, takes lessons in reading and writing, and becomes the town marshal.

Three Faces West (Republic, 1940). Dir., Bernard Vorhaus. Cast: John Wayne, Charles Coburn, Sigrid Gurie, Spencer Charters. Duke falls in love with the daughter of a surgeon who has migrated from Vienna; he leads the townspeople out of the Dust Bowl to Oregon.

The Long Voyage Home (United Artists, 1940). Dir., John Ford; prod., Walter Wanger. Cast: John Wayne, Thomas Mitchell, Ian Hunter, Barry Fitzgerald. Duke plays a Swedish sailor aboard a tramp steamer.

Seven Sinners (Universal, 1940). Dir., Tay Garnett; prod., Joe Pasternak. Cast: Marlene Dietrich, John Wayne, Albert Dekker, Broderick Crawford. A South Seas island tale in which Duke plays a Navy lieutenant.

A Man Betrayed (Republic, 1941). Dir., John H. Auer. Cast: John Wayne, Frances Dee, Edward Ellis, Ward Bond. A contemporary comedy-romance in which Duke plays a young lawyer who falls in love with a crooked politician's daughter. (Television title: *Wheel of Fortune.* British title: *Citadel of Crime.*)

Lady from Louisiana (Republic, 1941). Dir., Bernard Vorhaus. Cast: John Wayne, Ona Munson, Ray Middleton, Dorothy Dandridge. Duke is a lawyer who breaks up a political racket led by the father of the girl he falls in love with.

The Shepherd of the Hills (Paramount, 1941). Dir., Henry Hathaway; prod., Jack Moss. Cast: John Wayne, Betty Field, Harry Carey, Marjorie Main. Duke plays a young moonshiner who is reunited with his father, who had apparently deserted him in his youth.

FILMOGRAPHY

Lady for a Night (Republic, 1942). Dir., Leigh Jason. Cast: Joan Blondell, John Wayne, Ray Middleton, Philip Merivale. Duke plays a riverboat gambler in this Joan Blondell film.

Reap the Wild Wind (Paramount, 1942). Dir., Cecil B. DeMille. Cast: Ray Milland, John Wayne, Paulette Goddard, Raymond Massey. Duke plays the second lead as a ship's captain in this nineteenth-century sea saga.

The Spoilers (Universal, 1942). Dir., Ray Enright; prod., Frank Lloyd. Cast: Marlene Dietrich, Randolph Scott, John Wayne, Margaret Lindsay. Duke plays a gold miner and part-owner of a mine who resists attempts of swindlers.

In Old California (Republic, 1942). Dir., William McGann. Cast: John Wayne, Binnie Barnes, Albert Dekker, Helen Parrish. Duke plays a young Boston pharmacist who goes West and falls in love with a dance-hall girl.

Flying Tigers (Republic, 1942). Dir., David Miller. Cast: John Wayne, John Carroll, Anna Lee, Paul Kelly. Duke plays a fighter pilot commander in this, his first war film.

Reunion in France (MGM, 1942). Dir., Jules Dassin; prod., Joseph L. Mankiewicz. Cast: Joan Crawford, John Wayne, Reginald Owen, John Carradine. Duke plays a fighter pilot downed in Nazi-occupied France. (British title: *Mademoiselle France.*)

Pittsburgh (Universal, 1942). Dir., Lewis Seiler. Cast: Marlene Dietrich, Randolph Scott, John Wayne, Frank Craven. Duke plays a coal miner named Pittsburgh Markham, brash and ambitious, who manipulates his way to the top.

A Lady Takes a Chance (RKO, 1943). Dir., William A. Seiter; prod., Frank Ross. Cast: Jean Arthur, John Wayne, Charles Winninger, Phil Silvers. Duke plays a rodeo cowboy who falls for a sharp New York woman who's on vacation in the West.

In Old Oklahoma (Republic, 1943). Dir., Albert S. Rogell. Cast: John Wayne, Martha Scott, Albert Dekker, George "Gabby" Hayes. Duke is a turn-of-the-century cowboy who helps the Indians protect their land from the oil barons. Later reissued as *War of the Wildcats.*

FILMOGRAPHY

The Fighting Seabees (Republic, 1944). Dir., Edward Ludwig. Cast: John Wayne, Dennis O'Keefe, Susan Hayward, William Frawley. Duke plays a construction boss drawn into the war in the South Pacific.

Tall in the Saddle (RKO, 1944). Dir., Edwin L. Marin; prod., Robert Fellows. Cast: John Wayne, Ella Raines, Ward Bond, Audrey Long. Duke plays a cowboy who solves the mystery of his would-be-employer's death.

Flame of the Barbary Coast (RKO, 1945). Dir., Joseph Kane. Cast: John Wayne, Ann Dvorak, Joseph Schildkraut, William Frawley. Duke plays a Montana cowboy visiting San Francisco as the great 1906 earthquake strikes.

Back To Bataan (RKO, 1945). Dir., Edward Dmytryk; prod., Robert Fellows. Cast: John Wayne, Anthony Quinn, Beulah Bondi, Richard Loo. Duke plays an Army colonel who helps organize Philippine resistance on Bataan.

They Were Expendable (MGM, 1945). Dir., John Ford. Cast: Robert Montgomery, John Wayne, Donna Reed, Jack Holt, Ward Bond. Duke plays a Navy lieutenant in charge of a fleet of torpedo boats.

Dakota (Republic, 1945). Dir., Joseph Kane. Cast: John Wayne, Vera Hruba Ralston, Walter Brennan, Ward Bond. As a newly-wed, Duke becomes a pawn in a battle between his new bride and her railroad-tycoon father.

Without Reservations (RKO, 1946). Dir., Mervin LeRoy; prod., Jesse L. Lasky. Cast: Claudette Colbert, John Wayne, Don DeFore, Anne Triola. Duke plays a Marine flyer on leave who falls for a naive bestselling authoress.

Angel and the Badman (Republic, 1947). Dir., James Edward Grant; prod., John Wayne. Cast: John Wayne, Gail Russell, Harry Carey, Bruce Cabot. Duke's a gunfighter who's pacified by a Quaker girl and her family.

Tycoon (RKO, 1947). Dir., Richard Wallace; prod., Stephen Ames. Cast: John Wayne, Laraine Day, Sir Cedric Hardwicke, Judith Anderson. Duke plays a tunnel- and bridge-building engineer who builds a railroad tunnel through a mountain in South America.

Fort Apache (RKO, 1948). Dir., John Ford; prods., John Ford and Merian C. Cooper. Cast: John Wayne, Henry Fonda, Shirley Temple, John Agar. Duke plays a U.S. Cavalry captain in command at Fort Apache who is sympathetic to the Apache Indians led by Cochise.

Red River (United Artists, 1948). Dir., Howard Hawks. Cast: John Wayne, Montgomery Clift, Joanne Dru, Walter Brennan. Duke plays an uncompromising, hard-driving cattle baron in one of his best films.

Three Godfathers (MGM, 1949). Dir., John Ford; prods., John Ford and Merian C. Cooper. Cast: John Wayne; Pedro Armendariz; Harry Carey, Jr.; Ward Bond. Duke plays an outlaw leader who reforms by film's end.

Wake of the Red Witch (Republic, 1949). Dir., Edward Ludwig. Cast: John Wayne, Gail Russell, Gig Young, Adele Mara. Duke is a seagoing adventurer who wrestles with an octopus for a fortune in pearls in this South Seas adventure.

The Fighting Kentuckian (Republic, 1949). Dir., George Waggner; prod., John Wayne. Cast: John Wayne, Vera Hruba Ralston, Philip Dorn, Oliver Hardy. Duke plays a rifleman in the second Kentucky Regiment in this pre–Civil War saga.

She Wore a Yellow Ribbon (RKO, 1949). Dir., John Ford; prods., John Ford and Merian C. Cooper. Cast: John Wayne, Joanne Dru, John Agar, Ben Johnson. Duke plays an aging U.S. Cavalry officer in this excellent film.

Sands of Iwo Jima (Republic, 1949). Dir., Allan Dwan. Cast: John Wayne, John Agar, Adele Mara, Forrest Tucker. Duke got an Academy Award nomination for his performance as Sergeant John M. Stryker in this better-than-average war story.

Rio Grande (Republic, 1950). Dir., John Ford; prods., John Ford and Merian C. Cooper. Cast: John Wayne, Maureen O'Hara, Ben Johnson, J. Carrol Naish. Duke plays a middle-aged lieutenant colonel in the U.S. Cavalry.

FILMOGRAPHY

Operation Pacific (Warner Bros., 1951). Dir., George Waggner; prod., Louis F. Edelman. Cast: John Wayne, Patricia Neal, Ward Bond, Scott Forbes. Duke plays a submarine officer.

Flying Leathernecks (RKO, 1951). Dir., Nicholas Ray; prod., Edmund Grainger. Cast: John Wayne, Robert Ryan, Don Taylor, Janis Carter. Duke plays an unpopular but efficient commander of a marine fighter squadron in the South Pacific.

The Quiet Man (Republic, 1952). Dir., John Ford; prods., John Ford and Merian C. Cooper. Cast: John Wayne, Maureen O'Hara, Barry Fitzgerald, Ward Bond. Duke is a former prizefighter who returns to his father's native Ireland and finds a wife.

Big Jim McLain (Warner Bros., 1952). Dir., Edward Ludwig; prod., Robert Fellows. Cast: John Wayne, Nancy Olson, James Arness, Alan Napier. Duke is a House Un-American Activities Committee investigator fighting Communists in Hawaii.

Trouble Along the Way (Warner Bros., 1953). Dir., Michael Curtiz; prod., Melville Shavelson. Cast: John Wayne, Donna Reed, Charles Coburn, Tom Tully. Duke plays a college football coach.

Island in the Sky (Warner Bros., 1953). Dir., William A. Wellman; prod., Robert Fellows. Cast: John Wayne, Lloyd Nolan, James Arness, Andy Devine. Duke plays the pilot of a transport plane that's downed in the frozen wastelands of the North.

Hondo (Warner Bros., 1953). Dir., John Farrow; prod., Robert Fellows. Cast: John Wayne, Geraldine Page, Ward Bond, James Arness. Duke plays an ex-gunfighter who falls for a widow whose husband he has killed.

The High and the Mighty (Warner Bros., 1954). Dir., William A. Wellman; prod., Robert Fellows. Cast: John Wayne, Claire Trevor, Robert Stack, Laraine Day. Duke plays a commercial pilot who survived a plane crash in which he lost both his wife and child and who co-pilots a plane that is in danger of crashing at sea.

The Sea Chase (Warner Bros., 1955). Dir., John Farrow. Cast: John Wayne, Lana Turner, David Farrar, Tab Hunter. Duke plays a German who has opposed Hitler; one of his worst films.

FILMOGRAPHY

Blood Alley (Warner Bros., 1955). Dir., William A. Wellman. Cast: John Wayne, Lauren Bacall, Paul Fix, Joy Kim. Duke is rescued from a mainland Communist Chinese jail by a group of villagers who want him to help them escape to Hong Kong. He aids the entire village population by loading them aboard a ferry boat and making a dangerous three-hundred-mile run down the Formosa Strait to freedom.

The Conqueror (RKO, 1956). Dir., Dick Powell. Cast: John Wayne, Susan Hayward, Pedro Armendariz, Agnes Moorehead. Duke portrays Genghis Khan in possibly the worst film he ever made.

The Searchers (Warner Bros., 1956). Dir., John Ford; prods., Merian C. Cooper and C. V. Whitney. Cast: John Wayne, Vera Miles, Natalie Wood, Ward Bond. Duke plays a tough, independent loner in the post–Civil War era. One of his best films.

The Wings of Eagles (MGM, 1957). Dir., John Ford; prod., Charles Schnee. Cast: John Wayne, Maureen O'Hara, Dan Dailey, Ward Bond. Duke plays Navy flyer Frank "Spig" Wead in this biographical film of the flyer's life.

Jet Pilot (RKO, 1957). Dir., Josef Von Sternberg; prod., Jules Furthman. Cast: John Wayne, Janet Leigh, Jay C. Flippen, Paul Fix. Duke plays an Air Force colonel who falls in love with a female Russian pilot who has defected to the West.

Legend of the Lost (United Artists, 1957). Dir., Henry Hathaway. Cast: John Wayne, Sophia Loren, Rossano Brazzi. Duke plays an adventurous desert guide who discovers a hidden city in the Sahara.

I Married a Woman (RKO, 1958). Dir., Hal Kanter; prod., William Bloom. Cast: George Gobel, Diana Dors, Adolphe Menjou, John Wayne. Duke did a guest-star cameo as himself.

The Barbarian and the Geisha (20th Century-Fox, 1958). Dir., John Huston; prod., Eugene Frenke. Cast: John Wayne, Eiko Ando, Sam Jaffe, So Yamamura. Duke portrays the first counsul-general of Japan, Townsend Harris.

Rio Bravo (Warner Bros., 1959). Dir., Howard Hawks. Cast: John Wayne, Dean Martin, Angie Dickinson, Walter Brennan. Duke plays a sheriff in a border town.

FILMOGRAPHY

The Horse Soldiers (United Artists, 1959). Dir., John Ford; prods., John Lee Mahin and Martin Rackin. Cast: John Wayne, William Holden, Constance Towers, Hoot Gibson. Duke plays a colonel in the Union forces leading a company of soldiers on a mission into Confederate territory.

The Alamo (United Artists, 1960). Dir., John Wayne. Cast: John Wayne, Richard Widmark, Laurence Harvey, Richard Boone. Duke plays Colonel Davy Crockett in this epic film about one of America's most famous battles against the Mexican forces.

North to Alaska (20th Century-Fox, 1960). Dir., Henry Hathaway. Cast: John Wayne, Stewart Granger, Ernie Kovacs, Fabian. A comedy in which Duke is a partner in a rich gold mine.

The Comancheros (20th Century-Fox, 1961). Dir., Michael Curtiz; prod., George Sherman. Cast: John Wayne, Stuart Whitman, Lee Marvin, Ina Balin. Duke plays a captain in the Texas Rangers who has his hands full trying to extradite a man on murder charges.

The Man Who Shot Liberty Valance (Paramount, 1962). Dir., John Ford; prod., Willis Goldbeck. Cast: James Stewart, John Wayne, Lee Marvin, Vera Miles. Duke plays a strong and independent Westerner who comes to the aid of an idealistic lawyer in his feud with a gunman.

Hatari! (Paramount, 1962). Dir., Howard Hawks. Cast: John Wayne, Elsa Martinelli, Hardy Kruger, Red Buttons. Duke is the leader of big-game catchers who capture African animals for zoos.

The Longest Day (20th Century-Fox, 1963). Dirs., Ken Annakin, Andrew Marton, Bernhard Wicki, Darryl F. Zanuck, Gerd Oswald; prod., Darryl F. Zanuck. Cast: Eddie Albert, Richard Burton, Robert Mitchum, John Wayne. Duke played a small role as Lieutenant Colonel Benjamin Vandervoort in this epic dramatization of the D-Day invasion of Europe.

How the West Was Won (MGM, 1962). Dirs., John Ford, Henry Hathaway, George Marshall, Richard Thorpe; prod., Bernard Smith. Cast: John Wayne, Henry Fonda, Karl Malden, Robert Preston. Duke played a cameo as General William T. Sherman in this epic film.

FILMOGRAPHY

Donovan's Reef (Paramount, 1963). Dir., John Ford. Cast: John Wayne, Lee Marvin, Elizabeth Allen, Jack Warden. Duke is an ex-Navy officer who stays in the South Pacific after the war and buys a bar there. A good comedy.

McLintock! (United Artists, 1963). Dir., Andrew V. McLaglen; prod., Michael Wayne. Cast: John Wayne, Maureen O'Hara, Yvonne De Carlo, Patrick Wayne. A Western comedy in which Duke plays a tough entrepreneur who's so influential that the town's named after him.

Circus World (Paramount, 1964). Dir., Henry Hathaway; prod., Samuel Bronston. Cast: John Wayne, Claudia Cardinale, Rita Hayworth, Lloyd Nolan. Duke is a circus owner who takes his company to Europe. (British title: *The Magnificent Showman.*)

The Greatest Story Ever Told (United Artists, 1965). Dir., George Stevens. Cast: Max Von Sydow, Carroll Baker, Pat Boone, Victor Buono. A star-studded epic of the life of Christ in which Duke plays a cameo as a centurion who accompanies Christ to the cross.

In Harm's Way (Paramount, 1965). Dir., Otto Preminger. Cast: John Wayne, Kirk Douglas, Patricia Neal, Paula Prentiss. Duke plays the captain of a navy cruiser. He was suffering from cancer of the lung while making this film, but he didn't know it.

The Sons of Katie Elder (Paramount, 1965). Dir., Henry Hathaway; prod., Hal Wallis. Cast: John Wayne, Dean Martin, Martha Hyer, Michael Anderson, Jr. Duke's first film following his cancer operation. He plays a gunslinger, the eldest of four brothers who return to the family home for their mother's funeral.

Cast a Giant Shadow (United Artists, 1966). Dir., Melville Shavelson; prods., Melville Shavelson and Michael Wayne. Cast: Kirk Douglas, Yul Brynner, Senta Berger, Frank Sinatra, John Wayne. Duke plays a small part as General Mike Randolph in this biographical story of American Jew Mickey Marcus, who helped shape the Israeli Army.

The War Wagon (Universal, 1967). Dir., Burt Kennedy; prods., Marvin Schwartz/Batjac. Cast: John Wayne, Kirk Douglas, Howard Keel, Keenan Wynn. Duke plays the victim of a crooked lawman who has thrown him in jail to steal his land and gold from his mine.

El Dorado (Paramount, 1967). Dir., Howard Hawks. Cast: John Wayne, Robert Mitchum, James Caan, Charlene Holt. Duke plays a gunfighter for hire.

The Green Berets (Warner Bros.-Seven Arts, 1968). Dir., John Wayne; prod., Michael Wayne. Cast: John Wayne, David Janssen, Jim Hutton, Aldo Ray. Duke plays a colonel in the Green Berets who leads his troops in the Vietnam War.

Hellfighters (Universal, 1969). Dir., Andrew V. McLaglen; prod., Robert Arthur. Cast: John Wayne, Katharine Ross, Jim Hutton, Vera Miles. Duke plays an expert oil-fire fighter, a characterization styled on famous oil-fire fighter Red Adair.

True Grit (Paramount, 1969). Dir., Henry Hathaway; prod., Hal Wallis. Cast: John Wayne, Glen Campbell, Kim Darby, Robert Duvall. Duke plays a boozy, one-eyed U.S. marshal named Reuben J. "Rooster" Cogburn who helps a young girl find her father's murderer. The portrayal won Duke an Academy Award as best actor.

The Undefeated (20th Century-Fox, 1969). Dir., Andrew V. McLaglen; prod., Robert L. Jacks. Cast: John Wayne, Rock Hudson, Tony Aguilar, Lee Meriwether. Duke plays a man who resigns his commission as a colonel in the Union forces at the end of the Civil War and heads West, befriending a former Confederate colonel in wild-West civilian life.

Chisum (Warner Bros., 1970). Dir., Andrew V. McLaglen; prod., Andrew J. Fenady. Cast: John Wayne, Forrest Tucker, Christopher George, Pamela McMyler. Duke plays a cattle baron who fights corrupt businessmen, lawmen, and politicians to save his land and the land of his neighbors.

Rio Lobo (20th Century-Fox, 1970). Dir., Howard Hawks. Cast: John Wayne, Jorge Rivero, Jennifer O'Neill, Jack Elam. Duke plays a Civil War Union colonel who, after the war, settles his differences with a gang who stole a gold shipment and killed one of his officers.

FILMOGRAPHY

Big Jake (National General, 1971). Dir., George Sherman; prod., Michael Wayne. Cast: John Wayne, Richard Boone, Maureen O'Hara, Patrick Wayne. Duke plays a wealthy rancher whose grandson is kidnapped and who sets out to rescue him.

The Cowboys (Warner Bros., 1972). Dir., Mark Rydell. Cast: John Wayne, Roscoe Lee Browne, Bruce Dern, Colleen Dewhurst. Duke is an old rancher who's forced to make a long cattle drive with young boys as cowhands.

Cancel My Reservation (Warner Bros., 1972). Dir., Paul Bogart; prod., Gordon Oliver. Cast: Bob Hope, Eva Marie Saint, Ralph Bellamy. Duke makes a cameo appearance in one of Bob Hope's nightmares.

The Train Robbers (Warner Bros., 1973). Dir., Burt Kennedy; prod., Michael Wayne. Cast: John Wayne, Ann-Margret, Rod Taylor, Ben Johnson. Duke plays a man who agrees to help a young widow find and return the gold her husband had stolen.

Cahill, United States Marshal (Warner Bros., 1973). Dir., Andrew V. McLaglen; prod., Michael Wayne. Cast: John Wayne, George Kennedy, Gary Grimes, Neville Brand. Duke is a U.S. marshal who returns home from the trail to find that the sheriff and his deputy have been murdered and the bank robbed. (British title: *Cahill.*)

McQ (Warner Bros., 1974). Dir., John Sturges; prods., Jules Levy, Arthur Gardner, Lawrence Roman. Cast: John Wayne, Eddie Albert, Diana Muldaur, Colleen Dewhurst. Duke plays an uncompromising cop who seeks vengeance after his partner has been killed.

Brannigan (United Artists, 1975). Dir., Douglas Hickox; prods., Jules Levy, Arthur Gardner. Cast: John Wayne, Richard Attenborough, Mel Ferrer, Judy Geeson. Duke is a Chicago cop who goes to London to extradite a drug dealer.

Rooster Cogburn (Universal, 1975). Dir., Stuart Millar; prod., Hal Wallis. Cast: John Wayne, Katharine Hepburn, Richard Jordan, Strother Martin. Duke plays the boozy, one-eyed marshal, Reuben J. "Rooster" Cogburn, pursuing an outlaw gang. On the trail, he finds the elderly daughter of a minister (who has been killed by the gang he's trailing) and an Indian boy, both of whom accompany him on his pursuit.

The Shootist (Paramount, 1976). Dir., Don Siegel; prods., Mike Frankovich, William Self. Cast: John Wayne, Lauren Bacall, Ron Howard, James Stewart. Duke plays a gunfighter dying of cancer in this, his last, film.

The following are films in which Duke did not appear but which he had a hand in producing through his companies, Wayne-Fellows Productions and Batjac.

Bullfighter and the Lady (Republic, 1951). Dir., Budd Boetticher. Cast: Robert Stack, Gilbert Roland, John Hubbard, Joy Page. A Wayne-Fellows production.

Plunder of the Sun (Warner Bros., 1953). Dir., John Farrow; prod., Robert Fellows. Cast: Glenn Ford, Diana Lynn, Patricia Medina. A Wayne-Fellows production.

Ring of Fear (Warner Bros., 1954). Dirs., James Edward Grant, William A. Wellman (uncredited). Cast: Pat O'Brien, Clyde Beatty, Mickey Spillane, Gonzalez-Gonzalez. A Wayne-Fellows production.

Track of the Cat (Warner Bros., 1954). Dir., William A. Wellman. Cast: Robert Mitchum, Diana Lynn, Tab Hunter, William Hopper. A Wayne-Fellows production.

Goodbye, My Lady (Warner Bros., 1956). Dir., William A. Wellman. Cast: Walter Brennan, Phil Harris, Sidney Poitier, Louise Beavers. A Batjac production.

Seven Men From Now (Warner Bros., 1956). Dir., Budd Boetticher; prods., Andrew V. McLaglen, Robert E. Morrison. Cast: Randolph Scott, Lee Marvin, Stuart Whitmore, Gail Russell. A Batjac production.

Gun the Man Down (United Artists, 1956). Dir., Andrew V. McLaglen; prod., Robert E. Morrison. Cast: James Arness, Angie Dickinson, Emile Meyer, Harry Carey, Jr. A Batjac production.

FILMOGRAPHY

Man in a Vault (Universal/RKO, 1956). Dir., Andrew V. McLaglen; prod., Robert E. Morrison. Cast: William Campbell, Anita Ekberg, Paul Fix, Mike Mazurki. A Batjac production.

China Doll (United Artists, 1958). Dir., Frank Borzage. Cast: Victor Mature, Ward Bond, Johnny Desmond, Stuart Whitman. A Romina/Batjac production.

Escort West (United Artists, 1959). Dir., Francis D. Lyon; prods., Robert E. Morrison, Nate H. Edwards. Cast: Victor Mature, Noah Beery, Faith Domergue, Harry Carey, Jr. A Romina/Batjac production.

Hondo and the Apaches (MGM pilot for television). Dir., Lee H. Katzin; prod., Andrew J. Fenady. Cast: Ralph Taeger, Michael Rennie, Noah Beery, Jim Davis, Robert Taylor. A Batjac/Fenady production. Released in Great Britain 1967.

Other John Wayne appearances:

What Price Glory? (A John Ford Presentation, 1950) (Stage) This was a special performance on stage Grauman's Chinese Theatre of John Ford's old stock company. Duke played a soldier.

Rookie Of The Year (Screen Directors Playhouse) 1955 (Television) Directed by John Ford. Cast: John Wayne, Vera Miles, James Gleason, Ward Bond.

The Colter Craven Story (A *Wagon Train* television episode) Aired November 23, 1960. Directed by John Ford. Cast: Ward Bond, John Carradine, Carleton Young, Hank Worden. Duke played General Sherman under the name Michael Morris.

Flashing Spikes (Alcoa Premiere-television) Aired October 4, 1962. Directed by John Ford. Cast: James Stewart, Jack Warden, Patrick Wayne, Harry Carey, Jr., Edward Buchanan, John Wayne.

No Substitute For Victory (Alaska Pictures Corp.) 1970. Produced by Chuck Keen. Directed by Robert F. Slatzer. Cast: General Westmoreland, General Mark Clark, Mayor Sam Yorty. Duke was on-camera host and narrator of this 109 minute theatrical documentary on Viet Nam.

FILMOGRAPHY

Chesty (A John Ford Production, 1970) Duke was on-camera host and narrator of this 30 minute film depicting the life of war hero Lewis B. "Chesty" Puller.

The Challenge Of Ideas (U.S.A. Information Films, 1955) Cast: John Wayne, Helen Hayes, David Brinkley. This was an anti-communist documentary.

Directed by John Ford (American Film Institute Productions, 1971) Directed by Peter Bogdanovich. A two hour television tribute to Ford and the Western featuring John Wayne and other stars.

APPENDIX

IN addition to his movie and television work, Duke starred in his own radio series and narrated one long-playing phonograph record:

Three Sheets to the Wind (1942–43). Duke starred as an alcoholic detective in this twenty-six-episode radio series for the NBC Radio Network. The show was directed by movie director Tay Garnet and lasted only one season.

America, Why I Love Her (1973). This RCA Record album was written and produced by John Mitchum, Robert Mitchum's brother, a versatile character actor, musician, and songwriter. Duke did the narration.

INDEX

INDEX

INDEX

INDEX

INDEX

INDEX

INDEX

INDEX

INDEX

INDEX